First to the Parklands

Original Narratives from the History of Western Exploration

Edited By Jeffrey Eling

Second Edition

The Narrative Press
HISTORICAL ADVENTURE & EXPLORATION

To Nancy, Nick & Nina.

The Narrative Press
P.O. Box 2487, Santa Barbara, California 93120 U.S.A.
Telephone: (800) 315-9005 Web: www.narrativepress.com

ISBN 1-58976-247-9 (Paperback)

Produced in the United States of America

CONTENTS

Book II
Sea to Shining Sea 1840-60

Book III
The Great Surveys and the Closing of the Frontier
1861-1901

PROLOGUE

The West is a land of wonders and unlimited horizons, where segments have been set aside as parklands. This book is a collection of journals, diaries, articles, memoirs and reports of those Americans who were among the first to explore the future parklands: government agents, company traders, fur trappers, hunters, soldiers, surveyors, geologists and naturalists. Their journeys range throughout the West and its frontier history, across the expanse of the entire 19th century and the varied landscape of plains and mountains, forest and ocean, desert and stone.

At an earlier period of American history, the western frontier was just over the crest of the Appalachians. As settlement moved westward, the boundary moved to the Mississippi. Further west is the 100th meridian longitude, an invisible line that extends right down the middle of the country, where the land changes and the 'true West' begins. Once called "The Great American Desert," the Great Plains extend from the northern to the southern border and beyond. The trees fade away, the sky is clear, the air is dry and the plain stretches away into infinity until, finally, the mountains rise far, far away. Isolated buttes rise from the flat landscape and badlands are intricately carved into the soil. Mountains are on the far horizon for a long time before they are finally reached. Sweeping over the spine of the Rockies and down the other side, the landscape changes again. Rivers that have their beginnings in the snowy mountains carve deep canyons through a stony desert. Isolated ranges punctuate the Great Basin, on and on to the great wall of the Sierra Nevada and the volcanic cones of the Cascades. Over this final and formidable barrier, the land slopes away to the Pacific. The desert finally ends and its aridity compensated for by a moist, lush rainforest of towering trees, shining peaks and tumbling cascades, ending with dramatic headlands and sea stacks towering above the Pacific. Crossing over this region of the far west, explorers sometimes passed through the future parklands.

Explorers of European descent had begun to penetrate the American West as early as the 16th century. Conquistadors and friars had, for instance, encountered the Grand Canyon in earlier centuries but, remarkably, had almost nothing to say about it. Despite a long-standing presence of European claims to the area, by the time the Americans pushed into the region, it was still largely terra incognita. With the advent of the Romantic Movement, American culture was prepared to be profoundly affected by the dramatic landscapes found there. But these were not pleasure holidays. Rather, these were often ordeals of great hardship where the participants experienced hunger, thirst, brutal cold, searing heat, exhausting labor, Indian attacks, hordes of mosquitoes (with no DEET!) and more.

It cannot be said that these persons were actually the first non-natives to set foot in a particular area, but generally they did leave the first written accounts. Sometimes, an area like Yellowstone is discovered and rediscovered, until it is finally communicated to the general public. Sometimes, an area like Big Bend, Yosemite or Grand Canyon will be explored earlier in one section and later in another, or more thoroughly. Therefore, more than one account of a region's discovery will be included. The definition of parklands will be a loose one to cover any of the protected natural areas, primarily federal lands, including parks, monuments, scenic rivers and even forests. Coverage will be necessarily selective, taken from available written accounts.

The focus will be on the original narratives, but will preface each with discussions of context and setting. I have taken the liberty of correcting misspellings, punctuation and grammar in the journals so they will be more readable. The narratives begin in 1805 with the expedition of Lewis and Clark, the opening of the far western frontier. The frontier closed by 1890 in the push to the Pacific and the selections will end soon after. Generally, these narratives were written down during or near the events they describe, but often not published and made available until a later date, sometimes even many decades after the events. Any misconceptions, prejudices or fabrications of the authors are allowed to stand. The intent is to allow the explorers to tell us what they saw and to share in their adventures, but a correct interpretation of phenomena and events cannot be assumed in their reports. Their writings will be a series of windows into the history of exploration in the Far West – from fur trappers through railroad surveys, military campaigns, government-sponsored scientific surveys and private excursions. These include stories of human interest – of courage, tragedy, sacrifice and triumph in a land that has no equal.

BOOK I

OPENING OF THE FRONTIER
1805-40

The first section of journal entries is from the era of fur trappers and mountain men, inaugurated by the epic voyage of Lewis and Clark. It is fitting that the first entry should begin with an appropriate selection from their transcontinental crossing. Their immediate successors were parties motivated at the economic level by the lucrative trade in furs, an enterprise in North America for almost two centuries before the Americans entered the picture. Their predecessors were the French voyageurs moving into the Great Lakes and making their way by canoe deeper and deeper into Canada along its many lakes and rivers. Voyageurs had moved deep into the interior plains of America as well. The British were descending into the same general area from Hudson Bay and, later, from Montreal after taking over French Canada. The British explorer, Alexander Mackenzie, made the first transcontinental crossing in the 1790s by way of Canada's rivers, over a difficult portage across the far northern Rockies, thence down to the sea. This event much concerned Thomas Jefferson, when it became known through the publishing of Mackenzie's journal, prodding the President into action. The commission to send his secretary, Meriwether Lewis, up the Missouri, across the Rockies and down the Columbia was motivated by the same desire to find a suitable passage across the continent, where a trading post could be established on the Pacific and a profitable trade in furs opened across the ocean to the Far East. An easy passage was never found by any of the explorers before or after Lewis and Clark. The Americans did not spread across the continent because the geography opened up an easy passage (although South Pass did make it easier) but, rather, did so in spite of its many obstacles. This initial opening was encouraged, however, by a fortuitous event. In 1803, Napoleon agreed to sell the Louisiana Territory to the United States. This was a large territory that extended from the Mississippi River, north of Texas and south of Canada, all the way to the crest of the Rockies. The Americans did not only explore their newly acquired territory, however, but from the beginning crossed over into the territory of other nations; opening the Santa Fe Trail and probing for suitable routes to California and the Oregon country, the ultimate prizes sought for by the pioneers. By the 1840s, fashions changed and the West trapped out, causing the fur trade to collapse.

Yet, the mountain men who first tramped through this unknown wilderness were all initiating the opening of the Far Western frontier for the United States. They were also the first to leave a record of places seen – like Yellowstone, Yosemite and the Grand Tetons

Chapter I

UPPER MISSOURI
1805

from The Journal of Meriwether Lewis

The selected entry from the Lewis Journal describes the area now set aside as the Upper Missouri National Wild & Scenic River. It is followed by his description of the Great Falls of the Missouri River, a series of falls in the wilderness in 1805. Today, it is much reduced by use for hydroelectric power and is not a designated parkland. However, I have included it since it was a wild spectacle in primitive America. I have also included Lewis' curious adventures with wildlife in its vicinity.

William Clark & Meriwether Lewis

Lewis began his journey down the Ohio River in 1803; picking up Clark, a party of hardy volunteers, and much needed equipment and supplies on the way. They wintered just outside St. Louis and then ascended the Missouri in 1804; a long, laborious trip to the villages of the Mandan and Hidatsa Indians. They wintered in that harsh climate and were lucky to hire a French trapper named Charbonneau as interpreter, not because of his meager services, but rather the valuable knowledge and services of his Indian wife, Sacagawea. She was a Shoshone Indian captured by an Hidatsa war party. Her knowledge of Shoshone language and surrounding terrain would be immensely helpful as the Corps of Discovery pushed into the unknown beyond the Mandan/Hidatsa villages. The entry begins with the expedition leaving their winter quarters in the spring of 1805.

Ft. Mandan April 7, 1805

Our vessels consisted of six small canoes and two large pirogues. This little fleet, although not quite so respectable as those of Columbus or Capt. Cook, were still viewed by us with as much pleasure as those deservedly famed adventurers ever beheld theirs; and I dare say with quite as much anxiety for their safety and preservation. We were now about to penetrate a country at least two thousand miles in width, on which the foot of civilized man had never trodden. The good or evil it had in store for us was for experiment yet to determine, and these little vessels contained every article by which we expected to subsist or defend ourselves. However, as the state of mind in which we are generally gives the colouring to events, when the imagination is suffered to wander into futurity, the picture which now presented itself to me was a most pleasing one. Entertaining, as I do, the most confident hope of succeeding in a voyage, which had formed a darling project of mine for the last ten years, I could but esteem this moment of my departure as among the happiest of my life. The party are in excellent health and spirits, zealously attached to the enterprise, and anxious to proceed. Not a whisper or murmur of discontent is heard among them, but all act in unison, and with the most perfect harmony. . . .

Heading upriver, they enter the area of the Missouri Breaks. Here, Lewis has his first view of the Rocky Mountains (actually one of the outlying smaller ranges east of the Rockies).

Sunday May 26th

On arriving to the summit of one of the highest points in the neighborhood, I thought myself well repaid for my labor; as from this point I beheld the Rocky Mountains for the first time . . . these points of the Rocky Mountains were covered with snow and the sun shone on it in such manner as to give me the most plain and satisfactory view.

While I viewed these mountains, I felt a secret pleasure in finding myself so near the head of the heretofore conceived boundless Missouri; but when I reflected on the difficulties which this snowy barrier would most probably throw in my way to the Pacific, and the sufferings and hardships of myself and party in them, it in some measure counter balanced the joy I had felt during the first moments gazing on them. But as I have always held it a crime to anticipate evils, I will believe it to be a good comfortable road until I am compelled to believe differently. . . .

Wednesday May 29th

. . . Today we passed, on the starboard side, the remains of a vast many mangled carcasses of buffalo, which had been driven

over a precipice of 120 feet by the Indians and perished. The water appeared to have washed away a part of this immense slaughter, and still there remained the fragments of at least a hundred carcasses. They created a most horrid stench. In this manner, the Indians of the Missouri destroy vast herds of buffalo at a stroke.

For this purpose, one of the most active and fleet young men is selected and disguised in a robe of buffalo skin, having also the skin of the buffalo's head with the ears and horns fastened on his head in form of a cap. Thus caparisoned, he places himself at a convenient distance between a herd of buffalo and a precipice proper for the purpose, which happens in many places on this river for miles together.

The other Indians now surround the herd on the back and flanks, and at a signal agreed on all show themselves at the same time moving forward towards the buffalo. The disguised Indian, or decoy, has taken care to place himself sufficiently nigh the buffalo to be noticed by them when they take to flight. Running before them , they follow him at full speed to the precipice.

The cattle behind, driving those in front over and seeing them go, do not look or hesitate about following until the whole are precipitated down the precipice, forming one common mass of dead and mangled carcasses. The decoy, in the meantime, has taken care to secure himself in some cranny or crevice of the cliff, which he had previously prepared for that purpose. The part of the decoy, I am informed, is extremely dangerous. If they are not very fleet runners, the buffalo tread them under foot and crush them to death, and sometimes drive them over the precipice.

Friday May 31st

. . . The hills and river cliffs which we passed today exhibit a most romantic appearance. The bluffs of the river rise to the height of two to three hundred feet, and in most places is nearly perpendicular. They are formed of remarkable white sandstone, which is sufficiently soft to give way readily to the impression of water . . . we see the remains of ruins or elegant buildings. As we passed on, it seemed as if those scenes of visionary enchant-

ment would never have an end; for here it is too that nature presents to the view of the traveler vast ranges of walls of tolerable workmanship. So perfect indeed are those walls that I should have thought that nature had attempted here to rival the human art of masonry, had I not recollected that she had first begun her work. . . .

Thursday June 13th, 1805

I had proceeded about two miles, with Goodrich at some distance behind me, when my ears were saluted by the agreeable sound of falling water. Advancing a little further, I saw the spray arise above the plain like a column of smoke, which would frequently disappear again in an instant; caused, I presume, by the wind which blew pretty hard from the s.w. I did not, however, lose my direction to this point which soon began to make a roaring too tremendous to be mistaken for any cause short of the Great Falls of the Missouri.

I hurried down the hill, which was about 200 feet high and difficult of access, to gaze on this sublimely grand spectacle. . . . I wished for the pencil of Salvator Rosa or the pen of Thompson, that I might be able to give to the world some just idea of this truly magnificent and sublimely grand object, which has from the beginning of time been concealed from the view of civilized man; but this was fruitless and vain. . . .

On the following day, Lewis climbs alone upstream to more cascades.

Friday, June 14th, 1805

. . . A beautiful little island, well timbered, is situated about the middle of the river. On this island, in a cottonwood tree, an eagle has placed her nest. A more inaccessible spot she could not have found, for neither man nor beast dare pass these gulfs which separate her domain from these shores. The water is also broken as it descends over the upper fall, so that the spray or mist rises again to a considerable height.

. . . Just above this is another cascade of about 5 feet, above which the water's velocity began to abate. I ascended the hill behind me. From the summit, I overlooked a beautiful and

extensive plain, reaching from the river to the base of the snow-clad mountains. I saw the meandering course of the Missouri through this plain where immense herds of buffalo were feeding. Vast flocks of geese fed in the delightful pasture on either border. . . .

I descended the hill and headed to the bend of the Missouri where there was a herd of at least a thousand buffalo. . . I selected a fat buffalo and shot him through the lungs.

While I was gazing attentively on the poor animal discharging blood in streams from his mouth and nostrils, expecting him to fall any moment and forgetting to reload my rifle, a large white or brown bear came within 20 steps before I discovered him. I drew up my gun to shoot but at the same instant remembered that she was not loaded. He was too near for me to hope to perform this operation in time, as he was briskly advancing on me. It was an open level plain, not a bush within miles nor a tree within less than 300 yards. The river bank was sloping and not more than three feet deep. In short, there was no place where I could conceal myself from this monster before recharging my rifle. I thought of retreating in a brisk walk as fast as he was advancing, until I could reach a tree about 300 yards below me. I had no sooner turned about when he pitched at me, open mouthed and at full speed. I ran about 80 yards and found he gained on me fast. I ran into the water about waist deep and faced about, presenting the point of my espontoon. At that instant, he arrived at the edge of the water within about 20 feet of me.

The moment I put myself in this position of defense, he suddenly wheeled about as if frightened, declined the combat on such unequal grounds, and retreated with quite as great precipitation as he just before pursued me. As soon as I saw him run off, I returned to the shore and charged my gun. I saw him run through the level open plain about three miles, till he disappeared in the woods. During the whole of this distance he ran at full speed, sometimes looking behind him as if he expected pursuit.

I now began to reflect on this novel occurrence and endeavored to account for this sudden retreat of the bear . . . but the cause of his alarm still remains mysterious and unaccountable to me.

I was gratified that he had declined the combat. My gun reloaded, I felt confidence once more in my strength; and determined never again to suffer my piece to be empty longer than the time required to charge her.

Later, Lewis sees another carnivore which, like the grizzly bear, he has not encountered before this journey – the mountain lion. Later, he is charged by three bison before veering off.

I continued my route homewards and passed the buffalo which I had killed; but did not think it prudent to remain all night here where the succession of curious adventures wore the impression on my mind of enchantment. Sometimes, I thought it might be a dream, but the prickly pears which pierced my feet very severely after dark convinced me that I was really awake, and that it was necessary to make my way to camp.

It was sometime after dark before I returned to the party. I found them extremely uneasy for my safety. They had formed a thousand conjectures, all of which equally forebode my death. They had already agreed on the route each should take in the morning to search for me. I was much fatigued, but ate a hearty supper and took a good night's rest.

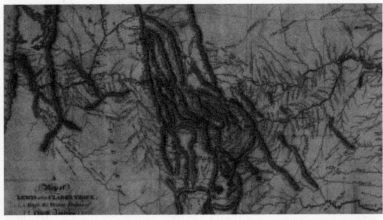

The map produced after the Lewis & Clark Expedition filled in many of the blank areas of earlier charts.

Chapter II

SOUTHERN ROCKIES –
GREAT SAND DUNES
1806-07

from Arkansaw Journey
by Zebulon Montgomery Pike

Even before Lewis and Clark returned, another expedition was sent out under the command of Zebulon Pike to explore the southwestern reaches of the Louisiana Territory. Following the Arkansas River to its sources, his party suffered greatly crossing the Rocky Mtns. in winter. These entries concern his failed attempt to ascend the Grand Peak, now called Pikes Peak, and the later passage through the Great Sand Dunes. After this, his party was taken captive by a Spanish force for trespassing into Spanish territory. It is believed by some that Pike had deliberately trespassed in order to be captured. This gave him an opportunity to spy on their dominions as he was marched down to Chihuahua, Mexico. Later, he was released. It is also believed that he was operating under orders from a traitor named General Wilkinson, governor of the Louisiana Territory and in league with Aaron Burr. There may have been a plan to carve out a separate empire under their command from the Louisiana Territory and the Internal Provinces of New Spain. Others doubt Pike's involvement in the Wilkinson-Burr conspiracy. In late 1806, Pike is ascending a peak in the Rockies.

Nov. 27th, 1806

Arose hungry, dry and extremely sore, from the inequality of the rocks on which we had lain all night. Yet, we were amply compensated for toil by the sublimity of the prospect below. The unbounded prairie was overhung with clouds, which appeared like the ocean in a storm, wave piled on wave and foaming, while the sky was perfectly clear where we were. Commenced our march up the mountain, and in about an hour arrived at the summit of this chain. Here we found snow middle-deep; no sign of beast or bird inhabiting this region. The summit of the Grand Peak, which was entirely bare of vegetation and covered with snow, now appeared at the distance of 15 miles from us. It was as high again as what we had ascended, and it would have taken a whole day's march to arrive at its base, when I believe no human being could have ascended to its pinnacle. This, with the condition of my soldiers, who had only light overalls on, no stockings, and were in every way ill provided to endure the inclemency of the region, dissuaded us. The bad prospect of killing anything to subsist on, with the further detention of two or three days which it must occasion, determined us to return. The clouds from below had now ascended the mountain and entirely enveloped the summit, on which rest eternal snows. We descended by a long, deep ravine, with much less difficulty than contemplated. Found all our baggage safe, but the provisions all destroyed. It began to snow, and we sought shelter under the side of a projecting rock, where all four made a meal on one partridge and a piece of deer's ribs the ravens had left us, being the first we had eaten in 48 hours.

Jan 28th, 1807

Followed down the ravine and discovered after some time that there had been a road cut out; on many trees various hieroglyphics were painted. After marching some miles, we discovered at a distance another chain of mountains. Nearer by, at the foot of the white mountains which we were then descending, were sandy hills. We marched past the outlet of the mountains, left the sandy desert to our right, and kept down between it and the mountain. When we encamped, I ascended one of the largest

"Rocky Mountains," by Albert Bierstadt

hills of sand, and with my glass could see a large river flowing nearly north by west and south by east through the plain. This river came out of the third chain of mountains. I returned to camp with the news of my discovery. The sand-hills extended up and down the foot of the white mountains about 15 miles, and appeared to be about 5 miles in width. Their appearance was exactly that of the sea in a storm, except as to color, not the least sign of vegetation existing thereon.

Chapter III

BLACK HILLS – BIGHORN MTNS. – GRAND TETONS – HELLS CANYON 1811

from Astoria, *by Washington Irving*

Washington Irving

The successful completion of the Lewis & Clark expedition was followed by other private excursions of fur trappers and traders. John Colter left the Lewis & Clark expedition on the return journey to join other trappers coming up the Missouri. It is known he was in the vicinity of the Grand Tetons and Yellowstone but he never kept a diary. Another expedition was sponsored by the wealthy entrepreneur John Jacob Astor. He also planned a transcontinental crossing, with a trading post established on the Pacific coast. He hired Wilson Price Hunt to lead a party overland and a ship, the *Tonquin*, sent by sea around the Horn to the mouth of the Columbia River. Although completed, the expedition could not be called a success. The trading post was abandoned. Most aboard the *Tonquin* were massacred by Indian traders; and the ship itself blown up while the Indians were on board, in retaliation by a hidden survivor still aboard the ship. The overland crossing also met with disaster. Many suffered horribly from hunger or thirst, heat or cold in the excruciating crossing of the Snake River Desert and the Blue Mountains of Oregon. Some died. One went insane. The significant discovery of South Pass was made on the return journey. This would be the easiest route for pioneers later on the Oregon Trail, but this information was kept private by John Jacob Astor.

John J. Astor

In almost all entries included in this volume, the narratives are written by the explorers themselves. Here, an exception is made and is again later with Captain Bonneville because the author relied on journals and interviews of western explorers while writing this in 1835.

While Mr. Hunt was diligently preparing for his arduous journey, some of his men began to lose heart at the perilous pros-

pect before them; but before we accuse them of want of spirit, it is proper to consider the nature of the wilderness into which they were about to adventure. It was a region almost as vast and trackless as the ocean, and, at the time of which we treat, but little known, excepting through the vague accounts of Indian hunters. A part of their route would lay across an immense tract, stretching north and south for hundreds of miles along the foot of the Rocky Mountains, and drained by

W. P. Hunt

the tributary streams of the Missouri and Mississippi. This region, which resembles one of the immeasurable steppes of Asia, has not inaptly been termed "the great American desert." It spreads forth into undulating and treeless plains, and desolate sandy wastes wearisome to the eye from their extent and monotony, and which are supposed by geologists to have formed the ancient floor of the ocean, countless ages since, when its primeval waves beat against the granite bases of the Rocky Mountains.

It is a land where no man permanently abides; for, in certain seasons of the year there is no food either for the hunter or his steed. The herbage is parched and withered; the brooks and streams are dried up; the buffalo, the elk, and the deer have wandered to distant parts, keeping within the verge of expiring verdure, and leaving behind them a vast uninhabited solitude, seamed by ravines, the beds of former torrents, but now serving only to tantalize and increase the thirst of the traveler. Occasionally the monotony of this vast wilderness is interrupted by mountainous belts of sand and limestone, broken into confused masses; with precipitous cliffs and yawning ravines, looking like the ruins of a world; or is traversed by lofty and barren ridges of rock, almost impassable, like those denominated the Black Hills. Beyond these rise the stern barriers of the Rocky Mountains, the limits, as it were, of the Atlantic world. The rugged defiles and deep valleys of this vast chain form sheltering places for restless and ferocious bands of savages, many of them the remnants of tribes, once inhabitants of the prairies, but broken up by war and violence, and who carry into their mountain haunts the fierce passions and reckless habits of desperadoes.

Such is the nature of this immense wilderness of the far West; which apparently defies cultivation, and the habitation of civilized life. . . .

Mr. Hunt and his party were now on the skirts of the Black Hills. . . . The wild recesses of these hills, like those of the Rocky Mountains, are retreats and lurking places for broken and predatory tribes, and it was among them that the remnant of the Cheyenne tribe took refuge, as has been stated, from their conquering enemies, the Sioux.

The Black Hills are chiefly composed of sandstone, and in many places are broken into savage cliffs and precipices, and present the most singular and fantastic forms; sometimes resembling towns and castellated fortresses. The ignorant inhabitants of plains are prone to clothe the mountains that bound their horizon with fanciful and superstitious attributes. Thus the wandering tribes of the prairies, who often behold clouds gathering round the summits of these hills, and lightning flashing, and thunder pealing from them, when all the neighboring plains are serene and sunny, consider them the abode of the genii or thunder-spirits who fabricate storms and tempests. On entering their defiles, therefore, they often hang offerings on the trees, or place them on the rocks, to propitiate the invisible "lords of the mountains," and procure good weather and successful hunting; and they attach unusual significance to the echoes which haunt the precipices. This superstition may also have arisen, in part, from a natural phenomenon of a singular nature. In the most calm and serene weather, and at all times of the day or night, successive reports are now and then heard among these mountains, resembling the discharge of several pieces of artillery. Similar reports were heard by Messrs. Lewis and Clark in the Rocky Mountains, which they say were attributed by the Indians to the bursting of the rich mines of silver contained in the bosom of the mountains. . . .

Whatever might be the supernatural influences among these mountains, the travelers found their physical difficulties hard to cope with. They made repeated attempts to find a passage through or over the chain, but were as often turned back by impassable barriers. Sometimes a defile seemed to open a practicable path, but it would terminate in some wild chaos of rocks and cliffs, which it was impossible to climb. The animals of these solitary regions were different from those they had been accustomed to. The black-tailed deer would bound up the ravines on their approach, and the bighorn would gaze fearlessly down upon them from some impending precipice, or skip playfully from rock to rock. . . .

Baffled in his attempts to traverse this mountain chain, Mr. Hunt skirted along it to the southwest, keeping it on the right; and still in hopes of finding an opening. At an early hour one day, he encamped in a narrow valley on the banks of a beautifully clear but rushy pool; surrounded by thickets bearing abundance of wild cherries, currants, and yellow and purple gooseberries.

While the afternoon's meal was in preparation, Mr. Hunt and Mr. M'Kenzie ascended to the summit of the nearest hill, from whence, aided by the purity and transparency of the evening atmosphere, they commanded a vast prospect on all sides.

Below them extended a plain, dotted with innumerable herds of buffalo. Some were lying down among the herbage, others roaming in their unbounded pastures, while many were engaged in fierce contests like those already described, their low bellowings reaching the ear like the hoarse murmurs of the surf on a distant shore.

Far off in the west they descried a range of lofty mountains printing the clear horizon, some of them evidently capped with snow. These they supposed to be the Bighorn Mountains, so called from the animal of that name, with which they abound. They are a spur of the great Rocky chain. The hill from whence Mr. Hunt had this prospect was, according to his computation, about two hundred and fifty miles from the Arikara village.

After crossing the waste between the Black Hills and the Bighorn chain, Irving notes the following Indian beliefs concerning the Rocky Mountains.

We have already noticed the superstitious feelings with which the Indians regard the Black Hills; but this immense range of mountains, which divides all that they know of the world, and give birth to such mighty rivers, is still more an object of awe and veneration. They call it "the crest of the world," and think that Wacondah, or the master of life, as they designate the Supreme Being, has his residence among these aerial heights. The tribes on the eastern prairies call them the mountains of the setting sun. Some of them place the "happy hunting grounds," their ideal paradise, among the recesses of these mountains; but say that they are invisible to living men. Here also is the "Land of Souls," in which are the "towns of the free and generous spirits," where those who have pleased the master of life while living, enjoy after death all manner of delights.

Wonders are told of these mountains by the distant tribes, whose warriors or hunters have ever wandered in their neighborhood. It is thought by some, after death, they will have to travel to these mountains and ascend one of their highest and most rugged peaks, among rocks and snows and tumbling torrents. After many moons of painful toil they will reach the summit, from whence they will have a view over the land of souls. There they will see the happy hunting grounds, with the souls of the brave and good living in tents in green meadows, by bright running streams, or hunting the herds of buffalo, and elk, and deer, which have been slain on earth. There, too, they will see the villages or towns of the free and generous spirits brightening in the midst of delicious prairies. If they have acquitted themselves well while living, they will be permitted to descend and enjoy this happy country; if otherwise they will be but tantalized with this prospect of it, and then hurled back from the mountain to wander about the sandy plains, and endure the eternal pangs of unsatisfied thirst and hunger. . . .

Making a circuit around the southern end of the Bighorn Mountains, they cross the Bighorn River Basin. They follow the Wind River toward its source in the mountains, then turn up another stream, reaching a pass where the Tetons are seen off in the distance.

In the course of the day, they came to a height that commanded an almost boundless prospect. Here one of the guides paused, and, after considering the vast landscape attentively, pointed to three mountain peaks glistening with snow, which rose, he said, above a fork of Columbia River. They were hailed by the travelers with that joy with which a beacon on a sea-shore is hailed by mariners after a long and dangerous voyage. It is true there was many a weary league to be traversed before they should reach these landmarks, for, allowing for their evident height and the extreme transparency of the atmosphere, they could not be much less than a hundred miles distant. Even after reaching them, there would yet remain hundreds of miles of their journey to be accomplished. All these matters were forgotten in the joy at seeing the first landmarks of the Columbia, that river which formed the bourne of the expedition. These remarkable peaks were known as the Tetons; as guiding points for many days to Mr. Hunt, he gave them the name of the Pilot Knobs. . . .

Being now well supplied with provisions, Mr. Hunt broke up his encampment on the 24th of September, and continued to the west. A march of fifteen miles, over a mountain ridge, brought them to a stream about fifty feet in width, which Hoback, one of their guides, who had trapped about the neighborhood when in the service of Mr. Henry, recognized for one of the head waters of the Columbia. The travelers hailed it with delight, as the first stream they had encountered tending toward their point of destination.

They kept along it for two days, during which, from the contribution of many rills and brooks, it gradually swelled into a small river. As it meandered among rocks and precipices, they were frequently obliged to ford it, and such was its rapidity, that the men were often in danger of being swept away. Sometimes the banks advanced so close upon the river, that they were obliged to scramble up and down their rugged promontories, or to skirt along their bases where there was scarce a foothold. Their horses had dangerous falls in some of these passes. One of them rolled, with his load, nearly two hundred feet down hill into the river, but without receiving any injury. At length they emerged from these stupendous defiles, and continued for several miles along the bank of Hoback's River, through one of the stern mountain valleys. Here it was joined by a river of greater magnitude and swifter current, and their united waters swept off through the valley in one impetuous stream, which, from its rapidity and turbulence, had received the name of the Mad River. At the confluence of these streams the travelers encamped. An important part in their arduous journey had been attained, a few miles from their camp rose the three vast snowy peaks called the Tetons, or the Pilot Knobs, the great landmarks of the Columbia, by which they had shaped their course through this mountain wilderness. By their feet flowed the rapid current of Mad River, a stream ample enough to admit of the navigation of canoes, and down which they might possibly be able to steer their course to the main body of the Columbia. The Canadian voyageurs rejoiced at the idea of once more launching themselves upon their favorite element; of exchanging their horses for canoes, and of gliding down the bosoms of rivers, instead of scrambling over the backs of mountains. Others of the party, also, inexperienced in this kind of traveling, considered their toils and troubles as drawing to a close. They had conquered the chief difficulties of this great rocky barrier, and now flattered themselves with the hope of an easy downward course for the rest of their journey. Little did they dream of the hardships and perils by land and water, which were yet to be encountered in the frightful wilderness that intervened between them and the shores of the Pacific!

The Snake River country was unfamiliar even to their hunter guides. They canoed down the Snake River and it became increasingly turbulent until disaster overtakes them.

The river again became rough and impetuous, and was chafed and broken by numerous rapids. These grew more and more dangerous, and the utmost skill was required to steer among them. Mr. Crooks was seated in the second canoe of the squadron, and had an old experienced Canadian for steersman, named Antoine Clappine, one of the most valuable of the voyageurs. The leading canoe had glided safely among the turbulent and roaring surges, but in following it, Mr. Crooks perceived that his canoe was bearing towards a rock. He called out to the steersman, but his warning voice was either unheard or unheeded. In the next moment they struck upon the rock. The canoe was split and overturned. There were five persons on board. Mr. Crooks and one of his companions were thrown amidst roaring breakers and a whirling current, but succeeded, by strong swimming, to reach the shore. Clappine and two others clung to the shattered bark, and drifted with it to a rock. The wreck struck upon the rock with one end, and swinging around, flung poor Clappine off into the raging stream, which swept him away, and he perished. His comrades succeeded in getting upon the rock, from whence they were afterwards taken off.

This disastrous event brought the whole squadron to a halt, and struck a chill into every bosom. Indeed they had arrived at a terrific strait, that forbade all further progress in the canoes, and dismayed the most experienced voyageur. The whole body of the river was compressed into a space of less than thirty feet in width, between two ledges of rocks, upwards of two hundred feet high, and formed a whirling and tumultuous vortex, so frightfully agitated as to receive the name of "The Caldron Linn." Beyond this fearful abyss, the river kept raging and roaring on, until lost to sight among impending precipices. . . .

The situation of the unfortunate travellers was now gloomy in the extreme. They were in the heart of an unknown wilderness, untraversed as yet by a white man. They were at a loss what route to take, and how far they were from the ultimate place of their destination, nor could they meet in these uninhabited wilds with any human being to give them information. The repeated accidents to their canoes had reduced their stock of provisions to five days' allowance, and there was now every appearance of soon having famine added to their other sufferings.

This last circumstance rendered it more perilous to keep together than to separate. Accordingly, after a little anxious but bewildered counsel, it was determined that several small detachments should start off in different directions, headed by the several partners. Should any of them succeed in falling in with friendly Indians, within a reasonable distance, and obtaining a supply of provisions and horses, they were to return to the aid of the main body: otherwise they were to shift for themselves, and shape their course according to circumstances; keeping the mouth of the Columbia River as their ultimate point of their wayfaring. Accordingly, three several parties set off from the camp at Caldron Linn, in opposite directions.

The various parties find no relief crossing the Snake River desert. The few Indians they encounter are in desperate poverty themselves, barely finding enough food for their own survival. In extreme suffering and despair, the separated parties each approach Hells Canyon. The narrative follows the fortunes of the main party under Hunt.

The month of December set in drearily, with rain in the valleys and snow upon the hills. They had to climb a mountain with snow to the midleg, which increased their painful toil. A small beaver supplied them with a scanty meal, which they eked out with frozen blackberries, haws, and choke-cherries, which they found in the course of their scramble. Their journey this day, though excessively fatiguing, was but thirteen miles; and all the next day they had to remain encamped, not being able to see half a mile ahead, on account of a snow-storm. Having nothing else to eat, they were compelled to kill another of their horses. The next day they resumed their march in snow and rain, but with all their efforts could only get forward nine miles, having for a part of the distance to unload the horses and carry the packs themselves. On the succeeding morning they were obliged to leave the river and scramble up the hills. From the summit of these, they got a wide view of the surrounding country, and it was a prospect almost sufficient to make them despair. In every direction they beheld snowy mountains, partially sprinkled with pines and other evergreens, and spreading a desert and toilsome world around them. The wind howled over the bleak and wintry landscape, and seemed to penetrate to the marrow of their bones. They waded on through the snow, which at every step was more than knee deep.

After toiling in this way all day, they had the mortification to find that they were but four miles distant from the encampment of the preceding night, such was the meandering of the river among these dismal hills. Pinched with famine, exhausted with fatigue, with evening approaching, and a wintry wild still lengthening as they advanced, they began to look forward with sad forebodings to the night's exposure upon this frightful waste. Fortunately they succeeded in reaching a cluster of pines about sunset. Their axes were immediately at work; they cut down trees, piled them in great heaps, and soon had huge fires "to cheer their cold and hungry hearts."

About three o'clock in the morning it again began to snow, and at daybreak they found themselves, as it were, in a cloud, scarcely being able to distinguish objects at the distance of a hundred yards. Guiding themselves by the sound of running water, they set out for the river, and by slipping and sliding contrived to get down to its bank. One of the horses, missing his footing, rolled down several hundred yards with his load, but sustained no injury. The weather in the valley was less rigorous than on the hills. The snow lay but ankle deep, and there was a quiet rain now falling. After creeping along for six miles, they encamped on the border of the river. Being utterly destitute of provisions, they were again compelled to kill one of their horses to appease their famishing hunger. . . .

The wanderers had now accomplished four hundred and seventy-two miles of their dreary journey since leaving the Caldron Linn; how much further they had yet to travel, and what hardships to encounter, no one knew.

On the morning of the 6th of December, they left their dismal encampment, but had scarcely begun their march when, to their surprise, they beheld a party of white men coming up along the opposite bank of the river. As they drew nearer, they were recognized for Mr. Crooks and his companions. When they came opposite, and could make themselves heard across the murmuring of the river, their first cry was for food; in fact, they were almost starved. Mr. Hunt immediately returned to the camp, and had a kind of canoe made out of the skin of the horse killed on the preceding night. This was done after the Indian fashion, by drawing up the edges of the skin with thongs, and keeping them distended by sticks or thwart pieces. In this frail bark, Sardepie, one of the Canadians, carried over a portion of the flesh of the horse to the famishing party on the opposite side of the river, and brought back with him Mr. Crooks and the Canadian, Le Clerc. The forlorn and wasted looks and starving condition of these two men struck dismay to the hearts of Mr. Hunt's followers. They had been accustomed to each other's appearance, and to the gradual operation of hunger and hardship upon their frames, but the change in the looks of these men, since last they parted, was a type of the famine and desolation of the land; and they now began to indulge the horrible presentiment that they would all starve together, or be reduced to the direful alternative of casting lots!

When Mr. Crooks had appeased his hunger, he gave Mr. Hunt some account of his wayfaring. On the side of the river along which he had kept, he had met with but few Indians, and those were too miserably poor to yield much assistance. For the first eighteen days after leaving the Caldron Linn, he and his men had been confined to half a meal in twenty-four hours; for three days following, they had subsisted on a single beaver, a few wild cherries, and the soles of old moccasins; and for the last six days their only animal food had been the carcass of a dog. They had been three days' journey further down the river than

Mr. Hunt, always keeping as near to its banks as possible, and frequently climbing over sharp and rocky ridges that projected into the stream. At length they had arrived to where the mountains increased in height, and came closer to the river, with perpendicular precipices, which rendered it impossible to keep along the stream. The river here rushed with incredible velocity through a defile not more than thirty yards wide, where cascades and rapids succeeded each other almost without intermission. Even had the opposite banks, therefore, been such as to permit a continuance of their journey, it would have been madness to attempt to pass the tumultuous current either on rafts or otherwise. Still bent, however, on pushing forward, they attempted to climb the opposing mountains; and struggled on through the snow for half a day until, coming to where they could command a prospect, they found that they were not half way to the summit, and that mountain upon mountain lay piled beyond them, in wintry desolation. Famished and emaciated as they were, to continue forward would be to perish; their only chance seemed to be to regain the river, and retrace their steps up its banks. It was in this forlorn and retrograde march that they had met Mr. Hunt and his party.

Mr. Crooks also gave information of some others of their fellow adventurers. He had spoken several days previously with Mr. Reed and Mr. M'Kenzie, who with their men were on the opposite side of the river, where it was impossible to get over to them. They informed him that Mr. M'Lellan had struck across from the little river above the mountains, in the hope of falling in with some of the tribe of Flatheads, who inhabit the western skirts of the Rocky range. As the companions of Reed and M'Kenzie were picked men, and had found provisions more abundant on their side of the river, they were in better condition and more fitted to contend with the difficulties of the country, than those of Mr. Crooks, and when he lost sight of them, were pushing onward, down the course of the river. . . .

The combined parties of Hunt and Crooks left the Hells Canyon of Snake River and crossed over the Blue Mountains of Oregon, no easy feat but they managed to get through to Astoria. There they met the parties of Reed, M'Kenzie and M'Lellan who related the tale of their passage through Hells Canyon and down the Columbia. The following narrative tells about their experiences.

They accordingly continued to follow the downward course of Snake River; clambering rocks and mountains, and defying all the difficulties and dangers of that rugged defile, which subsequently, when the snows had fallen, was found impassable by Messrs. Hunt and Crooks.

Though constantly near to the borders of the river, and for a great part of the time within sight of its current, one of their greatest sufferings was thirst. The river had worn its way in a deep channel through rocky mountains, destitute of brooks or springs. Its banks were so high and precipitous, that there was rarely any place where the travelers could get down to drink of its waters. Frequently they suffered for miles the torments of Tantalus; water continually within sight, yet fevered with the most parching thirst. Here and there they met with rainwater collected in the hollows of the rocks, but more than once they were reduced to the utmost extremity; and some of the men had recourse to the last expedient to avoid perishing.

Their sufferings from hunger were equally severe. They could meet with no game, and subsisted for a time on strips of beaver skin, broiled on the coals. These were doled out in scanty allowances, barely sufficient to keep up existence, and at length failed them altogether. Still they crept feebly on, scarce dragging one limb after another, until a severe snow-storm brought them to a pause. To struggle against it, in their exhausted condition, was impossible, so cowering under an impending rock at the foot of a steep mountain, they prepared themselves for that wretched fate which seemed inevitable.

At this critical juncture, when famine stared them in the face, M'Lellan casting up his eyes, beheld an ahsahta, or bighorn, sheltering itself under a shelving rock on the side of the hill above them. Being in a more active plight than any of his comrades, and an excellent marksman, he set off to get within shot of the animal. His companions watched his movements with breathless anxiety, for their lives depended upon his success. He made a cautious circuit; scrambled up the hill with the utmost silence, and at length arrived, unperceived, within a proper distance. Here leveling his rifle he took so sure an aim, that the bighorn fell dead on the spot; a fortunate circumstance, for, to pursue it, if merely wounded, would have been impossible in his emaciated state. The declivity of the hill enabled him to roll the carcass down to his companions, who were too feeble to climb the rocks. They fell to work to cut it up; yet exerted a remarkable self-denial for men in their starving condition, for they contented themselves for the present with a soup made from the bones, reserving the flesh for future repasts. This providential relief gave them strength to pursue their journey, but they were frequently reduced to almost equal straits, and it was only the smallness of their party, requiring a small supply of provisions, that enabled them to get through this desolate region with their lives.

Chapter IV

NORTH CASCADES
1814

from Fur Hunters of the Far West
by Alexander Ross

British fur traders were pushing down from Canada into the north-west about the same time as the Americans. Astoria was abandoned to British control with the outbreak of the War of 1812. Alexander Ross was one of the party who came to Astoria on board the *Tonquin* and shifted their allegiance to the British trading company. The British Northwest Co. established several forts along the coast and in the interior along the Columbia and Snake Rivers. One of these was Okanogan, located in central Washington State along the Columbia River. From this establishment, Alexander Ross discusses expeditions he took in the employ of the Northwest Co. The passage west across the North Cascades was a failed attempt to open a path across the mountains to the Pacific. It is unclear exactly what path Ross followed but was probably in the southern half of the park. The dense forested 'holes' of the North Cascades are vividly described. He is abandoned by his Indian guides due to illness and fear caused by a dramatic thunderstorm, forcing him to turn away from his goal. The selected entry begins several days after leaving Okanogan.

On the twenty-sixth (June) – We made an early start this morning, course as nearly as possible due west. Not half an hour had passed, before we had to steer to every point of the compass, so many impediments crossed our path. On entering the dense and gloomy forest I tried my pocket compass, but to very little purpose, as we could not in many places travel fifty yards in any one direction, so rocky and uneven was the surface over which we had to pass. . . .

On the twenty-ninth – This morning we started in a southerly direction, but soon got to the west again. Country gloomy, forests almost impervious, with fallen as well as standing timber. A more difficult route to travel never fell to man's lot. On the heights the chief timber is a kind of spruce fir, not very large, only two or three feet in diameter. The valleys were filled with poplar, alder, stunted birch, and willows. This range of mountains, lying in the direction of nearly s. and n. are several hundred miles in length. The tracks of wild animals crossed our path in every direction. The leaves and decayed vegetation were uncommonly thick on the surface of the ground, and the mice and squirrels swarmed, and had riddled the earth like a sieve. The fallen timber lay in heaps, nor did it appear that the fire ever passed in this place. The surface of the earth appeared in perfect confusion, and the rocks and yawning chasms gave to the whole an air of solemn gloom and undisturbed silence. My companions began to flag during the day.

On the thirtieth – The sixth day, in the evening, we reached a height of land, which on the east side is steep and abrupt. Here we found the water running in the opposite direction. My guide unfortunately fell sick at this place, and we very reluctantly had to wait for two days until he recovered, when we resumed our journey; but his recovery was slow, and on the second day he gave up altogether, and could proceed no further. We were still among the rugged cliffs and deep groves of the mountain, where we seldom experienced the cheering sight of the sun, nor could we get to any elevated spot clear enough to have a view of the surrounding country. By getting to the top of a tall tree, now and then, we got some relief, though but little, for we could seldom see to any distance, so covered was all around us with a thick and almost impenetrable forest. The weather was cold, and snow capped many of the higher peaks. In such a situation I found myself, and without a guide. To go forward without him was almost impossible; to turn back was labor lost; to remain where we were was anything but pleasant; to abandon the sick man to his fate was not to be thought of. The serious question then arose, what to do? At last we settled the matter, so that one of the Indians should remain with the guide, and the other accompany me, I still intending to proceed. We then separated, I taking care every now and then as we went along to mark with a small axe some of the larger trees to assist us on our way back, in case our compass got deranged, although, as I have already noticed, we but seldom used it while our guide was with us; but the case was different now, it was the only guide I had.

August fourth – We were early on the road this morning, and were favored occasionally with open ground. We had not gone far when we fell on a small creek running, by compass, w.s.w., but so meandering, that we had to cross and recross it upwards of forty times in the course of the day. The water was clear and cold and soon increased so much that we had to avoid it and steer our course from point to point on the north side. Its bottom was muddy in some places, in others stony, its banks low and lined with poplars, but so overhung with wood, that we could oftener hear than see the stream. On this unpromising stream, flowing, no doubt, to the Pacific, we saw six beaver lodges, and two of the animals themselves, one of which we shot. We shot a very fine otter also, and notwithstanding the season of the year, the fur was black. Tired and hungry, we put up at a late hour.

On the fifth – I slept but little during the night. My mind was too occupied to enjoy repose, so we got up and started at an early hour. Our journey today was through a delightful country of hill and dale, wood and plains. Late in the afternoon, however, we were disturbed and greatly agitated, by a fearful and continuous noise in the air, loud as thunder, but with no intervals. Not a breath of wind ruffled the air, but towards the southwest, from whence the noise came, the whole atmosphere was darkened, black, and heavy. Our progress was arrested; we stood and listened in anxious suspense for nearly half an hour, the noise still increasing, and coming, as it were, nearer and nearer to us. If I could compare it to anything, it would be to the rush of a heavy body of water, falling from a height; but when it came opposite to where we stood, in a moment we beheld the woods before it bending down like grass before the scythe! It was the wind, accompanied with a torrent of rain – a perfect hurricane, such as I had never witnessed before. It reminded me at once of those terrible visitations of the kind peculiar to tropical climates. Sometimes a slight tornado or storm of the kind has been experienced on the Oregon, but not often. The crash of falling trees, and the dark, heavy cloud, like a volume of condensed smoke, concealed from us at the time the extent of its destructive effects. We remained motionless until the storm was over. It lasted an hour, and although it was scarcely a quarter of a mile from us, all we felt of it was a few heavy drops of rain, as cold as ice, with scarcely any wind; but the rolling cloud passed on, carrying destruction before it, as far as the eye could follow. In a short time we perceived the havoc it had made by the avenue it left behind. It had leveled everything in its way to the dust; the very grass was beaten down to the earth for nearly a quarter of a mile in breadth.

The Indian I had along with me was so amazed and thunderstruck with superstition and fear at what he had seen, that his whole frame became paralyzed. He trembled, and sighed to get back. He refused to accompany me any further, and all I could either say or do could not turn him from his purpose.

Although he manages to threaten and cajole the Indian guide to stay with him, that night he gives Ross the slip. Unable to find his own way to the Pacific, he follows the same path back to the Indian guides. The attempt to reach the ocean was abandoned and they all returned to Fort Okanogan.

Chapter V

BADLANDS – BLACK HILLS
1823

from The Narrative of James Clyman

The following three selections come from the fur-trapping excursions sent out by William Ashley. One of his employees was Jedediah Smith, who led very early extensive expeditions throughout the Plains, Rockies and Great Basin to New Mexico, California and the Oregon country. On one of these, he would rediscover South Pass, the conduit for fur trappers and pioneers across the continent. This selection is taken from the expedition that was the first led by Jedediah Smith. The excerpt is taken from the diary of James Clyman, another young man hired by William Ashley. Diverted from the Missouri River by an attack from the Arikara Indians, it is believed this expedition passed through the Badlands, although he gives little description of it. Instead, he provides interesting tales of their sufferings and what they did to survive, including burying some of the men in sand up to their chins while the rest of the party went on to hunt for water. The grizzly bear attack on Jedediah Smith related here was close in time to the remarkable story of Hugh Glass. This tough frontiersman had been badly mauled by a grizzly in the area of northwestern South Dakota. Abandoned for dead by his companions (one was the young Jim Bridger), who feared an Indian attack was imminent, he managed to survive and crawl alone across hundreds of miles of wilderness – through the hot searing plains, surviving on rattlesnake meat, until he reached an outpost on the Missouri River. This and the story here of Jedediah Smith reflects the legendary toughness of the frontiersman.

Jedediah Smith

> . . . *About dark we all got collected, except two who had given out and were left buried in the sand all but their heads. Capt. Smith, being the last who was able to still walk, took some water back, then bringing up the exhausted men whom he had buried in the sand. . . .*

. . . Again we fell into a tract of country where no vegetation of any kind existed, being worn into knobs and gullies and extremely uneven. A loose, grayish colored soil, very soluble in water, ran thick as it moved, of a pale whitish color and remarkably adhesive. There came on a misty rain while we were in this pile of ashes and it loaded down our horses' feet in great lumps. It looked remarkable that not a foot of level land could be found, the narrow ravines going in all manner of direction and the cobble mounds of a regular taper from top to bottom, all of them of the precise same angle and the tops sharp. The whole of this region is moving to the Missouri River as fast as rain and thawing of snow can carry it. By inclining to the west, in a few hours we got on to smooth ground and soon cleared ourselves of mud. At length, we arrived at the foot of the Black Hills, which rises in a very slight elevation above the common plain. We entered a pleasant undulating pine region, cool and refreshing, so different from the hot, dusty plains we have been so long passing over. . . .

. . . Late in the afternoon, while passing through a brushy bottom, a large grizzly came down the valley. We being in single file on foot leading pack horses, he struck us about the center, then turning ran parallel to our line. Capt. Smith, being in the advance, ran to the open ground and as he emerged from the thicket, he and the bear met face to face. Grizzly did not hesitate a moment but sprang on the captain, taking him by the head first. Pitching and sprawling on the earth, he grabbed him by the middle, fortunately catching by the ball pouch and butcher knife, which he broke, but also breaking several of his ribs and cutting his head badly. None of us had any surgical knowledge and asked each other what was to be done. I asked the captain what was best. He said for someone to go for water and to get out a thread and needle and sew up the wounds around his head, which was bleeding freely. I got a pair of scissors, cut off his hair and began my first job of dressing wounds. Upon examination, I found the bear had taken nearly all of his head in his capacious mouth, close to his left eye on one side and close to his right ear on the other and had laid the skull bare to near the crown of the head, leaving a white streak where his teeth passed. One of his ears was torn from his head to the outer rim. After stitching all the other wounds in the best way I was capable and according to the captain's direction, I told him I could do nothing for his ear. "O, you must try to stitch it up some way

or other," said he. Then I put in my needle, stitching it through and through, over and over, laying the lacerated parts together as nice as I could with my hands. Water was found in about a mile when we moved on and encamped. The captain was able to mount his horse and ride to camp, where we pitched the only tent we had and made him as comfortable as circumstances would permit.

Chapter VI

FLAMING GORGE – DINOSAUR
1825

from The Narrative of William Ashley

William Ashley would split up his men into different parties and send them out in different directions to trap for beaver, later to meet again at a Rendezvous near the Wind River Mtns. After splitting up into different parties, this one was led down the Green River by Ashley himself, believing it to be the fabled Buenaventura that would lead them down an easy passage to the California coast. Not prepared for such wild rapids, his party abandoned the river and went overland after the journey described here. Later in 1849, William Manly, and in 1869, John Wesley Powell, passed through here with their exploring parties and discovered a spot where Ashley had carved his name and date onto the cliffs.

Downstream in Lodore Canyon, Powell also discovered the remains of a boat wreck and mistakenly believed it to be the remains of a disastrous one from the Ashley expedition. However, Ashley's narrative relates no such incident.

Ashley gives a more detailed description of Flaming Gorge while giving a briefer description of Dinosaur's canyons near the end. Apparently, they had to portage through most of Lodore Canyon.

After the departure of the land parties, I embarked with six men on Thursday, April 21, on board my newly made boat and began the descent of the river. . . .

Monday, April 25th . . . we arrived at the base of a lofty rugged mountain, the summit of which was covered with snow and bearing east and west. . . .

Flaming Gorge

Saturday, May 2nd: We continued our voyage about half a mile below our camp, when we entered between the walls of this range of mountains, which approach at this point to the waters' edge on either side of the river and rise almost perpendicular to *an immense height. The channel of the river is here contracted to the width of sixty or seventy yards, and the current (much increased in velocity) as it rolled along in angry submission to the serpentine walls that direct it, seemed constantly to threaten us with danger as we advanced. We, however, succeeded in descending about ten miles without any difficulty or material change in the aspect of things and encamped for the night. About two miles above this camp, we passed the mouth of a creek on the west side some fifteen yards wide, which discharged its water with great violence.*

Sunday, May 3rd: After progressing two miles, the navigation became difficult and dangerous, the river being remarkably crooked with more or less rapids every mile caused by rocks which had fallen from the sides of the mountain, many of which rise above the surface of the water and required our greatest exertions to avoid them. At twenty miles from our last camp, the roaring and agitated state of the water a short distance before us indicated a fall or some other obstruction of considerable magnitude. Our boats were consequently rowed to shore, along which we cautiously descended to the place from whence the danger was to be apprehended. It proved to be a perpendicular fall of ten or twelve feet produced by large fragments of rocks which had fallen from the mountain and settled in the river extending entirely across its channel and forming an impregnable barrier to the passage of loaded watercraft. We were therefore obliged to unload our boats of their cargoes and pass them empty over the falls by means of long cords which we had provided for such purposes. At sunset, our boats were reloaded and we descended a mile lower down and encamped.

Monday, May 4th: This day we made about forty miles. The navigation and mountains by which the river is bounded continues pretty much the same as yesterday. These mountains appear to be almost entirely composed of stratas of rock and various colors (mostly red) and are partially covered with a dwarfish growth of pine and cedar, which are the only species of timber to be seen.

They leave the canyons of Flaming Gorge and pass through the open area of Browns Hole.

Tuesday, May 5ᵗʰ: After descending six miles, the mountains gradually recede from the water's edge, and the river expands to the width of two hundred and fifty yards, leaving the river bottoms on each side from one to three hundred yards wide interspersed with clusters of small willows. We remained at our encampment here until the morning of the 7ᵗʰ, when we descended ten miles lower down and encamped on a spot of ground where several thousand Indians had wintered during the past season. Their camp had been judiciously selected for defense, and the remains of their work around it accorded with the judgment exercised in the selection. Many of their lodges remained as perfect as when occupied. They were made of poles two or three inches in diameter, set up in circular form, and covered with cedar bark.

Dinosaur

Friday, May 8ᵗʰ: We proceeded down the river about two miles, where it again enters between two mountains and affording a channel even more contracted than before (Lodore Canyon). *As we passed along between these massive walls, which in a great degree exclude from us the rays of heaven and presented a surface as impassable as their body was impregnable, I was forcibly struck with the gloom which spread over the countenances of my men; they seemed to anticipate (and not far distant, too) a dreadful termination of our voyage, and I must confess that I partook in some degree of what I supposed to be their feelings, for things around has had truly an awful appearance. We soon came to a dangerous rapid which we passed over with a slight injury to our boats. A mile lower down, the channel became so obstructed by the intervention of large rocks, over and between which the water dashed with such violence, as to render our passage in safety impracticable. The cargoes of our boats were therefore a second time taken out and carried about two hundred yards, to which place, after much labor, our boats were descended by means of cords. Thence we descended fifty miles to the mouth of a beautiful river emptying on each side, to which I gave the name of Mary's river* (Yampa River). *The navigation continued dangerous and difficult the whole way; the mountains equally lofty and rugged with their summits entirely covered with snow. Mary's river is one hundred yards wide, has a rapid current, and from every appearance very much confined between lofty mountains. A valley about two hundred yards wide extends one mile below the confluence of these rivers, then the mountain again on that side advances to the water's edge* (Echo Park). *Two miles lower down is a very dangerous rapid, and eight miles further the mountain withdraws from the river on the west side about a half mile.*

Here we found a luxurious growth of sweet-bark or round-leaf cottonwood and a number of buffalo, and succeeded by narrow river bottoms and hills. The former, as well as several islands, are partly clothed with a luxuriant growth of round-leaf cotton- wood and extend four miles down the river, where the moun- tains again close to the water's edge and are in appearance more terrific than any we had seen during the whole voyage. They immediately produce bad rapids, which follow in quick succession for twenty miles, below which, as far as I descended, the river is without obstruction. In the course of our passage through the several ranges of mountains, we performed sixteen portages, the most of which were attended with the utmost diffi- culty and labor.

The Ashley party exits from the lower end of Dinosaur and aban- dons the river.

Chapter VII

YELLOWSTONE
1827

from an article by Daniel Potts
in the Niles Register, *Oct. 6, 1827*

This is the first of three entries that describe early encounters with Yellowstone before 1840 by roaming bands of fur trappers. These are the earliest written accounts of Yellowstone but, somehow, their discoveries did not become public knowledge, although this first account appeared in the Philadelphia newspaper. It describes Yellowstone Lake and an encounter with the hostile Blackfoot Indians.

Sweet Lake, July 8, 1827: Shortly after writing to you last, I departed for the Blackfoot country much against my will, but I could not make a party for any other route. We took a northerly direction for about fifty miles, where we crossed Snake River at the forks of Henry and Lewis. At this place we were daily harassed by the Blackfoot. From thence we went up Henry's Fork, which bears north of east thirty miles, and crossed a large rugged mountain which separated the two forks. Then we went east up the other branch to its source, near the top of the great chain of Rocky Mountains, which separates the waters of the Atlantic from those of the Pacific. Many rivers have their beginning here; that of the Yellowstone has a large freshwater lake near its head at the very top of the mountains, about 100 by 40 miles in diameter, and as clear as crystal. On the south border of this lake are a number of hot boiling springs, some of water and others of most beautiful fine clay, resembling a mush pot, and throwing particles to the height of 20 to 30 feet. The clay is a white and pink color, and the water appears fathomless, as it appears to be entirely hollow underneath. There are also a number of places where pure sulphur is sent forth in abundance. While one of our men visited one, at an instant, the earth began a tremendous trembling, and he with difficulty made his escape, when an explosion took place, resembling that of thunder. During our stay, I heard it every day. Then we left by a circuitous route to the northwest.

Two others and myself pushed on in advance for the purpose of accumulating a few more beaver. In the act of passing through a narrow confine in the mountain, we were met head on by a large party of Blackfoot Indians, who, not knowing our number, fled into the mountains in confusion. We retired to a small grove of willows. Here we made every preparation for battle; after which, finding our enemy as much alarmed as ourselves, we mounted our horses, which we hastily loaded, and took the back retreat. We here put whips to our horses and they pursued us in close quarters until we reached the plains, where we left them behind. On this trip, one man was closely fired on by a party of Blackfoot; several others were closely pursued.

Chapter VIII

GRAND TETONS – YELLOWSTONE
1830-35

from Life in the Rocky Mountains
by Warren Angus Ferris

The second of three narratives in Yellowstone before 1840 was written and first published by a fur trapper in 1842. His writing style is sometimes overheated but is appropriate for the scenes he witnessed. These include the massive herds of charging bison, a wonderful view of Jackson Hole from Teton Pass and, finally, a visit to the Firehole Geyser basins of Yellowstone.

. . . Next day, oh, there they were, thousands and thousands of them! Far as the eye could reach the prairie was literally covered, and not only covered but crowded with them. In very sooth it was a gallant show; a vast expanse of moving, plunging, rolling, rushing life – a literal sea of dark forms, with still pools, sweeping currents, and heaving billows, and all the grades of movement from calm repose to wild agitation. The air was filled with dust and bellowings, the prairie was alive with animation. I never realized before the majesty and power of the mighty tides of life that heave and surge in all great gatherings of brute creation. The scene had here a wild sublimity of aspect, that charmed the eye with a spell of power, while the natural sympathy of life with life made the pulse bound and almost madden with excitement. Jove but it was glorious! and the next day too, the dense masses pressed on in such vast numbers, that we were compelled to halt, and let them pass to avoid being overrun by them in a literal sense. On the following day also, the number seemed if possible more countless than before, surpassing even the prairie-blackening accounts of those who had been here before us, and whose strange tales it had been our wont to believe the natural extravagance of a mere travelers' turn for romancing, but they must have been true, for such a scene as this our language wants words to describe, much less to exaggerate. On, on, still on, the black masses come and thicken – an ebbless deluge of life is moving and swelling around us!

. . . Leaving this, we passed the narrows, a corner of Jackson's Big Hole, crossed Lewis River, ascended the mountains, and on the 30th came into a region where the weather was fair, the sky cloudless above us, and the sun shining pleasantly, quite reverse to the appearance a short distance below. Gazing down, in the direction of Jackson's Hole, from our elevated position, one of the most beautiful scenes imaginable was presented to our view. It seemed quite filled with large bright clouds, resembling immense banks of snow, piled on each other in massive numbers, of the purest white, wreathing their ample folds in various forms and devious convolutions, and mingling in one vast embrace their shadowy substance.

. . . I had heard in the summer of 1833, while at rendezvous, that remarkable boiling springs had been discovered, on the sources of the Madison, by a party of trappers in their spring hunt; of which the accounts they gave were so very astonishing, that I determined to examine them myself, before recording their descriptions, though I had the united testimony of more than twenty men on the subject, who all declared they saw them, and that they really were as extensive and remarkable as they had been described. Having now an opportunity of paying them a visit, and as another or a better might not soon occur, I parted with the company after supper, and taking with me two Pend-O'reilles, set out at a round pace, the night being clear and comfortable. We proceeded over the plain about twenty miles, and halted until daylight on a fine spring, flowing into Camas Creek. Refreshed by a few hours sleep, we started again after a hasty breakfast, and entered a very extensive forest called the Piney Woods, which we passed through, and reached the vicinity of the springs about dark, having seen several small lakes or ponds, on the sources of the Madison. We rode about forty miles; which was a hard day's ride, taking into consideration the rough irregularity of the country through which we had traveled.

We regaled ourselves with a cup of coffee, and immediately after supper lay down to rest, sleepy, and much fatigued. The continual roaring of the springs, however, for some time prevented my going to sleep, and excited an impatient curiosity to examine them; which I was obliged to defer the gratification of until morning; and filled my slumbers with visions of water spouts, cataracts, fountains, jets d'eau of immense dimensions, etc., etc.

When I arose in the morning, clouds of vapor seemed like a dense fog to overhang the springs, from which frequent reports or explosions of different loudness, constantly assailed our ears. I immediately proceeded to inspect them, and might have exclaimed with the Queen of Sheba, when their full reality of dimensions and novelty burst upon my view, "the half was not told me."

From the surface of a rocky plain or table, burst forth columns of water, of various dimensions, projected high in the air, accompanied by loud explosions, and sulphurous vapors, which were highly disagreeable to the smell. The rock from which these springs burst forth, was calcareous, and probably extends some distance from them, beneath the soil. The largest of these wonderful fountains, projects a column of boiling water several feet in diameter, to the height of more than one hundred and fifty feet, accompanied with a tremendous noise. These explosions and discharges occur at intervals of about two hours. After having witnessed three of them, I ventured near enough to put my hand into the water of its basin; but withdrew it instantly, for the heat of the water in this immense cauldron was altogether too great for comfort, and the agitation of the water, the disagreeable effluvium continually exuding, and the hollow unearthly rumbling under the rock on which I stood, so ill accorded with my notions of personal safety, that I retreated back precipitately to a respectful distance. The Indians who were with me, were quite appalled, and could not by any means be induced to approach them. They seemed astonished at my presumption in advancing up to the large one, and when I safely returned, congratulated me on my "narrow escape." (It seems reasonable to conclude that the Indians were appalled because what Ferris was doing was dangerous, as he could have broken through the thin crust and burned himself to death in the scalding water. Nevertheless Ferris remarks the following.) *They believed them to be supernatural, and supposed them to be the production of the Evil Spirit. One of them remarked that hell, of which he had heard from the whites, must be in that vicinity. The diameter of the basin into which the water of the largest jet principally falls, and from the center of which, through a hole in the rock of about ten feet in diameter, the water spouts up as above related, may be about thirty feet. There are many other smaller fountains, that did not throw their waters up so high, but occurred at shorter intervals. In some instances, the volumes were projected obliquely upwards, and fell into the neighboring fountains or on the rock or prairie. But their ascent was generally perpendicular, falling in and about their own basins or apertures. These wonderful productions of nature, are situated near the center of a small valley, surrounded by pine-covered hills, through which a small fork of the Madison flows. Highly gratified with my visit to these formidable and magnificent fountains, jets, or springs, whichever the reader may please to call them, I set out after dinner to rejoin my companions. Again we crossed the Piney Woods, and encamped on the plains at Henry's Fork.*

Chapter IX

CHIMNEY ROCK / SCOTTS BLUFF – WIND RIVER MTNS. – HELLS CANYON
1832-34

from The Adventures of Captain Bonneville
digested from his journal by Washington Irving

Cptn. Benjamin Bonneville

Washington Irving again utilized the journals of western travelers, in this case to describe the places seen by Captain Bonneville. Bonneville was granted a leave of absence from the army ostensibly to lead a fur trapping expedition into the northwest. Many of the details of his activities are suspicious, however, from the perspective of gaining any wealth in furs. More likely he was on a scouting expedition to gauge the numbers and strength of Indian tribes, the British presence and the best location for establishing American forts to protect the expected wave of American pioneers.

The passages excerpted from Irving's book describe the landmarks of Chimney Rock and Scotts Bluff, and Bonneville's ascent of a prominent peak in the Wind River Mtns. There is a Mt. Bonneville, but it is not at all clear from the passage which mountain accords with the descriptive facts, this one or another. For dramatic effect, it is possible Irving has included information that would not be possible from any one peak. His discussion of their passage by the Snake River canyons and falls ends at Hells Canyon where the party is barred by the topography from proceeding any further on the Snake.

The country now became wild and broken. High bluffs advanced upon the river, and forced the travelers occasionally to leave its banks and wind their course into the interior. In one of the wild and solitary passes, they were startled by the trail of four or five pedestrians, whom they supposed to be spies from some predatory camp of either Arickara or Crow Indians. This obliged them to redouble their vigilance at night, and to keep especial watch upon their horses. In these rugged and elevated regions they began to see the black-tailed deer, a species larger than the ordinary kind, and chiefly found in rocky and mountainous countries. They had reached also a great buffalo range; Captain Bonneville ascended a high bluff, commanding an extensive view of the surrounding plains. As far as his eye could reach, the country seemed absolutely blackened by innumerable herds. No language, he says, could convey an adequate idea of the vast living mass thus presented to his eye. He remarked that the bulls and cows generally congregated in separate herds.

Opposite to this camp at this place was a singular phenomenon, which is among the curiosities of the country. It is called the Chimney. The lower part is a conical mound, rising out of the naked plain; from the summit shoots up a shaft or column, about one hundred and twenty feet in height, from which it derives its name. The height of the whole, according to Captain Bonneville, is a hundred and seventy-five yards. It is composed of indurated clay, with alternate layers of red and white sandstone, and may be seen at the distance of upwards of thirty miles.

On the 21ˢᵗ (of June), they encamped amidst high and beetling cliffs of indurated clay and sandstone, bearing the semblance of towers, castles, churches, and fortified cities. At a distance, it was scarcely possible to persuade one's self that the works of art were not mingled with these fantastic freaks of nature. They have received the name of Scott's Bluffs, from a melancholy circumstance. A number of years since, a party were descending the upper part of the river in canoes, when their frail barks were overturned and all their powder spoiled. Their rifles being thus rendered useless, they were unable to procure food by hunting, and had to depend upon roots and wild fruits for subsistence. After suffering extremely from hunger, they arrived at Laramie's Fork, a small tributary of the north branch of the Nebraska, about sixty miles above the cliffs just mentioned. Here one of the party, by the name of Scott, was taken ill; and his companions came to a halt, until he should recover health and strength sufficient to proceed. While they were searching round in quest of edible roots, they discovered a fresh trail of white men, who had evidently but recently preceded them. What was to be done? By a forced march they might overtake this party, and thus be able to reach the settlements in safety. Should they linger, they might all perish of famine and exhaustion.

Scott, however, was incapable of moving; they were too feeble to aid him forward, and dreaded that such a clog would prevent their coming up with the advance party. They determined, therefore, to abandon him to his fate. Accordingly, under pretense of seeking food, and such simples as might be efficacious in his malady, they deserted him and hastened forward upon the trail. They succeeded in overtaking the party of which they were in quest, but concealed their faithless desertion of Scott; alleging that he had died of disease.

On the ensuing summer, these very individuals visiting these parts in company with others, came suddenly upon the bleached bones and grinning skull of a human skeleton, which, by certain signs they recognized for the remains of Scott. This was sixty long miles from the place where they had abandoned him; and it appeared that the wretched man had crawled that immense distance before death put an end to his miseries. The wild and picturesque bluffs in the neighborhood of his lonely grave have ever since borne his name. . . .

They were now advancing diagonally upon the chain of Wind River Mtns., which lay between them and Green River valley. To coast round their southern points would be a wide circuit; whereas, could they force their way through them, they might proceed in a straight line. The mountains were lofty, with snowy peaks and cragged sides; it was hoped, however, that some practicable defile might be found. They attempted, accordingly, to penetrate the mountains by following up one of the branches of the Popo Agie, but soon found themselves in the midst of stupendous crags and precipices that barred all progress. Retracing their steps, and falling back upon the river, they consulted where to make another attempt. They were too close beneath the mountains to scan them generally, but they now recollected having noticed, from the plain, a beautiful slope rising, at an angle of about thirty degrees, and apparently without any break, until it reached the snowy region. Seeking this gentle acclivity, they began to ascend it with alacrity, trusting to find at the top one of those elevated plains which prevail among the Rocky Mountains. The slope was covered with coarse gravel, interspersed with plates of freestone. They attained the summit with some toil, but found, instead of a level, or rather undulating plain, that they were on the brink of a deep and precipitous ravine, from the bottom of which rose a second slope, similar to the one they had just ascended. Down into this profound ravine they made their way by a rugged path, or rather fissure of the rocks, and then labored up the second slope. They gained the summit only to find themselves on another ravine, and now perceived that this vast mountain, which had presented such a sloping and even side to the distant beholder on the plain, was shagged by frightful precipices, and seamed with longitudinal chasms, deep and dangerous.

In one of these wild dells they passed the night, and slept soundly and sweetly after their fatigues. Two days of more arduous climbing and scrambling only served to admit them into the heart of this mountainous and awful solitude; where difficulties increased as they proceeded. Sometimes they scrambled from rock to rock, up the bed of some mountain stream, dashing its bright way down to the plains; sometimes they availed themselves of the paths made by the deer and the mountain sheep, which, however, often took them to the brink of fearful precipices, or led to rugged defiles, impassable for their horses. At one place, they were obliged to slide their horses down the face of a rock, in which attempt some of the poor animals lost their footing, rolled to the bottom, and came near being dashed to pieces.

In the afternoon of the second day, the travelers attained one of the elevated valleys locked up in this singular bed of mountains. Here were two bright and beautiful little lakes, set like mirrors in the midst of stern and rocky heights, and surrounded by grassy meadows, inexpressibly refreshing to the eye. These probably were among the sources of those mighty streams which take their rise among these mountains, and wander hundreds of miles through the plains.

In the green pastures bordering upon these lakes, the travelers halted to repose, and to give their weary horses time to crop the sweet and tender herbage. They had now ascended to a great height above the level of the plains, yet they beheld huge crags of granite piled one upon another, and beetling like battlements far above them. While two of the men remained in the camp with the horses, Captain Bonneville, accompanied by the other man, set out to climb a neighboring height, hoping to gain a commanding prospect, and discern some practicable route through this stupendous labyrinth. After much toil, he reached the summit of a lofty cliff, but it was only to behold gigantic peaks rising all around, and towering far into the regions of the snowy atmosphere. Selecting one which appeared to be the highest, he crossed a narrow intervening valley, and began to scale it. He soon found that he had undertaken a tremendous task; but the pride of man is never more obstinate than when climbing mountains. The ascent was so steep and rugged that he and his companion were frequently obliged to clamber on hands and knees, with their guns slung upon their backs. Frequently exhausted with fatigue, and dripping with perspiration, they threw themselves upon the snow, and took handfuls of it to allay their parching thirst. At one place, they even stripped off their coats and hung them upon the bushes, and thus lightly clad, proceeded to scramble over these eternal snows. As they ascended still higher, there were cool breezes that refreshed and braced them, and springing with new ardor to their task, they at length attained the summit.

Here a scene burst upon the view of Captain Bonneville, that for a time astonished and overwhelmed him with its immensity. He stood, in fact, upon that dividing ridge which Indians regard as the crest of the world; and on each side of which, the landscape may be said to decline to the two cardinal oceans of the globe. Whichever way he turned his eye, it was confounded by the vastness and variety of objects. Beneath him, the Rocky

Mountains seemed to open all their secret recesses: deep, solemn valleys; treasured lakes; dreary passes; rugged defiles, and foaming torrents; while beyond their savage precincts, the eye was lost in an almost immeasurable landscape; stretching on every side into dim and hazy distance, like the expanse of a summer's sea. Whichever way he looked, he beheld vast plains glimmering with reflected sunshine; mighty streams wandering on their shining course toward either ocean, and snowy mountains, chain beyond chain, and peak beyond peak, till they melted like clouds into the horizon. For a time, the Indian fable seemed realized: he had attained that height from which the Blackfoot warrior, after death, first catches a view of the land of souls, and beholds the happy hunting grounds spread out below him, brightening with the abodes of the free and generous spirits. The captain stood for a long while gazing upon this scene, lost in a crowd of vague and indefinite ideas and sensations. A long-drawn inspiration at length relieved him from this enthrallment of the mind, and he began to analyze the parts of this vast panorama. A simple enumeration of a few of its features may give some idea of its collective grandeur and magnificence.

The peak on which the captain had taken his stand commanded the whole Wind River chain; which, in fact, may rather be considered one immense mountain, broken into snowy peaks and lateral spurs, and seamed with narrow valleys. Some of these valleys glittered with silver lakes and gushing streams; the fountain heads, as it were, of the mighty tributaries to the Atlantic and Pacific Oceans. Beyond the snowy peaks, to the south, and far, far below the mountain range, the gentle river, called the Sweet Water, was seen pursuing its tranquil way through the rugged regions of the Black Hills. In the east, the headwaters of Wind River wandered through a plain, until, mingling in one powerful current, they forced through their way through the range of Horn Mountains, and were lost to view. To the north were caught glimpses of the upper streams of the Yellowstone, that great tributary of the Missouri. In another direction were to be seen some of the sources of the Oregon, or Columbia, flowing to the northwest, past those towering landmarks the Three Tetons, and pouring down into the great lava plain; while, almost at the captain's feet, the Green River, or Colorado of the West, set forth on its wandering pilgrimage to the Gulf of California; at first a mere mountain torrent, dashing northward over a crag and precipice, in a succession of cascades, and tumbling into the plain where, expanding into an ample river, it circled away to the south, and after alternately shining out and disappearing into the mazes of the vast landscape, was finally lost in a horizon of mountains. The day was calm and cloudless, and the atmosphere so pure that objects were discernible at an astonishing distance. The whole of this immense area was enclosed by an outer range of shadowy peaks, some of them faintly marked on the horizon, which seemed to wall it in from the rest of the earth. . . .

For a long time, Captain Bonneville remained gazing around him with wonder and enthusiasm; at length the chill and wintry winds, whirling about the snow-clad height, admonished him to descend. He soon regained the spot where he and his companion had thrown off their coats, which were now gladly resumed, and, retracing their course down the peak, they safely rejoined their companions on the border of the lake. . . .

In the winter of 1833-34, they make their way down the Snake River until finally reaching the outskirts of Hells Canyon.

On the second day after this determination, they were again upon Snake River, but, contrary to their expectations, it was nearly free from ice. A narrow riband ran along the shore, and sometimes there was a kind of bridge across the stream, formed of old ice and snow. For a short time, they jogged along the bank, with tolerable facility, but at length came to where the river forced its way into the heart of the mountains, winding between tremendous walls of basaltic rock, that rose perpendicularly from the water's edge, frowning in bleak and gloomy grandeur. Here difficulties of all kinds beset their path. The snow was from two to three feet deep, but soft and yielding, so that the horses had no foothold, but kept plunging forward, straining themselves by perpetual efforts. Sometimes the crags and promontories forced them upon the narrow riband of ice that bordered the shore; sometimes they had to scramble over vast masses of rock which had tumbled from the impending precipices; sometimes they had to cross the stream upon the hazardous bridges of ice and snow, sinking to the knee at every step; sometimes they had to scale slippery acclivities, and to pass along narrow cornices, glazed with ice and sleet, a shouldering wall of rock on one side, a yawning precipice on the other, where a single false step would have been fatal. In a lower and less dangerous pass, two of their horses actually fell into the river; one was saved with much difficulty, but the boldness of the shore prevented their rescuing the other, and he was swept away by the rapid current.

In this way, they struggled forward, manfully braving difficulties and dangers, until they came to where the bed of the river was narrowed to a mere chasm, with perpendicular walls of rock that defied all further progress. Turning their faces now to the mountain, they endeavored to cross directly over it; but, after clambering nearly to the summit, found their path closed by insurmountable barriers.

Nothing now remained but to retrace their steps. To descend a cragged mountain, however, was more difficult and dangerous than to ascend it. They had to lower themselves cautiously and slowly, from steep to steep; and, while they managed with difficulty to maintain their own footing, to aid their horses by holding on firmly to the rope halters, as the poor animals stumbled among slippery rocks, or slid down icy declivities.

Thus, after a day of intense cold, and severe and incessant toil, amidst the wildest of scenery, they managed, about nightfall, to reach the camping ground, from which they had started in the morning, and for the first time in the course of their rugged and perilous expedition, felt their hearts quailing under their multiplied hardships. . . .

Later in their journey, they return to Hells Canyon further downstream.

If the scenery of the Way-lee-way had charmed the travelers with its mingled amenity and grandeur, that which broke upon them on once more reaching Snake River, filled them with admiration and astonishment. At times, the river was overhung by dark and stupendous rocks, rising like gigantic walls and battlements; these would be rent by wide and yawning chasms, that seemed to speak of past convulsions of nature. Sometimes the river was of a glassy smoothness and placidity; at other times it roared along in impetuous rapids and foaming cascades. Here, the rocks were piled in the most fantastic crags and precipices; and in another place, they were succeeded by delightful valleys carpeted with green-sward. The whole of this wild and varied scenery was dominated by immense mountains rearing their distant peaks into the clouds. "The grandeur and originality of the views, presented on every side," says Captain Bonneville, "beggar both the pencil and the pen. Nothing we had ever gazed upon in any other region could for a moment compare in wild majesty and impressive sternness, with the series of scenes which here at every turn astonished our senses, and filled us with awe and delight."

Chapter X

YOSEMITE
1833

from Narrative of the Adventures of Zenas Leonard
written by himself

Joseph Walker

Captain Bonneville sent a detachment of his party under the command of Joseph Walker toward the southwest across the Great Basin, over the Sierra Nevada and into California. The journal kept by one of the party, Zenas Leonard, describes their excruciating crossing of the mountains and the difficult descent down the steep cliffs of the Yosemite, where they encountered the massive sequoia redwoods. The lateness of the season causing the waterfalls to be much reduced in waterflow, may explain the lack of any significant reference to its famous waterfalls.

Oct. 16: Continued our course until the afternoon, when we arrived at what we took to be the top, where we again encamped, but without anything to eat for our horses, as the ground was covered with deep snow, which apparently lays on the north side of the peaks all year round. These peaks are generally covered with rocks and sand, totally incapable of vegetation; except on the south side, where grows a kind of juniper or gin shrub, bearing a berry tasting similar to gin. Here we passed the night without anything to eat except these gin berries, and some of the insects from the lake described above, which our men had gotten from the Indians. We had not suffered much from cold for several months previous to this; but this night, surrounded as we were with the everlasting snows on the summit of this mountain, the cold was felt with three-fold severity.

In taking a view the next morning of the extensive plains through which we had traveled, its appearance is awfully sub-

lime. As far as the eye can reach, you can see nothing but an unbroken level, tiresome to the eye to behold. . . .

The explorers continue their difficult passage through the deep snows, getting by on horse meat, not finding any game and not sure where they were.

We were at a complete stand. No one was acquainted with the country nor knew how wide the summit of this mountain was. We had traveled for five days since we arrived at what we supposed to be the summit and were still surrounded with snow and rugged peaks. The vigor of every man was almost exhausted and with nothing to give our poor horses, which were no longer any assistance in traveling, but a burden, for we had to help most of them along as we would an old and feeble man. . . .

Our situation was growing more distressing every hour, and all we now thought of was to extricate ourselves from this inhospitable region; and, as we were perfectly aware, traveling on foot was the only way of succeeding, we spent no time in idleness and scarcely stopped to view an occasional specimen of the wonders of nature's handy work. We traveled a few miles every day, still on the top of the mountain, and our course continually obstructed with snow, hills and rocks. Here we began to encounter many small streams which would shoot out from under these high snow banks, and after running a short distance in deep chasms which they have through ages cut in the rocks, precipitate themselves from one lofty precipice to another, until they are exhausted in rain below. Some of these precipices appeared to us to be more than a mile high. Some of the men thought that if we could succeed in descending one of these precipices to the bottom, we might thus work our way into the valley below (Yosemite Valley?). *Yet on making several attempts we found it utterly impossible for a man to descend, to say nothing of our horses. We were obliged to keep along the top of the dividing ridge between two of these chasms, which seemed to lead pretty near in the direction we were going – westward – in passing over the mountain, supposing it to run north and south. In this manner we continued until the 25th, without any particular occurrence, except that of our horses dying daily. Our course was very rough and tiresome, having to encounter one hill of snow and one edge of rocks after another. On the 25th every man appeared to be more discouraged and* *down spirited than ever. I thought that our position would soon be beyond hope if no prospect of getting off the mountain would now be discovered. This day we sent out several parties who returned in the evening without bringing the least good news; except one man, who was last coming, having separated from his companions, and brought a basket full of acorns to camp. These were the first acorns we had seen since we left the state of Missouri. These nuts were from an Indian who had them on his back traveling across the mountain to the east side. When the Indian saw our hunter, he dropped his basket of provisions and ran for his life. These nuts caused no little rejoicing in our camp, not only on account of their value as food, but because they gave us the gratifying evidence that a country mild and salubrious enough to produce acorns was not too far distant and must be vastly different from any we had passed through for a long time. We now felt agreeably surprised that we had succeeded so far and so prosperously, in a region of many miles in extent, where a native Indian could find nothing to eat in traversing the same route but acorns. . . .*

The next morning we resumed our journey, somewhat revived with the strong expectation that after a few days more tedious traveling, we would find ourselves in a country producing some kind of game by which we might restore our languid frames, and pasture to resuscitate the famished condition of our horses. We still found snow in abundance, but our course was not so much obstructed with rocks as formerly. In two or three days, we arrived at the brink of the mountain. This at first was a happy sight, but when we approached closer, it seemed to be so near perpendicular that it would be folly to attempt a descent. In looking over the plain below with the naked eye, you have one of the most singular views; from our great height the plain presents a dim yellow appearance; but on taking a view with the spy glass we found it to be a beautiful plain stretching towards the west into the far horizon. From the spot where we stood to the plain beneath must be at least a distance of three miles. As it is almost perpendicular, a person cannot look down without feeling as if he was wafted to and fro in the air, from the giddy height. A great many were the surmises as to the distance and direction to the nearest point on the Pacific. Captain Walker, who was a man well acquainted with geography, was of the opinion that it was not much further than we could see with the aid of our glass, as the plain had the appearance of a sea shore.

Here we encamped for the night, and sent men out to discover some convenient passage down towards the plain, who returned after an absence of a few hours and reported that they had discovered a pass or Indian trail which they thought would answer our purpose. They also saw some signs of deer and bear, which was equally joyful news, as we longed to have a taste of some palatable meat. The next morning, after pursuing our course a few miles along the edge of the mountain top, we arrived at the path discovered by our men. We immediately commenced the descent, gladly leaving the cold and famished region of snow behind. The mountain was extremely steep and difficult to descend, and the only way we could do so quickly was by taking a zigzag direction, first climbing along one side and then turning to the other, until we arrived at a ledge or precipice of rocks of great height extending eight to ten miles along the mountain. Here we halted and sent men in each direction as to ascertain if there was any possibility of getting over this obstruction. In the afternoon, our men returned without finding any safe passage through the rocks. Yet one man had succeeded in killing a small deer, which he carried all the way to camp on his back. This was dressed, cooked and eaten in less time than a hungry wolf would devour a lamb.

This was the first game larger than a rabbit we had killed since the 4th of August, when we killed the last buffalo near the Great Salt Lake, and the first we had eaten since our dried meat was exhausted 11 days before. During this time we had lived on stale and forbidden horse flesh. I was conscious that it was not such meat as a dog would feast on, but we were driven to extremes and had either to do this or die. It was the most unwholesome, as well as the most unpleasant food I ever ate or ever expect to eat, and I hope that no other person will be compelled to go through the same. It seemed to be the greatest cruelty to take your rifle, when your horse sinks to the ground from starvation, but still manifests a desire and willingness to follow you, and to shoot him in the head; then cutting him up and taking such parts of their flesh as extreme hunger alone will render it possible for a human being to eat. This we did several times, and it was the only thing that saved us from death. 24 of our horses died since we arrived on top of the mountain, 17 of which we ate the best parts.

When our men returned without finding any passage over the rocks, we searched for a place that was as smooth and gradual in the descent as possible. After finding one, we brought our horses, and fastening ropes around them, let them down one at a time without doing them any injury. Once we had our horses and baggage over the rocks, we continued our course down the mountain, which still continued very steep and difficult. After we were safely over the rocks, several of the men started out in search of game, although it was nearly night. The main body continued on down until we arrived at some green oak bushes, where we encamped for the night and to wait for our hunters. They returned soon after well paid for their labor, having killed two large black-tailed deer and a black bear, all very fat and in good eating order. This night we passed more cheerful and in better heart than any we had spent for a long time. Our meat was dressed and well cooked, and every man felt in good order to partake of it.

In descending the mountain this far, we now found but little snow and emerged into a country with some vegetation, having passed through several groves of green oak bushes, etc. The principal timber we came across was redwood, white cedar and the balsam tree. We continued down the side of the mountain at our leisure, finding the timber much larger and better, game more abundant and the soil more fertile. Here we found plenty of oak timber bearing a large quantity of acorns. On the evening of the 30th, we arrived at the foot or base of the mountain, having spent almost a month in crossing over. Along the base of this mountain, it is quite romantic. The soil is very productive, the timber is immensely large and plenty; and game, such as deer, elk, grizzly bear and antelopes are remarkably plenty. From the mountain out to the plain, a distance from 10 to 20 miles, the timber stands as thick as it could grow, and the land is well watered by a number of small streams rising here and there along the mountain. In the last two days, we have found some trees of the redwood species, incredibly large, some of which would measure from 16 to 18 fathoms round the trunk at the height of a man's head from the ground.

Chapter XI

SCOTTS BLUFF
1834

from Narrative of a Journey Across the Rocky Mountains
by John Kirk Townsend

The following narrative is written by a naturalist, an ornithologist in particular, who accompanied a mixed group of mountain men, missionaries and scientists led by Captain Nathaniel Wyeth. This was the first crossing along the route that came to be known as the Oregon Trail. Townsend's companion was the famous botanist Thomas Nuttall, who had invited the ornithologist along, so that they jointly investigated the 'new' flora and fauna of the West. The selection picks up where the party leaves the gentle prairies behind, and faces the tribulations of the High Plains, then the drama of the bluffs before encountering more beauties of animate Nature.

On the morning of the 24th of May we forded the Platte river, or rather its south fork, along which we had been traveling during the previous week. On the northern side, we found the country totally different in its aspect. Instead of the extensive and apparently interminable green plains, the monotony of which had become so wearisome to the eye, here was a great sandy waste, without a single green thing to vary and enliven the dreary scene. It was a change, however, and we were therefore enjoying it, and remarking to each other how particularly agreeable it was, when we were suddenly assailed by vast swarms of most ferocious little black gnats; the whole atmosphere seemed crowded with them, and they dashed into our faces, assaulted our eyes, ears, nostrils, and mouths, as though they were determined to bar our passage through their territory. These little creatures were so exceedingly minute that, singly, they were scarcely visible; and yet their sting caused such excessive pain, that for the rest of the day our men and horses were rendered almost frantic, the former bitterly imprecating, and the latter stamping, and kicking, and rolling in the sand, in tremendous, yet vain, efforts to rid themselves of their pertinacious little foes. It was rather amusing to see the whole com-

pany with their handkerchiefs, shirts, and coats, thrown over their heads, stemming the animated torrent, and to hear the greenhorns cursing their tormenters, the country, and themselves, for their foolhardiness in venturing on the journey. When we encamped in the evening, we built fires at the mouths of the tents, the smoke from which kept our enemies at a distance, and we passed a night of tolerable comfort, after a day of most peculiar misery.

The next morning I observed that the faces of all the men were more or less swollen, some of them very severely, and poor Captain W. was totally blind for two days afterwards.

25ᵗʰ. – We made a noon camp today on the north branch or fork of the river, and in the afternoon traveled along the bank of the stream. In about an hour's march, we came to rocks, precipices, and cedar trees, and although we anticipated some difficulty and toil in the passage of the heights, we felt glad to exchange them for the vast and wearisome prairies we had left behind. Soon after we commenced the ascent, we struck onto an Indian path very much worn, occasionally mounting over rugged masses of rock, and leaping wide fissures in the soil, and sometimes picking our way over the jutting crags, directly above the river. On the top of one of the stunted and broad spreading cedars, a bald eagle had built its enormous nest; and as we descended the mountain, we saw the callow young lying within it, while the anxious parents hovered over our heads, screaming their alarm.

In the evening we arrived upon the plain again; it was thickly covered with ragged and gnarled bushes of a species of wormwood, which perfumed the air, and at first was rather agreeable. The soil was poor and sandy, and the straggling blades of grass which found their way to the surface were brown and withered. Here was a poor prospect for our horses; a sad contrast indeed to the rich and luxuriant prairies we had left. On the edges of the little streams, however, we found some tolerable pasture, and we frequently stopped during the day to bait our poor animals in these pleasant places. . . .

The next morning the whole camp was suddenly aroused by the falling of all the tents. A tremendous blast swept as from a funnel over the sandy plain, and in an instant precipitated our frail habitations like webs of gossamer. The men crawled our from under the ruins, rubbing their eyes, and, as usual, muttering imprecations against the country and all that therein was; it was unusually early for a start, but we did not choose to pitch the tents again, and to sleep without them here was next to impossible; so we took our breakfast in the open air, devouring our well sanded provisions as quickly as possible, and immediately took to the road.

During the whole day a most terrific gale was blowing directly in our faces, clouds of sand were driving and hurtling by us, often with such violence as nearly to stop our progress, and when we halted in the evening, we could scarcely recognize each other's faces beneath their odious mask of dust and dirt. . . .

28ᵗʰ. – We fell in with a new species of game today; a large band of wild horses. They were very shy, scarcely permitting us to approach within rifle distance, and yet they kept within sight of us for some hours. Several of us gave them chase, in the hope of at least being able to approach sufficiently near to examine them closely, but we might as well have pursued the wind; they scoured away from us with astonishing velocity, their long manes and tails standing out almost horizontally, as they sprang along before us. Occasionally they would pause in their career, turn and look at us as we approached them, and then, with a neigh that rang loud and high above the clattering of the hoofs, dart their light heels into the air, and fly from us as before. We soon abandoned this wild chase, and contented ourselves with admiring their sleek beauty at a distance. . . .

The bluffs on the northern shore of the Platte, are, at this point, exceedingly rugged, and often quite picturesque; the formation appears to be simply clay, intermixed, occasionally, with a stratum of limestone, and one part of the bluff bears a striking and almost startling resemblance to a dilapidated feudal castle (Scott's Bluff). There is also a kind of obelisk, standing at a considerable distance from the bluffs, on a wide plain, towering to the height of about two hundred feet, and tapering to a small point at the top. This pillar is known to the hunters and trappers who traverse these regions, by the name of the "chimney" (Chimney Rock). Here we diverged from the usual course, leav-

ing the bank of the river, and entered a large and deep ravine between the enormous bluffs.

The road was very uneven and difficult, winding from amongst innumerable mounds six to eight feet in height, the space between them frequently so narrow as scarcely to admit our horses, and some of the men rode for upwards of a mile kneeling upon their saddles. These mounds were of hard yellow clay, without a particle of rock of any kind, and along their bases, and in the narrow passages, flowers of every hue were growing. It was a most enchanting sight; even the men noticed it, and more than one of our matter-of-fact people exclaimed, "beautiful, beautiful!" Mr. N. was here in his glory. He rode on ahead of the company, and cleared the passages with a trembling and eager hand, looking anxiously back at the approaching party, as though he feared it would come ere he had finished, and tread his lovely prizes under foot.

The distance through the ravine is about three miles. We then crossed several beautiful grassy knolls, and descending to the plain, struck the Platte again, and traveled along its bank.

Chapter XII

GRAND TETONS – YELLOWSTONE 1836-39

from Journal of a Trapper
by Osborne Russell

The last of three entries on Yellowstone before 1840 concerns a fur trapper who found himself in the future park on more than one occasion. The selection begins with an account of the Battle of Pierre's Hole just west of the Grand Tetons. His party crosses over the mountains into Jackson's Hole, then eastward and eventually northward across the rugged fastness of the Absaroka Mountains, along the southeastern and eastern borders of Yellowstone. Finally, they make their way into Lamar Valley, which Russell describes as an Eden-like setting. They continue west through Gardner's Hole and across the Gallatin Mountains out of the park. A second time they left Jackson Hole in a northeast direction and came to the Upper Yellowstone River, followed it down to Yellowstone Lake, which they circled around the east side. Missing the Yellowstone Canyon and Falls, they continued north to Lamar Valley, a place that once more affected Russell as paradise on earth. They continued to Gardner's Hole and exited north out of the park. On a third trip, they explored the Cascade Corner in the southwestern portion of the park. His last trip takes him through Yellowstone's major geyser basins, including descriptions of what could be Grand Prismatic Spring. They continued on to Yellowstone Lake and Lamar Valley (again missing Yellowstone Canyon and Falls). They hunted in the plains north of the park in Blackfoot country before returning to the park. This expedition ends in tragedy when the trappers are attacked by a party of Blackfoot near the shores of Yellowstone Lake. The narrative picks up at the battle of Pierre's Hole, on the west side of the Tetons. Jackson Hole is on the east side of the Tetons.

1836

June 24th *Crossed the mountain 12 miles east course and descended into the southwest extremity of a valley called Pierre's Hole, where we stayed the next day. This valley lies north and south in an oblong form, about 30 miles long and 10 wide, surrounded, except on the north, by wild and rugged mountains. The east range resembles mountains piled on mountains and capped with three spiral peaks which pierce the cloud. These peaks bear the French name of Tetons or Teats. The Snake Indians call them the hoary headed Fathers. This is a beautiful valley, consisting of a smooth plain, intersected by small streams and thickly clothed with grass and herbage, and abounds with buffalo, elk, deer, antelope. 27th We traveled to the north end of the valley and encamped on one of the numerous branches, which unite at the northern extremity to form a stream called Pierre's fork, which discharges its waters into Henry's Fork of Snake River. The stream on which we encamped flows directly from the Central Tetons and is narrowly skirted with cottonwood trees, closely intermingled with underbrush on both sides. We were encamped on the south side in a place partially clear of brush under the shade of the large cottonwoods. 28t About 9 AM, we were aroused by an alarm of "Indians." We ran to our horses. All was confusion – each one trying to catch his horses. We succeeded in driving them into camp, where we caught all but 6, which escaped into the prairie. In the meantime, the Indians appeared before our camp to the number of 60, of which 15 to 20 were mounted on horseback and the remainder on foot – all being entirely naked, armed with fusees, bows, arrows, etc. They immediately caught the horses which had escaped from us, and commenced riding to and fro within gunshot of our camp with all the speed their horses were capable of producing, without shooting a single gun for about 20 minutes, brandishing their war weapons and yelling at the top of their voices. Some had scalps suspended on small poles, which they waved in the air. Others had pieces of scarlet cloth with one end fastened round their head while the other trailed after them. After securing my horses, I took my gun, examined the priming, set the breech on the ground and hand on the muzzle with my arms folded, gazing at the novelty of this scene for some minutes; quite unconscious of danger until the whistling of balls about my ears gave me to understand that these were something more than mere pictures of imagination, and gave me assurance that these living centaurs were a little more dangerous than those I had been accustomed to see portrayed on canvas.*

The first gun was fired by one of our party, which was taken as a signal for attack on both sides. The well-directed fire from our rifles soon compelled them to retire from the front and take to the brush behind us, where they had the advantage until 7 or 8 of our men glided into the brush and concealing themselves until their left wing approached within about 30 ft. of them before they shot a gun. They then raised and attacked them in the flank. The Indians did not stop to return the fire, but retreated through the brush as fast as possible, dragging their wounded along with them and leaving their dead on the spot. In the meantime, myself and the remainder of our party were closely engaged with the centre and right. I took the advantage of a large tree which stood near the edge of the brush between the Indians and our horses. They approached until the smoke of our guns met I kept a large German horse pistol loaded by me in case they should make a charge when my gun was empty. When I first stationed myself at the tree, I placed a hat on some twigs which grew at the foot of it and would put it in motion by kicking the twig with my foot in order that they might shoot at the hat and give me a better chance at their heads. I soon found this sport was no joke, for the poor horses behind me were killed and wounded by the balls intended for me. The Indians stood the fight for about 2 hours, then retreated through the brush with a dismal lamentation. We then began to look about to find what damage they had done us. One of our comrades was found under the side of an old root, wounded by balls in 3 places in the right and one in the left leg below the knee, no bones having been broken. Another had received a slight wound in the groin. We lost 3 horses killed on the spot and several more wounded, but not so bad as to be unable to travel.

Towards night some of our men followed down the stream about a mile, found the place where they had stopped and laid their wounded comrades on the ground in a circle. The blood was still standing congealed in 9 places where they had apparently been dressing the wounds. 29th Stayed at the same place, fearing no further attempt by the same party of Indians. 30th Traveled up the main branch about 10 miles. July 1st Traveled to the s.e. extremity of the valley and encamped for the night. Our wounded comrade suffered very much in riding, although everything was done which lay in our power to ease his sufferings. A pallet was made upon the best gaited horse belonging to the party for him to ride on. One man was appointed to lead the animal. 2nd Crossed the Teton mountains in an east direction for about 15 miles. The ascent was very steep and rugged, covered with tall pines, but the descent was somewhat smoother.

Here we again fell on to Lewis fork, which runs in a southern direction through a valley about 80 miles long. . . . This valley is called Jackson Hole. . . . The whole is covered with wild sage and surrounded by high and rugged mountains, upon whose summits the snow remains during the hottest months in summer. . . . This valley, like all other parts of the country, abounds with game.

Here we again attempted to cross Lewis fork with a bull skin boat. July 4ᵗʰ Our boat being completed, we loaded it with baggage and crossed to the other side; but on returning, we ran it into some brush. It instantly filled and sunk, but without further accident than the loss of the boat. We had already forded half the distance across the river upon horse back and were now upon the other shore. We now began making a raft of logs that had drifted on the island. On this, when completed, we put the remainder of our equipment. About 2 PM, ten of us started on it toward the other side. We no sooner reached the rapid current than our raft (which was constructed of large timber) became unmanageable and all efforts to reach either side were vain. Fearing lest we should run on to the dreadful rapids to which we were fast approaching, we abandoned the raft and committed ourselves to the mercy of the current. We being all tolerably good swimmers except myself, I would have called for help, but at this critical period everyone had to shift for himself. Fortunately, I scrambled to the shore among the last swimmers. We were now on the side from whence we started without a single article of bedding, except an old cloth tent, while the rain poured incessantly. Fortunately, we had built a large fire previous to our departure on the raft, which was still burning.

I now began to reflect on the miserable condition of myself and those around me; without clothing, provisions or firearms, and drenched to the skin with the rain.

I thought of those who were, perhaps, at this moment celebrating the anniversary of our independence in my native land; or seated around tables loaded with the richest dainties that a rich, independent and enlightened country could afford. Or perhaps they were collected in the gay saloon, relating the heroic deeds of our ancestors, or joining in the nimble dance, forgetful of cares and toils. But here was a group of human beings crouched around a fire, which the rain was fast diminishing, meditating on their deplorable condition, not knowing at what moment we might be aroused by the shrill war cry of the hostile savages, with which the country was infested. All the while not an article of defense, except our butcher knives, remained in our possession.

The night, at length, came on and we lay down to wait the events of the morrow. Day light appeared and we started down along the shore in hope of finding something that might have got loose from the raft and drifted upon the beach. We had not gone a mile when we discovered the raft lodged on a gravel bar, which projected from the island, where it had been driven by the current. We hastened through the water waist deep to the spot where, to our great surprise and satisfaction, we found everything safe upon the raft in the same manner we had left it. We also discovered that the river could, with some difficulty, be forded on horseback at this place. Accordingly, we had our horses driven across to us, packed them up, mounted and crossed without further accident. The day being fair, we spent the remainder of it and the following day in drying our equipment. . . .

The party left the Tetons and spent many days among the Absaroka Mountains making their way east and north. All this time, they had a man wounded from the previous battle with them who required enormous assistance in getting him up and down the rugged mountain passes. Finally, they made their way over the Absarokas and down a tributary stream into Lamar Valley.

29th We descended the stream about 15 miles through the dense forest and, at length, came to a beautiful valley . . . surrounded by dark and lofty mountains. The stream, after running through the center in a n.w. direction, rushed down a tremendous cañon of basaltic rock just wide enough to admit its waters. The banks of the stream in the valley were low, and skirted in many places with beautiful cottonwood groves.

Here we found a few Snake Indians, comprising 6 men, 7 women and 10 children, who were the only inhabitants of this lonely and secluded spot. They were all neatly clothed in dressed deer and sheep skins of the best quality, and seemed to be perfectly contented and happy. They were rather surprised at our approach and retreated to the heights, where they might have a view of us without apprehending any danger. Having persuaded them of our pacific intentions, we succeeded in getting them to encamp with us. Their personal property consisted of one old butcher knife, nearly worn to the back, two old shattered fusees, which had long since become useless for want of ammunition, a small stone pot and about 30 dogs on which they carried their skins, clothing, provisions, etc. on their hunting excursions. They were well armed with bows and arrows pointed with obsidian. Their bows were beautifully wrought from sheep, buffalo and elk horns, secured with deer and elk sinews, ornamented with porcupine quills, and generally about 3 feet long. We obtained a large number of elk, deer and sheep skins from them of the finest quality, and three large, neatly dressed panther skins in return for awls, axes, kettles, tobacco, ammunition, etc. They would throw the skins at our feet and say "give us whatever you please for them and we will be satisfied. We can get plenty of skins but we do not often see the Tibuboes" (or People of the Sun). They said there had been a great many beaver on the branches of this stream, but they had killed nearly all of them and, being ignorant of the value of fur, had singed it off with fire in order to drip the meat more conveniently. They had seen whites some years previous, who had passed through the valley, and left a horse behind, but he had died during the first winter. They are never at a loss for fire, which they produce by the friction of two pieces of wood rubbed together with a quick and steady motion. One of them drew a map of the country around us on a white elk skin with a piece of charcoal. He explained the direction of the different passes, streams, etc. From them, we discovered that it was about one days travel in a s.w. direction to the outlet or northern extremity of the Yellowstone Lake. But the route, from his description, being difficult and beaver comparatively scarce, our leader gave up the idea of going to it this season, as our horses were much jaded and their feet badly worn.

Our geographer also told us that this stream united with the Yellowstone after leaving this valley, half a days travel in a west direction. The river then ran a long distance through a tremendous cut in the mountain in the same direction (Black Canyon of the Yellowstone), *and emerged into a large plain, the extent*

*of which was beyond his geographical knowledge or concep-
tion. 30th We stopped at this place and, for my own part, I
almost wished I could spend the remainder of my days like this,
where happiness and contentment seemed to reign in wild
romantic splendor, surrounded by majestic battlements which
seemed to support the heavens and shut out all hostile intrud-
ers. 31st We left the valley and descended the stream by a narrow, difficult path, winding among the huge fragments of
basaltic rock for about 12 miles. The trail came to an end and
the towering rocks seemed to overhang the river on either side,
forbidding further progress of man or beast, and obliged us to
halt for the night. About dark, some of our trappers came to
camp and reported one of their comrades to be lost or met with
some serious accident. The next day we concluded to stop at
this place. Four men went in search of him and returned at
night without any tidings of him whatever. It was agreed that
either his gun had burst and killed him or his horse had fallen
with him over some tremendous precipice. He was a man about
55 years of age and 30 years experience as a hunter. Our leader
concluded that further search was useless in this rocky, pathless
and pine covered country.*

*Aug. 2nd We forded the Yellowstone with some difficulty to the
south side. The river at this place is about 200 yards wide and
nearly swimming to horses* (Bannock Ford). *A short distance
below it rushes down a chasm with a dreadful roar, echoing
among the mountains. After crossing, we went up a steep and
narrow defile in a south direction. On gaining the summit in
about 3 miles, we found the country to open south and west of
us into rolling prairie hills. We descended the mountain and
encamped on a small stream running west. 3rd Traveled about
25 miles due west, the route broken and uneven in the latter part
of the day and some places thickly covered with pines. We
encamped at night in a valley called Gardners Hole. This valley
is about 40 miles in circumference surrounded, except on the
north and west, by low piney mountains. On the west is a high,
narrow range of mountains, running north and south, dividing
the waters of the Yellowstone from those of Gallatin fork of the
Missouri. We stopped in this valley until the 20th. The trappers
were continually employed in hunting and trapping beaver. 21st
We crossed the mountains through a defile in a west direction
and fell on to a small branch of the Gallatin.*

1837

We followed Lewis fork through the valley, crossing several large streams coming in from the east. We then left the valley and followed the river about 5 miles through a piece of rough piney country and came to Jackson Lake, which is formed by the river. . . . On the s.w. stands the 3 Tetons, whose dark frightful forms, rising abruptly from the lake and towering above the clouds, casts a gloomy shade upon the waters below. The water rushes in torrents down the awful precipices from the snow by which they are crowned.

Russell and his fellow trappers (including Jim Bridger) make their way north and east of the Tetons, trapping beaver along the way, until they make their way into the Upper Yellowstone Valley above the Lake. Just north of Yellowstone Lake, they encounter thermal activity in Pelican Valley.

. . . We encamped about 3 PM. After resting our horses about an hour, seven of us were ordered to go and hunt some streams running into the Yellowstone some distance below the lake. We started from the camp in an east direction, crossed the plain and entered the pines. After traveling about an hour through dense forests, we fell into a broken tract of country, which seemed to be all on fire at some distance below the surface. It being very difficult to get around this place, we concluded to follow an elk trail across it for about half a mile. The treading of our horses sounded like traveling on a plank platform covering an immense cavity in the earth, whilst the hot water and steam were spouting and hissing around us in all directions. As we were walking and leading our horses across this place, the horse that was before me broke through the crust with one hind foot, and the blue steam rushed forth from the hole. The whole place was covered with a crust of limestone of a dazzling whiteness, formed by the overflowing of the boiling water. Shortly after leaving this resemblance of the infernal regions, we killed a fat buck elk. We camped, at sunset, in a smooth grassy spot between two high shaggy ridges, watered by a small stream which came tumbling down the gorge behind us. As we had passed the infernal regions, we thought, as a matter of course, these must be a commencement of the Elysian fields and, accordingly, began preparing a feast. A large fire was soon blazing, encircled with sides of elk ribs and meat cut in slices

supported on sticks, down which the grease ran in torrents. The repast being over, the jovial tale goes round the circle. The peals of loud laughter break upon the stillness of the night, which after being mimicked in the echo from rock to rock, it dies away in the solitary gloom. Every tale puts an auditor in mind of something similar to it but under different circumstances, which being told the laughing part gives rise to increasing merriment and furnishes more subjects for good jokes and witty sayings such as Swift never dreamed of. Thus the evening passed, with eating, drinking and stories enlivened with witty humor until near midnight. All being wrapped in their blankets, lying around the fire, gradually falling to sleep one by one, until the last tale is encored by the snoring of the drowsy audience. The speaker takes the hint, breaks off the subject, and wrapping his blanket more closely about him, soon joins the snoring party. The light of the fire being superseded by that of the moon, just rising from behind the eastern mountain, a sullen gloom is cast over the remaining fragments of the feast. All is silent except the occasional howling of the solitary wolf on the neighboring mountain, whose senses are attracted by the flavors of roasted meat. Fearing to approach nearer, he sits upon a rock and bewails his calamities in piteous moans, which are re-echoed among the mountains. Aug 20th Crossed over a high rugged mountain about 12 miles n.e. and fell into the Secluded Valley, of which I have described in my last year's journal. Here we found some of those independent and happy natives, of whom I gave a description. We traded some beaver and dressed skins from them and hunted the streams running into the valley for several days. There is something in the wild romantic scenery of this valley which I cannot, nor will I, attempt to describe. The impressions made upon my mind while gazing from a high eminence on the surrounding landscape one evening, as the sun was gently gliding behind the western mountain and casting its gigantic shadows across the vale, were such as time can never efface from my memory. As I am neither poet, painter or romance writer, I must content myself to be what I am, a humble journalist; and leave this beautiful vale in obscurity until visited by some more skillful admirer of the beauties of nature, who may chance to stroll this way at some future period.

1838

This summer's excursion from Fort Hall leads them into the southwestern section of the park, where they encounter the many falls and cascades along the Bechler River.

After winding about among the fallen trees and rocks about 6 miles, we fell on to the middle branch of Henrys Fork; which is called by hunters "the falling fork," from the numerous cascades it forms whilst meandering through the forest, previous to its junction with the main river.... We ascended this stream, passing several beautiful cascades for about 12 miles; when the trail led us into a prairie 8 miles in circumference, where we found the camp just as the sun was setting.

1839

The party of trappers see more of Yellowstone this summer than any other, seeing many of their old favorite places and many new wonders besides. However, their halcyon summer ends in tragedy and Russell never returns to Yellowstone again.

We stopped at the fort (Fort Hall) until the 26th of June, then made up a party of 4 for the purpose of trapping in the Yellowstone and Wind River Mtns. . . . 9th We traveled around this lake to the inlet on the west side and came to another lake about the same size (Shoshone Lake). This has a small prairie on the west side, whilst the other is completely surrounded by thick pines. The next day, we traveled along the border of the lake till we came to the n.w. extremity, where we found about 50 springs of boiling hot water. We stopped here for some hours, as one of my comrades had visited this spot the year previous and he wished to show us some curiosities. The first spring we visited was about 10 feet in diameter, which threw up mud with a noise similar to boiling soap. Close about this were numerous others, similar to it, throwing up the hot mud and water 5 or 6 feet high. About 30 or 40 paces from these, along the side of a small ridge, the hot steam rushed forth from holes in the ground with a hissing noise, which could be heard a mile distant. On a near approach, we could hear the water bubbling under ground, some distance from the surface. The sound of our footsteps over this place was like thumping over a hollow vessel of immense size. In many places were peaks, from 2 to 6 feet high, formed of limestone deposited by the boiling water, which appeared of a snowy whiteness. The water, when cold, is perfectly sweet, except having a fresh limestone taste. After surveying these nat-

ural wonders for sometime, my comrade conducted me to what he called the "hour spring." At this spring, the first thing that attracts the attention is a hole about 15 inches in diameter, in which the water is boiling slowly about 4 inches below the surface. At length, it begins to boil and bubble violently. The water commences rising and shooting upwards, until the column arises to the height of sixty feet; from whence, it falls to the ground in drops on a circle of about 30 feet in diameter, being perfectly cold when it strikes the ground. It continues shooting up in this manner five or six minutes, sinks back to its former state of slowly boiling for an hour and then shoots forth as before. My comrade said he had watched the motions of this spring for one whole day and part of the night previous. He found no irregularity whatever in its movements. After surveying these wonders for a few hours, we left the place and traveled north about 3 miles over ascending ground. Then we descended a steep and rugged mountain 4 miles in the same direction, and fell on to the head branch of the Jefferson branch of the Missouri. The whole country was still thickly covered with pines, except here and there a small prairie. We encamped, set some traps for beaver, and stayed 4 days. At this place, there are also large numbers of hot springs, some of which have formed cones of limestone 20 feet high.

They are of a snowy whiteness, which makes a splendid appearance standing among the evergreen pines. Some of the lower peaks are very serviceable to the hunter in preparing his dinner when hungry, for here his kettle is always ready and boiling. Meat, being suspended in the water by a string, is soon prepared for his meal without further trouble.

. . . At length we came to a boiling lake about 300 ft. in diameter, forming nearly a complete circle. The stream, which arose from it, was of three distinct colors. From the west side, for one third of the diameter, it was white; in the middle it was pale red; and the remaining third on the east was a light sky blue (Grand Prismatic Spring?). *The water was a deep indigo blue, boiling like an immense caldron, and running over the white rock which had formed round the edges to the height of 4 or 5 feet by sloping gradually for 60 or 70 feet.*

Russell quickly skims over the next two weeks as they tour many of the same areas they had visited previously, like Secluded Valley and

Gardners Hole, trapping beaver at points along the way. Some of the party hunts buffalo on the Yellowstone plain outside the northern end of the park against the advice of Russell, who feared rousing the Blackfoot against them. Finally, they end up camping on the northeast side of Yellowstone Lake. Here, remembering every detail, Russell's fears are realized.

The next day we went to the lake and set our traps on a branch running into it near the outlet on the n.e. side. 28th After visiting my traps, I returned to the camp. After stopping about an hour or two, I took my rifle and sauntered down the shore of the lake, among the scattered groves of tall pines, until tired of walking about. The day being very warm, I took a bath in the lake for probably an hour and returned to camp about 4 PM. Two of my comrades took a walk among the pines hoping to kill an elk. They started off whilst the other was laying asleep. Sometime after they were gone, I went to a bale of dried meat, which had been spread in the sun 30 or 40 feet from the place where we slept. Here, I pulled off my powder horn and bullet pouch, laid them on a log, drew my butcher knife and began to cut. We were encamped about half a mile from the lake, on a stream running in a s.w. direction through a prairie bottom about a quarter of a mile wide. On each side of this valley arose a bench of land about 20 feet high, running parallel with the stream and covered with pines. On this bench we were encamped on the s.e. side of the stream. The pines, immediately behind us, were thickly intermingled with logs and fallen trees. After eating a few minutes, I arose and kindled a fire, filled my tobacco pipe and sat down to smoke. My comrade, whose name was White, was still sleeping. I cast my eyes towards the horses, which were feeding in the valley, and discovered the heads of some Indians, who were gliding round under the bench within 30 steps of me. I jumped to my rifle and aroused White. Looking towards my powder horn and bullet pouch, it was already in the hands of an Indian, and we were completely surrounded. We cocked our rifles and started through the ranks into the woods, which seemed to be completely filled with Blackfeet, who rent the air with their horrid yells. On presenting our rifles, they opened a space about 20 feet wide, through which we plunged. About the fourth jump, an arrow struck White on the right hip joint. I hastily told him to pull it out. As I spoke, another arrow struck me in the same place, but they did not retard our progress. At length, another arrow, striking through my right leg above the knee, benumbed the flesh so that I fell with my breast across a log. The Indian who shot me was within 8 feet, and made a spring towards me with his uplifted battle axe. I made a leap, avoided the blow, and kept hopping from log to log through a shower of arrows, which flew around us like hail, lodging in the pines and logs. After we had passed them about 10 paces, we wheeled about and took aim at them. They began to dodge behind the trees and shoot their guns. We ran and hopped about 50 yards further into the logs and bushes, then made a stand. I was very faint from the loss of blood. We set down among the logs, determined to kill the two foremost when they came up, and then die like men. We rested our rifles across a log. White, aiming at the foremost, and myself at the second, I whispered to him that when they turned their eyes toward us to pull the trigger. About 20 of them passed by us within 15 feet, without casting a glance towards us. Another file came round on the opposite side within 20 or 30 paces, closing with the first a few rods beyond us. All turned to the right and the next minute were out of sight among the bushes.

They were all well armed with fusees, bows and battle axes. We sat still, until the rustling among the bushes had died away. Then we arose and, after looking carefully around us, White asked in a whisper how far it was to the lake. I replied, pointing to the s.e., that it was a quarter of a mile. I was nearly fainting from the loss of blood and the want of water. We hobbled along 40 or 50 rods and I was obliged to sit down a few minutes, then go a little further and rest again. We managed in this way until we reached the bank of the lake. Our next object was to obtain some of the water, as the bank was very steep and high. White had been perfectly calm and deliberate until now when his con-versation became wild, hurried and despairing. He observed, "I cannot go down to that water for I am wounded all over and I shall die." I told him to sit down, while I crawled down and brought some back in my hat. This I effected with a great deal of difficulty. We then hobbled along the border of the lake for a mile and a half, when it grew dark and we stopped. We could still hear the shouting of the savages over their booty. We stopped under a large pine near the lake and I told White I could go no further. "Oh," said he, "let us go up into the pines and find a spring." I replied that there was no spring within a mile of us, which I knew to be a fact. "Well," said he, "if you stop here I shall make a fire." "Make as much as you please," I *replied angrily, "this is a poor time now to undertake to frighten me into measures." I then started to the water, crawling on my hands and one knee, returning in about an hour with some in my hat. While I was at this, he had kindled a small fire. Taking a draught of water from the hat, he exclaimed, "Oh dear, we shall die here, we shall never get out of these mountains." "Well," said I, "if you persist in thinking so you will die; but I can crawl from this place upon my hands and one knee, kill 2 or 3 elk, make a shelter of the skins and dry the meat until we are able to travel." In this manner, I persuaded him that we were not in half so bad a situation as we might be, although he was not in half so bad a situation as I expected, for on examination I found only a slight wound from an arrow on his hip bone. But he was not so much to blame, as he was a young man who had been brought up in Missouri the pet of the family and had never done or learned much of anything but horse racing and gambling whilst under the care of his parents (if care it can be called). I pulled off an old piece of a coat made of blanket (as he was entirely without clothing, except his hat and shirt). I set myself in a leaning position against a tree, ever and anon gathering such leaves and rubbish as I could without altering the position of my body. Keeping up a little fire in this manner, I miserably spent the night. The next morning, Aug 29th, I could not arise without assistance. White procured me a couple of sticks for crutches, by the help of which I hobbled to a small grove of pines about 60 yds. distant. We had scarcely entered the grove, when we heard a dog barking and Indians singing and talking. The sound seemed to be approaching us. They, at length, came near to where we were, to the number of 60. They commenced shooting at a large band of elk that were swimming in the lake, killed 4 of them, dragged them to shore and butchered them, which occupied about 3 hours. They then packed the meat in small bundles on their backs and traveled up along the rocky shore about a mile and encamped. We then left our hiding place, crept into the thick pines about 50 yds. distant and started in the direction of our encampment, in the hope of finding our comrades. My leg was very much swelled and painful, but I managed to get along slowly on my crutches by White carrying my rifle. When we were within about 60 rods of the encampment, we discovered the Canadian hunting round among the trees, as though he was looking for a trail. We approached him within 30 feet before he saw us, and he was so agitated by fear that he knew not whether to run or stand still.*

On being asked where Elbridge was, he said they came to the camp the night before at sunset. The Indians pursued them into the woods, where they separated and he saw him no more. At the encampment, I found a sack of salt. Everything else the Indians had carried away or cut to pieces. They had built 7 large conical forts near the spot; from which we supposed their number to have been 70 or 80, part of whom had returned to their village with the horses and plunder. We left the place heaping curses on the head of the Blackfoot Nation, which neither injured them or alleviated our distress. We followed down the shore of the lake and stopped for the night. My companions threw some logs and rubbish together, forming a kind of shelter from the night breeze, but in the night it took fire (the logs being pitch pine). The blaze ran to the tops of the trees. We removed a short distance, built another fire and laid by it until morning. We made a raft of dry poles and crossed the outlet upon it. We then went to a small grove of pines nearby and made a fire, where we stopped the remainder of the day, in hopes that Elbridge would see our signals and come to us, for we left directions on a tree at the encampment which route we would take. In the meantime, the Canadian went to hunt something to eat, but without success. I had bathed my wounds in salt water, and made a salve of beaver's oil and castoreum, which I had applied to them. This had eased the pain and drawn out the swelling in a great measure. The next morning I felt very stiff and sore, but we were obliged to travel or starve, as we had eaten nothing since our defeat, and game was very scarce on the west side of the lake.

. . . We had passed up the left hand fork on the 9ᵗʰ of July on horseback in good health and spirits, and came down on the right on the 31ˢᵗ of August on foot with weary limbs and sorrowful countenances. We built a fire and laid down to rest, but I could not sleep more than 15 or 20 minutes at a time, for the night was so very cold. We had plenty of meat, however, and made moccasins of raw elk hide. The next day, we crossed the stream and traveled down near to Jackson Lake on the west side, then took a small branch in a west direction to the head. We then had the Teton Mountains to cross, which looked like a laborious undertaking, as it was steep and the top covered with snow. We arrived at the summit, however, with a great deal of difficulty before sunset. After resting a few moments, we traveled down about a mile on the other side and stopped for the

night. After spending another cold and tedious night, we were descending the mountain through the pines at day light, and the next night reached Henrys Fork of Snake River.

As is evident from these three narratives, Yellowstone was discovered by several mountain men during the years when fur-trappers roamed the West. However, another three decades would pass before Yellowstone was officially discovered, both by Washburn's party and the general public. Russell's journal makes passing mention of Bridger as a member of their party. This is the famous Jim Bridger who later was guide for Captain Reynolds on his 1859 expedition, that failed in the attempt to cross the mountains into Yellowstone. Jim Bridger was famous for his telling of tall tales about places and events in the Old West. In the case of Yellowstone, his tales were not always so tall, as Captain Reynolds believed. For a number of years, there were hints of the wonders behind the towering mountains surrounding the Upper Yellowstone, including exaggerations of thousand foot waterfalls. Did the wonderland of fountains, burning lakes, thundering waterfalls and multicolored canyons exist? Not until 1870 did the answer come . . . it does!

BOOK II

SEA TO SHINING SEA
1840-60

In the next time period, Americans will decisively claim the entire span of the continent from the Atlantic to the Pacific. The era of the mountain man fur trapper is passing and the first wave of pioneers will head to the Far West in their covered wagons. Chimney Rock, Scotts Bluff and other dramatic buttes stand like sentinels along the Oregon Trail; and argonauts will hazard the daunting landscape of vast deserts and towering mountains on their way to the California gold fields. John Charles Fremont unfurls the Stars and Stripes atop a high mountain in the Wind River Mtns. in 1842, as an inspiration and beacon to the oncoming overlanders. An aggressive foreign policy under President Polk successfully realizes America's belief in its Manifest Destiny. Britain agrees to hand over the Oregon Country, while Americans invade Mexican territory. The Treaty of Guadalupe-Hidalgo in 1848 realizes America's continental ambitions. Military campaigns against Mexico and Indian nations along with mapping, railroad and boundary surveys will also discover new landscapes in places like Death Valley, Yosemite, Big Bend, Canyonlands, Petrified Forest, Glacier and the Grand Canyon.

Chapter I

WIND RIVER MTNS.
1842

from
Report of the Exploring Expedition to the Rocky Mountains
by Brevet Captain J. C. Fremont

Utilizing the mountain men (like Kit Carson) as guides, John Charles Fremont explored and surveyed much of the West, not for furs but to promote the national effort to expand across the continent. Under the sponsorship of his father-in-law, Senator Thomas Hart Benton, he received funding for at least some of his expeditions and many copies of his reports were printed by the government and made available to the

J. C. Fremont   general public. His maps improved geographical knowledge and his writings (improved by the literary abilities of his wife, Jessie Benton Fremont) inspired a whole generation to move west and stake their claims in Oregon and California. Fremont himself led the Bear Flag Revolt in California at the opening of the Mexican-American War.

This selection is taken from his early expedition to South Pass in 1842. Disregarding instructions, he took the impractical but inspired action of ascending what he thought was the highest peak in the Rocky Mountains. From the west side of the Wind River Mtns., he ascended by way of Island Lake to the top of Snow Peak, now called Mt. Fremont. The selection opens with the Pathfinder near the shores of the lake (Mountain Lake) later named for him at the western base of the Wind River Mtns.

August 10 – The air at sunrise is clear and pure, and the morning extremely cold, but beautiful. A lofty snow peak of the mountain is glittering in the first rays of the sun, which has not yet reached us. The long mountain wall to the east, rising two thousand feet abruptly from the plain, behind which we see the peaks, is still dark, and cuts clear against the glowing sky. A fog, just risen from the river, lies along the base of the mountain. Water froze last night, and fires are very comfortable. The scenery becomes hourly more interesting and grand, and the view here is truly magnificent; but, indeed, it needs something to repay the long prairie journey of a thousand miles. The sun has just shot above the wall, and makes a magical change. The whole valley is glowing and bright, and all the mountain peaks are gleaming like silver. . . . We were now approaching the loftiest part of the Wind River chain; and I left the valley a few miles from our encampment, intending to penetrate the mountains as far as possible with the whole party. We were soon involved in very broken ground, among long ridges covered with fragments of granite. Winding our way up a long ravine, we came unexpectedly in view of a most beautiful lake, set like a gem in the mountains. The sheet of water lay transversely across the direction we had been pursuing; and, descending the steep, rocky ridge, where it was necessary to lead our horses, we followed its banks to the southern extremity. Here a view of the utmost magnificence and grandeur burst upon our eyes. With nothing between us and their feet to lessen the effect of the whole height, a grand bed of snow-capped mountains rose before us, pile upon pile, glowing in the bright light of an August day. Immediately below them lay the lake, between two ridges, covered with dark pines, which swept down from the main chain to the spot where we stood. Here, where the lake glittered in the open sunlight, its banks of yellow sand and the light foliage of aspen groves contrasted well with the gloomy pines. . . . I was so much pleased with the beauty of the place, that I determined to make the main camp here, where our animals would find good pasturage, and explore the mountains with a small party of men. Proceeding a little further, we came suddenly upon the outlet of the lake, where it found its way through a narrow passage between low hills. Dark pines, which overhung the stream, and masses of rock, where the water foamed along, gave it much romantic beauty. Where we crossed, which was immediately at the outlet, it is two hundred and fifty feet wide, and so deep, that with difficulty we were able to ford it. Its bed was an accumulation of rocks, boulders and broad slabs, and large angular fragments, among which the animals fell repeatedly. . . .

After establishing a base camp where most of the men would be stationed, Fremont made preparations for the ascent of the prominent peak with a smaller party of men and mules

August 12 – Early in the morning we left the camp, fifteen in number, well armed, of course, and mounted on our best mules. A pack animal carried our provisions, with a coffee pot and kettle, and three or four tin cups. Every man had a blanket strapped over his saddle, to serve for his bed, and the instruments were carried by turns on their backs. We entered directly on rough and rocky ground; and, just after crossing the ridge, had the good fortune to shoot an antelope. We heard the roar, and had a glimpse of a waterfall as we rode along; and, crossing on our way two fine streams, tributary to the Colorado, in about two hours' ride we reached the top of the first row or range of the mountains. Here, again, a view of the most romantic beauty met our eyes. It seemed as if, from the vast expanse of uninteresting prairie we had passed over, Nature had collected

Illustration from Fremon's Report of the Wind River Mountains.

Illustration from Fremon's Report of the Wind River Mountains.

all her beauties together in one chosen place. We were over-looking a deep valley, which was entirely occupied by three lakes, and from the brink the surrounding ridges rose precipitously five hundred and a thousand feet, covered with the dark green of the balsam pine, relieved on the border of the lake with the light foliage of the aspen. They all communicated with each other; and the green of the waters, common to mountain lakes of great depth, showed that it would be impossible to cross them. The surprise manifested by our guides when these impossible obstacles suddenly barred our progress proved they were among the hidden treasures of the place, unknown even to the wandering trappers of the region. Descending the hill, we proceeded to make our way along the margin of the southern extremity. A narrow strip of angular fragments of rock sometimes afforded a rough pathway for our mules, but generally we rode along the shelving side, occasionally scrambling up, at a considerable risk of tumbling back into the lake.

The slope was frequently 60°; the pines grew densely together, and the ground was covered with the branches and trunks of trees. The air was fragrant with the odor of the pines; and I realized this delightful morning the pleasure of breathing that mountain air which makes a constant theme of the hunter's praise, and which now made us feel as if we had all been drinking some exhilarating gas. The depths of this unexplored forest were a place to delight the heart of a botanist. There was a rich undergrowth of plants, and numerous gay-colored flowers in brilliant bloom. We reached the outlet at length, where some freshly barked willows that lay in the water showed that beaver had been recently at work. There were some small brown squirrels jumping about in the pines, and a couple of large mallard ducks swimming about in the stream.

The hills on this southern end were low, and the lake looked like a mimic sea, as the waves broke on the sandy beach in the force of a strong breeze. There was a pretty open spot, with fine grass for our mules; and we made our noon halt on the beach, under the shade of some large hemlocks. We resumed our journey after a halt of about an hour, making our way up the ridge on the western side of the lake. In search of smoother ground, we rode a little inland; and, passing through groves of aspen, soon found ourselves again among the pines. Emerging from these, we struck the summit of the ridge above the upper end of the lake.

We had reached a very elevated point; and in the valley below, and among the hills, were a number of lakes at different levels; some two or three hundred feet above others, with which they communicated by foaming torrents. Even to our great height, the roar of the cataracts came up, and we could see them leaping down in lines of snowy foam. From this scene of busy waters, we turned abruptly into the stillness of a forest, where we rode among the open bolls of the pines, over a lawn of verdant grass, having strikingly the air of cultivated grounds. This led us, after a time, among masses of rock which had no vegetable earth but in hollows and crevices, though still the pine forest continued. Toward evening, we reached a defile, or rather a hole in the mountains, entirely shut in by dark pine-covered rocks.

A small stream, with a scarcely perceptible current, flowed through a level bottom of perhaps eighty yards width, where the grass was saturated with water. Into this the mules were turned, and were neither hobbled nor picketed during the night, as the fine pasturage took away all temptation to stray; and we made our bivouac in the pines. The surrounding masses were all of granite. While supper was being prepared, I set out on an excursion in the neighborhood, accompanied by one of my men. We wandered about among the crags and ravines until dark, richly repaid for our walk by a fine collection of plants, many of them in full bloom. Ascending a peak to find the place of our camp, we saw that the little defile in which we lay communicated with the long green valley of some stream, which, here locked up in the mountains, far away to the south, found its way in a dense forest to the plains.

Looking along its upward course, it seemed to conduct, by a smooth gradual slope, directly toward the peak, which, from long consultation as we approached the mountain, we had decided to be the highest of the range. Pleased with the discovery of so fine a road for the next day, we hastened down to the camp, where we arrived just in time for supper. Our table service was rather scant; and we held the meat in our hands, and clean rocks make good plates, on which we spread our maccaroni. Among all the strange places on which we had occasion to encamp during our long journey, none have left so vivid an impression on my mind as the camp of this evening. The disorder of the masses which surrounded us; the little hole through which we saw the stars overhead; the dark pines where we slept; and the rocks lit up with the glow of our fires, made a night picture of very wild beauty.

August 13 – The morning was bright and pleasant, just cool enough to make exercise agreeable, and we soon entered the defile I had seen the preceding day. It was smoothly carpeted with a soft grass, and scattered over with groups of flowers, of which yellow was the predominant color. Sometimes we were forced, by an occasional difficult pass, to pick our way on a narrow ledge along the side of the defile, and the mules were frequently on their knees; but these obstructions were rare, and we journeyed on in the sweet morning air, delighted at our good fortune in having found such a beautiful entrance to the mountains. This road continued for about three miles, when we suddenly reached its termination in one of the grand views which, at every turn, meet the traveler in this magnificent region. Here the defile up which we had traveled opened out into a small lawn, where, in a little lake, the stream had its source.

There were some fine asters in bloom, but all the flowering plants appeared to seek the shelter of the rocks, and to be of lower growth than below, as if they loved the warmth of the soil, and kept out of the way of the winds. Immediately at our feet a precipitous descent led to a confusion of defiles, and before us rose the mountains as we have represented them in the annexed view. It is not by the splendor of far-off views, which have lent such a glory to the Alps, that these impress the mind; but by a gigantic disorder of enormous masses, and a savage sublimity of naked rock, in wonderful contrast with innumerable green spots of a rich floral beauty, shut up in their stern recesses. Their wildness seems well suited to the character of the people who inhabit the country.

I determined to leave our animals here, and make the rest of our way on foot. The peak appeared so near, that there was no doubt of our returning before night; and a few men were left in charge of the mules, with our provisions and blankets. We took with us nothing but our arms and instruments, and as the day had become warm, the greater part left our coats. Having made an early dinner, we started again. We were soon involved in the most ragged precipices, nearing the central chain very slowly, and rising but little. The first ridge hid a succession of others; and when, with great fatigue and difficulty, we had climbed up five hundred feet, it was but to make an equal descent on the other side. All these intervening places were filled with small deep lakes, which met the eye in every direction, descending from one level to another, sometimes under bridges formed by huge fragments of granite, beneath which was heard the roar of the water. These constantly obstructed our path, forcing us to make long detours; frequently obliged to retrace our steps, and frequently falling among the rocks. Maxwell was precipitated toward the face of a precipice, and saved himself from going over by throwing himself flat on the ground. We clambered on, always expecting, with every ridge that we crossed, to reach the foot of the peaks, and always disappointed, until about 4 o'clock, when, pretty well worn out, we reached the shore of a little lake, in which there was a rocky island, and from which we obtained the view given in the frontispiece. We remained here a short time to rest, and continued on around the lake, which had in some places a beach of white sand, and in others was bound with rocks, over which the way was difficult and dangerous, as the water from innumerable springs made them very slippery.

By the time we had reached the further side of the lake, we found ourselves all exceedingly fatigued, and, much to the satis-faction of the whole party, we encamped. The spot we had cho-sen was a broad flat rock, in some measure protected from the winds by the surrounding crags, and the trunks of fallen pines afforded us bright fires. Nearby was a foaming torrent, which tumbled into the little lake about one hundred and fifty feet below us, and which, by way of distinction, we have called Island Lake. We had reached the upper limit of the piney region; as, above this point, no tree was to be seen, and patches of snow lay everywhere around us on the cold sides of the rocks. The flora of the region we had traversed since leaving our mules was extremely rich, and, among the characteristic plants, the scarlet flowers of the dodecatheon dentatum everywhere met the eye in great abundance. A small green ravine, on the edge of which we were encamped, was filled with a profusion of alpine plants in brilliant bloom. . . . I was taken ill shortly after we had encamped, and continued so until late in the night, with violent headache and vomiting. This was probably caused by the excessive fatigue I had undergone, and want of food, and perhaps, also, in some measure, by the rarity of the air. The night was cold, as a violent gale from the north had sprung up at sunset, which entirely blew away the heat of the fires. The cold, and our granite beds, had not been favorable to sleep, and we were glad to see the face of the sun in the morning. Not being delayed by any preparation for breakfast, we set out immediately.

On every side as we advanced was heard the roar of waters, and of a torrent, which we followed up a short distance, until it expanded into a lake about one mile in length. On the northern side of the lake was a bank of ice, or rather of snow covered with a crust of ice. Carson had been our guide into the mountains, and, agreeably to his advice, we left this little valley, and took to the ridges again; which we found extremely broken, and where we were again involved with precipices. Here were ice fields; among which we were all dispersed, seeking each the best path to ascend the peak. Mr. Preuss attempted to walk along the upper edge of one of these fields, which sloped away at an angle of about twenty degrees; but his feet slipped from under him, and he went plunging down the plane. A few hundred feet below, at the bottom, were some fragments of sharp rock, on which he landed; and though he turned a couple of somersaults, fortunately received no injury beyond a few bruises. Two of the men, Clement Lambert and Descoteaux, had been taken ill, and lay down on the rocks a short distance below; and at this point I was attacked with headache and giddiness, accompanied by vomiting, as on the day before. Finding myself unable to proceed, I sent the barometer over to Mr. Preuss, who was in a gap two or three hundred yards distant, desiring him to reach the peak, if possible, and take an observation there. He found himself unable to proceed further in that direction. . . . Carson, who had gone over to him, succeeded in reaching one of the snowy summits of the main ridge, whence he saw the peak towards which all our efforts had been directed, towering eight or ten hundred feet into the air above him. In the mean time, finding myself grow rather worse than better, and doubtful how far my strength would carry me, I sent Basil Lajeunesse, with four men, back to the place where the mules had been left.

We were now better acquainted with the topography of the country, and I directed him to bring back with him, if it were in any way possible, four or five mules, with provisions and blankets. With me were Maxwell and Ayer; and after we had remained nearly an hour on the rock, it became so unpleasantly cold, though the day was bright, that we set out on our return to the camp, at which we all arrived safely, straggling in one after the other. I continued ill during the afternoon, but became better towards sundown, when my recovery was completed by the appearance of Basil and four men, all mounted. The men who had gone with him had been too much fatigued to return, and were relieved by those in charge of the horses; but in his powers of endurance Basil resembled more a mountain goat than a man. They brought blankets and provisions, and we enjoyed well our dried meat and a cup of good coffee. We rolled ourselves up in our blankets, and with our feet turned to a blazing fire, slept soundly until morning.

August 15 – It had been supposed that we had finished with the mountains; and the evening before, it had been arranged that Carson should set out at daylight, and return to breakfast at the camp of the mules, taking with him all but four or five men, who were to stay with me and bring back the mules and instruments. Accordingly, at the break of day they set out. With Mr. Preuss and myself remained Basil Lajeunesse, Clement Lambert, Janisse, and Descoteaux. When we had secured strength for the day by a hearty breakfast, we covered what remained, which was enough for one meal, with rocks, in order that it might be safe from any marauding bird; and, saddling our mules, turned our faces once more towards the peaks. This time we determined to proceed quietly and cautiously, deliberately resolved to accomplish our object if it were within the compass of human means. We were of opinion that a long defile which lay to the left of yesterday's route would lead us to the foot of the main peak. Our mules had been refreshed by the fine grass in the little ravine at the Island camp, and we intended to ride up the defile as far as possible, in order to husband our strength for the main ascent. Though this was a fine passage, still it was a defile of the most rugged mountains known, and we had many a rough and steep slippery place to cross before reaching the end. In this place the sun rarely shone; snow lay along the border of the small stream which flowed through it, and occasional icy passages made the footing of the mules very insecure, and the rocks and ground were moist with the trickling waters in this spring of mighty rivers. We soon had the satisfaction to find ourselves riding along the huge wall which forms the central summits of the chain. There at last it rose by our sides, a nearly perpendicular wall of granite, terminating 2,000 to 3,000 feet above our heads in a serrated line of broken, jagged cones. We rose on until we came almost immediately below the main peak, which I denominated the Snow peak, as it exhibited more snow to the eye than any of the neighboring summits. Here were three small lakes of a green color, each of perhaps a thousand yards in diameter, and apparently very deep. These lay in a kind of chasm; and, according to the barometer, we had attained but a few hundred feet above the Island lake.

We managed to get our mules up to a little bench about a hundred feet above the lakes, where there was a patch of good grass, and turned them loose to graze. During our rough ride to this place, they had exhibited a wonderful surefootedness. Parts of the defile were filled with angular, sharp fragments of rock, three or four and eight or ten feet cube; and among these they had worked their way, leaping from one narrow point to another, rarely making a false step, and giving us no occasion to dismount. Having divested ourselves of every unnecessary encumbrance, we commenced the ascent. This time, like experienced travelers, we did not press ourselves, but climbed leisurely, sitting down as soon as we found breath beginning to fail. At intervals we reached places where a number of springs gushed from the rocks, and about 1,800 feet above the lakes came to the snow line. From this point our progress was uninterrupted climbing. Hitherto I had worn a pair of thick moccasins, with soles of parfleche; but here I put on a light thin pair, which I had brought for the purpose, as now the use of our toes became necessary to further advance. I availed myself of a sort of comb of the mountain, which stood against the wall like a buttress, and which the wind and the solar radiation, joined to the steepness of the smooth rock, had kept almost entirely free from snow. Up this I made my way rapidly. Our cautious method of advancing in the outset had spared my strength; and, with the exception of a slight disposition to headache, I felt no remains of yesterday's illness. In a few minutes we reached a point where the buttress was overhanging, and there was no other way of surmounting the difficulty than by passing around one side of it, which was the face of a vertical precipice of several hundred feet.

Putting hands and feet in the crevices between the blocks, I succeeded in getting over it, and, when I reached the top, found my companions in a small valley below. Descending to them, we continued climbing, and in a short time reached the crest. I sprang upon the summit, and another step would have precipitated me into an immense snow field five hundred feet below. To the edge of this field was a sheer icy precipice; and then, with a gradual fall, the field sloped off for about a mile, until it struck the foot of another lower ridge. I stood on a narrow crest, about three feet in width, with an inclination of about 20° N, 51° E. As soon as I had gratified the first feelings of curiosity, I descended, and each man ascended in his turn; for I would only allow one at a time to mount the unstable and precarious slab, which it seemed a breath would hurl into the abyss below. We mounted the barometer in the snow of the summit, and, fixing a ramrod in a crevice, unfurled the national flag to wave in the breeze where never flag waved before. During our morning's ascent, we had met no sign of animal life, except the small sparrow-like bird already mentioned. A stillness the most profound and a terrible solitude forced themselves constantly on the mind as the great features of the place. Here, on the summit, where the stillness was absolute, unbroken by any sound, and the solitude complete, we thought ourselves beyond the region of animated life; but while we were sitting on the rock, a solitary bee (bromus, the humble bee) came winging his flight from the eastern valley, and lit on the knee of one of the men.

It was a strange place, the icy rock and the highest peak of the Rocky Mountains, for a lover of warm sunshine and flowers; and we pleased ourselves with the idea that he was the first of his species to cross the mountain barrier – a solitary pioneer to foretell the advance of civilization. I believe that a moment's thought would have made us let him continue his way unharmed; but we carried out the law of this country, where all animated nature seems at war; and, seizing him immediately, put him in at least a fit place – in the leaves of a large book, among the flowers we had collected on our way.

The day was sunny and bright, but a slight shining mist hung over the lower plains, which interfered with our view of the sur-

rounding country. On one side we overlooked innumerable lakes and streams, the spring of the Colorado of the Gulf of California; and on the other was the Wind river valley, where were the heads of the Yellowstone branch of the Missouri; far to the north, we just could discover the snowy heads of the Trois Tetons, where were the sources of the Missouri and Columbia rivers; and at the southern extremity of the ridge, the peaks were plainly visible, among which were some of the springs of the Nebraska or Platte river. Around us, the whole scene had one main striking feature, which was that of terrible convulsion. Parallel to its length, the ridge was split into chasms and fissures; between which rose the thin lofty walls, terminated with slender minarets and columns, which is correctly represented in the view from the camp on Island lake. . . . Having now made what observations our means afforded, we proceeded to descend. We had accomplished an object of laudable ambition, and beyond the strict order of our instructions. We had climbed the loftiest peak of the Rocky Mountains, and looked down upon the snow a thousand feet below, and, standing where never human foot had stood before, felt the exultation of first explorers. It was about 2 o'clock when we left the summit; and when we reached the bottom, the sun had already sunk behind the wall, and the day was drawing to a close. It would have been pleasant to have lingered here and on the summit longer; but we hurried away as rapidly as the ground would permit; for it

Fremont ascending to the top of the "highest peak in the Rocky Mtns."

was an object to regain our party as soon as possible, not knowing what accident the next hour might bring forth.

We reached our deposit of provisions at nightfall. Here was not the inn which awaits the tired traveler on his return from Mount Blanc, or the orange groves of SouthAmerica, with their refreshing juices and soft fragrant air; but we found our little cache of dried meat and coffee undisturbed. Though the moon was bright, the road was full of precipices, and the fatigue of the day had been great. We therefore abandoned the idea of rejoining our friends, and lay down on the rock, and, in spite of the cold, slept soundly.

August 16 – We left our encampment with the daylight. We saw on our way large flocks of the mountain goat looking down on us from the cliffs. At the crack of a rifle, they would bound off among the rocks, and in a few minutes make their appearance on some lofty peak, some hundred or a thousand feet above. It is needless to attempt any further description of the country; the portion over which we traveled this morning was rough as imagination could picture it, and to us seemed equally beautiful. A concourse of lakes and rushing waters, mountains of rocks naked and destitute of vegetable earth, dells and ravines of the most exquisite beauty, all kept green and fresh by the great moisture in the air, and sown with brilliant flowers, and everywhere thrown around all the glory of most magnificent scenes: these constitute the features of the place, and impress themselves vividly on the mind of the traveler. It was not until 11 o'clock that we reached the place where our animals had been left, when we first attempted the mountains on foot. Near one of the still burning fires we found a piece of meat, which our friends had thrown away, and which furnished us a mouthful – a very scanty breakfast. We continued directly on, and reached our camp on the mountain lake at dusk. We found all well. Nothing had occurred to interrupt the quiet since our departure, and the fine grass and good cool water had done much to reestablish our animals. All heard with great delight the order to turn our faces homeward; and toward sundown of the 17th, we encamped again at the Two Buttes.

Chapter II

ROCKY MOUNTAIN
1843

from Scenes in the Rocky Mountains
by Rufus B. Sage

From 1841 to 1844, Rufus Sage roamed the Rocky Mountain West hunting, trading with Indians and soldiering with Texans against the Mexicans. Mostly, he wandered alone and with other mountain men on the high plains and front range of Colorado and New Mexico. One of his hunting excursions took him in the fall of 1843 into the southeastern quadrant of the present-day Rocky Mountain National Park. He refers successively to the area around Wild Basin, St. Mary's Lake and Moraine Park.

Sept. 25th. Having purchased a horse for the purpose, I proceeded to the mountains on a hunting excursion, where, unattended by any one, I had a further opportunity of testing the varied sweets of solitude.

My course lay directly west some eight miles to Soublet's creek, a considerable affluent of the Platte, heading at the base of Long's Peak; thence, continuing up its right hand branch, I penetrated into the mountains, on the second day, a distance of several miles and camped. One of the passes to Grand River, which is generally thought much the nearest route, leads up this branch.

The interval from the 27th to the 30th was devoted to exploration, and I ascended the main chain of the mountains left of Long's Peak. The usual height of this ridge is about ten thousand feet, upon which the stern chambers of deathless winter are repeatedly exposed to the eye. . . .

Sept. 30th. In the afternoon I raised camp and proceeded for ten or twelve miles, through a broad opening between two mountain ridges, bearing a northwesterly direction, to a large valley skirting a tributary of Thompson's creek, where, finding an abundance of deer, I passed the interval till my return to the Fort.

. . . The locality of my encampment presented numerous and varied attractions. It seemed, indeed, like a concentration of beautiful lateral valleys, intersected by meandering watercourses, ridged by lofty ledges of precipitous rock, and hemmed in upon the west by vast piles of mountains climbing beyond the clouds, and upon the north, south, and east, by sharp lines of hills that skirted the prairie; while occasional openings, like gateways, pointed to the far-spreading domains of silence and loneliness.

Easterly a wall of red sandstone and slate extended for miles northward and southward, whose counterscarp spread to view a broad and gentle declivity, decked with pines and luxuriant herbage, at the foot of which a lake of several miles in circumference occupies the centre of a basin-like valley, bounded in every direction by verdant hills, that smile upon the bright gem embosomed among them.

This valley is five or six miles in diameter, and possesses a soil well adapted to cultivation. It also affords every variety of game, while the lake is completely crowded with geese, brants, ducks, and gulls, to an extent seldom witnessed. What a charming retreat for some one of the world-hating literati! He might here hold daily converse with himself, Nature, and his God, far removed from the annoyance of man.

Four miles further north the traveler is brought to one of the main branches of Thompson's creek, up which is another pass to the waters of Grand River. This stream traces its way through a fertile valley, two or three miles broad, stretching from the prairie almost to the base of Long's Peak, a distance of nearly three miles. The valley is well timbered and admirably adapted to stock-raising.

The hills and mountains, enclosing it upon each side are also studded with forests of pine and cedar, while the entire section is stored with all of the usual varieties of game known to contiguous regions, in addition to its rich treasures of fruits, flowers and grasses.

In surveying, from a commanding summit, the vast prairie skirting the mountain range upon the east, several small lakes are discernible at different points. The water of these is usually brackish, and their shores, whitened by constant saline efflorescence, glisten in the sun's rays, and present a striking contrast with the surrounding verdure.

The mind is perfectly astounded at the immense expanse thus brought within the scope of vision. On a clear day, objects favorably situated no larger than an ox or a horse, may be seen at a distance of twenty miles, and the timber of creeks even for sixty or seventy miles. Here the beholder may scale beyond the clouds far heavenward, and gaze upon a world at his feet!

Chapter III

SOUTHERN ROCKIES
1847

from Adventures in Mexico and the Rocky Mountains
by George Frederick Ruxton

The British author was a born wanderer who, through all his travels, had fondest memories of his days spent wandering in the Rockies. On a diplomatic and commercial mission for his government, he traveled through Mexico and north into the Rockies during the outbreak of the Mexican War. His books are historically valuable for their accurate descriptions of mountain men trappers and their way of life. It is stretching it a bit to call him an explorer of this region, as Pike, Long and trappers had already traveled the area and accounts written. Still, it is another early and lyrical description of the Rockies, one in winter and another in spring, in two contrasting moods of Nature.

The mountain rises directly from the north end of the Vallecito, and is the dividing ridge between the waters of the Del Norte and the Arkansa, or Rio Napeste of the Mexicans. The ascent to the summit, from the western side, is short, but very steep; and the snow was of such a depth that the mules could hardly make their way to the top. Leading my horse by the bridle, I led the way, and at length, numbed with cold, I reached the summit, where is a level plateau of about a hundred square yards. Attaining this, and exposed to the full sweep of the wind, a blast struck me, carrying with it a perfect avalanche of snow and sleet, full in my front, and knocked me as clean off my legs as I could have been floored by a twenty-four pound shot.

The view from this point was wild and dismal in the extreme. Looking back, the whole country was covered with a thick carpet of snow, but eastward it was seen in patches only here and there. Beside me lay the main chain of the Rocky Mountains, Pike's Peak lifting its snowy head far above the rest; and to the southeast the Spanish Peaks towered like twin giants over the plains. Beneath the mountain on which I stood was a narrow valley, through which ran a streamlet bordered with dwarf oak and pine, and looking like a thread of silver as it wound through the plain. Rugged peaks and ridges, snow clad and covered with pine, and deep gorges filled with broken rocks, everywhere met the eye. To the eastward the mountains gradually smoothed away into detached spurs and broken ground, until they met the vast prairies, which stretched far as the eye could reach, and hundreds of miles beyond – a sea of seeming barrenness, vast and dismal. A hurricane of wind was blowing at the time, and clouds of dust swept along the sandy prairies, like the smoke of a million bonfires. On the mountaintop it roared and raved through the pines, filling the air with snow and broken branches, and piling it in huge drifts against the trees. The perfect solitude of this vast wilderness was almost appalling. From my position on the summit of the dividing ridge I had a bird's-eye view, as it were, over the ragged and chaotic masses of the stupendous chain of the Rocky Mountains, and the vast deserts which stretched away from their eastern bases; while, on all sides of me, broken ridges, and chasms and ravines, with masses of piled-up rocks and uprooted trees, with clouds of drifting snow flying through the air, and the hurricane's roar battling through the forest at my feet, added to the wildness of the scene, which was unrelieved by the slightest vestige of animal or human life. Not a sound, either of bird or beast, was heard – indeed the hoarse and stunning rattle of the wind would have drowned them, so loud it roared and raved through the trees. . . .

Later in his journey . . .

Daybreak in this wild spot was beautiful in the extreme. While the deep gorge in which I lay was still buried in perfect gloom, the mountaintops loomed grey and indistinct from out of the morning mist. A faint glow of light broke over the ridge which shut out the valley from the east, and, spreading over the sky, first displayed the snow-covered peak, a wreath of vapoury mist encircling it, which gradually rose and disappeared. Suddenly the dull white of its summit glowed with light like burnished silver; and at the same moment the whole eastern sky blazed, as it were, in gold, and ridge and peak, catching the refulgence, glittered with the beams of the rising sun, which at length, peeping over the crest, flooded at once the valley with its dazzling light.

Chapter IV

BADLANDS
1849

from "The Report of John Evans"
in Report of a Geological Survey of Wisconsin, Iowa, and
Minnesota; and Incidentally of a Portion of Nebraska
Territory *by David Dale Owen*

Another kind of voyage of discovery were the fossil hunting expeditions. Paleontology was a science in its infancy at that time. Many landscapes of the West, however, revealed the bones and fossils of extinct species, prehistoric remains from the very distant past. Such a place was the Badlands. This early description of the region was, as indicated by the title, an incidental extension of a geological survey into what was then called the Nebraska Territory but is, in fact, the extensive badlands of South Dakota. John Evans describes many of the fossilized creatures found but this selection is limited to his more interesting description upon seeing the Mauvaises Terres (Badlands).

After leaving the locality on Sage Creek, affording the above-mentioned fossils, crossing that stream, and proceeding in the direction of White River, about twelve or fifteen miles, the formation of the Mauvaises Terres proper bursts into view, disclosing, as here depicted, one of the most extraordinary and picturesque sights that can be found in the whole Missouri country.

From the high prairies, that rise in the background, by a series of terraces or benches, towards the spurs of the Rocky Mountains, the traveler looks down into an extensive valley, that may be said to constitute a world of its own, and which appears to have been formed, partly by an extensive vertical fault, partly by the long-continued influence of the scooping action of denudation.

The width of this valley may be about thirty miles, and its whole length about ninety, as it stretches away westwardly, towards the base of the gloomy and dark range of mountains known as the Black Hills. Its most depressed portion, three hundred feet below the general level of the surrounding country, is clothed with scanty grasses, and covered by a soil similar to that of the higher ground.

To the surrounding country, however, the Mauvaises Terres present the most striking contrast. From the uniform, monotonous, open prairie, the traveler suddenly descends, one or two hundred feet, into a valley that looks as if it had sunk away from the surrounding world; leaving standing, all over it, thousands of abrupt, irregular, prismatic, and columnar masses, frequently capped with irregular pyramids, and stretching up to a height of from one to two hundred feet, or more.

So thickly are these natural towers studded over the surface of this extraordinary region, that the traveler threads his way through deep, confined, labyrinthine passages, not unlike the narrow, irregular streets and lanes of some quaint old town of the European Continent. Viewed in the distance, indeed, these rocky piles, in their endless succession, assume the appearance of massive, artificial structures, decked out with all the accessories of buttress and turret, arched doorway and clustered shaft, pinnacle, and finial, and tapering spire.

One might almost imagine oneself approaching some magnificent city of the dead, where the labor and the genius of forgotten nations had left behind them a multitude of monuments of art and skill.

On descending from the heights, however, and proceeding to thread this vast labyrinth, and inspect, in detail, its deep, intricate recesses, the realities of the scene soon dissipate the delusions of the distance. The castellated forms which fancy had conjured up have vanished; and around one, on every side, is bleak and barren desolation.

Then, too, if the exploration be made in midsummer, the scorching rays of the sun, pouring down in the hundred defiles that conduct the wayfarer through this pathless waste, are reflected back from the white or ash-colored walls that rise around, unmitigated by a breath of air, or the shelter of a solitary shrub.

Chapter V

GUADALUPE MOUNTAINS
1849/1850

from The Journal of Captain R. B. Marcy &
from Personal Narrative of Explorations and Incidents
in Texas, New Mexico, California, Sonora and Chihuahua
by John Russell Bartlett

Guadalupe Mountains

Captain Randolph B. Marcy led many scouting expeditions across Texas and the Southwest in the middle years of the 19th century. He wrote government reports and personal reminiscences about his experiences and travels. The following is his report of escorting overlanders who are heading for the gold fields in California. Theirs was a southern route across the Texas Panhandle into Santa Fe. From there the gold seekers headed south down the Rio Grande and turned west into southern Arizona down the Gila River. In southern New Mexico, Marcy and his military escort broke off and headed east across a more southern region virtually unknown – Texas west of the Pecos and over Guadalupe Pass.(Marcy)

September 9 – Our course this morning, after leaving the Ojo del Cuerbo, was south 49° east, bearing directly for the peak of the Guadalupe, until we arrived nearly opposite to it on the west side; we then continued past it, gradually turning to the left around the hills at the base until we reached a rocky ravine which led us directly up to the foot of the towering cliff of the peak. We encamped near the head of the ravine, where there is a spring about 200 yards north of the road, and good grass. Animals must be driven up the ravine to the water, as the wagons cannot pass further than the turn of the road.

We had a good road today, with the exception of four miles of sand, and made twenty-three miles.

The Guadalupe range of mountains terminates at this place in an immense perpendicular bluff of light-colored sandstone, which rises to the enormous height of nearly two thousand feet, and runs off to the northeast towards the Pecos. . . .

September 10 – We remained in camp today until about 3 p.m., when, getting our wagon train up the hill, we found ourselves upon very high rolling table land, which our guide says descends from here to the Pecos river. As we have been continually ascending from the Rio Grande to this point, we are therefore now upon the summit level of two streams. As it rained most of the afternoon, we only made a short march of four miles, passing in a northeast direction around under the mountains, and encamped in a ravine which runs down through a large grove of pine timber from a gap in the Guadalupe mountains; there is a fine spring three hundred yards to the west of the road, which affords an abundant supply of water.

The mountains are covered on the eastern side with groves of large pine trees; and as this is the only kind of timber fit for building in the country, it may some day be useful. We have also seen a species of cedar with the bark resembling that of the oak, and very different from any we have ever seen before.

There are many varieties of the cactus and palmettos about the mountains, and we have this evening for the first time seen the maguey plant, which constitutes almost the only vegetable food that the Apaches and southern Comanches get for a great portion of the year. . . .

The Guadalupe is the last of the mountains between the Rio Grande and the Pecos.

. . . These wild and rocky mountain ranges are the places where several animals resort that are to be met with nowhere else. The grizzly bear (the most formidable animal of the continent) finds a lurking place in the caverns and thickets, and feeds upon the wild fruit that abounds here (Grizzly no longer exist here). The big-horn, or cimarron, is also seen skipping playfully from rock to rock upon the narrow overhanging crags, and cropping the

*short herbage which grows upon them: these, with the black-
tailed deer, are almost the only animals found upon these mountains. One of the latter was killed this evening, and we found it
very similar to the common fallow deer of the States, but much
larger. . . .*

*September 11 – As our animals were somewhat jaded from the
long marches we have made for a few days past, and as we had
a long journey before us, I remained in our camp of last night
until after dinner to give them rest, when we moved forward
over a good road to Independence spring, five miles.*

*Here we found two large springs of pure cold water, which boil
up from the ground and run off in a stream about the size of a
barrel, with a great supply of oak wood and grama grass near,
rendering it a most desirable place for encamping.*

*The country from the base of the mountains to this place is roll-
ing, and the soil good.*

*The peak of Guadalupe, and the general outline of the chain,
can be seen from here, and it appears to be impossible to pass
through it with wagons anywhere north of our route; and as the
defile is near the peak, which can be seen for many miles
around, it is a good landmark.*

It had been one year earlier when Marcy first opened up the route
across the Guadalupe Pass, returning from having given a military
escort to a group of overlanders on their way to the California gold
fields. In the year since, other argonauts had followed the route
through the area. Nevertheless, Bartlett's narrative is another early and
well-written description of the landmark. As commissioner of the
United States and Mexican Boundary Survey from 1850 to 1853, he
traveled throughout the borderlands region.

(Bartlett)

*November 9th – Up at four o'clock; took a hearty breakfast, and
was ready to move as soon as there was sufficient light to see
the road. Started at a lively pace, intending to make a good
march. The road was quite tortuous, winding among and over
hills, in a direction nearly west, towards the bold head of the
great Guadalupe Mountain, which had been before us some
eight or ten days. This is a most remarkable landmark, rising as*

it does far above all other objects, and terminating abruptly about three thousand feet above the surrounding plain. The sierra or mountain range which ends with it, comes from the northeast. It is a dark, gloomy-looking range, with bold and forbidding sides, consisting of huge piles of rocks, their debris heaped far above the surrounding hills. As it approaches its termination the color changes to a pure white, tinted with buff or light orange, presenting a beautiful contrast with other portions of the range, or with the azure blue of the sky beyond; for in this elevated region the heavens have a remarkable brilliancy and depth of color. . . .

The Guadalupe had been before us the whole day, and we all expected to reach it within a couple of hours after leaving camp. But hour after hour we drove directly towards it, without seeming to approach nearer; and finally, after journeying ten hours, the mountain seemed to be as distant as it was in the morning. Such is the great clearness of the atmosphere here, that one unused to measuring distances in elevated regions is greatly deceived in his calculations. When this mountain was first discovered we were more than one hundred miles off. Even then its features stood out boldly against the blue sky; and when the rays of the morning sun were shed upon it, it exhibited every outline of its rugged sides with as much distinctness as a similar object would in the old States at one fifth the distance. Often have I gazed at the Katskill Mountains in sailing down the Hudson; and though at a distance of but twelve miles, I never saw them as distinctly, as the Guadalupe Mountain appeared sixty miles off. . . .

November 10th – *Two hours before day my carriage driver was out with the mules to give them an early feed, while we managed to make a pot of tea from a canister, which I always carried with me for such occasions. This, with cold pork and hard bread, made our breakfast; but meagre as it was, it was taken with a relish. We then filled our leather water tank, and were on our journey before the sun peeped over the adjacent hills to our left. No sunrise at sea or from the mountain's summit could equal in grandeur that which we now beheld, when the first rays struck the snow-clad mountain, which reared its lofty head before us. The projecting cliffs of white and orange stood out in bold relief against the azure sky, while the crevices and gorges, filled with snow, showed their inequalities with a wonderful dis-*

tinctness. At the same time the beams of the sun playing on the snow produced the most brilliant and ever-changing iris hues. No painter's art could reproduce, or colors imitate, these gorgeous prismatic tints.

Five or six miles, over a hilly though very hard road, brought us to the base of the mountain, where we noticed a grove of live-oaks and pines, with water near them; but as it was too early to water our animals, we did not stop. At this spring a train was attacked a few months before we passed, and four men killed. As we now began to descend, I got out of the carriage, preferring to go on foot. I could thus the more readily lock and unlock the wheels when necessary. The road here, after passing through long defiles, winds for some distance along the side of the mountain. Now it plunges down some deep abyss, and then it suddenly rises again upon some little castellated spur, so that one almost imagines himself to be in a veritable fortress. Again we pass along the brink of a deep gorge, whose bottom, filled with trees, is concealed from our view, while the evergreen cedar juts forth here and there from the chasms in its sides. Winding and turning in every direction, we followed the intricacies of the Guadalupe Pass for at least six hours; and whenever the prospect opened before us, there stood the majestic bluff in all its grandeur, solitary and alone. In one place the road runs along the mountain on a bare rocky shelf not wide enough for two wagons to pass, and the next moment passes down through an immense gorge, walled by mountains of limestone, regularly terraced. As we were descending from this narrow ledge, the iron bolt which held the tongue of the carriage broke and let it drop. Nothing but iron would do to repair the injury; and after trying various expedients, a substitute for the broken bolt was found in the bail or handle of the tin kettle which held our provisions. This, being doubled and driven through the hole previously filled by the bolt, kept it in its place, while the tongue was supported by cords. By careful driving, and relieving the weight of the carriage by alighting when going over bad places, we got along tolerably well.

I regretted that we were not able to spend more time in this interesting Pass, the grandeur of which would, under any other circumstances, have induced us to linger; but we had too much at stake to waste a single hour. . . .

Chapter VI

YELLOWSTONE
1849/1851

from The Mormons, or, Latter-Day Saints
by J. W. Gunnison &
Life, Letters and Travels of Father Pierre-Jean DeSmet, S. J.
1801-1873
edited by Hiram Chittenden and Alfred Richardson

Hints of what lay on the Upper Yellowstone continued to crop up in various sources. Jim Bridger was more than once the source of this information, like the two excerpts quoted here. The dates given above are the times when Bridger related his memories to these two authors of visits he had made to Yellowstone in the past twenty years. The first is from Lt. Gunnison, whom Bridger guided to the Great Salt Lake in 1849. The second is from a letter of DeSmet, when he was with Bridger at an Indian peace council in 1851.

(Gunnison)

He has been very active, and traversed the region from the headwaters of the Missouri to the Del Norte – and along the Gila to the Gulf, and thence throughout Oregon and the interior of California. His graphic sketches are delightful romances. With a buffalo-skin and a piece of charcoal, he will map out any portion of this immense region, and delineate mountains, streams, and the circular valleys called 'holes,' with wonderful accuracy; at least we may so speak of that portion we traversed after his descriptions were given. He gives a picture, most romantic and enticing of the headwaters of the Yellowstone. A lake sixty miles long, cold and pellucid, lies embosomed amid high precipitous mountains. On the west side is a sloping plain several miles wide, with clumps of trees and groves of pine. The ground resounds to the tread of horses. Geysers spout up seventy feet high, with a terrific hissing noise, at regular intervals. Waterfalls are sparkling, leaping, and thundering down the precipices, and collect in the pool below. The river issues from this lake, and for fifteen miles roars through the perpendicular

Jim Bridger

canyon at the outlet. In this section are the Great Springs, so hot that meat is readily cooked in them, and as they descend on the successive terraces, afford at length delightful baths.

(DeSmet)

Near the source of the river Puante which empties into the Bighorn... is a place called Colter's Hell (just east of Yellowstone) *– from a beaver hunter of that name* (John Colter). *This locality is often agitated with subterranean fires. The sulphurous gases which escape in great volumes from the burning soil infect the atmosphere for several miles, and render the earth so barren that even the wild wormwood cannot grow on it. The beaver hunters have assured me that the frequent underground noises and explosions are frightful.*

However, I think that the most extraordinary spot in this respect, and perhaps the most marvelous of all the northern half of this continent, is in the very heart of the Rocky Mountains... between the sources of the Madison and Yellowstone. It reaches more than a hundred miles. Bituminous, sulphurous and boiling springs are very numerous in it. The hot springs contain a large quantity of calcareous matter, and form hills more or less elevated.

... The earth is thrown up very high, and the influence of the elements causes it to take the most varied and the most fantastic shapes. Gas, vapor and smoke are continually escaping by a thousand openings, from the base to the summit of the volcanic pile; the noise at times resembles the steam let off by a boat. Strong subterranean explosions occur, like those in 'Colter's Hell.' The hunters and Indians speak of it with a superstitious fear, and consider it the abode of evil spirits, that is to say, a kind of hell. Indians seldom approach it without offering some sacrifice, or at least without presenting the calumet of peace to the turbulent spirits, that they may be propitious. They declare that the subterranean noises proceed from the forging of warlike weapons: each eruption of earth is, in their eyes, the result of a combat between the infernal spirits, and becomes a monument of a new victory or calamity.

Near Gardiner river, a tributary of the Yellowstone, and in the vicinity of the region I have just been describing, there is a mountain of sulphur (Mammoth Hot Springs). *I have this report from Captain Bridger, who is familiar with every one of these mountains, having passed thirty years of his life near them.*

Chapter VII

FLAMING GORGE – DINOSAUR – DEATH VALLEY 1849-50

from Death Valley in '49
by William Lewis Manley

A major influx of immigrants enters California during the gold rush of '49. The following selection is taken from the memoirs of one of these gold seekers. Crossing the plains with overlanders in their covered wagons, he broke off with other young men to float down the Green River in a raft unsuitable for the wild rapids that lay downstream. Yet, western geography was still imperfectly understood by many. The group believed this was the fabled Buenaventura River, that would offer them easy passage to California; although, by now, Fremont had established that the Great Basin had no outlets to the sea. Passage through the canyons of Flaming Gorge and Dinosaur, and an informative exchange with a knowledgeable Indian chief ultimately dissuaded them. The party broke up and headed by land southwest across the Great Basin. Manley and Rogers linked up with a group of overlanders in a desperate crossing of the desert, reaching its nadir in Death Valley. The first part begins with Manley and the others preparing to descend the Green River. The second part tells the story of Manley and the second group in Death Valley. It is a tale with much human interest.

Upper Green River

About the first thing we did was to organize and select a captain; and, very much against my wishes, I was chosen to this important position. Six of us had guns of some sort. We had one regular axe and a large camp hatchet, and several very small hatchets. All our worldly goods were piled up on the bank, and we were alone.

An examination of the old ferry boat showed it to be in pretty good condition, the sand with which it had been filled keeping it very perfectly. We found two oars in the sand under the boat, and looked up some poles to assist us in navigation. Our cord-

age was rather scant but the best we could get and all we could muster. The boat was about twelve feet long and six or seven feet wide, not a very well proportioned craft, but having the ability to carry a pretty good load. We swung it up to the bank and loaded up our goods and then ourselves. It was not a heavy load for the craft, and it looked as if we were taking the most sensible way to get to the Pacific, and almost wondered that everybody was so blind as not to see it as we did.

This party was composed of W. L. Manley, M. S. McMahon, Charles and Joseph Hazelrig, Richard Field, Alfred Walton and John Rogers. We untied the ropes, gave the boat a push and commenced to move down the river with ease and comfort, feeling much happier than we would had we been going toward Salt Lake with the prospect of wintering there. . . .

Flaming Gorge

Thus far we had a very pleasant time, each taking his turn in working the boat while the others rested or slept. About the fifth day, when we were floating along in very gently running water, I had laid down to take a rest and a little sleep. The mountains here on both sides of the river were not very steep, but ran gradually for a mile or so. While I was sleeping the boat came around a small angle in the stream, and all at once there seemed to be a higher, steeper range of mountains right across the valley. The boys thought the river was coming to a rather sudden end and hastily awoke me, and for the life of me I could not say they were not right, for there was no way in sight for it to go. I remembered, while looking over a map the military men had, I found a place named Brown's Hole; and I told the boys I guessed we were elected to go on foot to California after all, for I did not propose to follow the river down any sort of a hole into any mountain. (Brown's Hole is actually further downstream between Flaming Gorge and Dinosaur.) *We were floating directly toward a perpendicular cliff, and I could not see any hole anywhere, nor any other place where it could go. Just as we were within a stone's throw of the cliff, the river turned sharply to the right and went behind a high point of the mountain that seemed to stand squarely on edge. This was really an immense crack or crevice, and seemed much wider at the bottom than it did at the top, 2,000 feet or more above our heads. Each wall seemed to lean in toward the water as it rose.*

We were now for some time between two rocky walls, between which the river ran very rapidly, and we often had to get out and work our boat over the rocks, sometimes lifting it off when it caught. Fortunately we had a good tow line, and one would take this and follow along the edge when it was, so he could walk. The mountains seemed to get higher on both sides as we advanced, and in places we could see quite a number of trees overhanging the river, and away up on the rocks we could see the wild mountain sheep looking down at us. They were so high that they seemed a mile away, and consequently safe enough. This was their home, and they seemed very independent, as if they dared us fellows to come and see them. There was an old cottonwood tree on the bank with marks of an axe on it, but this was all the sign we saw that anyone had ever been here before us. We got no game while passing through this deep cañon and began to feel the need of some fresh provisions very sorely.

We passed many deep, dark cañons coming into the main stream, and at one place, where the rock hung a little over the river and had a smooth wall, I climbed up above the high water mark which we could clearly see, and with a mixture of gunpowder and grease for paint, and a bit of cloth tied to a stick for a brush, I painted in fair sized letters on the rock, CAPT. W. L. MANLEY, U.S.A. We did not know whether we were within the bounds of the United States or not, and we put on all the majesty we could under the circumstances. (The United States had just acquired this territory from Mexico through the Treaty of Guadalupe-Hidalgo in 1848.) *I don't think the sun ever shone down to the bottom of the cañon, for the sides were literally sky-high; as the sky, and a very small portion of that, was all we could see.*

Just before night we came to a place where some huge rocks as large as cabins had fallen down from the mountain, completely filling up the river bed, and making it completely impassible for our boat. We unloaded it and while the boys held the stern line, I took off my clothes and pushed the boat out into the torrent, which ran around the rocks, letting them pay the line out slowly till it was just right. Then I sang out to "let go" and away it dashed. I grasped the bow line, and at the first chance jumped overboard and got to shore, when I held the boat and brought it in below the obstructions. There was some deep water below the rocks; and we went into camp. While some loaded the boat, others with a hook and line caught some good fish, which resembled mackerel.

While I was looking up toward the mountain top, and along down the rocky wall, I saw a smooth place about fifty feet above where the great rocks had broken out; and there, painted in large black letters, were the words "ASHLEY, 1824." This was the first real evidence we had of the presence of a white man in this wild place, and from this record it seems that twenty five years before some venturesome man had here inscribed his name. I have since heard there were some persons in St. Louis of this name, and of some circumstances which may link them with this early traveler. (See the above selection from the journal of William Ashley.)

When we came to look around, we found that another big rock blocked the channel 300 yards below, and the water rushed around it with a terrible swirl. So we unloaded the boat again and made the attempt to get around it as we did the other rocks. We tried to get across the river but failed. We now, all but one, got on the great rock with our poles, The one man was to ease the boat down with the rope as far as he could, then let go and we would stop it with our poles, push it out into the stream and let it go over. Yet, the current was so strong that when the boat struck the rock we could not stop it. The gunwale next to us rose, and the other went down, so that in a second the boat stood edgewise in the water, the bottom tight against the big rock, and the strong current pinned it there so tight that we could no more move it than we could move the rock itself.

This seemed a very sudden ending to our voyage. There were some very rapid thoughts as to whether we would not be safer among the Mormons than out in this wild country, afoot and alone. Our boat was surely lost beyond hope, and something must be done. I saw two pine trees, about two feet through, growing on a level place just below. I said to the men that we must decide between going afoot or making some canoes out of these pine trees. Canoes were decided on, and we never let the axes rest, night or day, till we had them completed. While my working shift was off, I took an hour or two for a little hunting. On a low divide, partly grown over with small pines and juniper, I found signs, old and new, of many elk, and so concluded the country was well stocked with noble game. The two canoes, when completed were about fifteen feet long and two feet wide, and we lashed them together for greater security. When we tried them we found they were too small to carry our load and us. We landed half a mile below, where there were two other pine trees – white pine – about two feet through, and much taller than the ones we had used. We set at work making a large canoe of these. I had to direct the work, for I was the only one who had ever done such work. We worked night and day at these canoes, keeping a big fire at night and changing off to keep the axes busy. This canoe we made twenty-five or thirty feet long and, when completed, they made me captain of it. Into it we loaded the most valuable things, such as provisions, ammunition, and cooking utensils. I had to take the lead, for I was the only skill-ful canoeist in the party. We agreed upon signals to give when danger was seen or game in sight and, leading off with my big canoe, we set sail again and went flying downstream.

This rapid rate soon brought us out of the high mountains and into a narrow valley when the stream became more moderate in its speed and we floated along easily enough.

They came out of Flaming Gorge, through the wide valley of Browns Hole and passed through the Gates of Lodore into Lodore Canyon.

Dinosaur

It took us two or three days to pass this beautiful valley (Brown's Hole), *and then we began to get into a rougher coun-try again, the cañons deeper and the water more tumultuous* (Lodore Canyon). *McMahon and I had the lead always, in the big canoe. The mountains seemed to change into bare rocks and get higher and higher as we floated along. After the first day of this, the river became so full of boulders that many times the only way we could continue was to unload the canoes and haul them over, load up and go ahead, only to repeat the same tactics in a very short time again. At one place, where the river was more than usually obstructed, we found a deserted camp, a skiff and some heavy cooking utensils. A notice, posted up on an alder tree, said that they had found the river route impractica-ble; and being satisfied that the river was so full of rocks and boulders that it could not be safely navigated, they had aban-doned the undertaking and were about to start overland toward Salt Lake. I took down the names of the parties at the time in my diary, which has since been burned, but I have now forgotten them entirely. They were all strangers to me. They had left behind such heavy articles as could not be carried on foot. This notice rather disconcerted us, but we thought we had better keep on and see for ourselves, so we did not follow them, but kept on down the rocky river. We found generally more boulders than water, and the down grade of the river bed was heavy.*

Some alders and willows grew upon the bank and up quite high on the mountains we could see a little timber. Some days we did not go more than four or five miles, and that was serious work, loading and unloading our canoes, and packing them over the boulders, with only small streams of water curling around between them. We went barefoot most of the time, for we were more than half of the time in the water, which roared and dashed so loud that we could hardly hear each other speak. We kept getting more and more venturesome and skillful, and managed to run some very dangerous rapids in safety.

On the high peaks above our heads we could see the Rocky Mountain sheep looking defiantly at us from their mountain fastnesses, so far away they looked no larger than jack rabbits. They were too far off to try to shoot at, and we had no time to try to steal up any nearer. At the rate we were making, food would be the one thing needful, and we were consuming it very fast. Sometimes we could ride a little ways, and then would come the rough-and-tumble with the rocks again.

One afternoon we came to a sudden turn in the river, more than a right angle, and, just below, a fall of two feet or more. This I ran in safety, as did the rest who followed and we cheered at our pluck and skill. Just after this the river swung back the other way at a right angle or more, and I quickly saw there was danger below and signaled them to go on shore at once, and lead the canoes over the dangerous rapids. I ran my own canoe near shore and got by the rapid safely, waiting for the others to come also. They did not obey my signals but thought to run the rapid the same as I did. The channel was straight here for 200 yards, without a boulder in it, but the stream was so swift that it caused great, rolling waves in the center, of a kind I have never seen anywhere else. The boys were not skillful enough to navigate this stream, and the suction drew them to the center where the great waves rolled them over and over, bottom side up and every way. The occupants of our canoe let go and swam to shore. Fields had always been afraid of water and had worn a life preserver every day since we left the wagons. He threw up his hands and splashed and kicked at a terrible rate, for he could not swim, but at last made solid ground. One of the canoes came down into the eddy below, where it lodged close to the shore, bottom up. Alfred Walton in the other canoe could not swim, but held on to the gunwale with a death grip, and it went on down through the rapids. Sometimes we could see the man and sometimes not, and he and the canoe took turns in disappearing. Walton had very black hair, and as he clung fast to his canoe his black head looked like a crow on the end of a log. Sometimes he would be under so long that we thought he must be lost, when up he would come again, still clinging manfully.

McMahon and I threw everything out of the big canoe and pushed out after him. I told Mc. to kneel down, so I could see over him to keep the craft off the rocks. By changing his paddle from side to side as ordered, he enabled me to make quick moves and avoid being dashed to pieces. We fairly flew, the boys said, but I stood up in the stern and kept it clear of danger, till we ran into a clear piece of river and overtook Walton clinging to the overturned boat. McMahon seized the boat and I paddled all to shore, but Walton was nearly dead and could hardly keep his grasp on the canoe. We took him to a sandy place and worked over him and warmed him in the sun till he came to life again, then built a fire and laid him up near to it to get dry and warm. If the canoe had gone on 20 yards further with him before we caught it, he would have gone into another long rapid and been drowned. We left Walton by the fire and crossing the river in the slack water, went up to where the other boys were standing, wet and sorry-looking, saying that all was gone and lost. Rogers put his hand in his pocket and pulled out three half dollars and said sadly, "Boys, this is all I am worth in the world." All the clothes he had were a pair of overalls and a shirt. If he had been possessed of a thousand in gold he would have been no richer, for there was no one to buy from and nothing to buy. I said to them, "Boys, we can't help what has happened, we'll do the best we can. Right our canoe, get the water out, and we'll go down and see how Walton is." They did as I told them, and lo and behold when the canoe rolled right side up, there were their clothes and blankets safe and sound. These light things had floated in the canoe and were safe. We now tried, by joining hands, to reach out far enough to recover some of the guns; but, by feeling with their feet, they found the bottom smooth as glass and the property all swept on below, no one knew where. The current was so powerful that no one could stand in it where it came up above his knees. The eddy, which enabled us to save the first canoe with the bedding and clothes, was caused by a great boulder as large as a house, which had fallen from above and partly blocked the stream. Everything that would sink was lost.

We all got into the two canoes and went down to Walton, where we camped and stayed all night for Walton's benefit. While we were waiting, I took my gun and tried to climb up high enough to see how much longer this horrible cañon was going to last. After many attempts, I could not get high enough to see in any direction. The mountain was all bare rocks in terraces, but it was impossible to climb from one to the other, and the benches were all filled with broken rocks that had fallen from above.

By the time I got back to camp, Walton was dry and warm and could talk. He said he felt better, and pretty good over his rescue. When he was going under the water, it seemed sometimes as if he never would come to the top again, but he held on and eventually came out all right. He never knew how he got to shore, he was so nearly dead when rescued.

The next morning Walton was so well we started on. We were now very poorly armed. My rifle and McMahon's shotgun were all the arms we had for seven of us, and we could make but a poor defense if attacked by man or beast, to say nothing of providing ourselves with food. The mountains on each side were very bare of timber, those on the east side particularly so, and very high and barren. Toward night we were floating along in a piece of slack water, the river below made a short turn around a high and rocky point almost perpendicular from the water (Echo Park). There was a terrace along the side of this point about fifty feet up, and the bench grew narrower as it approached the river. As I was coming down quite close under this bank, I saw three mountain sheep on the bench above. Motioning to the boys, I ran on shore and, with my gun in hand, crept down toward them, keeping a small pine tree between myself and the sheep. There were some cedar bushes on the point, and the pines grew about half way up the bank. I got in as good a range as possible and fired at one of them, which staggered around and fell down to the bottom of the cliff. I loaded and took the next largest one which came down the same way. The third one tried to escape by going down the bend and then creeping up a crevice, but it could not get away and turned back cautiously, which gave me time to load again and put a ball through it. I hit it a little too far back for instant death, but I followed it up, found it down and helpless, and soon secured it. I hauled this one down the mountain, and the other boy had the two others secure by this time. McMahon was so elated at my success that he said, "Manley, if I could shoot as you do I would never want any better business." And the other fellows said they guessed we were having better luck with one gun than with six, so we had a merry time after all. These animals were of a bluish color, with hair much finer than deer, and resembled a goat more than a sheep. These three were all females and their horns were quite straight, not curved like the big males. We cut the meat from the bones and broke them up, making a fine soup which tasted pretty good. They were in pretty good order, and the meat like very good mutton.

We kept pushing on down the river. The rapids were still dangerous in many places, but not so frequent nor so bad as the part we had gone over, and we could see that the river gradually grew smoother as we progressed.

After a day or two we began to get out of the cañons, but the mountains and hills on each side were barren and of a pale yellow caste, with no chance for us to climb up and take a look to see if there were any chances for us further along. We had now been obliged to follow the cañon for many miles, for the only way to get out was to get out endwise, climbing the banks being utterly out of the question. But these mountains soon came to an end, and there were some cottonwood and willows on the bank of the river, which was now so smooth we could ride along without the continual loading and unloading we had been forced to practice for so long. We had begun to get a little desperate at the lack of game, but the new valley, which grew wider all the time, gave us hope again, even if it was quite barren everywhere except back of the willow trees.

They had now exited out of Dinosaur and were floating down the river, when they met Chief Walker and his tribe. Manly tells the chief of their plan to continue down the river to California. His reply, in sign language, refers to the deep canyons and rapids they have just passed through in Flaming Gorge and Dinosaur, and then perhaps to the even more formidable canyons and rapids downstream in Canyonlands, Grand Canyon and elsewhere.

When I told Chief Walker this he seemed very much astonished, as if wondering why we were going down the river when we wanted to get west across the country. I asked him how many sleeps it was to the big water, and he shook his head, pointed out across the country and then to the river and shook his head again; by which I understood that water was scarce, out the way he pointed. He then led me down to a smooth sand bar on the river and then, with a crooked stick, began to make a map in the sand. First he made a long crooked mark, ten feet long or so, and pointing to the river to let me know that the mark in the sand was made to represent it. He then made a straight mark across near the north end of the stream, and showed the other streams which came into the Green river which I saw at once was exactly correct. Then he laid some small stones on each side of the cross mark, and making a small hoop of a willow twig, he rolled it in the mark he had made across the river, then flourished his stick as if he were driving oxen. Thus he repre-sented the emigrant road. He traced the branches off to the north where the soldiers had gone, and the road to California, which the emigrants took, all of which we could see was cor-rect. Then he began to describe the river down which we had come. A short distance below the road, he put some small stones on each side of the river to represent mountains. He then put down his hands, one on each side of the crooked mark and then raised them up again saying e-e-e-e-e-e as he raised them, to say that the mountains there were very high. Then he traced down the stream to a place below where we made our canoes; when he placed the stone back from the river further, to show that there was a valley there; then he drew them in close again further down, and piled them up again two or three tiers high, then placing both fists on them he raised them higher than the top of his head, saying e-e-e-e-e-e and looking still higher and shaking his head as if to say, "awful bad cañon," and thus he went on describing the river till we understood that we were near the place where we now were, and then pointed to his tepee, showing that I understood him all right. It was all cor-

rect, as I very well knew and assured me that he knew all about the country.

I became much interested in my newfound friend, and had him continue his map down the river. He showed two streams coming in on the east side and then he began piling up stones on each side of the river and then got longer ones and piled them higher and higher yet. Then he stood with one foot on each side of his river and put his hands on the stones and then raised them as high as he could, making a continued e-e-e-e-e as long as his breath would last, pointed to the canoe and made signs with his hands how it would roll and pitch in the rapids and finely capsize and throw us all out. He then made signs of death to show us that it was a fatal place. I understood perfectly plain from this that below the valley where we now were was a terrible cañon, much higher than any we had passed, and the rapids were not navigable with safety. Then Walker shook his head more than once and looked very sober, and said "Indiano" and reaching for his bow and arrows, he drew the bow back to its utmost length and put the arrow close to my breast, showing how I would get shot. Then he would draw his hand across his throat and shut his eyes as if in death to make us understand that this was a hostile country before us, as well as rough and dangerous. . . .

Having concluded to quit the river and head west by land again to California, Manley concludes with these words written over thirty years later.

Reading people of today, who know so well the geography of the American continent, may need to stop and think that in 1849 the whole region west of the Missouri River was very little known. The only men venturesome enough to dare travel over it were hunters and trappers who, by a wild life, had been used to all the privations of such a journey; and shrewd as the Indians themselves in the mysterious ways of the trail and the chase. Even these fellows had only investigated certain portions best suited to their purpose.

The Indians here have the reputation of being bloodthirsty savages, who took delight in murder and torture; but here, in the very midst of this wild and desolate country, we found a chief and his tribe, Walker and his followers, who were as humane and kind to white people as could be expected of anyone. I have often wondered at the knowledge of this man respecting the country, of which he was able to make us a good map in the sand, point out to us the impassable cañon, locate the hostile Indians, and many other points which were not accurately known by our own explorers for many years afterward. He undoubtedly saved our little band from a watery grave, for without his advice we would have gone on and on, far into the great Colorado cañon, from which escape would have been impossible and securing food another impossibility, while destruction by hostile Indians was among the strong probabilities of the case. So in a threefold way, I have for these more than forty years credited the lives of myself and comrades to the thoughtful interest and humane consideration of old Chief Walker. . . .

Death Valley

Manley and Rogers linked up with another group of overlanders, with whom they crossed the harsh desert of the Great Basin. In late 1849, they enter the Furnace Creek area of Death Valley and then turn south toward Badwater.

Bennett and Arcane now concluded not to wait for me to go ahead and explore out a way for them to follow, as I had done for a long time; but to go ahead, as it was evidently the best way to turn south and make our own road, and find the water and passes all for ourselves. So they hitched up and rolled down the cañon, and out into the valley and then turned due south. We had not gone long on this course before we saw that we must cross the valley and get over to the west side. To do this we must

Leaving Death Valley - The Manly party on the march after leaving their wangons.

cross through some water, and for fear the ground might be miry, I went to a sand hill near by and got a mesquite stick about three feet long with which to sound out our way. I rolled up my pants, pulled off my moccasins and waded in; having the teams stand still till I could find out whether it was safe for them to follow or not, by ascertaining the depth of the water and the character of the bottom (Badwater).

The water was very clear and the bottom seemed uneven, there being some deep holes. Striking my stick on the bottom it seemed solid as a rock, and breaking off a small projecting point I found it to be solid rock salt. As the teams rolled along, they scarcely roiled the water. It looked to me as if the whole valley, which might be a hundred miles long, might have been a solid bed of rock salt. Before we reached the water, there were many solid blocks of salt lying around covered with a little dirt on the top.

The second night we found a good spring of fresh water coming out from the bottom of the snow peak almost over our heads (Telescope Peak). *The small flow from it spread out over the sand and sank in a very short distance and there was some quite good grass growing around. There was no possible way to cross this high steep range of mountains anywhere to the north, and the Jayhawkers (another group of overlanders) had abandoned their wagons and burned them, and we could no longer follow on the trail they made. It seemed that there was no other alternative but for us to keep along the edge of the mountain to the south and search for another pass. Some who had Fremont's travels said that the range immediately west of us must be the one he described, on the west side of which was a beautiful country, of rich soil and having plenty of cattle, and horses, and containing some settlers, but on the east all was barren, dry, rocky, sandy desert as far as could be seen. We knew this eastern side answered well the description and believed that this was really the range described, or at least it was close by.*

We had to look over the matter very carefully and consider all the conditions and circumstances of the case. We could see the mountains were lower to the south, but they held no snow and seemed only barren rocks piled up in lofty peaks, and as we looked it seemed the most God-forsaken country in the world.

We had been in the region long enough to know the higher mountains contained most water, and that the valleys had bad water or none at all, so that while the lower altitudes to the south gave some promise of easier crossing it gave us no promise of water or grass, without which we must certainly perish. In a certain sense we were lost. The clear night and days furnished us with the means of telling the points of compass as the sun rose and set, but not a sign of life in nature's wide domain had been seen for a month or more. A vest pocketful of powder and shot would last a good hunter till he starved to death, for there was not a living thing to shoot great or small.

We talked over our present position pretty freely, and everyone was asked to speak his unbiased mind, for we knew not who might be right or who might be wrong, and someone might make a suggestion of the utmost value. We all felt pretty much downhearted. Our civilized provisions were getting so scarce that all must be saved for the women and children, and the men must get along some way on ox meat alone. It was decided not a scrap of anything that would sustain life must go to waste. The blood, hide and intestines were all prepared in some way for food. This meeting lasted till late at night. If some of them had lost their minds I should not have been surprised, for hunger swallows all other feelings. A man in a starving condition is a savage. He may be as bloodthirsty and savage as a wild beast, as docile and gentle as a lamb, or as wild and crazy as a terrified animal, devoid of affection, reason or thought of justice. We were none of us as bad as this, and yet there was a strange look in the eyes of some of us sometimes, as I saw by looking around, and as others no doubt realized for I saw them making mysterious glances in my direction.

Morning came and all were silent. The dim prospect of the future seemed to check every tongue. When one left a water hole he went away as if in doubt whether he would ever enjoy the pleasure of another drop. Every camp was sad beyond description, and no one can guide the pen to make it tell the tale as it seemed to us. When our morning meal of soup and meat was finished, Bennett's two teams, and the two of Arcane's concluded their chances of life were better if they could take some provisions and strike out on foot, and so they were given what they could carry, and they arranged their packs and bade us a sorrowful goodbye, hoping to meet again on the Pacific Coast.

There were genuine tears shed at the parting and I believe neither party ever expected to see each other in this life again.

. . . When in bed I could not keep my thoughts back from the old home I had left, where good water and a bountiful spread were always ready at the proper hour. I know I dreamed of taking a draft of cool, sweet water from a full pitcher and then woke up with my mouth and throat as dry as dust. The good home I left behind was a favorite theme about the campfire, and many a one told of the dream pictures, natural as life, that came to him of the happy Eastern home with comfort and happiness surrounding it, even if wealth was lacking. The home of the poorest man on earth was preferable to this place. Wealth was of no value here. A board of twenty dollar gold pieces could stand before us the whole day long with no temptation to touch a single coin, for its very weight would drag us nearer death. We could purchase nothing with it and we would have cared no more for it as a thing of value than we did the desert sands. We would have given much more for some of the snow which we could see drifting over the peak of the great snow mountains over our heads like a dusty cloud.

Deeming it best to spare the strength as much as possible, I threw away everything I could, retaining only my glass, some ammunition, sheath knife and tin cup. No unnecessary burden could be put on any man or beast, lest he lie down under it, never to rise again. Life and strength were sought to be husbanded in every possible way.

Leaving this camp where the water was appreciated we went over a road for perhaps 8 miles and came to the mouth of a rocky cañon leading up west to the summit of the range. This cañon was too rough for wagons to pass over. Out in the valley near its mouth was a mound about four feet high and in the top of this a little well held about a pailful of water that was quite strong of sulphur. When stirred, it would look quite black. About the mouth of the well was a wire grass that seemed to prevent it caving in. It seems the drifting sand had slowly built this little mound about the little well of water in a curious way. We spent the night here and kept a man at the well all night to keep the water dipped out as fast as it flowed, in order to get enough for ourselves and cattle. The oxen drank this water better than they did the brackish water of the former camp.

The plain was thinly scattered with sage brush, and up near the base of the mountain some greasewood grew in little bunches like currant bushes.

The men with wagons decided they would take this cañon and follow it up to try and get over the range, and not wait for me to go ahead and explore, as they said it took too much time and the provisions, consisting now of only ox meat, were getting more precarious every day. To help them all I could and, if possible, to be forewarned a little of danger, I shouldered my gun and pushed on ahead as fast as I could. The bottom was of sharp broken rock, which would be very hard for the feet of the oxen, although we had rawhide moccasins on them for some time, and this was the kind of foot-gear I wore myself. I walked on as rapidly as I could, and after a time came to where the cañon spread out into a kind of basin enclosed on all sides but the entrance, with a wall of high, steep rock, possible to ascend on foot but which would apparently bar the further progress of the wagons. I turned back utterly disappointed. I reached an elevation where I could look over the country east and south, and it looked as if there was not a drop of water in its whole extent, and there was no snow on the dark mountains that stretched away to the south. It seemed to me as if difficulties beset me on every hand. I hurried back down the cañon, but it was nearly dark before I met the wagons. By a mishap, I fell and broke the stock of my gun, over which I was very sorry, for it was an excellent one, the best I ever owned. I carried it in two pieces to the camp and told them the way was barred, at which they could hardly endure their disappointment. They turned back in the morning, as the cattle had nothing to eat here and no water, and not much of any food since leaving the spring; they looked terribly bad, and the rough road coming up had nearly finished them. They were yoked up and the wagons turned about for their return. They went better down hill, but it was not long before one of Bennett's oxen lay down, and could not be persuaded to rise again. This was no place to tarry in the hot sun, so the ox was killed and the carcass distributed among the wagons. So little draft was required that the remaining oxen took the wagon down. When within two or three miles of the water hole, one of Arcane's oxen also failed and lay down, so they turned him out, and when he had rested a little, he came on again for a while, but soon lay down again.

Arcane took a bucket of water back from camp and after drinking it and resting awhile, the ox was driven down to the spring.

This night we had another meeting to decide upon our course and determine what to do. At this meeting, no one was wiser than another, for no one had explored the country nor knew what to expect. The questions that now arose were: "How long can we endure the work in this situation?" "How long will our oxen be able to endure the great hardship on the small nourishment they receive?" "How long can we provide ourselves with food?"

We had a few small pieces of dry bread. This was kept for the children, giving them a little now and then. Our only food was in the flesh of the oxen, and when they failed to carry themselves along, we must begin to starve. It began to look as if the chances of leaving our bones to bleach upon the desert were the most prominent ones.

One thing was certain, we must move somewhere at once. If we stay here, we can live as long as the oxen do, and no longer. If we go on, it is uncertain where to go, to find a better place. We had guns and ammunition, to be sure, but of late we had seen no living creature in this desert wild. Finally, Mr. Bennett spoke, "Now I will make you a proposition. I propose that we select two of our youngest, strongest men and ask them to take some food and go ahead on foot to try to seek a settlement and food. We will go back to the good spring we have just left and wait for their return. It will surely not take them more than ten days for the trip, and when they get back we shall know all about the road, its character and how long it will take us to travel it. They can secure some other kind of food that will make us feel better, and when the oxen have rested a little at the spring, we can get out with our wagons and animals and be safe. I think this is the best and safest way. Now what do you all say?"

After a little discussion, all seemed to agree that this was the best, and now it remained to find the men to go. No one offered to accept the position of advance messengers. Finally, Mr. Bennett said he knew one man well enough to know that he would come back if he lived, and he was sure he would push his way through. "I will take Lewis if he will consent to go." I consented, though I knew it was a hazardous journey, exposed to

*all sorts of things, Indians, climate and probable lack of water;
but I thought I could do it and would not refuse. John Rogers, a
large strong Tennessee man, was then chosen as the other one,
and he consented also. . . .*

The two were supplied with whatever could be sacrificed from the
party staying behind to wait in Death Valley.

*Then we bade them all goodbye. Some turned away, too much
affected to approach us. Others shook our hands with deep feeling, grasping them firmly and heartily, hoping we would be successful and be able to pilot them out of this dreary place into a
better land. Everyone felt that a little food to make a change
from the poor dried meat would be acceptable. Mr. and Mrs.
Bennett and J.B. Arcane and wife were the last to remain when
the others had turned away. They had most faith in the plan and
felt deeply. Mrs. Bennett was the last, and she asked God to
bless us and bring some food to her starving children.*

*We were so much affected that we could not speak and silently
turned away, and took our course again up the cañon we had
descended the night before. After a while, we looked back and
when they saw us turn around, all the hats and bonnets waved
us a final parting. . . . We soon passed around a bend of the
cañon and walked on in silence.*

*We both of us meditated some over the homes of our fathers, but
took new courage in view of the importance of our mission and
passed on as fast as we could.*

*By night we were far up the mountain, near the perpendicular
rough peak, and far above us on a slope we could see some
bunches of grass and sage brush. We went to this and found
some small water holes. No water ran from them, they were so
small. Here we stayed all night. It did not seem very far to the
snowy peak to the north of us. Just where we were seemed the
lowest pass, for to the south were higher peaks and the rocks
looked as if they were too steep to get over.*

*Through this gap came a cold breeze, and we had to look
around to get a sheltered place in which to sleep. We lay down
close together, spoon fashion, and made the little blanket do as
cover for the both of us. In the morning we filled our canteens,*

which we had made by binding two powder cans together with strips of cloth, and started for the summit nearby. From this was the grandest sight we ever beheld. Looking east we could see the country we had been crawling over since November 4th. "Just look at the cursed country we have come over!" said Rogers as he pointed over it. To the north was the biggest mountain we ever saw, peaks on peaks and towering far above our heads, and covered with snow, which was apparently everlasting.

This mountain seemed to have very few trees on it, and in extent, as it reached away to the north, seemed interminable. South was a nearly level plain, and to the west I thought I could dimly see a range of mountains that held a little snow upon their summits, but on the main range to the south there was none. It seemed to me the dim snowy mountains must be as far as 200 miles away, but of course I could not judge accurately. After looking at this grand but worthless landscape long enough to take in its principal features, we asked each other what we supposed the people we left behind would think to see mountains so far ahead. We knew that they had an idea that the coast range was not very far ahead, but we saw at once to go over all these mountains and return within the limits of fifteen days, which had been agreed upon between us, would probably be impossible, but we must try as best we could, so down the rocky steep we clambered and hurried on our way. . . .

A month later, the two are returning to Death Valley with a mule, horses and supplies, having luckily reached a settlement after many difficulties and obstacles.

The range was before us, and we must get to the other side in some way. We could see the range for a hundred miles to the north, and along the base some lakes of water that must be salt. To the south it lowered, but very barren and ending in black, dry buttes. The horses must have food and water by night or we must leave them to die and, all things considered, it seemed to be the quickest way to camp to try and go up a rough looking cañon, which was nearly opposite us on the other side. So we loaded the mule and made our way down the rocky road to the ridge; and then left the Jayhawker's trail, taking our course more south, so as to get around a salt lake which lay directly before us. On our way we had to go close to a steep bluff, and cross a piece of ground that looked like a well-dried mortar bed, hard and smooth as ice, and thus got around the head of a small stream of clear water, salt as brine. We now went directly to the mouth of the cañon we had decided to take, and traveled up its gravelly bed. The horses now had to be urged along constantly to keep them moving. They held their heads down low, as they crept along, seemingly so discouraged that they would much rather lie down and rest forever than take another step. We knew they would do this soon, in spite of all our urging, if we could not get water for them. The cañon was rough enough where we entered it, and a heavy up grade too. This grew more and more difficult as we advanced, and the rough yellowish, rocky walls closed in nearer and nearer as we ascended.

A perpendicular wall, or rather rise, in the rocks was approached, and it was very difficult to persuade the horses to exert themselves and get up over the small obstruction; but the little mule skipped over as nimbly as a well-fed goat, and rather seemed to enjoy a little variety in the proceedings. After some coaxing and urging, the horses took courage to try the extra step and succeeded all right. We all moved on again, over a path that grew more and more narrow, more and more rocky under foot at every moment. We wound around, among and between the great rocks; and had not advanced very far before another obstruction, that would have been a fall of about three feet had water been flowing in the cañon, opposed our way. A small pile of lone rocks enabled the mule to go over all right, and she went on looking for every spear of grass, and smelling eagerly for water, but all our efforts were not enough to get the horses along another foot. It was getting nearly night and every minute without water seemed an age. We had to leave the horses and go on. We had deemed them indispensable to us, or rather to the extrication of the women and children, and yet the hope came to us that the oxen might help some of them out as a last resort. We were sure the wagons must be abandoned, and such a thing as women riding on the backs of oxen we had never seen. Still it occurred to us as not impossible, and although leaving the horses here was like deciding to abandon all for the feeble ones, we saw we must do it, and the new hope arose to sustain us for further effort. We removed the saddles and placed them on a rock, and after a few moments hesitation, moments in which were crowded torrents of wild ideas and desperate thoughts that were enough to drive reason from its throne, we left the poor animals to their fate and moved along. Just as we were passing out of sight, the poor creatures neighed pitifully after us, and one who has never heard the last despairing, pleading neigh of a horse left to die can form an idea of its almost human appeal. We both burst into tears, but it was no use, to try to save them we must run the danger of sacrificing ourselves and the little party we were trying so hard to save.

We found the little mule stopped by a still higher precipice or perpendicular rise of fully ten feet. Our hearts sank within us and we said that we should return to our friends as we went away, with our knapsacks on our backs, and the hope grew very small. The little mule was nipping some stray blades of grass as we came in sight. She looked around at us and then up the steep rocks before her with such a knowing, intelligent look of confidence, that it gave us new courage. It was a strange, wild place. The north wall of the cañon leaned far over the channel, overhanging considerably, while the south wall sloped back about the same, making the wall nearly parallel, and like a huge crevice descending into the mountain from above in a sloping direction.

We decided to try and get the confident little mule over this obstruction. Gathering all the loose rocks we could, we piled them up against the south wall. Beginning some distance below, putting up all those in the bed of the stream and throwing down others from narrow shelves above, we built a sort of inclined plane along the walls, gradually rising till we were nearly as high as the crest of the fall. Here was a narrow shelf, scarcely four inches wide, and a space from twelve to fifteen feet to cross to reach the level of the crest. It was all I could do to cross this space, and there was no foundation to enable us to widen it, so as to make a path for an animal. It was a forlorn hope, but we made the most of it. We unpacked the mule, and getting all our ropes together, made a leading line of it. Then we loosened and threw down all the projecting points of rocks we could, above the narrow shelf and every piece that was likely to come loose on the shelf itself. We fastened the leading line to her and, with one above and one below, we thought we could help her to keep her balance. If she did not make a misstep on that narrow way, she might get over safely. Without a moment's hesitation, the brave animal tried the pass. Carefully and steadily she went along, selecting a place before putting down a foot. When she came to the narrow ledge, she leaned gently on the rope, never making a sudden start or jump, but cautiously as a cat moved slowly along. There was now no turning back for her. She must cross this narrow place, over which I had to creep on hands and knees, or be dashed down fifty feet to a certain death. When the worst place was reached, she stopped and hesitated, looking back as well as she could. I was ahead with the rope, and I called encouragingly to her and talked to her a little. Rogers wanted to get all ready and holler at her as loud as he could and frighten her across, but I thought the best way was to talk to her gently, and let her move steadily.

I tell you, friends, it was a trying moment. It seemed to be weighed down with all the trials and hardships of many months. It seemed to be the time when helpless women and innocent children hung on the trembling balance between life and death. Our own lives we could save by going back, and sometimes it seemed as if we would perhaps save ourselves the additional sorrow of finding them all dead to do so at once. I was so nearly in despair that I could not help bursting in tears, and I was not ashamed of the weakness. Finally Rogers said, "Come Lewis," and I gently pulled the rope, calling the little animal to make a trial. She smelled all around and looked over every inch of the strong ledge, then took one careful step after another over the dangerous place. Looking back, I saw Rogers with a very large stone in his hand, ready to holler and perhaps kill the poor beast if she stopped. But she crept along, trusting to the rope for balance, till she was half way across; then another step or two, when calculating the distance closely, she made a spring and landed on a smooth bit of sloping rock below, that led up to the highest crest of the precipice and safely climbed to the top, safe and sound above the falls. The mule had no shoes and it was wonderful how her little hoofs clung to the smooth rock. We felt relieved. We would push on and carry food to the people; we would get them through some way; there could be no more hopeless moment than the one just past, and we would save them all.

It was the work of a little while to transfer the load up the precipice, and pack the mule again, when we proceeded. Around behind some rocks, only a distance beyond this place, we found a small willow bush and enough good water for a camp. This was a strange cañon. The sun never shone down to the bottom in the fearful place where the little mule climbed up, and the rocks had a peculiar yellow color. In getting our provisions up the precipice, Rogers went below and fastened the rope, while I pulled them up. Rogers wished many times we had the horses up safely where the mule was, but a dog could hardly cross the narrow path and there was no hope. Poor brutes, they had been faithful servants, and we felt sorrowful enough at their terrible fate.

We had walked two days without water, and we were wonderfully refreshed as we found it here. The way up this cañon was very rough and the bed full of sharp broken rocks in loose places, which cut through the bottoms of our moccasins and left us with bare feet upon the acute points and edges. I took off one of my buckskin leggings and gave it to Rogers, and with the other one for myself, we fixed the moccasins with them as well as we could. This enabled us to go ahead, but I think if our feet had been shod with steel, these sharp rocks would have cut through.

Starting early, we made the summit about noon, and from here we could see the place where we found a water hole and camped the first night after we left the wagons. Down the steep cañon we turned, the same one in which we had turned back with the wagons. Over the sharp broken pieces of volcanic rock that formed our only footing, we hobbled along with sore and tender feet. We had to watch for the smoothest place for every step, and then moved only with the greatest difficulty. The Indians could have caught us easily if they had been around, for we must keep our eyes on the ground constantly, and stop if we looked up and around. But we at last got down, and camped on the same spot where we had set out twenty-five days before to seek the settlements. Here was the same little water hole in the sand plain, and the same strong sulphur water which we had to drink the day we left. The mule was turned loose, dragging the same piece of rawhide she had attached to her when we purchased her. She ranged and searched faithfully for food, finding little except the small scattering of sage brush. She was industrious and walked around rapidly here and there, but at dark came into camp and laid down close to us to sleep.

There was no sign that anyone had been here during our absence, and if the people had gone to hunt a way out, they must either have followed the Jayhawker's trail or some other one. We were very afraid that they might have fallen victims to the Indians. Remaining in camp so long, it was quite likely they had been discovered by them, and it was quite likely they had been murdered for the sake of the oxen and camp equipage. It might be that we should find the hostiles waiting for us when we reached the appointed camping place, and it was small show for two against a party. Our mule and her load would be a great capture for them. We talked a great deal and said a great many things at that camp fire, for we knew we were in great danger, and we had many doubts about the safety of our people. That would soon be determined, and whether for joy or sorrow we could not tell.

From this place, as we walked along, we had a wagon road to follow in soft sand, but not a sign of a human footstep could we see, as we marched toward this, the camp of the last hope. We had the greatest fear that the people had given up on our return, had started out for themselves and that we should follow on, only to find them dead or dying. My pen fails me as I try to convey the feelings and thoughts of this trying hour. I can never hope to do so, but if the reader can place himself in my place, his imagination cannot form a picture that shall go beyond reality.

We were some seven or eight miles along the road, when I stopped to fix my moccasin while Rogers continued slowly along. The little mule went on ahead of both of us, searching all around for little bunches of dry grass, but always came back to the trail again and gave us no trouble. When I had started up again, I saw Rogers ahead leaning on his gun and waiting for me, apparently looking at something on the ground. As I came near enough to speak, I asked what he had found and he said, "Here is Capt. Culverwell, dead." He did not look much like a dead man. He lay upon his back, with arms extended wide, and his little canteen, made of two powder flasks, lying by his side. This looked indeed as if some of our saddest forebodings were coming true. How many more bodies should we find? Or should we find the camp deserted, and never find a trace of the former occupants.

We marched toward camp like two Indians, silent and alert, looking out for dead bodies and live Indians, for really we more expected to find the camp devastated by those rascals than to *find that it still contained our friends. To the east we could plainly see what seemed to be a large salt lake, with a bed that looked as if of the finest, whitest sand, but really a wonder of salt crystal. With dreary steps, we continued steadily forward. The little mule was the only unconcerned one of the party, ever looking for an odd blade of grass, dried in the hot dry wind, but yet retaining nourishment, which she preferred.*

About noon we came in sight of the wagons, still a long way off, but in the clear air we could make them out, and tell what they were, without being able to see anything more. Half a mile was the distance between us and the camp, before we could see very plainly, as they were in a little depression. We could see the covers had been taken off, and this was an ominous circumstance to us, for we feared the depredations of the Indians, in retaliation for the capture of their squashes. Perhaps they had shot our oxen before we left and they have slain them this time and the people too.

We surely left seven wagons. Now we could see only four, and nowhere the sign of an ox. They must have gone ahead with a small train, and left these four standing, after dismantling them.

No signs of life were anywhere about, and the thought of our hard struggles between life and death to go out and return, with the fruitless results that now seemed apparent, was almost more then human heart could bear. When should we know their fate? When should we find their remains, and how learn of their sad history, if we ourselves should live to get back again to settlements and life? If ever two men were troubled, Rogers and I surely passed through the furnace.

We kept as low and as much out of sight as possible, trusting very much to the little mule that was ahead, for we felt sure she would detect danger in the air sooner than we, and we watched her closely to see how she acted. She slowly walked along, looking out for food, and we followed a little way behind, but still no decisive sign to settle the awful suspense in which we lived and suffered. We became more and more convinced that they had taken the trail of the Jayhawkers, and we had missed them on the road, or they had perished before reaching the place where we turned from their trail.

One hundred yards now to the wagons and still no sign of life, no positive sign of death, though we looked carefully for both. We feared that perhaps there were Indians in ambush, and with nervous irregular breathing, we took counsel what to do. Finally, Rogers suggested that he had two charges in his shot gun and I seven in the Coll's rifle, and that I fire one of mine and await results before we ventured any nearer. If there were any of the red devils there, we could kill some of them before they got to us. Now, both closely watching the wagons, I fired the shot. Still as death and not a move for a moment. Then as if by magic, a man came out from under a wagon and stood up, looking all around, for he did not see us. Then he threw up his arms high over his head and shouted, "The boys have come! The boys have come!" Then other bare heads appeared, and Mr. Bennett and wife and Mr. Arcane came toward us as fast as they ever could. The great suspense was over. Our hearts were first in our mouths, then the blood all went away and left us almost fainting as we stood and tried to step. Some were safe, perhaps all of those nearest us, and the dark shadow of death that had hovered over us, and cast what seemed a pall upon every thought and action, was lifted and fell away, a heavy oppression gone. Bennett and Arcane caught us in their arms and embraced us with all their strength, and Mrs. Bennett, when she came, fell down on her knees and clung to me like a maniac in the great emotion that came to her, and not a word was spoken. If they had been strong enough, they would have carried us to camp upon their shoulders. As it was, they stopped two or three times, and turned as if to speak, but there was too much feeling for words, convulsive weeping would choke the voice.

All were a little calmer soon, and Bennett soon found voice to say, "I know you have found some place, for you have a mule," and Mrs. Bennett, through her tears, looked staringly at us, as she could hardly believe our coming back was a reality, and then exclaimed, "Good boys! O, you have saved us all! God bless you forever! Such boys should never die!" It was some time before they could talk without weeping. Hope almost died within them, and now when the first bright ray came, it almost turned reason from its throne. A brighter, happier look came to them than we had seen, and then they plied us with questions, the first of which was, "Where were you?"

We told them it must be 250 miles yet to any part of California where we could live. Then came the question, "Can we take our wagons?" "You will have to walk," was our answer, for no wagons could go over that unbroken road that we had traveled. As rapidly and carefully as we could, we told them of our journey, and the long distance between the water holes; that we had lost no time and yet had been twenty six days on the road; that for a long distance the country was about as dry and desolate as the region we had crossed east of this camp. We told them of the scarcity of grass, and all the reasons that had kept us so long from them.

We inquired after the others whom we had left in camp when we went away, and we were told all they knew about them. Hardly were we gone before they began to talk about the state of affairs which existed. They said that as they had nothing to live on but the oxen, it would be certain death to wait here and eat them up, and that it would be much better to move on a little every day to get nearer and nearer the goal before the food failed. Bennett told them they would know surely about the way when the boys returned, and knowing the road would know how to manage, what to expect and work for, and could get out successfully. But the general opinion of all but Mr. Bennett, Mr. Arcane and their families was, as expressed by one of them, "If those boys ever get out of this cussed hole, they are damned fools if they ever come back to help anybody."

Some did not stay more than a week after we were gone, but took their oxen and blankets and started on. They could not be content to stay idly in camp with nothing to occupy their minds or bodies. They could see that an ox, when killed, would feed them only a few days, and that they could not live long on them; and it stood them in hand to get nearer the western shore, as the less distance the more hope while the meat lasted. Bennett implored them to stay, as he was sure we could come back; and if most of them deserted him, he would be exposed to danger from the Indians, with no hope of a successful resistance against them.

But most seemed to think that to stay was to die, and it would be better to die trying to escape than to sit idly down and perish. These men seemed to think their first duty was to save themselves, and if fortunate, help others afterward. So they packed their oxen and left in separate parties, the last some two weeks before. They said that Capt. Culverwell went with the last party. I afterward learned that he could not keep up with them and turned to go back to the wagons again; and perished, stretched out upon the sand as we saw him, dying all alone, with no one to transmit his last words to family or friends. Not a morsel to eat, and the little canteen by his side empty. A sad and lonely death indeed!

The small remaining party now makes preparations to continue their trek out of Death Valley, across the mountains and into the fertile, settled valley beyond. To have a chance of making it, they must leave behind any unnecessary provisions, as it is impossible to take the wagons. The women cannot bear to leave their finest dress behind, so they dress themselves and their children in their best clothes for the journey. To transport the youngest children, they take their strongest shirts and in the words of Mr. Bennett, "turned the sleeves inside, sewed up the necks, then sewed the two shirts together by the tail, and when these are placed on the ox they will make two pockets for the youngest children, and we think the two others will be able to cling to his back with the help of a band around the body of the ox to which they can cling to, with their hands." They determine the best route is to leave Death Valley the way Manley and Rogers returned. One of the smallest children was suffering from poor nourishment and seemed near death but she now began to improve slowly. A glimmer of hope came to the party as they made ready.

. . . High overhead was the sun, and very warm indeed on that day in the fore part of February 1850, when the two children were put on Old Crump (one of the oxen) to see if he would let them ride. The two small children were placed in the pockets on each side, face outward, and they could stand or sit as they should choose. George and Melissa were placed on top and given hold of the strap that was to steady them in their place. I now led up Mrs. Bennett's ox, and Mr. Bennett helped his wife to mount the animal, on whose back as soft a seat as possible had been constructed. Mrs. Arcane in her ribbons was now helped to her seat on the back of Old Brigham (another ox) and she carefully adjusted herself to position, and arranged her dress and ornaments to suit, then took hold of the strap that served to hold on by, as there were no bridles on these two.

Rogers led the march with his ox; Bennett and I started the others along, and Arcane followed with Old Crump and the children. Bennett and Arcane took off their hats and bade the old camp good-bye. The whole procession moved, and we were once more going toward our journey's end, we hoped. The road was sandy and soft, the grade practically level. Everything went well for about four miles, when the pack on one of the oxen near the lead got loose and turned over to one side, which he no sooner saw thus out of position, then he tried to get away from it by moving sidewise. Not getting clear of the objectionable load in this way, he tried to kick it off, and thus really got his foot in it, making matters worse instead of better. Then he began a regular waltz and bawled at the top of his voice in terror. Rogers tried to catch him, but his own animal was so frisky that he could not hold him and do much else, and the spirit of fear soon began to be communicated to the others, and soon the whole train seemed to be taken crazy.

They would jump up high and then come down, sticking their fore feet as far as possible into the sand after which, with elevated tails, and terrible plunges would kick and thrush and run till the packs came off, when they stopped apparently quite satisfied. Mrs. Bennett slipped off her ox as quick as she could, grabbed her baby from the pocket on Old Crump, and shouting to Melissa and George to jump, got her family into safe position in pretty short order. Arcane took his Charley from the other pocket and laid him on the ground, while he devoted his own attention to the animals. Mrs. Arcane's ox followed suit, and waltzed around in the sand, bawled at every turn, fully as bad as any of the others. But Mrs. Arcane proved to be a good rider, and hard to unseat, clinging desperately to her strap as she was tossed up and down, and whirled about at a rate enough to make any one dizzy. Her many fine ribbons flew out behind like the streamers from a mast-head, and the many fancy fixin's she had donned fluttered in the air in gayest mockery. Eventually she was thrown, but without the least injury to herself, yet somewhat disordered in raiment. When I saw Bennett, he was standing half bent over laughing, in almost hysterical convulsion, at the entirely impromptu circus, which had so suddenly performed an act not on the program. Arcane was much pleased and laughed heartily when he saw no one was hurt. We did not think the cattle had so much life and so little sense as to waste their energies so uselessly. The little mule stepped out one side and looked on in amazement, without disarranging any article of her load.

Mrs. Bennett, carrying her baby and walking around to keep out of the way, got very much exhausted and sat down on the sand. Her face was as red as if the blood were about to burst through the skin, and she was perspiring freely. We carried a blanket and spread it down for her, while we gathered in the scattered baggage. Then the oxen were got together again, and submitted to being loaded up again, as quietly as if nothing had happened. Myself and the women had to mend the harness considerably. Arcane and his ox went back for some water, while Rogers and Bennett took the shovel and went ahead about a mile to cover up the body of Capt. Culverwell, for some of the party feared the cattle might be terrified at seeing it. All this took so much time that we had to make a camp of it right here.

We put the camp kettle on two stones, built a fire, put in some beans and dried meat cut very fine. It cooked till Arcane came with more water, which was added and thickened with a little of the unbolted flour, making a pretty good nutritious soup which we all enjoyed. We had to secure the animals, for there was neither grass nor water for them, and we thought they might not be in so good spirits another day.

We had little trouble in packing up again in the morning, and concluded to take a nearer route to the summit, so as to more quickly reach the water holes where Rogers and I camped on our first trip over the country. This would be a hard rocky road on its course leading up a small rocky cañon, hard on the feet of the oxen; so they had to be constantly urged on, as they seemed very tender footed. They showed no disposition to go on a spree again and, so far as keeping the loads on, behaved very well indeed. The women did not attempt to ride but followed on, close after Old Crump and the children, who required almost constant attention, for in their cramped position they made many cries and complaints. To think of it, two children cramped up in narrow pockets, in which they could not turn around, jolted and pitched around over the rough road, made them objects of great suffering to themselves and anxiety and labor on the part of the mothers.

Mrs. Bennett said she would carry her baby if she could, but her own body was so heavy for her strength that she could not do it. Bennett, Rogers and myself hurried the oxen all we could, so that we could reach the water; and let Bennett go back with some to meet the rest and refresh them for the end of the day's march. He could take poor Martha from the pocket and carry her in his arms, which would be a great relief for her. Arcane also took his child when he met them, throwing away his double barrel gun saying, "I have no use for you."

When the women reached camp, we had blankets already spread down for them, on which they cast themselves, so tired as to be nearly dead. They were so tired and discouraged, they were ready to die, for they felt they could not endure many days like this.

We told them this was the first day and they were not used to exercise, therefore more easily tired than after they became a little used to it. We told them not to be discouraged, for we knew every water hole, and all the road over which we would pilot them safely. They would not consent to try riding again, after their circus experience, and Mrs. Arcane said her limbs ached so much she did not think she could even go on the next day. They had climbed over the rocks all day, and were lame and sore, and truly thought they could not endure such another day. The trail had been more like stairs than a road in its steep ascent, and our camp was at a narrow pass in the range. The sky was clear and cloudless, as it had been for so long thus far upon this route. No rain had fallen, and only once a little snow that came to us like manna in the desert. For many days we had been obliged to go without water, both we and our cattle, and over the route we had come we had not seen any sign of a white man's presence older than our own. I have no doubt we were the first to cross the valley in this location, a visible sink hole in the desert.

The women did not recover sufficient energy to remove their clothing, but slept as they were, and sat up and looked around with uncombed hair in the morning, perfect pictures of dejection. We let them rest as long as we could, for their swollen eyes and stiffened joints told how sadly unprepared they were to go forward at once. The sun came out early and made it comfortable, while a cool and tonic breeze, came down from the great snow mountain, the very thing to brace them up after a thorough rest.

The slope to the east was soon met by a high ridge, and between this and the main mountain was a gentle slope scattered over with sage brush, and a few little stools of bunch grass here and there between. This gave our oxen a little food and, by dipping out the water from the holes and letting them fill up again, we managed to get water for camp use and to give the animals nearly all they wanted.

While waiting for the women, Bennett and Arcane wanted to go out and get a good view of the great snowy mountain I had told them so much about. The best viewpoint was near our camp, perhaps three or four hundred yards away, and I went with them. This place, where we now stood, was lower than the mountains either north or south, but were difficult to climb and gave a good view in almost every direction. There, on the backbone of the ridge, we had a grand outlook, but some parts of it brought back doleful recollections. They said they had traveled in sight of that mountain for months and seen many strange formations, but never one like this as from this point. It looked to be seventy-five miles to its base, and to the north and west there was a succession of snowy peaks that seemed to have no end. Bennett and Arcane said they never before supposed America contained mountains so grand with peaks that so nearly seemed to pierce the sky. Nothing except a bird could ever cross such steep ranges as that one.

West and south it seemed level, and low, dark, barren buttes rose from the plain, but never high enough to carry snow, even at this season of the year. I pointed out to them the route we were to follow, noting the prominent points, and it could be traced for fully one hundred and twenty-five miles from the point on which we stood. This plain, with its barren ranges and buttes, is now known as the Mojave Desert. This part of the view they seemed to study over, as if to fix every point and water hole upon their memory. We turned to go to camp, but no one looked back on the country we had come over since we first made out the distant snow peak, now so near us, on November 4th, 1849. The only butte in this direction that carried snow was the one where we captured the Indian and where the squashes were found.

The range east of us, across the low valley, was barren to look upon as a naked, single rock. There were peaks of various heights and colors, yellow, blue, fiery red and nearly black. It looked as if it might sometimes have been the center of a mammoth furnace. I believe this range is known as the Coffin Mountains. It would be difficult to find earth enough in the whole of it to cover a coffin.

Just as we were ready to leave and return to camp, we took off our hats, and then overlooking the scene of so much trial, suffering and death, spoke the thought uppermost in our minds saying, "Goodbye Death Valley!" Then we turned away and made our steps toward camp. Ever after this, in speaking of this long and narrow valley over which we had crossed into its nearly central part, and on the edge of which the lone camp was made for so many days, it was called Death Valley.

Many accounts have been given to the world as to the origin of the name and by whom it was thus designated, but ours were the first visible footsteps, and we the party which named it the saddest and most dreadful name that came to us first from its memories.

Chapter VIII

REDWOOD
1849

*from "The Discovery of Humboldt Bay"
in* Humboldt Times, *Spring 1856
by Lewis Keysor Wood*

As a consequence of the gold rush, many immigrants leaped over the intervening empty spaces of the West into California. Resident explorers, on various enterprises, soon cris-crossed the new state discovering its wondrous landscapes and flora. The expedition related here crossed through the Redwoods region on the way to discovering Humboldt Bay. The expedition was led by Josiah Gregg, author of *Commerce of the Prairies*, a classic work about the Santa Fe Trail. The narrative was written by Lewis Keysor Wood, one of the members of the expedition. It was a miserable wet winter in northern California. This, and the difficult terrain, took its toll upon the disposition of the party.

The month of October, 1849, found me on the Trinity river, at a point now called Rich Bar. How I came there and from whence, over what route, by what conveyance, or for what object, it matters not; suffice it to say that I was there, and that, too without provisions, poorly clad, and worse than all, in this condition at the commencement of a California winter. The company at this place numbered some forty persons, most of whom were in much the same situation and condition as myself. Near the bar was an Indian ranch, from which, during the prevalence of the rain that was now pouring down as if in contemplation of a second flood, we received frequent visits. From them we learned that the ocean was distant from this place not more than eight days' travel, and that there was a large and beautiful bay, surrounded by fine and extensive prairie lands.

The rainy season, having now, to all appearances set in, alternate rain and snow continually falling – a scanty supply of provisions for the number of persons now here, and scarcely a probability of the stock being replenished before the rains *should cease, the idea was conceived of undertaking an expedition with the view to ascertaining whether the bay, of which the Indians had given a description, in reality existed. Among the first and most active in getting up and organizing the expedition, was a gentleman by the name of Josiah Gregg, a physician by profession, formerly of Missouri. He had with him all the implements necessary to guide us through the uninhabited, trackless region of country that lay between us and the point to be sought. No one seemed better qualified to guide and direct an expedition of this kind than he. Upon him, therefore, the choice fell to take command. The number of persons that had expressed a desire to join the company up to this time, was twenty-four. The day fixed upon by the Captain for setting out was the 5th day of November. In the meantime, whatever preparations were necessary and in our power, were made. The Captain had negotiated with the chief of the rancheria for two of his men to act as guides. Nothing more remaining to be done, all were anxiously awaiting the arrival of the day fixed upon, and a cessation of the rain, which was still falling in torrents.*

The day of departure arrived, but with it came no change in the weather, save an occasional change from rain to snow. Many of the party now began to exhibit a marked desire to withdraw and abandon the expedition. The two Indian guides refused to go, assigning as a reason, that the great storm we had experienced on the river had been a continuous snow storm in the mountains, and that the depth of the snow would present an insuperable barrier to our progress, and endanger the safety of the whole party, at attempting the passage. This was sufficient for those who had manifested a desire to withdraw; and the number was speedily reduced to eight men, including the Captain whose determination was only the more fixed, because too large a number had abandoned the expedition. . . .

Owing to this great diminution in the number of the party, it became necessary before setting out, to examine the condition of our commissary department – from which it was ascertained that the stock of provisions had suffered even greater diminution than had the company in point of numbers. The articles found were flour, pork, and beans, and of these scarcely sufficient for ten days' rations. Notwithstanding this, an advance was determined upon, and, accordingly we broke up camp. Here commenced an expedition, the marked and prominent fea-

tures of which were constant and unmitigated toil, hardship, privation and suffering. Before us, stretching as far as the eye could see, lay mountains, high and rugged, deep valleys and difficult cañons, now filled with water by the recent heavy rains. . . .

Our progress up to this time had been very slow. The distance traveled per day did not exceed an average of seven miles. The appearance of the country now seemed to change – the mountain ridges were less high and abrupt than those over which we had passed, but much more densely covered with timber. Our belief now was that twelve miles further travel would bring us, if not to the coast, at least to a more level country, when our advance would be more rapid and attended with less difficulty and suffering. We therefore resumed our journey with lighter hearts and more buoyant hopes.

Our calculation of the distance to the coast or valley, subsequently proved to be not far from correct. The redwood forests, however, through which we had to pass, were more dense and difficult to penetrate than any before; consequently our progress was in proportion retarded. Dr. Gregg frequently expressed a desire to measure the circumference of some of these giants of the forest, and occasionally called upon some one of us to assist him. Not being in the most amiable state of mind and feeling at this time, and having neither ambition to gratify nor desire to enlighten the curious world, we not infrequently answered his calls with shameful abuse. His obstinate perseverance, however, in one or two instances, resulted in success. One redwood tree was measured whose diameter was found to be twenty-two feet, and it was no unusual thing to find these trees reaching the enormous height of three hundred feet. This may excite incredulity abroad, but trees have since been found in this redwood forest of much greater dimensions.

Through this forest we could not travel to exceed two miles a day. The reason for this was the immense quantity of fallen timber that lay upon the ground in every conceivable shape and direction, and in very many instances one piled upon another so that the only alternative left us was literally to cut our way through. To go around them was often as impossible as to go over them. We were obliged, therefore, constantly to keep two men ahead with axes, who, as occasion required, would chop into and slab off sufficient to construct a sort of platform by means of which the animals were driven upon the log and forced to jump off on the opposite side. There was not the least sign indicative of the presence of any of the animal creation; indeed, it was almost as impenetrable for them as for us, and doubtless was never resorted to save for purpose of shelter.

On the evening of the third day from our bear camp, as we called it, our ears were greeted with the welcome sound of the surf rolling and beating upon the sea shore. There was no doubt or mistake about it this time. The lofty tops caught the sound, which the deep stillness of a night in a forest rendered the more plainly audible and echoed it back to our attentive ears.

The following morning Messrs. Wilson and Van Duzen proposed to go to the coast in advance of the company, and at the same time to mark out the best route for the animals; to which proposition all agreed, and accordingly they left the camp. In the evening of the same day they returned, bringing the glad tidings that they had reached the sea shore, and it was not more than six miles distant.

At an early hour in the morning we resumed our journey with renewed spirits and courage. For three long days did we toil in these redwoods. Exhaustion and almost starvation, had reduced the animals to the last extremity. Three had just died, and the remainder were so much weakened and reduced, that it constituted no small part of our labor and annoyance in assisting them to get up when they had fallen, which happened every time they were unfortunate enough to stumble against the smallest obstacle that lay in their path, and not a single effort would they make to recover their feet, until that assistance came. At length we issued from this dismal forest prison, in which we had so long been shut up, into the open country, and at the same instant in full view of that vast world of water – the Pacific ocean. . . .

The party discovers Humboldt Bay and after leaving the area, disagreements and recriminations lead to the breakup of the party into two separate groups taking separate paths to San Francisco. Wood is severely injured in a fight with grizzlies during their return. Dr. Gregg dies of starvation during the return with the other party.

Chapter IX

YOSEMITE
1851

from Discovery of the Yosemite
and the Indian War of 1851
Which Led to That Event
by Lafayette Houghton Bunnell

*Photos of Yosemite by Carleton Watkins are among the earliest
in existence.*

The following is an historical account written thirty years after the event. The author participated as a volunteer in a pacification campaign sent against the Indians residing in the Yosemite region. The excerpts selected are of his responses to the landscape, with brief reference to their finding and capture of the Yosemite tribe. No battle was fought. The chief, Ten-ie-ya, and his tribe surrendered to the soldiers and were escorted out. Unlike the Walker expedition of 1833, the rediscovery of Yosemite in 1851 now became public knowledge and others soon visited the region. It became the first wilderness park in 1864, but established by the state of California rather than the federal government.

During the winter of 1849-50, while ascending the old Bear Valley trail from Ridley's ferry, on the Merced river, my attention was attracted to the stupendous rocky peaks of the Sierra Nevada. In the distance an immense cliff loomed, apparently to the summit of the mountains. Although familiar with nature in her wildest moods, I looked upon this awe-inspiring column with wonder and admiration. While vainly endeavoring to realize its peculiar prominence and vast proportions, I turned from it with reluctance to resume the search for coveted gold; but the impressions of that scene were indelibly fixed in my memory. Whenever an opportunity afforded, I made inquiries concerning the scenery of that locality. But few of the miners had noticed any of its special peculiarities. On a second visit to Ridley's, not long after, that towering mountain which had so profoundly interested me was invisible, an intervening haze obscuring it from view. A year or more passed before the mysteries of this wonderful land were satisfactorily solved.

During the winter of 1850-51, I was attached to an expedition that made the first discovery of what is now known as the Yosemite Valley. While entering it, I saw at a glance that the reality of my sublime vision at Ridley's ferry, forty miles away, was before me. The locality of the mysterious cliff was there revealed – its proportions enlarged and perfected.

The discovery of this remarkable region was an event intimately connected with the history of the early settlement of that portion of California. During 1850, the Indians in Mariposa county, which at that date included all the territory south of the divide of the Tuolumne and Merced rivers within the valley proper of the San Joaquin, became very troublesome to the miners and settlers. Their depredations and murderous assaults were continued until the arrival of the United States Indian commissioners in 1851, when the general government assumed control over them. Through the management of the commissioners, treaties were made, and many of these Indians were transferred to locations reserved for their special occupancy. . . .

We found the traveling much less laborious than before, and it seemed but a short time after we left the Indians before we suddenly came in full view of the valley in which was the village, or rather the encampments of the Yosemite. The immensity of rock I had seen in my vision on the Old Bear Valley trail from Rid-

ley's Ferry was here presented to my astonished gaze. The mystery of that scene was here disclosed. My awe was increased by this nearer view. The face of the immense cliff was shadowed by the declining sun; its outlines only had been seen at a distance. This towering mass

"Fools our fond gaze, and greatest of the great,
Defies at first our Nature's littleness,
Till, growing to its growth, we thus dilate
Our spirits to the size of that they contemplate."

That stupendous cliff is now known as "El Capitan," and the plateau from which we had our first view of the valley, as Mount Beatitude.

It has been said that "it is not easy to describe in words the precise impressions which great objects make upon us." I cannot describe how completely I realized this truth. None but those who have visited this most wonderful valley, can even imagine the feelings with which I looked upon the view that was there presented. The grandeur of the scene was but softened by the haze that hung over the valley – light as gossamer – and by the clouds which partially dimmed the higher cliffs and mountains. This obscurity of vision but increased the awe with which I beheld it, and as I looked, a peculiar exalted sensation seemed to fill my whole being, and I found my eyes in tears with emotion.

During many subsequent visits to this locality, this sensation was never again so fully aroused. It is probable that the shadows fast clothing all before me, and the vapory clouds at the head of the valley, leaving the view beyond still undefined, gave a weirdness to the scene, that made it so impressive; and the conviction that it was utterly indescribable added strength to the emotion. It is not possible for the same intensity of feeling to be aroused more than once by the same object, although I never looked upon these scenes except with wonder and admiration. . . .

Although we repeatedly discovered fresh trails leading from the different camps, all traces were soon lost among the rocks at the base of the cliffs. The debris or talus not only afforded places for temporary concealment, but provided facilities for escape without betraying the direction. If by chance a trail was followed for a while, it would at last be traced to some apparently inaccessible ledge, or to the foot of some slippery depression in the walls, up which we did not venture to climb. While scouting up the Ten-ie-ya cañon, above Mirror Lake, I struck the fresh trail of quite a large number of Indians. Leaving our horses, a few of us followed up the tracks until they were lost in the ascent up the cliff. By careful search they were again found and followed until finally they hopelessly disappeared.

Tiring of our unsuccessful search, the hunt was abandoned, although we were convinced that the Indians had in some way passed up the cliff.

During this time, and while descending to the valley, I partly realized the great height of the cliffs and high fall. I had observed the height we were compelled to climb before the talus had been overcome, though from below this appeared insignificant, and after reaching the summit of our ascent, the cliffs still towered above us. It was by instituting these comparisons while ascending and descending, that I was able to form a better judgment of altitude; for while entering the valley – although, as before stated, I had observed the towering height of El Capitan – my mind had been so preoccupied with the marvelous, that comparison had scarcely performed its proper function.

Yosemite Falls

The level of the valley proper now appeared quite distant as we looked down upon it, and objects much less than full size. As night was fast approaching, and a storm threatened, we returned down the trail and took our course for the rendezvous selected by Major Savage, in a grove of oaks near the mouth of Indian Cañon.

While on our way down, looking across to and up the south or Glacier Cañon, I noticed its beautiful fall, and planned an excursion for the morrow. I almost forgot my fatigue, in admiration of the solemn grandeur within my view; the lofty walls, the towering domes and numerous waterfalls; their misty spray blending with the clouds settling down from the higher mountains.

The duties of the day had been severe on men and horses, for beside fording the Merced several times, the numerous branches pouring over cliffs and down ravines from the melting snow, rendered the overflow of the bottom lands so constant that we were often compelled to splash through the watercourses that later would be dry. These torrents of cold water, commanded more especial attention, and excited more comment than did the grandeur of the cliffs and waterfalls. We were not a party of tourists, seeking recreation, nor philosophers investigating the operations of nature. Our business there was to find Indians who were endeavoring to escape from our charitable intentions toward them. But very few of the volunteers seemed to have any appreciation of the wonderful proportions of the enclosing granite rocks; their curiosity had been to see the stronghold of the enemy, and the general verdict was that it was gloomy enough.

Tired and wet, the independent scouts sought the camp and reported their failure. Gilbert and Chandler came in with their detachments just at dark, from their tiresome explorations of the southern branches. Only a small squad of their commands climbed above the Vernal and Nevada falls; and seeing the clouds resting upon the mountains above the Nevada Fall, they retraced their steps through the showering mist of the Vernal, and joined their comrades, who had already started down its rocky gorge. These men found no Indians, but they were the first discoverers of the Vernal and Nevada Falls, and the Little Yosemite. They reported what they had seen to their assembled comrades at the evening campfires. Their names have now passed from my memory – not having had an intimate personal acquaintance with them – but according to my recollection they belonged to the company of Capt. Dill. . . .

Finally the soldiers track the Indian tribe down after climbing out of the valley into the high country. The Yosemites give themselves up and are escorted out by the troops.

Vernal Falls

In order to take the most direct route to the valley, Captain Bol-
ing selected one of the young Yosemite Indians to lead the way
with our regular guide. Being relieved of the charge of Ten-ie-
ya, I took my usual place on the march with the guide. This
position was preferred by me, because it afforded ample oppor-
tunity for observation and time for reflection; and beside, it was
in my nature to be in advance. The trail followed, after leaving
the lake, led us over bare granite slopes and hidden paths, but
the distance was materially shortened. A short distance below
the bottom land of the lake, on the north side of the cañon and
at the head of the gorge, the smooth, sloping granite projects
like a vast roof over the abyss below. As we approached this,
our young guide pointed toward it.

By close observation I was able to discover that the trail led up
its sloping surface, and was assured by the guide that the trail
was a good one. I felt doubtful of the Captain's willingness to
scale that rocky slope, and halted for him to come up. The Cap-
tain followed the trail to its termination in the soil, and saw the
cause of my having halted.

Upon the discoloration of the rock being pointed out as the con-
tinuation of the trail, he glanced up the granite slope and said,

"Go on, but be watchful, for a slide into the gorge would bring as certain death as a slide from that San Joaquin trail, which I have not yet forgotten." Some of the command did not fancy this any more than they did the Ten-ie-ya trail down Indian Cañon. We all pulled off our boots and went up this slope bare-footed. Seeing there was no real danger, the most timid soon moved up as fearless as the others. I, with the advance, soon reached the soil above, and at the top halted until the Indians and our straggling column closed up. As I looked about me, I discovered, unfolding to my sight, one of the most charming views in this sublimest scenery of nature. During the day before, we had looked with astonishment on the almost boundless peaks, and snow-capped mountains, to be seen from the Mt. Hoffman divide. But here some of the same views appeared illuminated. In our ascent up the mountain, we had apparently met the rising sun. The scene was one long to be remembered for its brilliancy, although not describable.

. . . Although not sufficiently elevated to command a general outlook, the higher ridges framing some of the scenery to the north and eastward of us, the westerly view was boundless. The transparency of the atmosphere was here extreme, and as the sun illuminated the snow-clad and ice-burnished peaks, the scene aroused the enthusiasm of the command to a shout of glad surprise.

The recollections of the discomforts of the night were banished by the glory of the morning as here displayed. Even the beauties of the Yosemite, of which I was so ardent an admirer, were for the moment eclipsed by this gorgeously grand and changing scene. The aurora that had preceded the rising sun was as many-hued, and if possible more glorious, than the most vivid borealis of the northern climes. But when the sun appeared, seemingly like a sudden flash, amidst the distant peaks, the climax was complete. My opportunities for examining the mountain scenery of the Sierra Nevada above the immediate vicinity of the Yosemite, was such as to only enable me to give a somewhat general description, but the views that I had during our explorations afforded me glimpses of the possibilities of sublime mountain scenery, such as I had never before comprehended, although familiar with the views afforded from some of the peaks of Mexico and the Rocky Mountains. I doubt even if the

Yellowstone, supreme in some of its attractions, affords such varied and majestic beauty.

Looking back to the lovely little lake, where we had been encamped during the night, and watching Ten-ie-ya as he ascended to our group, I suggested to the Captain that we name the lake after the old chief, and call it Lake Ten-ie-ya. . . .

When Ten-ie-ya reached the summit, he left his people and approached where the Captain and a few of us were halting. . . . I called him up to us, and told him that we had given his name to the lake and river. At first, he seemed unable to comprehend our purpose, and pointing to the group of glistening peaks, near the head of the lake, said, "It already has a name; we call it Py-we-ack." Upon my telling him that we had named it Ten-ie-ya, because it was upon the shores of the lake that we had found his people, who would never return to it to live, his countenance fell and he at once left our group and joined his own family circle. His countenance as he left us indicated that he thought the naming of the lake no equivalent for the loss of his territory.

. . . As he moved off to hide his sorrow, I pitied him. As we resumed our march over the rough and billowy trail, I was more fully impressed with the appropriateness of the name for the beautiful lake. Here, probably, his people had built their last wigwams in their mountain home. From this lake we were leading the last remnant of his once dreaded tribe, to a territory from which it was designed they should never return as a people. My sympathies, confirmed in my own mind, a justness in thus perpetuating the name of Ten-ie-ya. . . .

. . . The next day we broke camp and moved down to the lower end of the valley near where we camped on the first night of our discovery, near the little meadow at the foot of the Mariposa Trail.

At sunrise the next morning, or rather as the reflections on the cliffs indicated sunrise, we commenced our ascent of the steep trail. As I reached the height of land where the moving column would soon perhaps forever shut out from view the immortal Rock Chief, my old sympathies returned, and leaving the command to pursue its heedless way, I climbed to my old perch where Savage had warned me of danger. As I looked back upon

El Capitan, his bald forehead was cooling in the breeze that swept by me from the "Summer land" below, and his cheerful countenance reflected back the glory of the rising sun. Feeling my own inferiority while acknowledging the majesty of the scene, I looked back from Mt. Beatitude, and quoting from Byron, exclaimed,

Yosemite!
"Thy vales of evergreen, thy hills of snow
Proclaim thee Nature's favorite now."

We reached the Fresno without the loss of a captive, and as we turned them over to the agent, we were formally commended for the success of the expedition.

Chapter X

BIG BEND
1852

from correspondence of M. T. W. Chandler
in Report on the United States and Mexican Boundary Survey
by William H. Emory

After the Mexican War, a boundary survey was led by William
Emory along the entire Mexican border. Part of this survey led through
Big Bend. Tyler Chandler was personally responsible for surveying
the region. This is his report to Major Emory. When possible, the party
followed the river by boat or by marching along the river bank, on
either the Mexican or American side. The first part is through the river
canyons of the Bofecillos Mountains in present-day Big Bend Ranch
State Park. Comanche Pass refers to the area around Lajitas, at the
very border of the national park. The name refers to the practice of
Comanche Indians crossing over the river here, on their frequent raids
into Mexico. Santa Helena Canyon (San Carlos in the report) was
impassible. The party was divided at Marsical Canyon (Sierra San
Vincente in the report). Difficulties of terrain caused them to abandon
a passage through Boquillas Canyon.

Fort Duncan, December 1, 1852

*Sir: In accordance with your directions, I have the honor to
make the following report on the topographical survey of that
portion of the Rio Grande intrusted to my charge. The survey
commenced a few miles above Fort Leaton, in the neighborhood of the Presidio del Norte, and extended to a point about
one hundred and twenty-five miles above the mouth of the Rio
Pecos, embracing a section of country which for ruggedness
and wildness of scenery is perhaps unparalleled.*

*The appearance of the valley in the vicinity of Fort Leaton, with
its succession of plains and arable bottoms, forms a contrast to
the rugged country beyond. From this valley, which is from one
to three miles wide on each side of the river, we suddenly enter
the range of the Bofecillos mountains, through which the river*

has found or forced a passage, forming extensive rapids at its entrance.

A narrow path along the river on the American side is the only means of passage in the immediate vicinity of the stream; and numerous rocks and branches of trees obstruct even this narrow trail.

Camp of the Boundary Survey.

The cañon of the Bofecillos mountains is less rugged in its character than those met with subsequently. Although the passage of a mule train on the immediate borders of the river is utterly impossible, there is on the American side a valley extending nearly parallel to the course of the stream, at a distance varying from two thousand to three thousand feet; along this passes an extensive Indian trail, but to all appearances not recently used. (The scenic highway, El Camino del Rio, follows this route today.) *Dangerous and long rapids occur where the river leaves the cañon, and the country loses entirely the features which characterize the north side of the Bofecillos range. The hills approach and recede from the river in varied succession; nearly always, however, admitting the possibility of carrying the line of survey along the river bottom, at least as far as the Comanche Pass. Scarcely a tree or branch of the smallest size marks the hill-sides or summits, and it is only on the immediate border of the river that the eye, wearied by the continued succession of sterile plains, is relieved by the sight of verdure; and this only when the rocky barriers recede sufficiently for a narrow strip of soil to form.*

Comanche Pass, on the Rio Bravo, the most celebrated and frequently used crossing place of the Indians, was found to be just below this Bofecillos range; here broad, well-beaten trails lead to the river from both sides. A band of Indians, under the well known chief, Mano (hand), crossed the river at the time of our visit; they had come, by their own account, from the headwaters of Red river, and were on their way to Durango, in Mexico – no doubt on a thieving expedition.

At this pass, the hills on either side are less elevated, and to the northwest the depression seems to extend many miles. Below the crossing the river passes through a country varying but little from that which was met with above. The San Carlos mountains rise in front to a considerable height. The strips of bottom land now become narrow, and occur at longer intervals.

The passage of the river through these mountains is grand and imposing. The entrance is shown in the accompanying sketch; dashing with a roaring sound over the rocks, the stream, when it reaches the cañon, suddenly becomes noiseless, and is diminished to a sixth of its former width; it enters the side of this vast mountain, which seems cut to its very base to afford a passage to the waters. On the right of the entrance, the rock is rounded and smoothed by the action of the water into an artificial appearance; on the opposite side the mountain receives the river in its full force. It is impossible to keep along the edge of the stream in its course through the mountain, and just as impossible to navigate it. The rapids and falls which occur in quick succession, make the descent in boats entirely impracticable (Santa Helena Canyon).

A detour by San Carlos was rendered necessary, and the river was again reached at a point some twenty miles below the lower termination of the cañon. It is in the passage through these mountains that the well defined "rapids of the Rio Grande" occur, which from their extent, and their near approach to a perpendicular line in their descent, merit the name of "falls." From the edge of the cañon the river may be seen far below, at a distance so great as to reduce it in appear-

ance to a mere thread; and from this height the roar of the rapids and falls is scarcely perceptible.

It was impossible to approach them in consequence of the rugged nature of the country; the fall of the river at this point, however, may be estimated at twelve feet, without including the rapids above and below. The stream is hemmed in by the cañon for ten miles, and then leaves it with the same abruptness that marks its entrance.

It was here found necessary to cross the mule train from the Mexican side, where it had traveled since the commencement of the survey. This was effected, though with considerable difficulty, at one of the usual crossings of the Indians. Near this point, for some distance above and below, the country is more open, the valleys broader, and are susceptible of cultivation; the bottom land is, however, limited by an elevated bank of gravel. There is also an abundance of cottonwood and mezquite timber.

Whenever the spectator was elevated sufficiently to see beyond the valley of the river, two prominent peaks were always presented to his view. One of these marks a summit in the range of the Mexican Sierra Carmel; and the other, from its peculiar shape and great height, was long and anxiously watched during the progress of our survey. From many places on the line it was taken as a prominent point on which to direct the instrument; and, though the face of the country might change during our progress down the river, still, unmistakable and unchangeable, far above the surrounding mountains, this peak reared its well known head. The windings of the river, and the progress of our survey, led us gradually nearer to this point of interest, and it was found to be a part of a cluster, rather than range, of mountains on the American side, known as "Los Chisos." For this peak, a view of which is here given, we have proposed the name of Mount Emory.

After passing this range of mountains, the survey was carried on with less labor than was previously encountered until we reached the Sierra San Vincente. Through these mountains the river forces its way, forming a cañon that equals the San Carlos in many places both in ruggedness and grandeur (Marsical Canyon). *A small party only could attempt the survey of this part of the line; and the command was divided, one party accompanying the mule train, and the other, under my personal charge, crossed the mountains. Here we experienced another series of falls or sharp rapids far down in the abyss along which the river finds its difficult course; the roaring of the waters announced a more than usual disturbance, and the boats soon encountered difficulties which, for one of them at least, were insurmountable. In this, as in other cañons, it was impossible to carry the line nearer the bed of the river than the summits of the adjoining hills. Two days were necessary to overcome the obstructions of the passage through this cañon, from the top of which we thought we saw a comparatively smooth country extending nearly to the Sierra Carmel, the highest range of mountains seen on the Mexican side of the river. On a high mesa of gravel, some sixty feet above the level of the river bottom, is situated the old presidio of San Vincente, one of the ancient military posts that marked the Spanish rule in this country, long since abandoned; the adobe walls are crumbling to decay, and scarcely a stick of timber remains in the whole enclosure, except in that part devoted to the chapel. The line of survey was connected with this place at a point distinguished by a survey flag, and distinctly pointed out in a note left, in accordance with your orders, for Señor Salazar, of the Mexican Commission.*

Continuing the survey from the Sierra de San Vincente, it was soon found that what in the distance seemed to be a smooth and open country was really rough and broken. It proved to be a country cut up with deep arroyos, presenting to the survey almost insurmountable obstacles. Passing these arroyos, a wild valley, nearly at right angles with the course of the river, preceded the approach to the cañon of Sierra Carmel, another of those rocky dungeons in which the Rio Grande is for a time imprisoned (Boquillas Canyon). No description can give an idea of the grandeur of the scenery through these mountains. There is no verdure to soften the bare and rugged view; no overhanging trees or green bushes to vary the scene from one of perfect desolation. Rocks are here piled one above another, over which it was with the greatest labor that we could work our way. The long detours necessarily made to gain but a short distance for the pack-train on the river were rapidly exhausting the strength of the animals, and the spirit of the whole party began to flag. The loss of the boats, with provisions and clothing, had reduced the men to the shortest rations, and their scanty wardrobes scarcely afforded enough covering for decency. The sharp rocks of the mountains had cut the shoes from their feet, and blood, in many instances, marked their progress through the day's work. Beyond the Sierra Carmel the river seemed to pass through an almost interminable succession of mountains: cañon succeeded cañon; the valleys, which alone had afforded some slight chances for rest and refreshment, had become so narrow and devoid of vegetation that it was quite a task to find grass sufficient for the mules. At a point some few miles below Sierra Carmel, it was supposed that a better pathway could be found on the Mexican side of the river. Just above the entrance of the river into a small cañon a place was chosen, which seemed to afford the most feasible opportunity for fording the river. With great difficulty the whole train was passed over without loss. With this slight interruption, the line of survey was carried on until it reached a point since shown to be about one hundred and twenty-five miles above the mouth of the Pecos. Here the work was suspended, owing to the failure of provisions and the means of transportation on the river. With the whole party we passed down on the Mexican side through the town of Santa Rosa, and arrived at Fort Duncan after a long and tedious journey. It is but proper, in justice to Messrs. Thompson and Phillips, the gentlemen associated with me as assistants, to mention their names as an expression of my appreciation of their exertions. To Mr. Phillips, for his able assistance and unvarying industry, I feel especially indebted.

I have forborne any but an incidental allusion to the difficulties of the survey under my charge, leaving it for yourself, so well acquainted with the character of the country gone over, to appreciate these difficulties, and thus excuse any deficiencies that may have occurred in the work.

I have the honor to be, very respectfully, your obedient servant,

M. T. W. CHANDLER,
Assistant in charge of party U. S.
and Mexican Boundary Commission

Chapter XI

PETRIFIED FOREST
1853

from Diary of a Journey
from the Mississippi to the Coasts of the Pacific
by Baldwin Mollhausen

Many railroad surveys cris-crossed the West in the 1850s and 1860s looking for a suitable passage for the Transcontinental Railroad to tie the country together. Captain Sitgreaves led a survey in 1851 that passed just south of Petrified Forest and made passing mention of seeing some samples of petrified trees. Another railroad survey crossed through the Petrified Forest in 1853, as discussed in the following monograph by a German scientist connected with the expedition. The first part of the excerpt may describe the area around El Malpais. The second clearly describes Petrified Forest. This party was the first of many that, unfortunately, carted away examples of the petrified specimens.

We traveled the following day over a gradually ascending plain, and although the forms of the mountains near us, as well as of those that still lay far off in the misty distance, awakened strong interest, the landscape became more attractive when, after a march of eight miles, we began again to descend, and found ourselves near the San Jose, which, coming from the northwest, watered a small valley and then flowed towards the south. Here we came first upon the streams of lava which traverse the country for miles like long black walls; and we perceived that we were now near the chief furnace of these volcanic regions, namely, some days' journey to the south of Mount Taylor.

Active volcanoes, that tower to a majestic height above a country, and send up columns of smoke to the clouds, doubtless tend much to beautify the regions where they are found; but the remains of extinct cones have a very different and commonly very disagreeable effect on the surrounding scenery. The lifeless form of what was once a wildly-raging, earth-shaking, burning mountain is almost spectral in its aspect; but the inquiring trav-

eler can calmly pursue his researches in the bed of the once fiery stream, and refresh himself at the sweet cool fountain that bubbles forth from its black stony veins. The place where we encamped on the 14th of November, though generally answering to this description, was not entirely destitute of the ornament of vegetation. The strips of meadow land had indeed lost their pleasant verdure and their flowers, and donned the faded livery of autumn; but the dwarf cedars that crowned the low rugged hills and the tops of the broad rocks had remained untouched by the destructive frost that nightly covered all objects with its icy crust. Between these dwarf cedars we laid down before a blazing fire and enjoyed a plentiful supper of roast ducks, having made prize of a considerable number of that savoury fowl among the reeds of the neighboring stream and on the flooded lowlands. . . .

On the 2nd of December, as we were toiling along, over or through the loose sandy soil, having just quitted the dreary valley where we had passed a very uncomfortable night, we found our progress arrested by a broad ravine that it was impossible for the wagons to cross, so that the whole procession had to turn to the south to seek for a way down, though it extended north and south as far as the eye could reach. Some antelopes that had leaped down by a shorter way tempted Mr. Campbell, Dr. Kennerly, and myself to follow them, though that was certainly no easy task, for the banks were excessively steep and composed of red sand mingled with masses of gypsum, and rent in all directions by the rains. The loose earth gave way continually beneath the hoofs of our mules, but between slipping and scrambling we got somehow to the bottom, where we found the ground so much broken by torrents of rain that our progress became still more difficult. Immense masses of water must sometimes rush through this valley, though at the time of our arrival we found only the narrow dry bed of a stream, showing here and there a pool of bitter brackish water, where the sandstone rock had prevented its trickling through. The valley is called by the Americans the Rio Secco, or Dry River, though at this part it might deserve the name of the Petrified Forest.

As we proceeded further we really thought we saw before us masses of wood that had been floated hither, or even a tract of woodland where the timber had been felled for the purposes of cultivation. Trees of all sizes lay irregularly scattered about, and amongst them stumps with the roots that had been left standing; some of them were more than sixty feet long, and of corresponding girth, and looking as if they had been cut into regular blocks, whilst broken branches and chips lay heaped up nearby. On a closer examination we found they were fossil trees that had been gradually washed bare by the torrents and had broken off by their own weight, and that, singularly enough, in logs of from one to three feet in length. We measured some of the largest trunks, and found one of five feet in diameter. Many of them were hollow – many looked as if half-burnt, and they were mostly of a dark color, but not so much as to prevent the bark, the burnt places, the rings, and the cracks in the wood from being clearly discernible. In some of the blocks appeared the most beautiful blending of agate and jasper colors; and, in others, which had yielded to the influence of the weather and fallen to pieces, there were bits so brilliantly tinted that if polished and set they would have made elegant ornaments; others, again, had not yet lost the original color of their wood, and looked so like decaying beams of deal that one felt tempted to convince oneself, by the touch, of their petrifaction. If you pushed these they fell into pieces that had the appearance of rotten planks. We collected small specimens of all these various kinds of fossil trees, and regretted that as our means of transport were so small we had to content ourselves with fragments, which certainly showed the variety of the petrifaction, but not the dimensions of the blocks.

We sought in vain for impressions of leaves and plants, and the only thing we found besides the trunks and blocks were the remains of some tree-like ferns, that we took at first for broken antlers of stags. We had to renounce our intention of making our way further to the south, along the river Secco, for we found its bed piled up more and more wildly with masses of earth and stones, and saw new chasms opening across our path. It was not without difficulty that we again made our way out of this rugged valley, and followed the track of our wagons along the high bank; but when, after a brisk ride of fourteen miles, we reached the encampment we found our tents pitched on a spot where it was evidently possible to cross to the other side of the Rio Secco; and we therefore proposed to undertake the task on the following morning with renewed strength. The evening, as usual, was cold, and so much the more disagreeable, as we were in want of fuel; for though there lay near us what looked like enormous masses of wood they were of the kind that one could only get a spark out of by means of a steel.

On the 2nd of December we managed to get down into the dry bed of the river – a laborious task, but effected without accident; and we then pursued our way along it for some distance further. All the way we went we saw in the side ravines, great heaps of petrifactions gleaming with such splendid colors that we could not resist the temptation to alight repeatedly and knock off a piece, now of crimson, now of golden yellow, and then another, glorious in many rainbow dyes.

Chapter XII

GLACIER
1854

from a report of James Doty
in Reports of Explorations and Surveys,
to Ascertain the Most Practicable and Economical
Route for a Railroad
from the Mississippi River to the Pacific Ocean, Vol. 1
by Isaac I. Stevens

This is another of the reports from the railroad surveys conducted by the federal government during 1853-54. The most far northern survey between the 47th and 49th degrees latitude was conducted by Isaac I. Stevens, who instructed James Doty to conduct a survey closest to the Canadian border at the 49th parallel. This took him to the region of Glacier, along the eastern side of the mountains, investigating Chief Mountain, a couple of mountain lakes, and Cut Bank Pass.

May 28 – . . . Immediately after passing this point, we obtained a view of the chief of King mountain (Chief Mountain), which is a bare rocky peak of a square form, standing at a distance of five or six miles from the main chain, and connected with it by a

One of James Alden's paintings of the Glacier region during the 1859 Boundary Survey along the 49th parallel.

high ridge wooded with pine. In seventeen miles came to a broad valley, the sides of which are wooded with pine and poplar; and in the bottom, five hundred feet below us, we saw the blue water of a mountain lake. This is the well-known Chief Mountain lake. (Lower St. Marys Lake?) *It takes its name from the Chief mountain, so called in honor of Mr. Roan, a gentleman who has been many years in charge of Edmonton House, a Hudson's Bay Company's post on the south fork of the Saskatchewan river. Descending into the valley, in four miles we reached the lake, and encamped in a beautiful prairie bordering it.*

May 29 – Moved up the lake three miles to its inlet, and encamped. In this camp we remained until June 5th, having been so unwell during that time as to be unable to travel, or do more than make short explorations and observe the latitude. . . .

Connected with Chief Mountain lake is another, three-fourths of a mile wide, and extending nine miles into the mountain in the form of a bow, and I therefore called it "Bow lake." (Upper St. Marys Lake?) *It is shut in by mountains coming close down to the water, and has no valley susceptible of cultivation. . . .*

Several lodges and numerous signs of Indians were seen in this vicinity, and I presume they were made by Kootenaies who come here stealthily to hunt. It was at first supposed that there must be a good pass in this vicinity, but a close examination satisfied me that such is not the case.

Numerous little streams emptying into these lakes are filled with beaver dams and beaver, this industrious animal having been left in quiet possession of this country since the low price of its fur has rendered it unprofitable to trap them. Elk, moose, and deer are abundant, and salmon trout of a large size are taken in the lakes. . . .

On the 8th we started on the return trip, striking for the Cut Bank river, but taking a course farther from the mountains than when coming up. . . .

On the 9th, left Cut Bank river and pursued the same route by which we came up, this being in fact the only route where the stream can be crossed in high water. Observed today great quantities of the camash, now in full bloom. It is a beautiful dark-blue flower, bell-shaped, and growing single on a stem ten to fifteen inches high. The camash is particularly abundant in the vicinity of Marias river, near the mountain. . . .

The next day was devoted to making further explorations of this pass. Following the old lodge trail, now no more than a narrow footpath – although the decayed stumps and trunks of trees clearly indicated that a broad road had once been cleared – in two miles found that the stream forked: keeping the left hand branch, came in six miles to where it forks in many branches, all heading in rugged mountains on the right hand, or north-west.

Doty continues south to an overlook of Marias Pass, just south of the present-day park, which A. W. Tinkham had explored the year before as part of the railroad survey. In time a railroad was built through this pass.

Chapter XIII

ORGAN PIPE CACTUS
1855

from "Report of Lieutenant N. Michler"
in Report on the United States and Mexican Boundary Survey
by William H. Emory

Previously, this same survey contained the Chandler report on Big Bend. Part of this same boundary survey later followed the revised boundary on the Arizona-Mexico border acquired by the Gadsden Purchase of 1853. First, Michler discusses the march from Fort Yuma east to the Mexican town of Sonoyta and their return. Later, after following the Gila river route to Tucson, his party heads south to the border then west again to the town of Sonoyta. These survey marches brought them to the Organ Pipe Cactus region near Sonoyta.

The road continues along the course of the subterranean stream until you reach the Rancho de Sonoyta, thirteen miles and a half further on. From the junction to within a short distance of this place, a heavy road of one hundred and thirty miles, you look on a desert country. Near Sonoyta it is well covered with mezquite timber; in the valley, to the east of the town, there is some salt grass; but to the west, as far as the Colorado, scarce a blade is to be seen. A dull, wide waste lies before you, interspersed with low sierras and mounds, covered with black, igneous rocks. The soil is a mixture of sand and gravel; the reflection from its white surface adds still greater torment to the intense and scorching heat of the sun. Well do I recollect the ride from Fort Yuma to Sonoyta and back, in the middle of August, 1855. It was the most dreary and tiresome I have ever experienced. Imagination cannot picture a more dreary, sterile country, and we named it the "Malpais." The burnt lime-like appearance of the soil is ever before you; the very stones look like the scoria of a furnace; there is no grass, and but a sickly vegetation, more unpleasant to the sight than the barren earth itself; scarce an animal to be seen – not even the wolf or the hare to attract the attention, and, save the lizard and the horned frog, naught to give life and animation to this region. The eye may watch in vain for the flight of a bird; to add to all is the knowledge that there is not one drop of water to be depended upon from Sonoyta to the Colorado or Gila. All traces of the road are sometimes erased by the high winds sweeping the unstable soil before them, but death has strewn a continuous line of bleached bones and withered carcasses of horses and cattle, as monuments to mark the way. . . .

Later in the year, Michler's party is coming from the east following the boundary line and monuments set up along the way. They pass the prominent peak of Baboquivari and eventually into the Organ Pipe Cactus region, following a scouting party send ahead.

The town of Sonoyta is the door of the State of Sonora, from the California side. It is a resort for smugglers, and a den for a number of low, abandoned Americans, who have been compelled to fly from justice. Some few Mexican rancheros had their cattle in the valley near by. It is a miserable poverty-stricken place, and contrasts strangely with the comparative comfort of an Indian village of Papagos within sight.

The Papagos wander over the country from San Javier as far west as the Tinajas Altas. They were at one time a formidable tribe, and waged unceasing war against the Mexicans. Having sustained repeated losses, they at length sought their God, who is said to dwell upon the high peak of Babuquivari, to ask his aid and countenance in their last grand fight with their enemies. They assembled their families and herds of horses and cattle within an amphitheatre enclosed by the mountain ridges, and battled it manfully for many days at its entrance; but their God could not turn the fate of war, and they suffered an overpowering defeat; since that time they have been quiet and peaceable.

. . . North of Sonoyta, and about forty miles distant, is a rugged serrated range of mountains called "Sierra del Ajo" (now within Organ Pipe Cactus), represented to be rich in copper, gold and silver. A company was engaged in attempts at mining, but, from the scarcity of water, with little hopes of success. The great distance necessary to transport the ore on pack-mules before reaching navigation, will render their efforts futile and unprofitable.

Chapter XIV

MOUNT RAINIER
1857

from "Ascent of Mount Rainier"
in The Overland Monthly, May 1875
by Lt. Col. A. V. Kautz

The following article relates the failed attempt of the author and
his party to ascend the peak on a private excursion of soldiers from a
fort in Washington Territory. The article appeared in 1875 and the
author was evidently unaware that the mountain had been successfully
ascended in 1870.

*In the summer of 1857 I was stationed at Fort Steilacoom,
Washington Territory. This post was located near the village of
Steilacoom, on the waters of Puget Sound. . . .*

*I was at that time a first-lieutenant, young, and fond of visiting
unexplored sections of the country, and possessed of a very prevailing passion for going to the tops of high places. My quarters
fronted Mount Rainier, which is about sixty miles nearly east of
Fort Steilacoom in an air line. On a clear day it does not look
more than ten miles off, and looms up against the eastern sky
white as the snow with which it is covered, with a perfectly
pyramidal outline, except at the top, which is slightly rounded
and broken. It is a grand and inspiring view, and I had
expressed so often my determination to make the ascent, without doing it, that my fellow officers finally became incredulous,
and gave to all improbable and doubtful events a date of occurrence when I should ascend Mount Rainier.*

*My resolution, however, took shape and form about the first of
July. . . . I made preparations after the best authorities I could
find, from reading accounts of the ascent of Mont Blanc and
other snow mountains. We made for each member of the party
an alpenstock of dry ash with an iron point. We sewed upon our
shoes an extra sole, through which were first driven four-penny
nails with the points broken off and the heads inside. We took*

with us a rope about fifty feet long, a hatchet, a thermometer, plenty of hard biscuit, and dried beef such as the Indians prepare.

Information relating to the mountain was exceedingly meagre; no white man had ever been near it, and Indians were very superstitious and afraid of it. The southern slope seemed the least abrupt, and in that direction I proposed to reach the mountain; but whether to keep the high ground, or follow some stream to its source, was a question. Leshi, the chief of the Nesquallies, was at that time in the guard-house, awaiting his execution, and as I had greatly interested myself to save him from his fate, he volunteered the information that the valley of the Nesqually River was the best approach after getting above the falls. He had some hope that I would take him as a guide; but finding that out of the question, he suggested Wah-pow-e-ty, an old Indian of the Nesqually tribe, as knowing more about the Nesqually than any other of his people. . . .

About noon on the 8ᵗʰ of July we finally started. The party consisted of four soldiers – two of them equipped to ascend the mountain, and the other two to take care of our horses when we should be compelled to leave them. We started the soldiers on the direct route, with orders to stop at Mr. Wren's, on the eastern limit of the Nesqually plains, ten or twelve miles distant, and wait for us, while the doctor and I went by the Nesqually Reservation in order to pick up old Wah-pow-e-ty, the Indian guide.

We remained all night at Wren's, and the next morning entered that immense belt of timber with which the western slope of the Cascade Range is covered throughout its entire length. . . .

. . . We calculated to be gone about six days. Each member of the party had to carry his own provisions and bedding; everything was therefore reduced to the minimum. Each took a blanket, twenty-four crackers of hard bread, and about two pounds of dried beef. We took Dogue (a German) and Carroll (an Irishman) with us; they were both volunteers for the trip; one carried the hatchet and the other the rope. I carried a field-glass, thermometer, and a large-sized revolver. Wah-pow-e-ty carried his rifle, with which we hoped to procure some game. The sol-

diers carried no arms. Bell and Doneheh were left behind to take care of the horses and extra provisions, until our return.

We each had a haversack for our provisions, and a tin canteen for water. The doctor very unwisely filled his with whisky instead of water. . . .

We did not get started until about eleven o'clock on the fourth morning. After cutting up a deer which Wah-pow-e-ty brought in early in the morning, we dried quite a quantity of it by the fire. As we anticipated, it proved of much assistance, for we already saw that six days would be a very short time in which to make the trip. By night we reached a muddy tributary coming in from the north, and evidently having its source in the melting snows of Rainier. The summit of the mountain was visible from our camp, and seemed close at hand; but night set in with promise of bad weather. . . . Our camp was at the foot of a mountain spur several thousand feet high, and the river close at hand. The gloomy forest, the wild mountain scenery, the roaring of the river, and the dark overhanging clouds, with the peculiar melancholy sighing which the wind makes through a fir forest, gave to our camp at this point an awful grandeur.

On the fifth morning the clouds were so threatening, and came down so low on the surrounding mountains, that we were at a loss what course to pursue – whether to follow up the main stream or the tributary at our camp, which evidently came from the nearest snow. We finally followed the main stream, which very soon turned in toward the mountain, the valley growing narrower, the torrent more and more rapid, and our progress slower and slower, especially when we were compelled to take to the timber. We often crossed the torrent, of which the water was intensely cold, in order to avoid the obstructions of the forest. Sometimes, however, the stream was impassable, and then we often became so entangled in the thickets as almost to despair of farther advance. Early in the evening we reached the foot of an immense glacier and camped. For several miles before camping the bed of the stream was paved with white granite bowlders, and the mountain gorge became narrower and narrower. The walls were in many places perpendicular precipices, thousands of feet high, their summits hid in the clouds. Vast piles of snow were to be seen along the stream – the remains of avalanches – for earth, trees, and rocks were inter-mingled with snow.

As it was near night we camped, thinking it best to begin the ascent in the early morning; besides, the weather promised to become worse. The foliage of the pine-trees here was very dense, and on such a cloudy day it was dark as night in the forest. The limbs of the trees drooped upon the ground, a disposition evidently given to them by the snow, which must be late in disappearing in this region.

We followed thus far the main branch of the Nesqually, and here it emerged from an icy cavern at the foot of an immense glacier. The ice itself was of a dark-blue tinge. The water was white, and whenever I waded the torrent my shoes filled with gravel and sand. The walls of this immense mountain gorge were white granite, and, just where the glacier terminated, the immense vein of granite that was visible on both sides seemed to form a narrow throat to the great ravine, which is much wider both above and below. . . .

We made our camp under a pine of dense foliage, whose limbs at the outer end drooped near the ground. . . . Night set in with a drizzling rain, and a more solitary, gloomy picture than we presented at that camp it is impossible to conceive. Tired, hungry, dirty, clothes all in rags – the effects of our struggles with the brush – we were not the least happy; the solitude was oppressive. The entire party, except myself, dropped down and did not move unless obliged to. I went up to the foot of the glacier, and explored a little before night set in. . . .

On the morning of the sixth day we set out again up the glacier. A drizzling rain prevailed through the night, and continued this morning. We had a little trouble in getting upon the glacier, as it terminated everywhere in steep faces that were very difficult to climb. Once up, we did not meet with any obstructions or interruptions for several hours, although the slippery surface of the glacier, which formed inclined planes of about twenty degrees, made it very fatiguing with our packs. About noon the weather thickened; snow, sleet, and rain prevailed, and strong winds, blowing hither and thither, almost blinded us. The surface of the glacier, becoming steeper, began to be intersected by immense crevasses crossing our path, often compelling us to travel sev-

Returning was far easier and more rapid than going. The snow was much harder and firmer. We passed over in three hours, coming down, what required ten in going up. We were greatly fatigued by the day's toil, and the descent was not accomplished without an occasional rest of our weary limbs. In one place the snow was crusted over, and for a short distance the mountain was very steep, and required the skillful use of the stick to prevent our going much faster than we desired. The soldier lost his footing, and rolled helplessly to the foot of the declivity, thirty or forty yards distant, and his face bore the traces of the scratching for many a day after, as if he had been through a bramble-bush.

We found the Indian and Carroll in the camp. The latter had a long story to tell of his wanderings to find camp, and both stated that the fatigue was too much for them. There was no complaint on the part of any of us about the rarity of the atmosphere. The doctor attributed to this cause the fact that he could not go but a few yards at a time, near the summit, without resting; but I am inclined to think this was due to our exhaustion. My breathing did not seem to be the least affected.

We were much disappointed not to have had more time to explore the summit of the mountain. We had, however, demonstrated the feasibility of making the ascent. Had we started at dawn of day we should have had plenty of time for the journey. . . .

The night was very cold and clear after our return. We had some idea of making another ascent; but an investigation into the state of our provisions, together with the condition of the party generally, determined us to begin our return on the morning of the eighth day. The two soldiers had eaten all their bread but one cracker each. The doctor and I had enough left, so that by a redistribution we had four crackers each, with which to return over a space that had required seven days of travel coming. We, of course, expected to be a shorter time getting back; but let it be ever so short, our prospect for something to eat was proportionately much more limited. We had more meat than bread, thanks to the deer the Indian had killed, and we depended greatly on his killing more game for us going back. But this dependence, too, was cut off; the Indian was snow-blind, and needed our help to guide him. His groans disturbed us during the night, and what was our astonishment in the morning to find his eyelids closed with inflammation, and so swollen that he looked as if he had been in a free fight and got the worst of it. He could not have told a deer from a stump the length of his little old rifle. . . .

As we returned we had more leisure to examine and clearer weather to see the glacier than we had coming up. . . .

The noise produced by the glacier was startling and strange. One might suppose the mountain was breaking loose, particularly at night. Although, so far as stillness was concerned, there was no difference between day and night, at night the noise seemed more terrible. It was a fearful crashing and grinding that was going on. . . .

The great stillness and solitude were also very oppressive; no familiar sounds; nothing except the whistle of the animal before mentioned and the noise of the glacier's motion was to be heard, and if these had not occurred at intervals the solitude would have been still more oppressive. We were glad to get down again to the Nesqually, where we could hear its roar and see its rushing waters. The other members of the party were so tired and worn, however, that they seemed to observe but little, and as we were now on our homeward way, their thoughts were set only on our camp on the Mishawl, with its provisions and promise of rest. . . .

Exhausted and starving, clothes in rags, and seriously ill, the party returns to the military post on the eleventh day.

Chapter XV

GRAND CANYON
1858

from Report upon the Colorado River of the West
by Lt. Joseph C. Ives

In late 1857, Lt. Joseph Ives assembled his group at the mouth of the Colorado River. They made the very difficult ascent by steamboat up the river until they reached the extreme western end of the Grand Canyon (today under Lake Mead) in March of 1858. The purposes of the expedition were both scientific and military – to study the geology and open a transportation route by way of the Colorado River. The first was successful, but the second was bound to fail and did. The illustrations in the report by Edward Mollhausen and F.W. Egloffstein, and even some references in the text, echo Gustave Dore's illustrations of the inferno in the *Divine Comedy* and *Paradise Lost*, perhaps capturing the mood of the party rather than the realistic features of the landscape. Others had earlier seen the canyon from the rim, back to the time of Spanish explorers like Cardenas and Garces. An American fur trapper, James O. Pattie, had also followed along the rim in 1831. The Ives expedition appears to be the first to explore its depths.

Camp 53, Round island, March 1 – We have now entered a region that has never, as far as any records show, been visited by whites, and are approaching a locality where it is supposed that the famous "Big Cañon" of the Colorado commences; every point of the view is scanned with eager interest. We can distinctly see to the north the steep wall of one side of the gorge where the Colorado breaks through the Black mountains. Whether this is the "Big Cañon" or not it is certainly of far grander proportions than any which we have thus far traversed.

At the head of the Cottonwood valley we threaded a canon, formed by the passage of the river through a spur that connects the Black and Dead mountain ranges. It was only two or three miles in extent, and the sides were of moderate height, but the gorgeous contrast and intensity of color exhibited upon the rocks exceeded in beauty anything that had been witnessed of a similar character. Various and vivid tints of blue, brown, white, purple, and crimson, were blended with exquisite shading upon the gateways and inner walls, producing effects so novel and surprising as to make the cañon, in some respects, the most picturesque and striking of any of these wonderful mountain passes. . . . .

Camp 57, mouth of Black cañon, March 8 – Between Mount Davis and the Black mountains the river flows between gravel bluffs and the foot-hills of the latter chain. The view in all directions was intercepted, and before we were conscious of its neighborhood a sudden turn around the base of a conical peak disclosed the southern portal of the Black cañon directly in front. The Black mountains were piled overhead in grand confusion, and through a narrow gateway flanked by walls many hundreds of feet in height, rising perpendicularly out of the water, the Colorado emerged from the bowels of the range.

A rapid, a hundred yards below the mouth of the cañon, created a short detention, and a strong head of steam was put on to make the ascent. After passing the crest the current became slack, the soundings were unusually favorable, and we were shooting swiftly past the entrance, eagerly gazing into the mysterious depths beyond, when the Explorer, with a stunning crash, brought up abruptly and instantaneously against a sunken rock. For a second the impression was that the cañon had fallen in. The concussion was so violent that the men near the bow were thrown overboard; the doctor, Mr. Mollhausen, and myself, having been seated in front of the upper deck, were precipitated head foremost into the bottom of the boat; the fireman, who was pitching a log into the fire, went half-way in with it; the boiler was thrown out of place; the steampipe doubled up; the wheel-house torn away; and it was expected that the boat would fill and sink instantly by all, but Mr. Carroll, who was looking for an explosion from the injured steam pipes. Finding, after a few moments had passed, that she still floated, Captain Robinson had a line taken into the skiff, and the steamer was towed alongside of a gravelly spit a little below; it was then ascertained that the stem of the boat, where the iron flanges of the two bow sections were joined, had struck fair upon the rock, and that, although the flanges were torn away, no hole had been made, and the hull was uninjured. The other damages were such as a day or two of labor could repair. . . . .

Nearly three days have elapsed since the accident, and everything is restored to its former condition. I have thought it would be imprudent, after this experience of sunken rocks, to attempt the passage of the cañon without making a preliminary reconnaissance in the skiff. A second escape of the boat, in the event of a similar encounter with a rock, would be too much to hope for; and should she be sunk in the cañon, and there be nothing to swim to but perpendicular walls five hundred or a thousand feet high, the individuals on board would be likely to share the fate of the steamer. The carpenter has been working at the skiff, to put it in a more serviceable condition, and two or three oars have been mended; tomorrow the captain, the mate, and myself, are going to make an attempt to ascend the cañon. . . .

Camp 59, head of Black cañon, March 10 – The skiff having been put in tolerable order, a bucket full of corn and beans, three pairs of blankets, a compass, and a sextant and chronometer were stowed away in it, and a little before sunrise the captain, mate, and myself commenced the exploration of the cañon. My companions each pulled a pair of sculls, and with considerable vigor; but as the current has a flow of three miles an hour we could not make rapid progress. We had proceeded a quarter of a mile, and had just rounded the first bend, when one of the sculls snapped, reducing by half our motive power. There was, fortunately, a current of air drawing in the right direction through the narrow gorge, and, with the odd scull and a blanket, an apology for a sail was rigged, which, at intervals, rendered great assistance.

In a few minutes, having passed what may be called the outworks of the range, we fairly entered its gigantic precincts, and commenced to thread the mazes of a cañon, far exceeding in vastness any that had been yet traversed. The walls were perpendicular, and more than double the height of those in the Mojave mountains, rising, in many places, sheer from the water, for over a thousand feet. The naked rocks presented, in lieu of the brilliant tints that had illuminated the sides of the lower passes, a uniform somber hue, that added much to the solemn and impressive sublimity of the place. The river was narrow and devious, and each turn disclosed new combinations of colossal and fantastic forms, dimly seen in the dizzy heights overhead, or through the sunless depths of the vista beyond. With every mile the view became more picturesque and imposing, exhibiting the same romantic effects and varied transformations that were displayed in the Mojave cañon, but on an enlarged and grander scale.

Rapids were of frequent occurrence, and at every one we were obliged to get out of the skiff, and haul it over. Eight miles from the mouth of the cañon, a loud sullen roaring betokened that something unusual was ahead, and a rapid appeared which was undoubtedly the same that had been described by Ireteba (an Indian guide). *Masses of rock filled up the sides of the channel. In the centre, at the foot of the rapid, and rising five feet above the surface of the water, was a pyramidal rock, against which the billows dashed as they plunged down from above, and glanced upwards, like a water spout.* . . .

Several rapids followed, at short distances, all of which would be troublesome to pass at the present depth of water. The constant getting out of the boat, and the labor of dragging it through these difficult places, made our progress for some miles exceedingly tedious and fatiguing. As sunset was approaching we came to a nook in the side of the cañon, four miles above the Roaring rapid, where a patch of gravel and a few pieces of driftwood, lodged upon the rocks, offered a tolerable camping place, and we hauled the skiff upon the shingle, and stopped for the night. There was no need of keeping a watch, with two grim lines of sentinels, a thousand feet high, guarding the camp. Even though we could have been seen from the verge of the cliff above, our position was totally inaccessible. . . .

This morning, as soon as the light permitted, we were again upon our way. The ascent of the river was attended with as much labor as it had been the day before; for though none of the rapids were of so violent a character, they were of constant occurrence. The wind still held to the south, and the blanket sail was again set to great advantage.

The cañon continued increasing in size and magnificence. No description can convey an idea of the varied and majestic grandeur of this peerless water-way. Wherever the river makes a turn the entire panorama changes, and one startling novelty after another appears and disappears with bewildering rapidity. Stately facades, august cathedrals, ampitheatres, rotundas, castellated walls, and rows of time-stained ruins, surmounted by every form of tower, minaret, dome, and spire, have been moulded from the cyclopean masses of rock that form the mighty defile. The solitude, the stillness, the subdued light, and the vastness of every surrounding object, produce an impression of awe that ultimately becomes almost painful. As hour after hour passed we began to look anxiously ahead for some sign of an outlet from the range, but the declining day brought only fresh piles of mountains, higher, apparently, than any before seen. We had made up our minds to pass another night in the cañon, and were searching for a spot large enough to serve as a resting-place, when we came into a narrow passage, between two mammoth peaks, that seemed to be nodding to each other across the stream, and unexpectedly found, at the upper end, the termination of the Black cañon.

Low hills of gravel intercepted the view, and prevented us from seeing far into the unknown region beyond. A mile above the cañon the river swept the base of a high hill, with salient angles, like the bastions of a fort. At the base was a little ravine, which offered a camping place that would be sheltered from observation, and we drew the skiff out of the water, determining not to proceed any further till tomorrow. Leaving the mate to take charge of the boat, the captain and myself ascended the hill, which is over a thousand feet high. A scene of barren and desolate confusion was spread before us. We seemed to have reached the focus or culminating point of the volcanic distur-bances that have left their traces over the whole region south. In almost every direction were hills and mountains heaped together without any apparent system or order. A small open area intervened between camp and a range to the north, and we could trace the course of the river as it wound towards the east, forming the Great Bend. In the direction of the Mormon road to Utah, which is but twenty miles distant, the country looked less broken, and it was evident that there would be no difficulty in opening a wagon communication between the road and the river. We tried to discover the valley of the Virgen, but could see no indication of any stream coming in from the northwest. The view in that direction was partially obstructed by another sum-mit of Fortification Rock.

Not a trace of vegetation could be discovered, but the glaring monotony of the rocks was somewhat relieved by grotesque and fanciful varieties of coloring. The great towers that formed the *northern gateway of the cañon were striped with crimson and yellow bands; the gravel bluffs bordering the river exhibited brilliant alternations of the same hues, and not far to the east, mingled with the gray summits, were two or three hills, altogether of a blood-red color, that imparted a peculiarly ghastly air to the scene.*

The approach of darkness stopped further observations, and we descended to camp, having first taken a good look, in every direction, for the smoke of Indian camp-fires, but without discovering any. In making the sixteen miles from last night's bivouac, we have had to labor hard for thirteen hours, stemming the strong current, and crossing the numerous rapids, and being thoroughly exhausted, depend for security tonight more upon our concealed position than upon any vigilance that is likely to be exhibited.

Camp 57, foot of Black cañon, March 12 – Skirting the base of Fortification Rock, we ascended the river a couple of miles, and came to the mouth of a stream about the size of Bill Williams' Fork, as the latter was when we passed it. We disembarked, and followed for some distance along its border. The appearance of the bed and the banks indicated the existence, during some seasons, of a wide and deep river. It was now but a few inches deep. The water was clear, and had a strong brackish taste. This fact, and its position, led me to suppose that we were at the mouth of the Virgen, but I could scarcely believe that the river could ever present so insignificant an appearance.

I now determined not to try to ascend the Colorado any further. The water above the Black Cañon had been shoal, and the current swift. Rapids had occurred in such quick succession as to make navigation almost impossible, and there would be no object in proceeding beyond the Great Bend. The difficulties encountered in the cañon were of a character to prevent a steamboat from attempting to traverse it at low water, and we had seen driftwood lodged in clefts fifty feet above the river, betokening a condition of things during the summer freshet that would render navigation more hazardous at that season than now. It appeared, therefore, that the foot of the Black Cañon should be considered the practical head of navigation, and I concluded to have a reconnaissance made to connect that point with the Mormon road, and to let this finish the exploration of the navigable portion of the Colorado.

The ascent of the Colorado River had to be abandoned, of course, although Ives suggests that a combination of the lower Colorado with the Mormon road opens up the country into Utah. There were tensions at the time between the United States and the Mormon kingdom of Zion; in fact, war was just barely averted in 1858. Ives may have been thinking of this when suggesting an alternate route into Utah. Nevertheless, Ives now turned back and divided his party. One descended the river back to Ft. Yuma near the mouth of the Colorado River, while he led a party by land around the southern rim of the Grand Canyon. This would involve a couple of excursions down side canyons to the canyon floor.

Camp 67, Big Cañon of the Colorado, April 3 – The two Hualpais preserved the credit of the Indian employees by being punctual to their engagement, and led off in company with the Mojaves as we ascended the ravine from Peacock's spring. It was a cool lovely morning, and a favorable day for travel. After proceeding a mile or two we issued from the hills and entered a region totally different from any that had been seen during the expedition. A broad table-land, unbroken by the volcanic hills that had overspread the country since leaving Fort Yuma, extended before us, rising in a gradual swell towards the north. The road become hard and smooth, and the plain was covered with excellent grass. Herds of antelope and deer were seen bounding over the slopes. Groves of cedar occurred, and with every mile became more frequent and of larger size. At the end of ten miles the ridge of the swell was attained, and a splendid panorama burst suddenly into view. In the foreground were low table-hills, intersected by numberless ravines; beyond these a lofty line of bluffs marked the edge of an immense cañon; a wide gap was directly ahead, and through it were beheld, to the extreme limit of vision, vast plateaus, towering one above the other thousands of feet in the air, the long horizontal bands broken at intervals by wide and profound abysses, and extending a hundred miles to the north, till the deep azure blue faded into a light cerulean tint that blended with the dome of the heavens. The famous "Big Cañon" was before us; and for a long time we paused in wondering delight, surveying that stupendous formation through which the Colorado and its tributaries break their way. . . .

Our guides, becoming impatient of the detention, plunged into a narrow and precipitous ravine that opened at our feet, and we followed as well as we could, stumbling along a rough and rocky pathway. The Hualpais were now of great assistance, for the ravines crossed and forked in intricate confusion; even Ireteba, who had hitherto lead the train, became at a loss how to proceed, and had to put the little Hualpais in front. The latter, being perfectly at home, conducted us rapidly down the declivity. The descent was great and the trail blind and circuitous. A few miles of difficult traveling brought us into a narrow valley flanked by steep and high slopes; a sparkling stream crossed its centre, and a gurgling in some tall grass near by announced the presence of a spring. The water was delicious. The grass in the neighborhood was sparse, but of good quality.

This morning we left the valley and followed the course of a creek down a ravine, in the bed of which the water at intervals sank and rose for two or three miles, when it altogether disappeared. The ravine soon attained the proportions of a cañon. The bottom was rocky and irregular, and there were some jump-offs over which it was hard to make the pack animals pass. The vegetation began to disappear, leaving only a few stunted cedars projecting from the sides of the rugged bluffs. The place grew wilder and grander. The sides of the tortuous cañon became loftier, and before long we were hemmed in by walls two thousand feet high. The scenery much resembled that in the Black Cañon, excepting that the rapid descent, the increasing magnitude of the colossal piles that blocked the end of the vista, and the corresponding depth and gloom of the gaping chasms into which we were plunging, imparted an unearthly character to a way that might have resembled the portals of the infernal regions. Harsh screams issuing from aerial recesses in the cañon sides and apparitions of goblin-like figures perched in the rifts and hollows of the impending cliffs, gave an odd reality to this impression. At short distances other avenues of equally magnificent proportions came in from one side or the other; and no trail being left on the rocky pathway, the idea suggested itself that were the guides to desert us our experience might further resemble that of the dwellers in the unblest abodes –in the difficulty of getting out. . . .

Camp 69, Cedar Forest, April 5 – A short walk down the bed of Diamond river, on the morning after we had reached it, verified

*the statement of Ireteba, and disclosed the famous Colorado
cañon. The view from the ridge, beyond the creek to which the
Hualpais had first conducted us, had shown that the plateaus
further north and east were several thousand feet higher than
that through which the Colorado cuts at this point, and the
cañons proportionately deeper; but the scene was sufficiently
grand to well repay for the labor of the descent. The cañon was
similar in character to others that have been mentioned, but on
a larger scale, and thus far unrivalled in grandeur. Mr. Mollhausen has taken a sketch, which gives a better idea of it than
any description. The course of the river could be traced for only
a few hundred yards, above or below, but what had been seen
from the tableland showed that we were at the apex of a great
southern bend. The walls, on either side, rose directly out of the
water. The river was about fifty yards wide. The channel was
studded with rocks, and the torrent rushed through like a mill-
race. . . .*

Eventually, they ascend back out of the canyon onto the plateau.
They are abandoned by their Hualpais guides and sometimes lose their
way. Ascending into an even higher tableland, they wait out a terrific
storm of wind and sleet.

*Our altitude is very great. During the last march the ascent was
continuous, and the barometer shows an elevation of nearly
seven thousand feet. A still higher plateau rises towards the
north. The cañon Colorado is not far distant, and we must be
opposite to the most stupendous part of the "Big Cañon." The
bluffs are in view, but the intervening country is cut up by side
cañons and cross ravines, and no place has yet been seen that
presents a favorable approach to the gigantic chasm.*

Their journey now takes them away from the main chasm of the
Grand Canyon of the Colorado and toward the narrower chasm of the
Little Colorado, where they make a dramatic descent.

*Camp 73, Colorado plateau, April 12 – Two miles beyond the
snow camp some lagoons were discovered – one of them large
enough to be called a pond. I recognized the place as having
been described by the Hualpais to Ireteba, but of the position I
had not been able to form a correct idea. As we advanced
towards the northeast, long undulating swells followed each
other and intercepted the view. The snow storm had extended*

over but a limited area, and the road, at first heavy, in the course of an hour or two became dry and good. The pines disappeared, and the cedars gradually diminished. To our regret the patches of grass also were less frequently met with, and the little seen was of poor quality. Each slope surmounted disclosed a new summit similar to that just passed, till the end of ten miles, when the highest part of the plateau was attained, and a sublime spectacle lay spread before us.

Towards the north was the field of plateaus and cañons, already seen and described, and shooting out from these a line of magnificent bluffs, extending eastward an enormous distance, marked the course of the cañon of the Little Colorado. Further south, eighty miles distant, towered the vast pile of the San Francisco mountain, its conical summit covered with snow, and sharply defined against the sky. Several other peaks were visible a little to the right, and half way between us and this cluster of venerable and mighty volcanoes was the "Red Butte," described by Lieutenant Whipple, standing in isolated prominence upon the level plain. On the north side of the Colorado appeared a short range of mountains, close to the cañon, which had been previously hidden by the intervening plateaus.

A march of twenty miles having been made, and no sign of water appearing, we had to put up with a dry camp. The grass was miserable, and altogether the mules fared badly. During the night the herders were negligent, and at daybreak nearly a hundred of the animals were missing. They had taken the back trail for the lagoons, but having started late and traveled leisurely were overtaken not many miles from camp. The trip did not render them better fitted for the day's journey, which had to be delayed until they were brought back.

The sun was oppressively warm, and every place whose appearance gave promise of water was carefully searched, but without success. Ten miles conducted us to the head of a ravine, down which was a well-beaten Indian trail. There was every prospect therefore that we were approaching a settlement similar to that of the Hualpais, on Diamond river. The descent was more rapid than the former had been, and in the course of a few miles we had gone down into the plateau one or two thousand feet, and the bluff on either side had assumed stupendous proportions. Still no signs of habitations were visible. The worn-out and

*thirsty beasts had begun to flag, when we were brought to a
standstill by a fall a hundred feet deep in the bottom of the
cañon. At the brink of the precipice was an overhanging ledge
of rocks, from which we could look down as into a well upon the
continuation of the gorge far below. The break reached completely across the ravine, and the side walls were nearly perpendicular. There was no egress in that direction, and it seemed
a marvel that a trail should be found leading to a place where
there was nothing to do but to return. A closer inspection
showed that the trail still continued along the cañon, traversing
horizontally the face of the right hand bluff. A short distance off
it seemed as though a mountain goat could scarcely keep its
footing upon the slight indentation that appeared like a thread
attached to the rocky wall, but a trial proved that the path,
though narrow and dizzy, had been cut with some care into the
surface of the cliff, and afforded a foothold level and broad
enough both for men and animals. I rode upon it first, and the
rest of the party and the train followed – one by one – looking
very much like a row of insects crawling upon the side of a
building. We proceeded for nearly a mile along this singular
pathway, which preserved its horizontal direction. The bottom
of the cañon meanwhile had been rapidly descending, and there
were two or three falls where it dropped a hundred feet at a
time, thus greatly increasing the depth of the chasm. The
change had taken place so gradually that I was not sensible of
it, till glancing down the side of my mule I found that he was
walking within three inches of the brink of a sheer gulf a thousand feet deep; on the other side, nearly touching my knee, was
an almost vertical wall rising to an enormous altitude. The
sight made my head swim, and I dismounted and got ahead of
the mule, a difficult and delicate operation, which I was thankful to have safely performed. A part of the men became so giddy
that they were obliged to creep upon their hands and knees,
being unable to walk or stand. In some places there was barely
room to walk, and a slight deviation in a step would have precipitated one into the frightful abyss. I was a good deal alarmed
lest some obstacle should be encountered that would make it
impossible to go ahead, for it was certainly impracticable to
return. After an interval of uncomfortable suspense the face of
the rock made an angle, and just beyond the turn was a projection from the main wall with a surface fifteen or twenty yards
square that would afford a foothold. The continuation of the
wall was perfectly vertical, so that the trail could no longer fol-*

*low it, and we found that the path descended the steep face of
the cliff to the bottom of the cañon. It was a desperate road to
traverse, but located with a good deal of skill – zigzagging
down the precipice, and taking advantage of every crevice and
fissure that could afford a foothold. It did not take long to discover that no mule could accomplish this descent, and nothing
remained but to turn back. We were glad to have even this priv-
ilege in our power. The jaded brutes were collected upon the little summit where they could be turned around, and then
commenced to re-perform the hazardous journey. The sun shone
directly into the cañon, and the glare reflected from the walls
made the heat intolerable. The disappointed beasts, now two
days without water, with glassy eyes and protruding tongues,
plodded slowly along, uttering the most melancholy cries. The
nearest water, of which we had knowledge, was almost thirty
miles distant. There was but one chance of saving the train, and
after reaching an open portion of the ravine the packs and the
saddles were removed, and two or three Mexicans started for
the lagoons mounted upon the least exhausted animals, and
driving the others loose before them. It was somewhat dangerous to detach them thus far from the main party, but there was
no help for it. Some of the mules will doubtless give out before
the night march is over, but the knowledge that they are on their
way to water will enable most of them to reach it in spite of
their weariness and the length of the way. . . .*

*Camp 73, Colorado plateau, April 14 – Lieutenant Tipton, Mr.
Egloffstein, Mr. Peacock, and myself, with a dozen men, formed
the party to explore the cañon. It was about five miles to the
precipice. The descent of the latter was accomplished without
serious trouble. In one or two places the path traversed smooth
inclined ledges, where the insecure footing made the crossing
dangerous. The bottom of the cañon, which from the summit
looked smooth, was covered with hills, thirty or forty feet high.
Along the centre we were surprised to find an inner cañon, a
kind of under cellar, with low walls at the starting point, which
were soon converted into lofty precipices, as the base of the
ravine sank deeper and deeper into the earth. Along the bottom
of this gorge we followed the trail, distinctly seen when the surface was not covered with rocks. Every few moments, low falls
and ledges, which we had to jump or slide down, were met with,
till there had accumulated a formidable number of obstacles to
be encountered in returning. Like other cañons, it was circui-*

tous, and at each turn we were impatient to find something novel or interesting. We were deeper in the bowels of the earth than we had ever been before, and surrounded by walls and towers of such imposing dimensions that it would be useless to attempt describing them; but the effects of magnitude had begun to pall, and the walk from the foot of the precipice was monotonously dull; no sign of life could be discerned above or below. At the end of thirteen miles from the precipice an obstacle presented itself that there seemed to be no possibility of overcoming. A stone slab, reaching from one side of the cañon to the other, terminated the plane which we were descending. Looking over the edge it appeared that the next level was forty feet below. This time there was no trail along the side bluffs, for these were smooth and perpendicular. A spring of water rose from the bed of the cañon not far above, and trickled over the ledge, forming a pretty cascade. It was supposed that the Indians must have come to this point merely to procure water, but this theory was not altogether satisfactory, and we sat down upon the rocks to discuss the matter.

Mr. Egloffstein lay down by the side of the creek, and projecting his head over the ledge to watch the cascade, discovered a solution to the mystery. Below the shelving rock, and hidden by it and the fall, stood a crazy looking ladder, made of rough sticks bound together with thongs of bark. It was almost perpendicular, and rested upon a bed of angular stones. The rounds had become rotten from the incessant flow of water. Mr. Egloffstein, anxious to have the first view of what was below, scrambled over the ledge and got his feet upon the upper round. Being a solid weight, he was too much for the insecure fabric, which commenced giving away. One side fortunately stood firm, and holding on to this with a tight grip, he made a precipitate descent. The other side and all the rounds broke loose and accompanied him to the bottom in a general crash, effectually cutting off the communication. Leaving us to devise means of getting him back, he ran to the bend to explore. The bottom of the cañon had been reached. He found that he was at the edge of a stream, ten or fifteen yards wide, fringed with cottonwoods and willows. The walls of the cañon spread out for a short distance, leaving room for a narrow belt of bottom land, on which were fields of corn and a few scattered huts.

A place was found near the ledge where one could clamber a little way up the wall, and we thus got a view of the valley. The river was nearly as large as the Gila at low water, and, with the exception of that stream, the most important tributary of the Colorado between its mouth and our position. The cañon Mr. Egloffstein saw could not be followed far; there were cascades just below. He perceived, however, that he was very near to its mouth, though perhaps a thousand feet greater altitude, and an Indian pointed out the exact spot where it united with the cañon of the Rio Colorado. . . .

Having looked at all that was to be seen, it now remained to get Mr. Egloffstein back. The slings upon the soldiers' muskets were taken off and knotted together, and a line thus made which reached to the bottom. Whether it would support his weight was a matter of experiment. The general impression was that it would not, but of the two evils – breaking his neck or remaining among the Yampais – he preferred the former, and fastened the strap around his shoulders. It was a hard straight lift. The ladder pole was left, and rendered great assistance both to us and the rope, and the ascent was safely accomplished. We invited the Indian to follow Mr. Egloffstein's example, but this he energetically declined. The examination being finished, it was time to return. On leaving camp we had expected to be back before night, and had brought along neither provisions nor overcoats. An hour or two earlier, finding that the day was rapidly slipping by, two of the party were directed to go back and tell those who had remained that we might be detained till the next day, and in that case to forward in the morning something to eat. We walked as fast as possible, in order to get out of the cañon before dark, but the ascent was laborious, and the trail, made in coming down over the rocks, difficult to follow. Numerous branch cañons, all looking alike, would have rendered it easy to become lost had the trail been once departed from. Night came before the foot of the precipice where the train had stopped was reached. It was impossible to distinguish the way in the dark, and we had to halt. A few minutes previously the tracks of the two men that had been sent ahead had been noticed diverging from the proper course, and it was concluded that they were wandering astray somewhere in the labyrinth. After nightfall, as is always the case in these regions, it became bleak and cold. Some of the party, attired for a walk under a hot sun, had not even their coats. The cañon was as dark as a dungeon. The sur-

*face of the ground being covered with rocks, a recumbent posi-
tion was uncomfortable, and the rocks being interspersed with
prickly pear and some other varieties of cactaceæ it would have
been unwise to walk about. The choice, therefore, lay between
sitting down and standing still, which two recreations we
essayed alternately for twelve hours that might have been, from
the sensations of the party, twelve days. As soon as it was light
enough to see the way we put our stiffened limbs in motion.
Climbing the precipice was severe work. The summit once
attained, it was but five miles to camp, but the violent exercise
of the ascent, coming after a twenty-four hours' abstinence
from food and rest, and a walk of more than thirty miles over a
difficult road, proved so exhausting that, during the last stretch,
two or three of the men broke down, and had to have coffee and
food sent back to them before they could proceed. . . .*

*The region east of camp has been examined today. The extent
and magnitude of the system of cañons in that direction is
astounding. The plateau is cut into shreds by these gigantic
chasms, and resembles a vast ruin. Belts of country miles in
width have been swept away, leaving only isolated mountains
standing in the gap. Fissures so profound that the eye cannot
penetrate their depths are separated by walls whose thickness
one can almost span, and slender spires that seem tottering
upon their bases shoot up thousands of feet from the vaults
below.*

*Towards the southeast, also, for a great distance, the surface is
furrowed by these abysses. They appear to extend nearly to the
San Francisco mountains, and bar all progress eastward.
Northward we can proceed no further, and the only course is to
go back to the nearest water as a starting point, and from
thence strike south, and, heading these formidable barriers,
cross Flax river, and again travel north upon the opposite side
of that stream.*

*The mules were brought back this evening; only two were lost;
the others reached the lagoon. Tomorrow morning we shall
return to that place, and after making an examination of the
cañons northwest of the trail proceed to follow the remaining
route now open to us.*

Camp 74, Forest lagoons, April 18 – Midway between the last camp and the lagoons, a trail was encountered leading towards another point of the Big Cañon. With a small detachment I left the main party and followed its course. It headed directly for the north side mountains – the peaks already spoken of as seen upon the opposite bank of the Colorado. We traveled till dark; the trail ended near some deserted huts that resembled those seen at the Yampais village; they were in the midst of a pine grove; there was no water in the neighborhood, and the Yampais, who doubtless make this place their summer resort, must be compelled to send to the bottom of the cañon for their supply.

The country became rough and so much cut up by ravines that it was impossible to approach very closely to the main river. A good view was obtained of the walls of the Flax river cañon, and its mouth approximately located. The junction was below the mouth of the Colorado, but of its smaller affluent.

We had to camp without water, and it being the second day that the animals had had nothing to drink, a great part of them broke from the herders as soon as their saddles were removed, and made a stampede for the lagoons. Barely enough were left to pack the few articles that had been brought.

Another reconnaissance has since been made on foot from the lagoons westward. A line thirty miles in extent was traversed, with results similar to those previously obtained. An excellent view was had of the Big Cañon. The barometric observations upon the surface of the plateau, and at the mouths of Diamond and Cataract rivers, showed that the walls of this portion of the cañon were over a mile high. The formation of the ground was such that the eye could not follow them the whole distance to the bottom, but as far down as they could be traced they appeared almost vertical. . . .

Our reconnoitering parties have now been out in all directions, and everywhere have been headed off by impassable obstacles. The positions of the main watercourses have been determined with considerable accuracy. The region last explored is, of course, altogether valueless. It can be approached only from the south, and after entering it there is nothing to do but to leave. Ours has been the first, and will doubtless be the last, party of whites to visit this profitless locality. It seems intended by nature that the Colorado river, along the greater portion of its lonely and majestic way, shall be forever unvisited and undisturbed.

The terrible chasm of the Civil War lies between them, but John Wesley Powell will begin his great adventure just eleven years later. Then Ives' last prophecy is proven untrue.

Chapter XVI

CANYONLANDS
1859

from Report of the Exploring Expedition
from Santa Fe, New Mexico, to the Junction of the Grand and
Green Rivers of the Great Colorado of the West, in 1859,
Under the Command of Capt. J. N. Macomb
by Prof. J. S. Newberry

The author of this report, John Newberry, accompanied both the
Ives expedition to the Grand Canyon and the Macomb expedition here
to the confluence of the Grand and Green Rivers. Starting from Santa
Fe, the group crossed southwestern Colorado and into eastern Utah,
which is where the excerpt begins. Note that the Cañon Colorado mentioned in the report is not meant to be the Colorado River itself, nor is
Labyrinth Cañon the one with the same name on the lower Green
River just above the Confluence. Rather, these are tributary canyons of
the Colorado the group follows through the northern reaches of the
Needles section of Canyonlands. Note, too, that in this time period
Grand River refers to the Colorado River above the Confluence. His is
the first written description of the intricate topography of needles,
buttes and mazelike canyons in the park. Although they were led to
believe that they were seeing the location of the Confluence from atop
the high butte (the ultimate goal of their journey), in later years it was
established by others that they were confused by the topography and
assurances of Indian guides.

*August 22 – Started this morning for the junction of Grand and
Green Rivers, Captain Macomb, Lieutenant Cogswell, Mr. Dim-
mock, Mr. Campean, myself, and three servants forming the
party. On leaving camp we struck southwest, gradually ascending for six miles, when we reached the brink of a magnificent
cañon twelve hundred feet in depth, called, from the prevailing
color of its walls, Cañon Colorado, into which with great difficulty we descended. . . . This part of the cañon is exceedingly
grand and beautiful, both from the form and coloring of its
walls. A few pinons and cedars cling to the sides and crown the
summits of the walls, while scattered cottonwoods and thickets*

of willow, with here and there a small tree of a new and peculiar species of ash, form a narrow thread of vegetation along its bottom. This, and many similar gorges, form the channels through which the drainage of the western slope of the Sierra Abajo reaches the Colorado. Twelve miles from the Ojo Verde the several cañons unite by the elimination of their dividing walls, and debouch into a comparatively open country. Descending the cañon we, therefore, at its mouth come out upon a third distinct plateau, from which the mesa cut by the Cañon Colorado had been removed; its edges receding in magnificent broken walls south and northwest. From this point the view swept westward over a wide extent of country, in its general aspects a plain, but everywhere deeply cut by a tangled maze of cañons, and thickly set with towers, castles, and spires of most varied and striking forms; the most wonderful monuments of erosion which our eyes, already experienced in objects of this kind, had beheld. Near the mesa we were leaving stand detached portions of it in every possible form, from broad, flat tables to slender cones crowned with pinnacles of the massive sandstone which forms the perpendicular faces of the walls of the Cañon Colorado. These castellated buttes are from one thousand to fifteen hundred feet in height, and no language is adequate to convey a just idea of the strange and impressive scenery formed by their grand and varied outlines. Toward the west the view reached some thirty miles, there bounded by long lines and bold angles of mesa walls similar to those behind us, while in the intervening space the surface was diversified by columns, spires, castles, and battlemented towers of colossal but often beautiful proportions, closely resembling elaborate structures of art, but in effect far surpassing the most imposing monuments of human skill. In the southwest was a long line of spires of white stone, standing on red bases, thousands in number, but so slender as to recall the most delicate carving in ivory or the fairy architecture of some Gothic cathedral; yet many, perhaps most, were over five hundred feet in height, and thickly set in a narrow belt or series some miles in length. Their appearance was so strange and beautiful as to call out exclamations of delight from all our party.

Next to the pinnacles the most striking objects in our view were buttes of dark, chocolate-covered rock, which had weathered into exact imitation of some of the feudal castles of the Old World; yet, like all the other features in the scene, they were on a gigantic scale. These buttes are composed of the liver-colored sandstones and chocolate shales of the walls of the Cañon Colorado, which consist of a great number of alternations of thinner or thicker layers of sandstone with those of shale. This structure in erosion gives rise to many curious and beautiful results, such as a beaded appearance in columns, while harder or thicker layers form their capitals and bases. It also produces what seem to be walls of masonry, with frieze and cornice.

Soon after issuing from the mouth of Cañon Colorado, the little intermittent stream which traverses it begins to cut the floor of the rocky plain that borders the Colorado River, and, following that stream as the only possible avenue through which we could reach our destination, we were soon buried in a deep and narrow gorge, which is thence continuous till it joins the greater cañon of Grand River. This cañon, from its many windings and the many branches which open into it, we designated by the name of Labyrinth Cañon. Its walls are from one to two hundred feet in height, so that there is no egress from it for many miles. The bottom is occupied with cottonwoods, and thickets of narrow-leaved willow, cane, and salt-bush; all of which, with fallen rocks, quicksands, and deep water-holes, made the passage through it almost impossible. Some two miles below the head of Labyrinth Cañon we came upon the ruins of a large number of houses of stone, evidently built by the Pueblo Indians, as they are similar to those on the Dolores, and the pottery scattered about is identical with that before found in so many places. It is very old but of excellent quality, made of red clay coated with white, and handsomely figured. Here the houses are built in the sides of the cliffs. A mile or two below we saw others crowning the inaccessible summits – inaccessible except by ladders – of picturesque detached buttes of red sandstone, which rise to the height of one hundred and fifty feet above the bottom of the cañon. Similar buildings were found lower down, and broken pottery was picked up upon the summits of the cliffs overhanging Grand River; evidence that these dreadful cañons were once the homes of families belonging to that great people formerly spread over all this region now so utterly sterile, solitary, and desolate. . . .

Descending the cañon till night came upon us, we made our camp under the overhanging cliffs on the north side, where some potholes in the rocky bottom promised us a supply of water.

August 23, Camp 29 to Grand River – Leaving servants and packs in camp, we today descended the Cañon of Labyrinth Creek, to its junction with Grand River. Until within a mile of the junction, the character of the cañon remains the same; a narrow gorge, with vertical sides, from 150 to 300 feet in height, its bottom thickly grown with bushes and obstructed with fallen rocks and timber, passable but with infinite difficulty. At the place mentioned above, however, our progress was arrested by a perpendicular fall, some 200 feet in height, occupying the whole breadth of the cañon, and to reach Grand River it was necessary to scale the walls which shut us in. This we accomplished with some difficulty on the south side, to find ourselves upon the level of the rocky plain into which we sunk when entering the cañon. The view we here obtained was most interesting, yet too limited to satisfy us. Looking down into the cañon we had been following, we could see it deepening by successive falls until, a mile below, it opened into the greater cañon of Grand River, a dark yawning chasm, with vertical sides, in which we caught glimpses of the river 1,500 feet below where we stood. On every side we were surrounded by columns, pinnacles, and castles of fantastic shapes, which limited our view, and by impassable cañons, which restricted our movements. South of us, about a mile distant, rose one of the castle-like buttes, which I have already mentioned, and to which, though with difficulty, we made our way. This butte was composed of alternate layers of chocolate-colored sandstone and shale, about 1,000 feet in height; its sides nearly perpendicular, but most curiously ornamented with columns and pilasters, porticos and colonnades, cornices and battlements, flanked here and there with tall outstanding towers, and crowned with spires so slender that it seemed as though a breath of air would suffice to topple them from their foundations. To accomplish the object for which we had come so far, it seemed necessary that we should ascend this butte. The day was perfectly clear and intensely hot; the mercury standing at 92° in the shade, and the red sandstone, out of which the landscape was carved, glowed in the heat of the burning sunshine. Stripping off nearly all our clothing, we made the attempt, and after two hours of most arduous labor succeeded in reaching the summit. The view which there burst upon us was such as amply repaid us for all our toil. It baffles description, however, and I can only hope that our sketches will give some faint idea of its strange and unearthly character.

The great cañon of the Lower Colorado, with its cliffs a mile in height, affords grander and more impressive scenes, but those having far less variety and beauty of detail than this. From the pinnacle on which we stood the eye swept over an area some fifty miles in diameter, everywhere marked by features of more than ordinary interest; lofty lines of massive mesas rising in successive steps to form the frame of the picture; the interval between them more than 2,000 feet below their summits. A great basin or sunken plain lay stretched out before us as on a map. Not a particle of vegetation was anywhere discernible; nothing but bare and barren rocks of rich and varied colors shimmering in the sunlight. Scattered over the plain were thousands of the fantastically formed buttes to which I have so often referred in my notes; pyramids, domes, towers, columns, spires, of every conceivable form and size. Among these by far the most remarkable was the forest of Gothic spires, first and imperfectly seen as we issued from the mouth of the Cañon Colorado. Nothing I can say will give an adequate idea of the singular and surprising appearance which they presented from this new and advantageous point of view. Singly, or in groups, they extend like a belt of timber for a distance of several miles. Nothing in nature or in art offers a parallel to these singular objects, but some idea of their appearance may be gained by imagining the island of New York thickly set with spires like that of Trinity church, but many of them full twice its height. Scarcely less striking features in the landscape were the innumerable cañons by which the plain is cut. In every direction they ran and ramified deep, dark, and ragged, impassable to everything but the winged bird. Of these the most stupendous was that of Grand River, which washes two sides of the base of the pinnacle on which we stood, a narrow chasm, as we estimated, full 1,500 feet in depth, into which the sun scarcely seemed to penetrate. At the bottom the whole breadth of this cañon is occupied by the turbid waters of Grand River, here a sluggish stream, at least with no current visible to us who were more than 2,000 feet above it. In this great artery a thousand lateral tributaries terminate, flowing through channels precisely like that of Labyrinth Creek; underground passages by which intermittent floods from the distant highlands are conducted through this country, producing upon it no other effect than constantly to deepen their own beds. Toward the south the cañon of Grand River was easily traced. Perhaps four miles below our position it is joined by another great chasm coming in from the northwest, said by the Indians to be that of Green River. From the point where we were it was inaccessible, but we had every reason to credit their report in reference to it.

After reaching the elevated point from which we obtained this view, I neglected to take the rest I so much needed, but spent the little time at may command in endeavoring to put on paper some of the more striking features of the scene before us. Standing on the highest point, I made a hasty panoramic sketch of the entire landscape. The effect had, however, nearly cost me dear; for before I had completed the circle of the horizon I was seized with dreadful headache, giddiness, and nausea, and, alone as I then was, had the greatest difficulty in rejoining my companions.

Chapter XVII

NORTH CASCADES
1859

from The Journal of Henry Custer

Many of the American records from the Northwest Boundary Survey were lost. However, one unpublished manuscript, left by a Swiss topographer with the survey, was discovered many years later. The following excerpt taken from his journal discusses one day in mid-August in the alpine country of the North Cascades. He enthusiastically describes his crossing of Whatcom Pass and descent to Little Beaver Creek

After proceeding over these fine meadows for some distance, we finally reached the brink of a deep precipice, some 2,000-3,000 feet deep, and below it we discerned the waters of a creek wending its way in a due n.e. course, through a wide gorge in the mountains. This is, undoubtedly, the sought for tributary of the Skagit.

Presently, our attention was attracted by one of the most magnificent sights I ever had the good fortune to behold. It was an immense glacier which covered the mountainside on our left. It extended uninterruptedly over nearly a square mile of surface. Its foot was close to the borders of the stream, which originates in it. From thence, it rises, forming a solid wall of pure ice, to a height of over 5,000 feet near to the summit of a very high mountain.

This mountain, which has the Indian name Wila-kin-ghaist, is one of the highest and most prominent peaks in this section of the Cascade Mountains. Its altitude I judge to be from 9,000-9,500 feet high, up to this lower summit, as already stated, this glacier extends – a vast, unbroken mass of solid ice.

Nothing ever seen before could compare to the matchless grandeur of this feature in nature. All the surrounding mountains to the east of us, and there are many of them, vanish before it into

insignificance in comparison with this colossus of glaciers. Imagine the Niagara Falls, tens of times magnified in height and size, and this vast sheet of falling water instantly crystallized and rendered permanently solid, and you have a somewhat adequate idea of the immensity of this natural phenomena. . . .

As above stated, the surrounding mountains to the east, which are high and exceedingly broken, are covered at intervals with glaciers and extend in an almost unbroken continuation over an area of many square miles.

Altogether, this section of the Cascade Mountains is worthy to stand beside the most famous mountains in the Alps of Europe, visited by thousands of admiring travelers. To reach these mountain solitudes, the traveler has to undergo considerable hardship, as we are here considerably beyond the limits of hotels, guides, and other luxuries of the civilized world. But whoever will take the pains to reach the heart of these mountains will be amply repaid by the many interesting and uncommon sights he will behold. . . .

We found, by closer inspection, that the descent from this plateau where we stood, and which forms the divide to the creek bottom, was over 3,000 feet and, from its almost perpendicular inclination, almost impractical. No alternative could be found but to risk it, or to make a long circuit to our left by ascending the mountains on this side, and continue along their summit until an easier descent to the creek bottoms could be found.

As it was already late, I concluded to risk the steep descent. By keeping well to our left, we succeeded in overcoming the difficulties of this descent, the steepest and most dangerous I have ever made. Had it not been for the bushes and small trees, which gave us occasional support, we would have found it impractical. As it was, it could only be overcome with the utmost caution on our part, by using our hands, arms, legs and sticks freely in a multitude of novel positions. Once to have lost foothold here, nothing would have been left to the unlucky climber but to resign himself to the inevitable fate of being dashed to pieces on the sharp and frightful rocks below.

By a piece of good luck, which did not desert us here, as well as in other localities of a similar nature, we all reached the valley of the creek, without encountering any accident. Below we found a creek of considerable size, originating as already observed in the adjacent glacier. This creek, as all the waters originating immediately in glaciers, has a most peculiar sky blue color, which increases in intensity as we descend the creek valley, and becomes finally dark blue, resembling almost the blue liquid coming from a dyer's vat.

We found a good camp near the banks of a creek in an open forest. Opposite us is the magnificent glacier, below it we see numerous cascades, hundreds of feet high, sending their dust-like waters over the rocky precipitous cliffs of the adjacent mountains, all intent to increase the volume of the creek near us.

Chapter XVIII

BIGHORN CANYON
(YELLOWSTONE)
1859

from Report on the Exploration of the Yellowstone River
by Bvt. Brig. Gen. W. F. Raynolds

Raynolds led the two year expedition throughout the high northern plains. They followed the Missouri River to the Yellowstone River and then part way up the Bighorn River. There they encountered the Big-horn Canyon.

Thursday, September 8 – From our camp we can distinctly trace the Bighorn up its valley to this immense wall, rising over 3,000 feet in height, and crossing the course of the stream at right angles. The river here is large, deep, and nearly 300 feet in width, and yet at this distance there are no evidences of its cutting its way through this rocky barrier, and nothing in the confirmation of the hills and spurs in the remoter ranges indicates the course of its channel. Its remarkable cañon is famous throughout the west, and as from this point our route would bear off southeastward towards the Platte, it was decided to visit this great natural curiosity this afternoon. I was accompanied by Dr. Hayden, Mr. Schonborn, and Mr. Wilson, and we rode up the banks of the Bighorn until a bend compelled its abandonment.

It was only after an hour's ride that the apparently smooth face of the lofty mountain wall afforded the slightest evidence of being broken, and two hours elapsed before we reached the foot of the cañon. . . .

The cañon is one of the most remarkable sights upon the continent. The river here narrows to a width of less than 150 feet, and bursts out through reddish tinted walls of perpendicular rock over 300 feet in height. Its current at this point is slow, but undoubtedly its course among the mountains is marked by successions of rapids and cascades.

We pushed up its banks until we reached the impassable wall of perpendicular rock, and after affording time for sketching and geological observations returned to camp. Bridger claims to have descended the lower cañon of the Bighorn some years since upon a raft during his service as a trapper with the American Fur Company, and his descriptions of the grandeur of the scenery along its banks are glowing and remarkable.

He portrays a series of rugged cañons, the river forming among jagged rocks between lofty overhanging precipices, whose threatening arches shut out all sunlight, interspersed with narrow valleys, teeming with luxuriant verdure, through whose pleasant banks the stream flows as placidly as in its broad valleys below. The conformation of the country – my measurements showing the mountains to be over 3,000 feet in height – render all these marvels natural, and if it were possible I should be glad to attempt the exploration of the cañon myself.

Crossing over to the Powder River, they followed it and crossed over to the Platte River, wintering at Ft. Laramie. In 1860, they followed the Wind River to its headwaters.

Heavy snows in May and June prevented them from crossing over the passes into the Upper Yellowstone as planned, forcing them to do a circuit around the west side of the Yellowstone region. They saw the Tetons, marched through Pierre's Hole and eventually followed the Missouri River back downstream.

Raynolds relied on Jim Bridger as a guide on this general surveying expedition. Bridger had wandered much of the region as a fur trapper and had himself been in Yellowstone. Raynolds was intrigued by the mountain man's tales of the Yellowstone region. While others might dismiss them as another of Bridger's famous tall tales, Raynolds believed them and was deeply frustrated and disappointed by their failure to get over the high snowy passes. This is how Raynolds relates the situation in his introduction to the report.

Beyond these is the valley of the Upper Yellowstone, which is, as yet, a terra incognita. My expedition passed entirely around, but could not penetrate it. My intention was to enter it from the head of Wind River, but the basaltic ridge previously spoken of intercepted our route and prohibited the attempt. After this obstacle had thus forced us over on the western slope of the Rocky Mountains, an effort was made to recross and reach the district in question; but, although it was June, the immense body of snow baffled all our exertions, and we were compelled to content ourselves with listening to marvelous tales of burning plains, immense lakes, and boiling springs, without being able to verify these wonders. . . . Had our attempt to enter this district been made a month later in the season, the snow would have mainly disappeared, and there would have been no insurmountable obstacles to overcome. I cannot doubt, therefore, that at no very distant day the mysteries of this region will be fully revealed, and though small in extent, I regard the valley of the Upper Yellowstone as the most interesting unexplored district in our widely expanded country.

If it had not been for all that snow, Raynolds would have become the official discoverer of Yellowstone ten years prior to the Washburn expedition. On a further note, Raynolds speaks of the tall tales of Bridger over the winter months while at Ft. Laramie.

He contends that near the headwaters of the Columbian river, in the fastnesses of the mountains, there is a spring gushing forth from the rocks near the top of the mountain. The water when it issues forth is cold as ice, but it runs down over the smooth rock so far and so fast that it is 'hot at the bottom.'

In Washburn's journal of 1870, while crossing the Firehole River at a spot warmed by an underground thermal spring, he exclaims, "Here is the river which Bridger said was hot at the bottom!"

BOOK III

THE GREAT SURVEYS
AND THE CLOSING OF THE FRONTIER
1861-1901

In the third time period, the remaining blank spaces on the map of the West are filled in due to the work of great surveys. These scientific surveys were aided by the building of the transcontinental railroad, being constructed in the 1860s and completed by 1869. In-depth exploration of the western wonderlands was also furthered by the proximity of new settlements in the west. These surveys of Josiah Whitney, Clarence King, John Wesley Powell and Ferdinand Hayden were thorough scientific surveys to further knowledge of geography, geology, botany, paleontology, archeology and ethnology. Important scientific works were produced as a part of these surveys. The dramatic topography of the Colorado Plateau came to light for the first time. After being discovered, rediscovered and discountenanced as fable, the wonders of the Yellowstone were finally revealed to the general public. A new appreciation of these and other natural wonders was realized through the paintings of Thomas Moran, the drawings of William Henry Holmes and the photographs of William Henry Jackson. These excursions brought to the general public a more intimate knowledge of the West, made known through articles in magazines for general consumption. These decades also saw the last remaining pockets of Indian resistance swept away. Such military campaigns also crossed through unknown landscapes.

After the great surveys, private excursions filled in the last remote corners of the west. The 1890 census showed that the frontier had closed, as expounded by the historian Frederick Jackson Turner. This was seen as a significant turning point in American History, and the selections will end soon after. It is a logical end to this journey of historical discovery.

Chapter I

LASSEN VOLCANIC –
KINGS CANYON
1863-64

from The Journal of William H. Brewer

The first of the great surveys was carried out in the state of California in the first half of the 1860s, far removed from the battlefields of the Civil War. This in-depth survey throughout the length and breadth of California provides us with the first documented ascent of Lassen's Peak and crossing of the dramatic topography of Kings Canyon. Note that William Brewer mistakenly names Mt. Shasta as the highest in the state. In fact, several peaks surpass it, in particular, Mt. Whitney, the highest in the lower 48. Clarence King was along on this survey. His book, *Mountaineering in the Sierra Nevada*, recounts his ascent of several notable peaks during this survey. This ascent of Lassen Peak was, of course, prior to the eruption of 1912 which caused the area to be elevated to national park status. The surveying party's encounters with grizzlies is no longer likely, as they have since disappeared from California.

Fort Crook, October 5, 1863

September 26, we made our first ascent of Lassen's Peak – King and I and the three friends who had come with us from their camp. We were up and off early, were on the summit before ten o'clock, and spent five hours there.

We had anticipated a grand view, the finest in the state, and it fully equaled our expectations, but the peak is not so high as we estimated, being only about 11,000 feet. The day was not entirely favorable – a fierce wind, raw and chilly, swept over the summit, making our very bones shiver. Clouds hung over a part of the landscape. Mount Shasta, eighty miles distant, rose clear and sharp against a blue sky, the top for six thousand feet rising above a stratum of clouds that hid the base. It was grand. Most of the clouds lay below us at the north. The great valley was very indistinct in the haze at the south, but the northern part was very clear.

A few days later, they climb Lassen Peak again when the weather has improved.

First up a canyon for a thousand feet, then among rocks and over snow, crisp in the cold air, glittering in the bright moonlight. At four we are on the last slope, a steep ridge, now on loose bowlders and sliding gravel, now on firmer footing. We avoid the snow slopes – they are too steep to climb without cutting our way by steps. We are on the south side of the peak, and the vast region in the southeast lies dim in the soft light of the moon – valleys asleep in beds of vapor, mountains dark and shadowy.

At 4:30 appears the first faint line of red in the east, which gradually widens and becomes a livid arch as we toil up the last steep slope.

We reach the first summit, and the northern scene comes in view. The snows of Mount Shasta are still indistinct in the dusky dawn. We cross a snow field, climb up bowlders, and are soon on the highest pinnacle of rock. It is still, cold, and intensely clear. The temperature rises to 25° – it has been 18°.

The arch of dawn rises and spreads along the distant eastern horizon. Its rosy light gilds the cone of red cinders across the crater from where we are. Mount Shasta comes out clear and well defined; the gray twilight bathing the dark mountains below grows warmer and lighter, the moon and stars fade, the shadowy mountain forms rapidly assume distinct shapes, and day comes on apace.

As we gaze in rapture, the sun comes on the scene, and as it rises, its disk flattened by atmospheric refraction, it gilds the peaks one after another, and at this moment the field of view is wider than at any time later in the day. The Marysville Buttes rise from the vapory plain, islands in a distant ocean of smoke, while far beyond appear the dim outlines of Mount Diablo and Mount Hamilton, the latter 240 miles distant.

North of the bay of San Francisco the Coast Range is clear and distinct, from Napa north to the Salmon Mountains near the Klamath River, Mount St. Helena, Mount St. John, Yalloballey, Bullet Chup, and all its other prominent peaks are in distinct view, rising in altitude as we look north.

But rising above all is the conical shadow of the peak we are on, projected in the air, a distinct form of cobalt blue on a ground of lighter haze, its top as sharp and its outlines as well defined as are those of the peak itself – a gigantic spectral mountain, projected so high in the air that it seems far higher than the original mountain itself – but, as the sun rises, the mountain sinks into the valley, and, like a ghost, fades away at the sight of the sun.

The snows of the Salmon Mountains glitter in the morning sun, a hundred miles distant. But the great feature is the sublime form of Mount Shasta towering above its neighboring mountains – truly a monarch of the hills. It has received some snow in the late storms, and the "snow line" is as sharply defined and as level as if the surface of an ocean had cut it against the mountain side.

Through the gaps we catch glimpses of the Siskiyou Mountains, and, east of Mount Shasta, the mere summits of some of the higher snow mountains of Oregon.

In the northeast is the beautiful valley of Pit River, with several sharp volcanic cones rising from it; while chain appears beyond chain in the dim distance, whose locality I cannot say, for we have no maps of that region.

In the east, valley and mountain chain alternate until all becomes indistinct in the blue distance. The peaks about Pyramid Lake are plainly seen. Honey Lake glistens in the morning sun – it seems quite near.

In the southeast we look along the line of the Sierra, peak beyond peak, until those near Lake Bigler form the horizon. The mere summit of Pyramid Peak is visible, but the Yuba Buttes, Pilot Peak, and a legion of lesser heights are very distinct. The valleys between these peaks are bathed in smoke.

Nearer, in this direction, are several beautiful valleys – Indian Valley, the Big Meadows, Mountain Meadows, and others – but all are dry and brown.

Like many philanthropists, in looking at the distant view I have almost forgotten that nearer home, just about the peak itself. Great tables of lava form the characteristic features; for Lassen's Peak, like Mount Shasta, is an extinct volcano (Lassen will have a violent eruption in 1912). *The remains of a crater exist, a hollow in the center, with three or four peaks, or cones, rising around it. The one we are on is the highest. The west cone has many red cinders, and looks red and scorched. A few miles north of the peak are four cones, the highest above nine thousand feet high, entirely destitute of all vegetation, scorched and broken. The highest is said to have been active in 1857.*

The lava tables beneath are covered with dark pine forests, here and there furrowed into deep canyons or rising into mountains, with pretty valleys hidden between.

Several lower peaks about us are spotted with fields of snow, still clean and white, sometimes of rose color with the red microscopic plant, as in the arctic regions.

Little lakes bask in the sunlight here and there, as blue as the sky above them. Twelve are in sight. And the Boiling Lake is in view, with clouds of white steam rising through the trees in the clear, cold, mountain air.

Here and there from the dark forest of pines that forms the carpet of the hills curls the smoke from some hunter's camp or Indian's fire.

Many volcanic cones rise, sharp and steep, some with craters in their tops, into which we can see – circular hollows, like great nests of fabulous birds.

On the west, the volcanic tables slope to the great central valley. The northern part of this, from Tehama to Shasta City, is very distinct and clear, with its forests and farms and orchards and villages, a line of willows marking the course of the Sacramento River. Farther south, smoke and haze obscure the plain.

But in all this wide view there appear no green pastures or lovely green herbage. Dark green forests, almost black, lie beneath us; desolate slopes, with snow and scattered trees, lie around us, and all the valleys are dry and sere. All is as unlike the mountains of the eastern states, or the Alps, as it is possible for one mountain scene to be unlike another.

As the sun rises it is truly wonderful how distinct Mount Shasta is. Its every ridge and canyon and snow field look so plain that one can scarcely believe that it lies eighty miles distant in air line – a weary way and much farther by any road or trail.

The valleys become more smoky, and the distant Sierra more indistinct, dark and jagged lines rising above the haze.

Until 10 AM not a cloud obscures the sky, then graceful cirri creep over from the Pacific, light and feathery.

The day wears on. The sun is warm and the air balmy. Silence broods over the peak – no sound falls on the ear, save occasionally, when a rock, loosed by last night's frost and freed by the day's thaw, rumbles down the steep slope, and all is silent again.

Now and then a butterfly or bird (of arctic species) flits over the summit and among the rocks, but both are silent.

Before 2 PM the smoke increases in the valleys, until the great central valley looks like an indistinct ocean, without surface or shores. Mountain valleys become depths of smoke that the sight cannot penetrate. The distant views fade away in haze, and the landscape looks dreamy. . . .

Continuing their survey of California, next summer they were exploring in the Sierra Nevada. Ascending into the mountains, they encounter grizzlies along the way, as well as giant rattlesnakes.

In camp on the south fork of Kings River, July 7

. . . We were working back toward high peaks, where we hoped to discover the sources of Kings, Kaweah, and Kern rivers, geographical problems of some considerable interest and importance. We got back as far as we could and camped at an altitude

of 9,750 feet, by a rushing stream, but with poor feed. Wood was plenty, dry, from trees broken by avalanches in winter. A beautiful little lake was near us. About five miles east lay the high granite cone we hoped to reach – high and sharp, its sides bristling with sharp pinnacles.

Saturday, July 2, we were up at dawn, and Hoffman and I climbed this cone, which I had believed to be the highest of this part of the Sierra. We had a rough time, made two unsuccessful attempts to reach the summit, climbing up terribly steep rocks, and at last, after eight hours of very hard climbing, reached the top. The view was yet wilder than we have ever seen before. We were not on the highest peak, although we were a thousand feet higher than we anticipated any peaks were. We had not supposed there were any over 12,000 or 12,500 feet, while we were actually up over 13,000, and there were a dozen peaks in sight beyond as high or higher!

Such a landscape! A hundred peaks in sight over thirteen thousand feet – many very sharp – deep canyons, cliffs in every direction almost rivaling Yosemite, sharp ridges almost inaccessible to man, on which human foot has never trod – all combined to produce a view the sublimity of which is rarely equaled, one which few are privileged to behold.

There is not so much snow as in the mountains farther north, not so much falls in winter, the whole region is drier, but all the higher points, above 12,000 feet are streaked with it, and patches occur as low as 10,500 feet. The last trees disappear at 11,500 feet – above this desolate bare rocks and snow. Several small lakes were in sight, some of them frozen over.

The view extended north eighty to ninety miles, south nearly as far – east we caught glimpses of the desert mountains beyond Owens Valley – west to the Coast Range, 130 or more miles distant.

On our return we slid down a slope of snow perhaps eight hundred feet. We came down in two minutes the height that we had been over three hours in climbing. We got back very tired, but a cup of good tea and a fine venison soup restored us.

King and Gardner went on to ascend one of the highest peaks in the vicinity, one of several ascents King wrote about in his classic book, *Mountaineering in the Sierra Nevada*. Back together, they all took the long, steep descent into the dramatic canyon of the South Fork of Kings River.

July 23

I am spending today in camp, the first for two weeks and I will go on with my story.

We got into the canyon of the South Fork of Kings River, and forded the stream, which is quite a river where we crossed, and camped at a fine meadow in the valley. It was a very picturesque camp, granite precipices rising on both sides to immense height. The river swarmed with trout; I never saw them thicker. The boys went fishing and soon caught about forty, while the soldiers caught about as many more.

We left there the next morning and worked up the valley about ten miles. Next to Yosemite this is the grandest canyon I have ever seen. It much resembles Yosemite and almost rivals it. A pretty valley of flat half a mile wide lies along the river, in places rough and strewn with bowlders, and in others level and covered with trees. On both sides rise tremendous granite precipices, of every shape, often nearly perpendicular, rising from 2,500 feet to above 4,000 feet. They did not form a continuous wall, but rose in high points, with canyons coming down here and there, and with fissures, gashes, and gorges. The whole scene was sublime – the valley below, the swift river roaring by, the stupendous cliffs standing against a sky of intensest blue, the forests through which we rode. We would look up through the branches and see the clear sky and grand rocks, or occasionally, as we crossed an open space, we would get more comprehensive views.

We camped at the head of this valley by a fine grassy meadow where the stream forked. On both sides rose grand walls of granite about three thousand feet high, while between the forks was a stupendous rock, bare and rugged, over four thousand feet high. We luxuriated on trout for the next two meals. The rattlesnakes were thick – four were killed this day.

The next day, July 20, we started in different directions. Hoff-man and Gardner climbed the cliffs on the south side. They got up two thousand feet above them which they could not scale. I explored a side canyon, to the south, where the Indian foot trail ran, to see if we could get out that way with our animals. I had a grand climb, but found the way entirely inaccessible for horses. I followed up a canyon, the sides grand precipices, with here and there a fine waterfall or series of cascades, making a line of foam down the cliffs. I climbed over bowlders and through brush, got up above two very fine waterfalls, one of which is the finest that I have seen in this state outside of Yosemite. I had a hard day's work.

In the meantime a soldier had explored another canyon, and reported that we could get out to the north that way, so the next day we started, and came to this camp. It was worse than any of our other trails. We are not over 5 miles from our last camp, and have come up over four thousand feet!

It was heavy for our animals. Twice we had very steep slopes for a thousand feet together, where it seemed at first that no animal could get up with a pack. Once our pack horse fell, turned a complete somersault over a bowlder, and landed below squarely on his feet, when he kept on his way as if nothing had happened. His pack remained firm and he was not hurt in the least. Fortunately it was not so steep there. There were places where if an animal had once started he would have rolled several hundred feet, but all went safely over. We camped at a little over nine thousand feet where we are now, by a meadow on the hillside where we have a grand view of the peaks in front and the canyon beneath us.

Yesterday Gardner and Hoffman went on a peak about twelve thousand feet, which commands a comprehensive view of all the ground we have been over lately; while two soldiers, Dick, and I explored ahead for a trail. We were unsuccessful, but we got on a ridge over eleven thousand feet high that commands a stu-pendous view. The deep canyons on all sides, the barren granite slopes, clear little lakes that occupy the beds of ancient gla-ciers, the sharp ridges, the high peaks, some of them rising to above fourteen thousand feet, like huge granite spires – all lay around, forming a scene of indescribable sublimity.

After various explorations, the party makes their way over a high pass out of Kings Canyon and down into the desert east of the Sierra Nevada.

Camp 189, on the middle fork of the San Joaquin
August 5, 1864

. . . Some prospectors had come over the summit to this place, as I told you, and we resolved to follow their trail, assuming that where they went we could go. Tuesday, July 26, we started and got about eleven miles, a hard day's work, for we rose 4,300 feet. First we went up a steep, rocky slope of 1,000 to 1,500 feet, so steep and rough that we would never have attempted it had not the prospectors already been over it and made a trail in the worst places – it was terrible. In places the mules could scarcely get a foothold where a canyon yawned hundreds of feet below; in places it was so steep that we had to pull the pack animals up by main strength. They show an amount of sagacity in such places almost incredible. Once Nell fell on a smooth rock, but Dick caught her rope and held her – she might have gone into the canyon below and, with her pack, been irretrievably lost. We then followed up the canyon three or four miles and then out by a side canyon still steeper. We camped by a little meadow, at over nine thousand feet. Near camp a grand smooth granite rock rose about three thousand feet, smooth and bare.

July 27 we went over the summit, about twelve miles. The summit is a very sharp granite ridge, with loose bowlders on both sides as steep as they will lie. It is slow, hard work getting animals over such a sliding mass. It is 11,600 feet high, far above trees, barren granite mountains all around, with patches of snow, some of which were some distance below us – the whole scene was one of sublime desolation. Before us, and far beneath us lay Owens Valley, the desert Inyo Mountains beyond, dry and forbidding. Around us on both sides were mountains fourteen thousand feet high, beneath us deep canyons.

We descended down the canyon of Little Pine Creek and camped at a little meadow, in full view of the valley below and the ridges beyond, which were peculiarly illumined by the setting sun. On both sides of us were great rocky precipices. Dur-

*ing the day's progress we passed a number of beautiful little
lakes.*

*Thursday, July 28, we were up at dawn and went to Owens
River, sixteen miles. Six miles brought us out of the canyon on
the desert   then ten miles across the plain in the intense heat,
and we camped on the river bank, without shade or shelter, the
thermometer 96° in the shade, 156° in the sun. Yesterday in the
snow and ice – today in the heat! It nearly used us up.*

Chapter II

LITTLE MISSOURI BADLANDS *1864*

from The Report of General Alfred Sully

This is the first written description of the Little Missouri Badlands in the vicinity of present-day Theodore Roosevelt National Park. It seems likely that fur trappers would have been in the area long before 1864, as it is readily accessible from the Missouri River but, if so, none wrote about it. General Sully was leading a march in pursuit of Indians responsible for a massacre of whites in Minnesota. His report tries to put the best face on a failed campaign, while leaving a vivid description of the terrain.

From the Yellowstone River, August 13, 1864

On the fifth day of August we came in sight of the Bad Lands, which extend along the Little Missouri, the valley being about twenty miles across; through the middle of this valley runs the river. When I came in sight of this country from the top of the tableland we were marching on, I became alarmed, and almost despaired of ever being able to cross it; and should have been very much tempted, had I rations enough, to turn back. But on a close examination of my rations, I found I only had rations for six days longer; by some mistake of my commissary I suppose, but he is not with me to explain, as I left him back at Fort Rice. I, therefore, had to reduce the bread ration one-third and all the other stores, except meat, one-half, so as to make it last me to the river. We camped that night with little or no grass, and but a few holes of muddy rain water.

I have not sufficient power of language to describe the country in front of us. It was grand, dismal, and majestic. You can imagine a deep basin, 600 feet deep and twenty-five miles in diameter, filled with a number of stones and oven-shaped knolls of all sizes, from twenty feet to several hundred feet high, sometimes by themselves, sometimes piled up into large heaps on top of one another, in all conceivable shapes and confusion. Most of these hills were of a gray clay, but many of a light brick color, of burnt clay; little or no vegetation. Some of the sides of the hills, however, were covered with a few scrub cedars. Viewed in the distance, at sunset, it looked exactly like the ruins of an ancient city.

My Indian guide appeared to be confident of success and, trusting to him, I started next morning. By dint of hard digging, we succeeded by nightfall in reaching the banks of the Little Missouri, about twelve miles. I regret very much some gentleman well acquainted with geology and mineralogy did not accompany the expedition, for we marched through a most wonderful and interesting country. . . .

We now reached the river in the middle of the Bad Lands. Having dug our way down to this point, it was now necessary to dig our way out. I, therefore, so ordered a strong working party, with four companies of cavalry, under charge of Lieutenant Colonel Pattee, 7ᵗʰ Iowa Cavalry. I remained in camp to allow the animals to rest and pick up what grass could be found around, there being very little to be found. Some few of the men, however, without orders, took their horses into the timber beyond the pickets, leaving their saddles and arms in camp. A small party of the Indians crawled up and fired on them, creating a stampede. Most of the men ran away, leaving their horses. The Indians succeeded in getting a few away, but three or four men having some courage mounted their horses bareback and gave chase, causing the Indians to drop all the horses. All were retaken, save one or two. A company was soon in pursuit, but the Indians escaped through some of the numerous ravines and forests. . . .

By evening the working party under Colonel Pattee returned, having cut three miles of the road. A part of the company, however, by accident had been left behind. They were surrounded by Indians and were near being cut off, but by a hasty retreat they succeeded in getting through the deep gorge where the road was cut, the Indians firing at them from the tops of the hills. They pursued them to the river and showed themselves on the top of the high bluffs opposite my camp, firing into my camp. But a few shells from Jones' battery soon scattered them, and with the exception of a little picket-firing there was no more trouble that night. I now knew I had come upon the Indians I had fought

*about a week ago, and in the worst possible section of country I
could possibly wish to encounter an enemy.*

*My road lay through a succession of mountain gorges, down
deep ravines, with perpendicular bluffs, so narrow only one
wagon could pass at a time, intersected with valleys, down
which the Indians could dash onto any point of my train.
Stretched out in a single line we were extended from three to
four miles. . . .*

*After marching about three miles we came onto the Indians
strongly posted in front and on the flanks of a deep mountain
pass. They were dislodged after some little trouble, the shells
from Jones' battery doing good execution; and the advance
with other troops pushed on, while the pioneer party made the
road. The Indians attacked me on the flanks and rear at the
same time, but on all occasions they were repulsed with heavy
loss by troops nearby, and thus we advanced fighting, hunting a
road and digging it out, till we reached a small lake and spring
about ten miles from our starting point. . . .*

*At the spring there was, for a short time, quite a brisk little skir-
mish, the Indians trying to keep us from the only water we had
that day; and the day was so hot that the animals were suffering
very much, having had not much to eat for two days. Part of
Colonel McLaren's 2nd Minnesota did most of the work here.
One of his companies in advance got separated from the rest
and surrounded; they however got into a hollow and defended
themselves, until relieved by other companies sent out from
Colonel Thomas' command. Their loss, however, was slight in
comparison to their danger. Unfortunately, this day I lost the
services of my guide; he was shot, having ventured too far in the
advance. He was the only one who knew the country over which
we were marching.*

*The next morning we moved forward. The Indians were in front
of us appearing as if they intended to give us battle. . . . We
advanced without much trouble, with a little skirmishing in
front, and also an attack in rear. The enemy were repulsed on
all sides. It was evident, in spite of all their boasting, all fighting was out of them. A few miles brought us out to an open
country, and the last we saw of the Indians was a cloud of dust
some six or eight miles off, running as fast as they could. They*

were better mounted than we were. . . . It is certain, however, their loss was very heavy. The same Indians I fought before were engaged, besides Cheyenne, Brules, Minneconjous, and others from the south.

After marching six miles this day, we came to the place where the Indians left about thirty hours before my arrival. From the size of their camp, or rather bivouac, for they had pitched no lodges; I should judge all the Indians in the country had assembled there. The space they occupied was over one mile long and half a mile wide, besides which we discovered camps all over the country, close by this spot. . . . We continued our way across the country to the Yellowstone, which we reached on the 12th of August, over a section of country I never wish to travel again; our animals half dead with hunger; the grass entirely eaten off.

Chapter III

JOHN DAY FOSSIL BEDS
1864-71

from "The Rocks of the John Day Valley"
in The Overland Monthly, *May, 1871*
by Thomas Condon

Following the passage of many emigrants along the Oregon Trail, settlements sprang up in the Willamette Valley and along the Columbia River. Eastern Oregon, arid and barren, remained an unexplored region until the 1860s. Hearing of a cavalry detachment that had passed through the region and seeing the fossils they had discovered in the John Day Valley, the geologist Thomas Condon spent several years exploring the region. As a consequence, he discovered not only its landscape; but by looking closer, even the deep well of the past – countless eons of geological processes and the coming and going of past flora and fauna.

. . . There are many residents of the Pacific Slope who will remember having journeyed from The Dalles, on the Columbia River, to Cañon City, among the Blue Mountains. For sixty miles or more the road passes over volcanic materials, which have drifted there from the Cascade Range. Twenty miles farther, and this outflow thins out into a mere capping of basalt on the hill-tops. The hills themselves, and the foundations on which they stand, are here found to be sedimentary rock, wonderfully filled with the abundant records of former animal and vegetable life. Oldest of all in sight is the old ocean-bed of the Cretaceous period, with its teeming thousands of marine shells, as perfect today in their rocky bed as those of our recent seashores; their cavities often filled with calcareous spar or chalcedony, as if to compensate for the loss of their own proper marine hues. Next in ascending order come the freshwater deposits of the earlier Tertiaries, so full of the leaf-prints of the grand old forests that, during that age of semi-tropical climate, covered those lake-shores. The marine rocks form the outer rim, or shore-line, of what was in those early times a lake, of irregular outline, extending from Kern Creek Hill on the west to Cañon City on

the east, and from the hills north of the John Day River to the Crooked River Valley on the south. Within this lake-depression, whose former muddy sediment is now elevated into chalky hills, so despised for their alkaline waters and unproductive soils, the geologist feels at home. How strangely out of place a score of palm-trees, a hundred yew-trees, or even a bank of ferns, would seem here now! And yet here these once lived, and died, and were buried; and beautiful beyond description are their fossil remains even now, as they are unburied.

Seen from the summit of Kern Creek Hill – its western border – this vast amphitheatre of lesser hills presents a wild, wonderful grouping of varied outlines and colors. A spur of the Blue Mountains – its nearest point, forty miles away – covered with a dense forest, forms the dark background of the view. The varying shades of brown that characterize the older marine rocks rise in vast border masses, almost treeless and shrub-less, in an inner, irregular circle, while the lighter shades that fill the deeper depressions of the central portion mark the later sedimentary deposits; and then, like vast ink-blots on a painting, one sees, here and there, a protruding mass of dark-colored trap. Through the heart of this wild region winds the John Day River, running westward until it passes the middle ground of the picture, and then turning northward to join the Columbia.

This stream, so insignificant in appearance, has done wonderful work among these hills. The river itself was, in the olden time, merely a series of connecting links between a chain of lakes that extended from the Blue Mountains to the Cascades of the Columbia. It has for unnumbered ages gone on excavating vast gorges and cañons, as all other streams in central Oregon have done, till lake after lake was drained off, and their beds laid dry, stripped of enduring moisture, and slowly changed to a tree-less desert. The deep excavations that resulted could hardly fail to lay bare important records of the past, cutting as they do through the whole extent of the Tertiary periods. . . .

Condon goes on to discuss the discovery of bones of ancient creatures, like the Oreodon and early species of the horse, buried in the ashes of an ancient and massive volcanic eruption.

Chapter IV

SHOSHONE FALLS
1868

from "The Falls of the Shoshone"
in Overland Monthly, Oct. 1870
by Clarence King

Along with the other great surveys of the time was the 40th parallel survey, close to the route of the nearly-completed Transcontinental Railroad. We have already been with Clarence King in the California survey conducted by William Brewer in 1863-64. We join him again on a side-trip from the 40th parallel survey to the Shoshone Falls on the Snake River. Today, it is reduced in flow by diversion for hydroelectric power and irrigation, and is not a designated parkland. However, at one time, it was one of the great natural spectacles of the American West. Like the Great Falls of the Missouri, we shall include it within our anthology. No doubt, this waterfall had been seen by others before King, but it is the earliest written description I can find. The Astorians may have been the first Euro-Americans to have seen it. Their fatal wreck had been just a little upstream at the Cauldron Linn. They walked downstream from there, according to Irving, and he describes the deep canyons and cascades they saw, but no description he gives fits these thundering falls.

In October, 1868, with a small detachment of a United States Geological Survey, the writer crossed the Goose Creek Mountains, in northern Utah, and descended by the old Fort Boise road to the level of the Snake Plain. A gray, opaque haze hung close to the ground, and shut out the distance. The monotony of the sage-desert was overpowering. We would have given anything for a good outlook; but for three days the mists continued, and we were forced to amuse ourselves by chasing occasional antelopes.

The evening we camped on Rock Creek was signalized by a fierce wind from the northeast. It was a dry storm, which continued with tremendous fury through the night, dying away at daybreak, leaving the heavens brilliantly clear. We were break-

"Shoshone Falls," Timothy O'Sullivan

fasting when the sun rose, and shortly afterward, mounting into the saddle, headed toward the cañon of the Shoshone. The air was cold and clear. The remotest mountain peaks upon the horizon could be distinctly seen, and the forlorn details of their brown slopes stared at us as through a vacuum. A few miles in front the smooth surface of the plain was broken by a ragged, zigzag line of black, which marked the edge of the farther wall of the Snake Cañon. A dull, throbbing sound greeted us. Its pulsations were deep, and seemed to proceed from the ground beneath our feet. Leaving the cavalry to bring up the wagon, my two friends and I galloped on, and were quickly upon the edge of the cañon-wall. We looked down into a broad, circular excavation, three-quarters of a mile in diameter, and nearly seven hundred feet deep. East and north, over the edges of the cañon, we looked across miles and miles of the Snake Plain, far on to the blue, boundary mountains. The wall of the gorge opposite us, like the cliff at our feet, sank in perpendicular bluffs nearly to the level of the river; the broad excavation being covered by rough piles of black lava, and rounded domes of trachyte rock. A horizon as level as the sea; a circling wall, whose sharp edges were here and there battlemented in huge, fortress-like masses; a broad river, smooth and unruffled, flowing quietly into the middle of the scene, and then plunging into a labyrinth of rocks, tumbling over a precipice two hundred feet high, and flowing westward in a still, deep current, disappear behind a black promontory. It is a strange, savage scene: a monotony of pale-blue sky, olive and gray stretches of desert, frowning walls of jetty lava, deep beryl-green of river-stretches, reflecting, here and there, the intense solemnity of the cliffs, and in the centre a dazzling sheet of foam. In the early morning light, the shadows of the cliffs were cast over half the basin, defining themselves in sharp outline here and there upon the river. Upon the foam of the cataract one point of the rock cast a cobalt-blue shadow. Where the river flowed around the western promontory, it was wholly in shadow, and of a deep sea-green. A scanty growth of coniferous trees fringed the brink of the lower cliffs, overhanging the river. Dead barrenness is the whole sentiment of the scene. The mere suggestion of trees clinging here and there along the walls, serves rather to heighten than relieve the forbidding gloom of the place. Nor does the flashing whiteness, where the river tears itself among the rocky islands, or rolls in spray down the cliff, brighten the aspect. In contrast with its brilliancy, the rocks seem darker and more wild. The descent of four hundred feet, from our stand-point to the level of the river above the falls, has to be made by a narrow, winding path, among rough ledges of lava. We were obliged to leave our wagon at the summit, and pack down the camp equipment and photographic apparatus upon carefully led mules. By midday, we were comfortably camped on the margin of the left bank, just above the brink of the falls. My tent was pitched upon the edge of a cliff, directly overhanging the rapids. From my door I looked over the edge of the falls, and, whenever the veil of mist was blown aside, I could see for a mile down the river. The lower half of the cañon is excavated in a gray, porphyritic trachyte. It is over this material that the Snake falls. Above the brink, the whole breadth of the river is broken by a dozen small, trachyte islands, which the water has carved into fantastic forms: rounding some into low domes, sharpening others into mere pillars, and now and then wearing out deep caves. At the very brink of the fall a few twisted evergreens cling with their roots to the rock, and lean over the abyss of foam with something of that air of fatal fascination which is apt to take possession of men.

In plan the fall re-curves upstream in a deep horseshoe, resembling the outline of Niagara. The total breadth is about seven hundred feet, and the greatest height of a single fall about one hundred and ninety. Among the islands above the brink are several beautiful cascades, where portions of the river pour over in lace-like forms. The whole mass of the fall is one ever-varying sheet of spray. In the early spring, when swollen by the rapidly melted snows, the river pours over with something like the grand volume of Niagara, but, at the time of my visit, it was wholly white foam. . . . The sheet of foam plunges almost vertically into a dark, beryl-green, lake-like expanse of the river. Immense volumes of foam roll up from the cataract-base, and, whirling about in the eddying winds, rise often a thousand feet into the air. When the wind blows down the cañon, a gray mist obscures the river for half a mile; and when, as is usually the case in the afternoon, the breezes blow eastward, the foam-cloud curls over the brink of the fall, and hangs like a veil over the upper river. On what conditions depends the height to which the foam-cloud rises from the base of the fall, it is apparently impossible to determine. Without the slightest wind, the cloud of spray often rises several hundred feet above the cañon-wall, and again, with apparently the same conditions of the river and atmosphere, it hardly reaches the brink of the fall. The incessant roar, reinforced by a thousand echoes, fills the cañon. From out this monotone, from time to time, rise strange, wild sounds, and now and then may be heard a slow, measured beat, not unlike the recurring fall of breakers. . . . The whole edge of the cañon is deeply cleft in vertical crevasses. The actual edge is usually formed of irregular blocks and prisms of lava, poised upon their ends in an unstable equilibrium, ready to be tumbled over at the first leverage of the frost. Hardly an hour passes without the sudden boom of one of those rock-masses falling upon the ragged débris piled below.

Night is the true time to appreciate the full force of the scene. I lay and watched it by the hour. The broken rim of the basin profiled itself upon a mass of drifting clouds where torn openings revealed gleams of pale moonlight and bits of remote sky trembling with misty stars. Intervals of light and blank darkness hurriedly followed each other. For a moment the black gorge would be crowded with forms. Tall cliffs, ramparts of lava, the rugged outlines of islands huddled together on the cataract's brink, faintly luminous from breaking over black rapids, the swift, white leap of the river, and a ghostly, formless mist through which the cañon-walls and far reach of the lower river were veiled and unveiled again and again. A moment of this strange picture, and then a rush of black shadow, when nothing could be seen but the breaks in the clouds, the rim of the basin, and a vague, white centre in the general darkness.

"Camp of the 40th Parallel Survey above Shoshone Falls,"
Timothy O'Sullivan

After sleeping on the nightmarish brink of the falls, it was no small satisfaction to climb out of the Dantean gulf and find myself once more upon a pleasantly prosaic foreground of sage. Nothing more effectually banishes the melotragic state of the mind than the obtrusive ugliness and abominable smell of this plant. From my feet a hundred miles of it stretched eastward. A half-hour's walk took me out of sight of the cañon, and as the wind blew westward, only occasional indistinct pulsations of the fall could be heard. The sky was bright and cloudless, and arched like a cheerful vacuum over the meaningless disk of the desert.

I walked for an hour, following an old Indian trail which occa-sionally approached within seeing distance of the river, and then, apparently quite satisfied, diverged again into the desert. When about four miles from the Shoshone, it bent abruptly to the north, and led to the edge of the cañon. Here again the nar-row gorge widened into a broad theatre, surrounded as before by black, vertical walls, and crowded over its whole surface by rude piles and ridges of volcanic rock. The river entered it from the east through a magnificent gateway of basalt, and, having reached the middle, flows on either side of a low, rocky island, and plunges in two falls into a deep, green basin. . . .

After ten days devoted to walking around the neighborhood and studying the falls and rocks, we climbed to our wagon, and rested for a farewell look at the gorge. It was with great relief that we breathed the free air of the plain, and turned from the rocky cañon where darkness, and roar, and perpetual cliffs had bounded our senses, and headed southward, across the noiseless plain. Far ahead rose a lofty, blue barrier, a mountain wall, marbled upon its summit by flecks of perpetual snow. A deep notch in its profile opened a gateway. Toward this, for leagues ahead of us, a white thread in the gray desert marked the winding of our road. . . .

He refers to two other great falls, Niagara and Yosemite, in contrast to the setting one finds at Shoshone Falls.

No sheltering pine or mountain distance of up-piled Sierras guards the approach to the Shoshone. You ride upon a waste – the pale earth stretched in desolation. Suddenly you stand upon a brink. As if the earth had yawned, black walls flank the abyss. Deep in the bed a great river fights its way through the labyrinth of blackened ruins, and plunges in foaming whiteness over a cliff of lava. You turn from the brink as from a frightful glimpse of the Inferno, and when you have gone a mile the earth seems to have closed again. Every trace of the cañon has vanished, and the stillness of the desert reigns.

Chapter V

ROCKY MOUNTAIN
1868

from an article in Rocky Mountain News, *1868*
by William N. Byers

Preliminary to Powell's descent of the Colorado River, he made a trip to the Rockies of Colorado. There, his group explored the headwaters of the Colorado River, at that time called the Grand River above the Confluence. Only the river below the Confluence was called the Colorado River. The other main tributary above the Confluence was called the Green River then and now. The Confluence is located where the Green and Grand Rivers meet in eastern Utah, now in the center of Canyonlands N.P. This is the spot almost reached by the Macomb party in 1859 (see above selection by J. S. Newberry). Powell's boat trip in 1869 would follow the Green River from Wyoming to the Confluence and then down the lower Colorado to the lower end of the Grand Canyon. During this first trip, exploring topography in Colorado, the Powell group would make the first documented ascent of Long's Peak. (The mountain was first seen from the plains by the Stephen Long party back in 1820.) The account is written by a newspaperman with the party, whose article appeared in the Denver newspaper.

August 20 – The party destined for the ascent of Long's Peak, consisting of Major J. W. Powell, W. H. Powell, L. W. Keplinger, Sam'l Garman, Ned E. Farrell, John C. Sumner, and the writer, left camp at the west side of Grand Lake, each mounted, and with one pack mule for the party. The mule was laden with ten days' rations, though we expected to make the trip in much less time. Each man carried his bedding under or behind his saddle, a pistol at his belt, and those not encumbered with instruments took their guns. We had two barometers and two sets of thermometers.

Crossing the Grand where it leaves the lake, we made one-half its circuit, around the northern shore, through a dense mass of brush and fallen timber, and at a point directly opposite our

camp on the eastern shore, began the ascent of the
mountain. . . .

*Turning away from the lake at right angles, we followed up a
sharp, narrow ridge, very steep, rocky and almost impassable
on account of the fallen timber. Progress was necessarily slow,
and we were full three hours making the first four miles. Then
we entered green timber and got along much faster. In about
seven miles from the starting point we reached the limit of timber growth and wound along the crest of the sharp, rocky ridge
which forms the divide between the two streams mentioned. The
route is very rough and tortuous. On either side, thousands of
feet below, are chains of little lakes, dark and solitary-looking
in their inaccessibility. About five miles from the timberline we
camped for the night, turning down, for that purpose, to the
edge of the timber on our right. The barometer showed an altitude of about 11,500 feet, and the frost was quite sharp.*

*August 21 – Our start was over much the same kind of country
traversed in the afternoon yesterday; skirting around the side of
a very lofty mountain; clambering over broken rocks, or climbing up or down to get around impassable ledges. In some places
we pass over great snow banks, which are really the best traveling we find. At the end of a mile we came to an impassable precipice, which subsequent exploration proved to extend from the
summit of the mountain on the left down to the stream on our
right, and thence down parallel with it. We spent the day in
searching for a place to get down or around it, but without success, and were compelled to go into camp, like the night before,
at the timberline. We had proved one thing, that horses and
mules could go no further, and we made preparations for proceeding on foot. The animals were turned loose to feed on the
short, young grass of the mountain side; the trail by which we
came down being barricaded by a few loose stones and a pole
or two to prevent their going back. Escape in any other direction was impossible.*

*August 22 – We were off at seven o'clock; each man with biscuit
and bacon in his pockets for two days' rations. One or two carried blankets, but most preferred doing without to carrying
them. Arms were also left behind. After some search a place
was found where we descended the precipice – not without risk
– then crossed a little valley, just at the timberline, and began*

the ascent of the range directly over a huge mountain which had the appearance of extending quite to Long's Peak. Gaining its summit, we found ourselves still further from our destination than we supposed we were the day before. Descending its precipitous northern face – which upon looking back appeared utterly impassable – we followed for a mile along a very low ridge, then turned eastward along a similar ridge, which connects Long's Peak with the range. It has been generally supposed that the great mountain was a part of the range, though occupying an acute angle in it, but such is not the case. It is not less than two miles from the range, and all its waters flow toward the Atlantic. Following up this ridge, it soon culminated in a very lofty mountain, only a few hundred feet lower than Long's, but with a crest so narrow that some of the party became dizzy in traveling along it. This, we supposed, would lead us to the great mountain, but found the route cut off by impassable chasms when yet more than a mile distant. There remained but one route – to descend to the valley and climb again all that we had already twice made.

Turning to the right, we clambered down with infinite labor to the valley of a branch of St. Vrain, where we went into camp at the extreme timberline. Some explorations were made, however, preparatory to tomorrow's labor; the most important by Mr. Keplinger, who ascended to within about 800 feet of the summit, and did not return until after dark. We became very uneasy about him, fearing that he would be unable to make his way down in safety. A man was sent to meet him, and bonfires kindled on some high rocks near us. An hour after dark they came in; Mr. K with the report that the ascent might be possible, but he was not very sanguine. The night was a most cheerless one, with gusts of wind and sprinkles of rain; our only shelter under the sides of an immense boulder, where we shivered the long hours through.

August 23 – Unexpectedly the day dawned fair, and at six o'clock we were facing the mountain. Approaching from the south, our course was over a great rockslide and then up a steep gorge, down which the broken stone had come. In many places it required the assistance of hands, as well as feet, to get along, and the ascent at best was very laborious. There was no extraordinary obstacle until within seven or eight hundred feet of the summit. Above that point the mountain presents the appearance, in every direction, of being a great block of granite, perfectly smooth and unbroken. Close examination, however, removed this delusion in some degree, and we were most agreeably surprised to find a passable way, though it required great caution, coolness, and infinite labor to make headway; life often depending upon a grasp of the fingers in a crevice that would hardly admit them. Before ten o'clock the entire party stood upon the extreme summit without accident or mishap of any kind.

The Peak is a nearly level surface, paved with irregular blocks of granite, and without vegetation of any kind, except a little gray lichen. The outline is nearly a parallelogram – east and west – widening a little toward the western extremity, and five or six acres in extent. On the eastern end are some large boulders, giving it an apparent altitude of ten or fifteen feet above the remainder of the surface. Along the northern edge, and especially at the northwest corner, the surface rounds off considerably, though the general appearance is almost that of a perfect level.

Barometric and thermometric observations were taken to determine altitude, and a monument erected to commemorate our visit. A record of the event with notes of the instrumental readings was deposited, along with other mementoes, in a tin case in the monument, and from a flag staff on its summit a flag was unfurled and left floating in the breeze. After nearly three hours' stay on the Peak we began the descent, which occupied two hours. A snow squall enveloped us on the way down, but it lasted for only a few minutes. Over thirty alpine lakes were counted from the summit.

Our way back was by the headwaters of St. Vrain; three considerable branches of which were crossed. The valley of each is filled with lakes alternated with great fields of snow. The latter is strewn with grasshoppers, which could be gathered by wagon loads. Upon these the bears were feasting, and the country seems to be literally infested with them. We saw two, and the tracks of others in every snowbank and soft spot of ground. We stopped for the night on the most westerly branch of the St. Vrain, and spent a second night without blankets around a camp fire, yet more cheerless because we were out of "grub."

August 24 – Without breakfast to eat or baggage to pack, we had no impediment to an early start, and had almost reached the summit of the range before old Sol's greeting. Our path was up a great gorge, over a snowfield, then a frozen lake – a small part clear of ice – and then more snow to the summit. Then down an easier slope with grass, and boulders, and great black ledges, to the head of the Grand, and our old camp, where our stock had been left. A hasty but a hearty breakfast, and then we saddled up and retraced our trail along the mountain ridge, through the tangled, fallen timber, and around the lake to our old and pleasant camp. We had been gone only five days; had been eminently successful, and of course were satisfied; the more so because the mountain had always before been pro- nounced inaccessible, and ours was the first party that had ever set foot upon its summit.

Chapter VI

YELLOWSTONE
1869

from "The Valley of the Upper Yellowstone"
in The Western Monthly, *July 1870,*
by Charles W. Cook & David E. Folsom

Charles W. Cook

In the 1860s, stronger indications of what lay on the Upper Yellowstone came from reports of prospectors who ventured into the region. These reports would appear in regional newspapers where truth was mixed with fiction regarding Yellowstone and its features. Tall tales were told which cast doubts in many people's minds about the veracity of all that was heard about Yellowstone. However, for those paying attention, it was becoming more evident that some things unusual were on the Upper Yellowstone. One expedition led by Walter deLacy even produced a rough map of the region used by the Folsom, Cook & Peterson party, as well as by the Washburn party the following year. DeLacy's own journal of his trip to the region was published after the Washburn report made Yellowstone known to the public at large.

The Cook/Folsom journal was published in an abbreviated form in the above-cited Chicago publication the following year, but only received limited attention. All copies, except one kept by Nathaniel Langford, were lost due mainly to a fire at the offices of *The Western Monthly*. Langford re-printed this truncated journal over 20 years later. Eventually, some 50 years later, Cook attempted to re-write an amplified account of their journey. It is the abbreviated report published originally in 1870 that follows.

The country around the headwaters of the Yellowstone River, although frequently visited by prospectors and mountain men, is still to the world of letters a veritable terra incognita. Environed by mountain chains that are covered by a dense growth of timber, making all approaches to it seem difficult, it has no regularly traveled route, and no party of emigrants on their way to the Pacific slope has ever passed through it; nor has any expedition under the patronage of the Government yet attempted to penetrate its fastnesses. The hardy prospectors, searching in this region for new 'diggings' have hitherto failed to find gold in paying quantities; but have always returned to repeat the tales of wonderful waterfalls a thousand feet in height, of innumerable hot springs of surprising magnitude, and of vast tracts of country covered with the scoria of volcanoes – some of which were reported to be in active operation.

William & Jessie Peterson

Owing to the fact that this class of men had gained a reputation for indulging in flights of fancy when recounting their adventures, these reports were received with considerable incredulity until it was noticed that, however much the accounts of different parties differed in detail, there was a marked coincidence in the descriptions of some of the most prominent features of the country.

In 1867, an exploring expedition from Virginia City, Montana Territory, was talked of, but for some unknown reason – probably for the want of a sufficient number to engage in it – it was abandoned. The next year another was planned, which ended like the first – in talk. Early in the summer of 1869, the newspapers throughout the Territory announced that a party of citizens from Helena, Virginia City, and Bozeman, accompanied by some of the officers stationed at Fort Ellis, with an escort of soldiers, would leave Bozeman about the fifth of September, for the Yellowstone country, with the intention of making a thorough examination of all the wonders with which that region was said to abound. The party was expected to be limited in numbers, and to be composed of some of the most prominent men in the Territory, and the writer felt extremely flattered when his earnest request to have his name added to the list was granted. He joined with two personal friends in getting an outfit, and then waited patiently for the other members of the party to perfect their arrangements. About a month before the day fixed for starting, some of the members began to discover that pressing business engagements would prevent their going. Then came news from Fort Ellis, that owing to some changes made in the

disposition of troops stationed in the Territory, the military por-
tion of the party would be unable to join the expedition; and our
party, which had now dwindled down to ten or twelve persons,
thinking it would be unsafe for so small a number to venture
where there was a strong possibility of meeting with hostile
Indians, also abandoned the undertaking. But the writer and his
two friends before mentioned, believing that the dangers to be
encountered had been magnified, and trusting by vigilance and
good luck to avoid them, resolved to attempt the journey at all
hazards. . . .

We pushed on up the valley, following the general course of the
river as well as we could, but frequently making short detours
through the foothills, to avoid the deep ravines and places
where the hills terminated abruptly at the water's edge. On the
eighth day out, we encountered a band of Indians – who, how-
ever, proved to be Sheepeaters, and friendly; the discovery of
their characters relieved our minds of apprehension, and we
conversed with them as well as their limited knowledge of
English and ours of pantomime would permit. For several
hours after leaving them, we traveled over a high rolling table-
land, diversified by sparkling lakes, picturesque rocks, and
beautiful groves of timber. Two or three miles to our left, we
could see the deep gorge which the river, flowing westward, had
cut through the mountains (Black Canyon of the Yellowstone).
The river soon after resumed its northern course; and from this

"Camp of the Survey, upon the southwest arm of
Yellowstone Lake"
by William Henry Jackson

point to the falls, a distance of twenty-five or thirty miles, it is believed to flow through one continuous cañon, through which no one has ever been able to pass. At this point we left the main river, intending to follow up the east branch for one day (Lamar Valley), *then to turn in a southwest course and endeavor to strike the* (Yellowstone) *river again near the falls. . . .*

They mis-identify the Absaroka Mountains as the Bighorn and Wind River Ranges, based on the same geographical misconceptions as the Washburn party.

September 18th – the twelfth day out – we found that ice had formed one-fourth of an inch thick during the night, and six inches of snow had fallen. The situation began to look a little disagreeable; but the next day was bright and clear, with promise of warm weather again in a few days. Resuming our journey, we soon saw the serrated peaks of the Bighorn Range (Absaroka) *glistening like burnished silver in the sunlight, and, overtowering them in the dim distance, the Wind River Mountains seemed to blend with the few fleecy clouds that skirted their tops; while in the opposite direction, in contrast to the barren snow-capped peaks behind us, as far as the eye could reach, mountain and valley were covered with timber, whose dark green foliage deepened in hue as it receded, till it terminated at the horizon in a boundless black forest. Taking our bearings as well as we could, we shaped our course in the direction in which we supposed the falls to be.*

They now pass through some backcountry thermal areas.

The next day, we came to a gentle declivity at the head of a shallow ravine, from which steam rose in a hundred columns and united in a cloud so dense as to obscure the sun. In some places it spurted from the rocks in jets not larger than a pipestem; in others it curled gracefully up from the surface of boiling pools from five to fifteen feet in diameter. In some springs the water was clear and transparent; others contained so much sulphur that they looked like pots of boiling yellow paint. One of the largest was as black as ink. Near this was a fissure in the rocks, several rods long and two feet across in the widest place at the surface, but enlarging as it descended. We could not see down to any great depth, on account of the steam but the ground echoed beneath our tread with a hollow sound, and we could hear the waters surging below, sending up a dull, resonant roar like the break of the ocean surf into a cave. At these springs but little water was discharged at the surface, it seeming to pass off by some subterranean passage. About half a mile down the ravine, the springs broke out again. Here they were in groups, spreading out over several acres of ground. One of these groups – a collection of mud springs of various colors, situated one above the other on the left slope of the ravine – we christened "The Chemical Works." The mud, as it was discharged from the lower side, gave each spring the form of a basin or pool. At the bottom of the slope was a vat, ten by thirty feet, where all the ingredients from the springs above were united in a greenish-yellow compound of the consistency of white lead. Three miles further on we found more hot springs along the sides of a deep ravine, at the bottom of which flowed a creek twenty feet wide. Near the bank of the creek, through an aperture four inches in diameter, a column of steam rushed with a deafening roar, with such force that it maintained its size for forty feet in the air, then spread out and rolled away in a great cloud toward the heavens. We found here inexhaustible beds of sulphur and saltpetre. Alum was also abundant; a small pond in the vicinity, some three hundred yards long and half as wide, contained as much alum as it could hold in solution, and the mud along the shore was white with the same substance, crystallized by evaporation.

On September 21ˢᵗ, a pleasant ride of eighteen miles over an undulating country brought us to the great cañon (Grand Canyon of the Yellowstone), two miles below the falls; but there being no grass convenient, we passed on up the river to a point half a mile above the upper falls, and camped on a narrow flat, close to the river bank. We spent the next day at the falls – a day that was a succession of surprises. . . . Above our camp the river is about one hundred and fifty yards wide, and glides smoothly along between gently-sloping banks (Hayden Valley); but just below, the hills crowd in on either side, forcing the water into a narrow channel, through which it hurries with increasing speed, until, rushing through a chute sixty feet wide, it falls in an unbroken sheet over a precipice one hundred and fifteen feet in height (Upper Falls). It widens out again, flows with steady course for half a mile between steep timbered bluffs four hundred feet high, and again narrowing in till it is not more than seventy-five feet wide, it makes the final fearful leap of three hundred and fifty feet (Lower Falls). The ragged edges of the precipice tear the water into a thousand streams – all united together, and yet apparently separate – changing it to the appearance of molten silver; the outer ones decrease in size as they increase in velocity, curl outward, and break into mist long before they reach the bottom. This cloud of mist conceals the river for two hundred yards, but it dashes out from beneath the rainbow-arch that spans the chasm, and thence, rushing over a succession of rapids and cascades, it vanishes at last, where a sudden turn of the river seems to bring the two walls of the cañon together. Below the falls, the hills gradually increase in height for two miles, where they assume the proportions of mountains. Here the cañon is at least fifteen hundred feet deep, with an average width of twice that distance at the top. For one-third of the distance downwards the sides are perpendicular – from thence running down to the river in steep ridges crowned by rocks of the most grotesque form and color; and it required no stretch of the imagination to picture fortresses, castles, watch-towers, and other ancient structures, of every conceivable shape. In several places near the bottom, steam issued from the rocks; and, judging from the indications, there were at some former period hot springs or steam-jets of immense size along the wall.

The next day we resumed our journey, traversing the northern slope of a high plateau between the Yellowstone and Snake Rivers. Unlike the dashing mountain stream we had thus far followed, the Yellowstone was in this part of its course wide and deep, flowing with a gentle current along the foot of low hills, or meandering in graceful curves through broad and grassy meadows (Hayden Valley). *Some twelve miles from the falls we came to a collection of hot springs that deserve more than a passing notice* (Mud Volcano region). *These, like the most we saw, were situated upon a hillside; and as we approached them we could see the steam rising in puffs at regular intervals of fifteen or twenty seconds, accompanied by dull explosions which could be heard half a mile away, sounding like the discharge of a blast underground. These explosions came from a large cave than ran back under the hill, from which mud had been discharged in such quantities as to form a heavy embankment twenty feet higher than the floor of the cave, which prevented the mud from flowing off; but the escaping steam had kept a hole, some twenty feet in diameter, open up through the mud in front of the entrance to the cave. The cave seemed nearly filled* with mud, and the stream rushed out with such volume and force as to lift the whole mass up against the roof and dash it out into the open space in front; and then, as the cloud of steam lifted, we could see the mud settling back in turbid waves into the cavern again. Three hundred yards from the mud-cave was another that discharged pure water; the entrance to it was in the form of a perfect arch, seven feet in height and five in width. A short distance below these caves were several large sulphur springs, the most remarkable of which was a shallow pool seventy-five feet in diameter, in which clear water on one side and yellow mud on the other were gently boiling without mingling.

September 24th, we arrived at Yellowstone Lake, about twenty miles from the falls.

. . . Its shores – whether gently sloping mountains, bold promontories, low necks, or level prairies – are everywhere covered with timber. The lake has three small islands, which are also heavily timbered. The outlet is at the northwest extremity. The lake abounds with trout, and the shallow water in its coves afford feeding ground for thousands of wild ducks, geese, pelicans, and swans.

We ascended to the head of the lake, and remained in its vicinity for several days, resting ourselves and our horses, and viewing the many objects of interest and wonder. Among these were springs differing from any we had previously seen (West Thumb). They were situated along the shore for a distance of two miles, extending back from it about five hundred yards and into the lake perhaps as many feet. The ground in many places gradually sloped down to the water's edge, while in others the white chalky cliffs rose fifteen feet high – the waves having worn the rock away at the base, leaving the upper portion projecting over in some places twenty feet. There were several hundred springs here varying in size from miniature fountains to pools or wells seventy-five feet in diameter and of great depth; the water had a pale violet tinge, and was very clear, enabling us to discern small objects fifty or sixty feet below the surface. In some of these, vast openings led off at the side; and as the slanting rays of the sun lit up these deep caverns, we could see the rocks hanging from their roofs, their water-worn sides and rocky floors, almost as plainly as if we had been traversing their silent chambers. These springs were intermittent, flowing *or boiling at irregular intervals. The greater portion of them were perfectly quiet while we were there, although nearly all gave unmistakable evidence of frequent activity. Some of them would quietly settle for ten feet, while another would as quietly rise until it overflowed its banks, and send a torrent of hot water sweeping down to the lake. At the same time, one near at hand would send up a sparkling jet of water ten or twelve feet high, which would fall back into its basin, and then perhaps instantly stop boiling and quietly settle into the earth, or suddenly rise and discharge its waters in every direction over the rim; while another, as if wishing to attract our wondering gaze, would throw up a cone six feet in diameter and eight feet high, with a loud roar. These changes, each one of which would possess some new feature, were constantly going on; sometimes they would occur within the space of a few minutes, and again hours would elapse before any change could be noted. At the water's edge, along the lake shore, there were several mounds of solid stone, on the top of each of which was a small basin with a perforated bottom; these also overflowed at times, and the hot water trickled down on every side. Thus, by the slow process of precipitation, through the countless lapse of ages, these stone monuments have been formed. A small cluster of mud springs near by claimed our attention. They were like hollow truncated cones and oblong mounds, three or four feet in height. These were filled with mud, resembling thick paint of the finest quality – differing in color, from pure white to the various shades of yellow, pink, red, and violet. Some of these boiling pots were less than a foot in diameter. The mud in them would slowly rise and fall as the bubbles of escaping steam, following one after the other, would burst upon the surface. During the afternoon, they threw mud to the height of fifteen feet for a few minutes, and then settled back to their former quietude.*

As we were about departing on our homeward trip, we ascended the summit of a neighboring hill, and took a final look at Yellowstone Lake. Nestled among the forest-crowned hills which bounded our vision, lay this inland sea, its crystal waves dancing and sparkling in the sunlight, as if laughing with joy for their wild freedom. It is a scene of transcendent beauty, which has been viewed by but few white men; and we felt glad to have looked upon it before its primeval solitude should be broken by the crowds of pleasure-seekers which at no distant day will throng its shores.

September 29th, we took up our march for home. Our plan was to cross the range in a northwesterly direction, find the Madison River, and follow it down to civilization. Twelve miles brought us to a small triangular-shaped lake, about eight miles long, deeply set among the hills. We kept on in a northwesterly direction, as near as the rugged nature of the country would permit; and on the third day came to a small irregularly shaped valley, some six miles across in the widest place, from every part of which great clouds of steam arose. From descriptions which we had had of this valley, from persons who had previously visited it, we recognized it as the place known as "Burnt Hole," or "Death Valley.". . . We descended into the valley, and found that the springs had the same general characteristics as those I have already described, although some of them were much larger and discharged a vast amount of water. One of them, at a little distance, attracted our attention by the immense amount of steam it threw off; and upon approaching it we found it to be an intermittent geyser in active operation. The hole through which the water was discharged was ten feet in diameter, and was situated in the centre of a large circular shallow basin, into which the water fell. There was a stiff breeze blowing at the time, and by going to the windward side and carefully picking our way over convenient stones, we were enabled to reach the edge of the hole. At that moment the escaping steam was causing the water to boil up in a fountain five or six feet high. It stopped in an instant, and commenced settling down – twenty, thirty, forty feet – until we concluded that the bottom had fallen out; but the next instant, without any warning, it came rushing up and shot into the air at least eighty feet, causing us to stampede for higher ground. It continued to spout at intervals of a few minutes, for some time; but finally subsided, and was quiet during the remainder of the time we stayed in the vicinity. We followed up the Madison five miles, and there found the most gigantic hot springs we had seen. They were situated along the river bank, and discharged so much hot water that the river was blood-warm a quarter of a mile below. One of the springs was two hundred and fifty feet in diameter, and had every indication of spouting powerfully at times. The waters from the hot springs in this valley, if united, would form a large stream; and they increase the size of the river nearly one-half. Although we experienced no bad effects from passing through the "Valley of Death," yet we were not disposed to dispute the propriety of giving it that name. It seemed to be shunned by all *animated nature. There were no fish in the river, no birds in the trees, no animals – not even a track – anywhere to be seen; although in one spring we saw the entire skeleton of a buffalo that had probably fallen in accidentally and been boiled down to soup.*

Leaving this remarkable valley, we followed the course of the Madison – sometimes through level valleys, and sometimes through deep cuts in mountain ranges – and on the fourth of October emerged from a cañon, ten miles long and with high and precipitous mountain sides, to find the broad valley of the Lower Madison spread out before us. Here we could recognize familiar landmarks in some of the mountain peaks around Virginia City. From this point we completed our journey by easy stages, and arrived at home on the evening of the eleventh. We had been absent thirty-six days – a much longer time than our friends had anticipated – and we found that they were seriously contemplating organizing a party to go in search of us.

Chapter VII

FLAMING GORGE – DINOSAUR – CANYONLANDS – GLEN CANYON – GRAND CANYON 1869

from "The Cañons of the Colorado"
in Scribner's Monthly, *Jan., Feb., Mar. 1875*
by John Wesley Powell

1869 was a banner year on the western frontier. The Transcontinental Railroad was officially completed. Folsom, Cook and Peterson discovered Yellowstone. And John Wesley Powell made his epic descent of the Green and Colorado River canyons. Here is the narrative as it appeared in three installments of a periodical, later expanded into book form for *Exploration of the Colorado River and its Cañons.* Reading the descriptions of the landscape and the explorers' interesting experiences causes this narrative of Powell's and the following one by Langford to seem like the climax of this anthology. The remaining mysteries of the west are about to be revealed in the canyons of the Colorado and the wonders of the Yellowstone.

The Colorado River is formed by the junction of the Grand and the Green. Grand River has its source in the Rocky Mountains, five or six miles west of Long's Peak. . . . A group of little alpine lakes that receive their waters from perpetual snow banks discharge into a common reservoir known as Grand Lake – a beautiful sheet of water, whose quiet surface reflects towering cliffs and crags of granite on its eastern shore, and stately pines and firs on its western margin.

Green River heads near Fremont's Peak in the Wind River Mountains. This river, like the last, has its sources in alpine lakes fed by everlasting snows. Thousands of these little lakes with deep, cold, emerald waters, are embosomed among the crags of the Rocky Mountains. These streams, born in the gloomy solitudes of the upper mountain region, have a strange and eventful history as they pass down through gorges, tumbling in cascades and cataracts until they reach the hot, arid plains of the lower Colorado, where the waters that were so clear above, empty muddy floods into the Gulf of California. . . .

The upper two-thirds of the basin rises from four to eight hundred feet above the level of the sea. This higher region is set on the east, north and west, with ranges of snow-clad mountains attaining an altitude above the sea varying from eight thousand to fourteen thousand feet.

Very little water falls within the basin, but, all winter long, snows fall on its mountain-crested rim, filling the gorges, half burying the forests, and covering the crags and peaks with a mantle woven by the winds from the waves of the sea. When the summer sun comes, these snows melt and tumble down the mountain-sides in millions of cascades. Ten million cascade brooks unite to form ten thousand torrent creeks; ten thousand torrent creeks unite to form a hundred rivers beset with cataracts; a hundred roaring rivers unite to form the Colorado, which rolls a mad, turbid stream into the Gulf of California. . . .

About the basin are mountains; within the basin are cañon gorges; the stretches of land from cañon brink to cañon brink are of naked rock or drifting sands, with here and there lines of volcanic cones, and with black scoria and ashes scattered about. These cañon gorges and desert wastes have prevented the traveler from penetrating the country, so that, until the Colorado River Exploring Expedition was organized, it was almost unknown; yet, enough had been seen to foment rumor, and many wonderful stories have been told in the hunter's cabin and explorer's camp. Stories were related of parties having entered the gorge in boats and having been carried down with fearful velocity into whirlpools, where all were overwhelmed in the abyss of waters; others of underground passages for the great river into which boats had passed, never to be seen again. It was currently believed that the river was lost under the rocks for several hundred miles. There were other accounts of great falls whose roaring music could be heard on the distant mountain summits. There were stories current of parties wandering on the brink of the cañon vainly endeavoring to reach the stream below, and perishing with thirst at last, in sight and sound of its tantalizing waters.

The Indians, too, have woven the mysteries of the cañons into the myths of their religion. Long ago there was a great and wise chief who mourned the death of his wife and would not be comforted until Tah-vwoats, one of the Indian gods, came to him and told him that she was in a happier land, and offered to take him there that he might see for himself, if, upon his return, he would cease to mourn. The great chief promised. Then Tah-vwoats made a trail through the mountains that lie between that beautiful land, the balmy region in the Great West, and this, the desert home of the poor Nu-ma. This trail was the cañon gorge of the Colorado. Through it he led him; and when they had returned, the deity exacted from the chief a promise that he would tell no one of the joys of that land, lest, through discontent with the circumstances of this world, the people should desire to go to Heaven. Then he rolled a river into the gorge, a raging stream that should engulf any who might attempt to enter thereby. More than once have I been warned by the Indians not to enter this cañon; they considered it disobedience to the gods and contempt of their authority, and believed that it would surely bring their wrath upon me.

For two years previous to the exploration I had been making some geological studies among the heads of the cañons running into the Colorado from the east, and a desire to explore the Grand Cañon itself grew upon me. Early in the spring of 1869 a small party was organized for this enterprise. Boats were built in Chicago and transported by rail to the point where the Union Pacific Railroad crosses Green River. With these we were to descend the Green into the Colorado, and the Colorado down to the foot of the Grand Cañon.

On the 24^{*th*} *of May the good people of Green River City turned out to see us start. We raised our little flag, pushed the boats from shore, and the swift current carried us down.*

Our boats were four in number – three built of oak, stanch and strong, double-ribbed, with double stern and stern-posts, and further strengthened by bulk heads, dividing each into three compartments. Two of these, the fore and aft, were decked, forming water-tight cabins. The little vessels were twenty-one feet long, and were capable of carrying about four thousand pounds each, and, without the cargoes, could be transported by four men. The fourth boat was made of pine, very light, but six-

teen feet in length, with a sharp cut-water, and every way built for fast rowing, and divided into compartments as the others.

We took with us rations deemed sufficient to last ten months, expecting to stop over for the winter at some point about midway down the stream. We also took tools for repairing boats and building cabins. For scientific work we had sextants, chronometers, barometers, thermometers, compasses, and other instruments.

The flour was divided into three equal parts, the meat and other articles of our rations, in the same way. Each of the larger boats had an axe, hammer, saw, auger, and other tools, so that all were loaded alike.

We distributed the cargoes in this way, that we might not be entirely destitute of some important article should any one of the boats be lost. In the small boat we packed a part of the scientific instruments, three guns, and three small bundles of clothing only. In this boat I proceeded in advance to explore the channel.

J. C. Sumner and William H. Dunn were my boatmen in the "Emma Dean." Then followed "Kitty Clyde's Sister," manned by W. H. Powell and G. Y. Bradley. Next, the "No Name," with O. G. Howland, Seneca Howland, and Frank Goodman; and last came the "Maid of the Cañon," with W. R. Hawkins and Andrew Hall. . . .

Our boats were heavily loaded, and only with the utmost care was it possible to float on the rough river without shipping water. Our way for nearly fifty miles was through the Green River Bad Lands, a region of desolation. The rocks are sandstone and shale, gray and buff, red and brown, blue and black strata in many alternations, lying nearly horizontal, and almost without soil or vegetation; but they are all very soft and friable, and are strangely carved by the rains and streams. The fantastic rain-sculpture imitates architectural forms, and suggests rude and weird statuary. Standing on some high point, you can look off in every direction over a vast landscape, with salient rocks and cliffs glittering in the evening sun. At such a time dark shadows are settling in the valleys and gulches, and the heights are made higher, and the depths deeper, by the glamour and witchery of light and shade. Away to the south the Uinta Mountains stretch in a long line – high peaks piercing the sky, and snow fields glittering like lakes of molten silver, and pine forests in somber green, and rosy clouds playing around the borders of huge black masses; and heights and depths, and clouds and mountains, and snow fields, and forests, and rocklands are blended into one grand view.

The journey to the foot of the mountains was made with no more important incident than the breaking of an oar in some ugly rapid, or the killing of a mountain sheep on a cliff that overhangs the river.

(Flaming Gorge)

The general course of the Green here is to the south. The Uinta Mountains have an east and west direction, and stand directly athwart the course of the stream; yet it glides along quietly as if a mountain range were no formidable obstruction to its progress. It enters the range by a flaring, brilliant red gorge, that may be seen from the north-west a score of miles away. The great mass of the mountain ridge through which the gorge is cut is composed of bright vermilion rocks, but they are surmounted by broad bands of mottled buff and gray, and these bands come down with a gentle curve to the water's edge on the nearer slope. This is the head of the first cañon which we were to explore, an introductory one to a series made by the river through this range. We named it "Flaming Gorge." The cliffs or walls on either side we found to be about twelve hundred feet high.

On the 30th of May we started down the mysterious cañons, with some anxiety. The old mountaineers had told us it could not be run; we had heard the Indians say: "Water heap catch 'em!" But all were eager for the trial. Entering Flaming Gorge, we quickly ran through it on a swift current, and emerged into a little park. Half a mile below, the river wheeled sharply to the left, and we turned into another cañon cut into the mountain. We entered the narrow passage; on either side the walls rapidly increased in altitude; on the left were overhanging ledges and cliffs five hundred, a thousand, fifteen hundred feet high; on the right the rocks were broken and ragged; the water filled the channel from cliff to cliff. Then the river turned abruptly around *a point to the right, and the water plunged swiftly down among the great rocks. And here we had our first experience with cañon rapids. I stood up on the deck of my boat to seek a way between the wave-beaten rocks. All untried as we were with such waters, the moments were filled with intense anxiety. Soon our boats reached the swift current; a stroke or two, now on this side, now on that, and we threaded the narrow passage with exhilarating velocity, mounting the high waves whose foaming crests dashed over us, and plunging into the troughs until we reached the quiet water below. And then came a feeling of great relief; our first rapid was run. Another mile and we came out into the valley again. . . .*

Soon we left the valley and entered another short cañon, very narrow at first, but widening below as the walls increased in altitude. The river was broad, deep, and quiet, and its waters mirrored towering rocks. Kingfishers were playing about the stream, and so we adopted as the name, "Kingfisher Cañon."

At the foot of this cañon the river turned to the east, past a point which was rounded to the shape of a dome; on its sides little cells had been carved by the action of the water, and in these pits, which cover the face of the dome, hundreds of swallows had built their nests; and as they flitted about the rock they looked like swarms of bees, giving to the whole the appearance of a colossal bee-hive, of the old-time form; and so we named it "Bee-Hive Point."

One evening when we camped near this point, I went out into a vast amphitheater, rising in a succession of terraces to a height of eighteen hundred or two thousand feet. Each step of this amphitheater was built of red sandstone, with a face of naked, red rock and glucose clothed with verdure; so that the amphitheater was surrounded by bands of red and green. The evening sun lit up the rocks and the cedars, and its many-colored beams danced on the waves of the river. The landscape reveled in sunshine.

Below Bee-Hive Point we came to dangerous rapids, where we toiled along for some days, making portage or letting our boats down the stream with lines. Now and then we had an exciting ride; the river rolled down at a wonderful rate, and where there were no rocks in the way, we made almost railroad speed. Here and there the water rushed into a narrow gorge, the rocks on the sides rolled it into the center in great waves, and the boats went bounding over these like things of life. Some the waves would break and their waters roll over the boats, which made much bailing necessary, and obliged us to stop occasionally for that purpose. At one time we made a run of twelve miles in an hour, including stoppages.

The spring before, I had a conversation with an old Indian, who told me about one of his tribe attempting to run this cañon: "The rocks," he said, holding his hands above his head, his arms vertical, and looking between them to the heavens, "the rocks h-e-a-p, h-e-a-p high; the water go h-oo-woogh, h-oo-woogh; water-pony (boat) h-e-a-p buck; water catch 'em! no see 'em Injun any more! no see 'em squaw any more! no see 'em papoose any more!" Those who have seen these wild Indian ponies rearing alternately before and behind, or "bucking" as it is called in the vernacular, will appreciate his description.

One day we came to calm water, but a threatening roar was heard in the distance below. Slowly approaching the point from which the sound issued, we came near the falls and tied just above them on the left. Here we were compelled to make a portage; so we unloaded the boats, fastened a long line to the bow, and one to the stern of the little boat, and moored her close to the brink of the fall. Then the bow-line was taken below and made fast, the stern-line was held by five or six men, and the boat let down as long as they could hold her against the rushing waters; then, letting go one end of the line, it ran through the ring, the boat leaped over the fall, and was caught by the lower rope. In this way the boats were passed beyond the fall. Then we built a trail among the rocks, along which we carried our stores, rations and clothing, and the portage was completed after a day's labor. On a high rock, by which our trail passed, we found the inscription: "Ashley 18-5;" the third figure was obscure, some of the party reading the date 1835, some 1855. (In fact, it was 1825.)

James Baker, an old-time mountaineer, once told me about a party of men starting down the river, and Ashley was named as one of them. The story runs that the boat was swamped and some of the party drowned in one of the cañons below. (As we have seen they were not drowned – see the "Journal of William Ashley" above.)

The word "Ashley" was a warning to us, and we resolved on great caution. We named the cataract "Ashley Falls." The river is very narrow at that point, the right wall vertical for two or three hundred feet, and the left towering to a great height with a vast pile of broken rock lying between the foot of the cliff and the water. Some of the rocks broken from the ledge above have tumbled into the channel and caused this fall. One great cubical block, thirty or forty feet high, stands in the middle of the stream, and the waters, parting to either side, plunge down about twelve feet and are broken again by smaller rocks into a rapid below. Immediately below the falls the water occupies the entire channel, there being no talus at the foot of the cliffs.

Near the foot of this cañon there is a little park, which is simply the widening of the cañon into a little valley; this we called "Red Cañon Park." Reaching this on the third of June, we spread our rations, clothing, etc., on the ground to dry, and several of the party went out for a hunt. I took a walk of five or six miles up to a pine-grove park, its grassy carpet bedecked with crimson flowers set in groups on the stems of pear-shaped cactus plants; patches of painted cups were seen here and there with yellow blossoms protruding through scarlet bracts; little blue-eyed flowers were peeping through the grass, and the air was filled with fragrance from the white blossoms of a spiræa; a mountain brook ran through the midst, ponded below by beaver dams. This quiet place formed a great contrast to the one I had just left.

The next day we ran down to Brown's Park, and found a quiet river through this valley until we reached the Gate of Lodore, the entrance to the Cañon of Lodore.

(Dinosaur)

On the 7th of June three of us climbed to the summit of the cliff on the left and found its altitude above camp to be 2,086 feet. The rocks are split with fissures, deep and narrow, sometimes a hundred feet or more to the bottom. Lofty pines find root in such fissures as are filled with loose earth and decayed vegetation. On a rock we found a pool of clear cold water caught from a shower, which had fallen the evening before. After drinking of this we walked to the brink of the cañon and looked down to the water below. The cañon walls are buttressed on a grand scale, and deep alcoves are excavated; rocky crags crown the cliffs, and the river rolls below. At noon we returned to camp. The sun shone in splendor on the vermilion walls, shaded into green and gray where the rocks were lichened over; the river filled the channel from wall to wall, and the cañon opened like a beautiful doorway to a region of glory. But at evening, when the sun was going down and the shadows were setting in the cañon, the vermilion gleams and roseate hues, blended with tints of green and gray, slowly changed to somber brown above, and black shadows crept over them below. Then it seemed the shadowy portal to a region of gloom. Through this gateway we were to enter on our voyage the next day.

Entering the cañon, we found, until noon, a succession of rapids, over which our boats had to be taken by lines. . . .

One night we were camped on the right bank, on a little shelving rock between the river and the foot of the cliff. With night comes gloom into these great depths. After supper we sat by our fire made of drift-wood caught by the rocks, and told stories of wild life. It was late before we spread our blankets on the beach. Lying down, we looked up through the cañon and saw that only a little of the blue heaven appeared overhead – a crescent of blue sky with but two or three constellations peering down upon us. I did not sleep for some time, as the excitement of the day had not worn off. Soon I saw a bright star that appeared to rest on the very verge of the cliffs overhead on the east. Slowly it seemed to float from its resting-place on the rocks over the cañon. At first it appeared like a jewel set on the brink of the cliff, but as it moved out from the rock I almost wondered that it did not fall. In fact it did seem to descend in a gentle curve, as though the bright sky, in which the stars were set, was spread across the cañon, resting on either wall, and swayed down by its own weight. The star appeared to be in the cañon, so high were the walls. I soon discovered that it was the bright star Vega, so it occurred to us to designate that part of the wall as "The Cliff of the Harp."

Very slowly we made our way through this cañon, often climbing on the rocks at the edge of the water for a few hundred

yards, to examine the channel before running it. One afternoon
we came to a place where it was necessary to make a portage.
The little boat was landed, and the others signaled to come up.
Where these rapids, or broken falls, occur, usually the channel
is suddenly narrowed by rocks, which have tumbled down from
the cliffs, or have been washed in by lateral streams. Immedi-
ately above the narrow rocky channel on one or both sides,
there is often a bay of quiet water, in which it was easy to land.
Sometimes the water descends with a smooth, unruffled surface
from the broad, quiet spread above, into the narrow, angry
channel below, by a semicircular sag. Great care was taken not
to pass over the brink into this deceptive pit, but above it we
could row with safety. At this point I walked along the bank to
examine the ground, leaving one of the men with a flag to guide
the other boats to the landing place. I soon saw one of the boats
make shore all right, and felt no more concerned; but a minute
after, I heard a shout, and, looking around, saw one of the boats
shoot down the center of the sag. It was the "No Name," with
Captain Howland, his brother, Seneca Howland, and Frank
Goodman. I felt that its going over was inevitable, and ran to
save the third boat. A few minutes more and she turned the point
and headed for the shore. Then I started down stream and
scrambled along to look for the boat that had gone over. The
first fall was not great, only ten or twelve feet, and we often had
run such; but below, the river tumbled down again for forty or
fifty feet in a channel filled with dangerous rocks that broke the
waves into whirlpools and beat them into foam. I passed around
a great crag just in time to see the boat strike a rock, and,
rebounding from the shock, careen and fill the open compart-
ment with water. Two of the men lost their oars. Then she swung
around and was carried down at a rapid rate, broadside on, for
a few yards, and, striking amidships on another rock with great
force, was broken quite in two, and the men were thrown into
the river. The larger part of the boat still floated buoyantly; this
they soon seized, and drifted down the river past the rocks for a
few hundred yards to a second rapid filled with huge bowlders.
Here the boat struck again, was dashed to pieces, and the men
and fragments were carried beyond my sight. Running along, I
turned a bend and saw a man's head above the water, dashed
about by the waves in a whirlpool below a great rock. It was
Frank Goodman clinging to the rock for his life. Then I saw
Howland trying to go to his aid from an island on which he had
been washed. Soon he came near enough to reach Frank with a

pole, which he extended toward him. The latter let go the rock, grasped the pole, and was pulled ashore. Seneca Howland was washed farther down the island, and was caught by some rocks, and, though somewhat bruised, managed to get ashore in safety.

And now the three men were on an island with a swift, dangerous river on either side and a fall below. The "Emma Dean" was soon brought down, and Sumner, starting above, as far as possible, pushed out. Right skillfully he plied his oars, and a few strokes set him on the island at the proper point. Then they all pulled the boat up stream, until they stood in water up to their necks. One sat on a rock and held the boat until the others were ready to pull, then he gave the boat a push, clung to it with his hands and climbed in as they pulled for the mainland, which they reached in safety. We were as glad to shake hands with them as if they had returned from a voyage around the world, and had been wrecked on a distant coast. We named the scene of this incident "Disaster Falls."

The next day, making a portage in the remaining boats, we discovered, a little below, some fragments of an old boat, an old dutch bake-oven, some tin plates and other articles, doubtless the relics of Ashley's party, whom I have before mentioned. (Doubtful, actually. Powell goes on to relate a legend about Ashley's supposed wreck here, believing it to be fact.)

. . . Below, we found rocks, rapids, falls, and made our portages. At many places the Cañon of Lodore has deep, dark alcoves set between massive buttresses. In these alcoves grow beautiful mosses and delicate ferns, while springs burst out from the farther recesses and wind in silver threads over floors of sand. At one place we found three cataracts in quick succession where we were compelled to make three difficult portages, and we named the place "Triplet Falls."

. . . At one place we had to make a portage of more than half a mile past a wild confusion of waves and rocks, which we called "Hell's Half Mile."

One day we stopped for a late dinner at the mouth of a brook on the right. This little stream comes down from a distant mountain in a deep side cañon. We set out to explore it, but were soon cut off from further progress up the gorge by a high rock over which the brook ran in a smooth sheet; the rock was not quite vertical, and the water did not plunge over in a fall. Then we climbed up to the left for an hour, until we were a thousand feet above the river, and six hundred above the brook. Just before us the cañon divided, one little stream coming down on the right and another on the left, and we could look away up either of these cañons through an ascending vista to cliffs, and crags, and towers, a mile back, and two thousand feet overhead.

To the right were a dozen gleaming cascades; pine and firs stood on the rocks, and aspens overhung the brooks. The rocks below were red and brown set in deep shadows, but above they were buff and vermilion. The light above, made more brilliant by the bright-tinted rocks, and the shadows below, made more gloomy by the somber hues of the brown walls, increased the apparent depth of the cañons, and it seemed a long way up to the world of sunshine and open sky, and a long way down to the cañon floor. Never before had I received such an impression of the vast height of these cañon walls; not even at the Cliff of the Harp, when the very heavens seemed to rest on their summits.

Late the same afternoon we made a short run to the mouth of another little brook coming down from the left into an alcove filled with luxuriant vegetation. Here camp was made with a group of cedars on one side, and a dense mass of box-elders and dead willows on the other. I went out to explore the alcove, and while away a whirlwind came on, scattering the fire among the dead willows and cedar spray. Soon there was a conflagration. The men rushed for the boats, leaving behind all that they could not readily seize at the instant, and even then they had their clothing burned and hair singed, and Bradley had his ears scorched. The cook filled his arms with the mess-kit, and jumping into a boat stumbled and fell, and away went our cooking utensils into the river. Our plates were gone, our spoons were gone, our knives and forks were gone. "Water catch 'em; h-e-a-p catch 'em!" When on the boats, the men were compelled to cut loose, as the flames, running out on the overhanging willows, scorched them. Loose on the stream they must go down, for the water was too swift to make head-way against it, and just below was a rapid filled with rocks. On they drifted, no channel explored, no signal to guide them. Just at this juncture I chanced to see them, but had not discovered the fire, and the strange movements of the men filled me with astonishment.

Down the rocks I clambered and ran to the bank. When I arrived they had landed. Then we all went back to the late camp to see if anything left behind could be saved. Some of the clothing and bedding that had been taken out of the boats, a few tin cups, a basin and a camp kettle, were all that was left.

The next day we ran down to the mouth of the Yampa River. The journey from the Gate of Lodore was marked by disasters and toils. At the junction of the Yampa and Green we found a beautiful park, enclosed on every side by towering walls of gray sandstone, smooth and vertical. There are three river entrances into the park – one down the Green, one down the Yampa, and one up the Green; there is a fourth entrance by a side cañon that comes in from the south. Elsewhere this park is unapproachable. The way through the Cañon of Lodore is a difficult and dangerous one. The course of the Yampa for forty miles above its mouth is through another cañon; it also is difficult and dangerous. Green River runs through a cañon below Echo Park, beset with rocks and interrupted by falls. So it may be said that the park has but one practicable entrance, that by a side cañon so narrow in many places that a horseman could scarcely ride through it; yet we found a trail down this side cañon, and evidences that the Indians had camped in this beautiful park; in fact, it had been described to me the year before. The park itself is a beautiful natural garden, with grasses and flowering plants, shrubs, and trees – just large enough for a farm.

Here we encamped for two or three days, for the purpose of repairing boats, drying rations, and to make the observations necessary to determine the latitude and longitude of the junction of the two rivers.

Opposite our camp the wall was high and vertical. The river running to the south for a mile and a half, turns back upon itself, and the two stretches of river, the first south, the second north, are separated by a wall in many places but ten to twenty feet wide and eight hundred feet high, and, on the east, everywhere vertical or overhanging. I wished to climb this wall for the purpose of measuring its altitude, so one day Bradley and I took the little boat and pulled up stream as far as possible, in order to reach a place where the wall was so broken that it seemed practicable to climb it. We landed on a little talus of rocks at the foot of the wall, but found that we must go still far-

ther up the river; so we scrambled on until we reached a place where the river sweeps against the wall. Here we found a shelf along which we could pass, and then were ready for the climb. We started up a gulch, then passed to the left, on a bench along the wall; then up again, over broken rocks; then we reached more benches, along which we worked until we found more broken rocks and crevices; by which we climbed still up, until we had ascended six or eight hundred feet. Here we were met by a sheer precipice.

Looking about, we found a place where it seemed possible to climb. I went ahead, Bradley handed the barometer to me, and followed; so we proceeded stage by stage until we were nearly to the summit. Here, by making a spring, I gained a foothold in a little crevice and grasped an angle of the rock overhead. I found I could get up no farther, and could not step back, for I dared not let go with my hand, and could not reach foothold below without; so I called to Bradley for help. He found a way by which he could get to the top of the rock over my head, but could not reach me. He looked around for some stick or limb of a tree, but found none. Then he suggested that he had better help me with the barometer case, but I feared I could not hold on to it. The moment was critical. I was standing on my toes, and my muscles began to tremble. It was sixty or eighty feet to the foot of the precipice. If I lost my hold I should fall to the bottom, and then perhaps roll over the bench and still farther down the cliff. At that instant it occurred to Bradley to take off his drawers, which he did, and swung them down to me. I hugged close to the rock, let go with my hand, seized the dangling legs, and, with his assistance, was enabled to gain the top.

Then we walked out on a peninsular rock, made the necessary observations for determining its altitude above camp, and returned, finding an easy way down.

On the 21st of June we left Echo Park; our boats floated along the long peninsular rock until we turned abruptly to the southwest and entered another cañon. The walls were high and vertical, the cañon narrow, and the river filled the whole space below, so that there was no landing-space at the foot of the cliff.

The Green is greatly increased by the Yampa, and we now had a much larger river. All this volume of water, confined as it was in a narrow channel, and rushing with great velocity, was set eddying and spinning into whirlpools by projecting rocks and short curves, and the waters waltzed their way through the cañon. The cañon was much narrower than any we had seen. With difficulty we managed our boats. They spun about from side to side; we knew not where we were going, and found it impossible to keep them headed down the stream. At first this caused us great alarm, but we soon found there was but little danger, and that we really were making progress on our way. It was the merry mood of the river to dance through this deep, dark gorge, and right gaily did we join in the sport. But our revel was interrupted by a cataract. We succeeded in landing against the wall, and after three or four hours' labor passed the difficult point.

In like manner, spinning in eddies, making portages, and riding with exciting velocity along portions of the river where the fall was great but the rocks were few, we made our way through Whirlpool Cañon, and camped, on the 23rd of June, on an island in a beautiful little park.

The next day Bradley and I started early to climb the mountain to the east; we found its summit to be nearly three thousand feet above camp, and it required some labor to scale it; but from its top – what a view! The walls were set with crags, and peaks, and buttressed towers, and overhanging domes. Turning to the right, the park was below us, with its island groves reflected by the deep, quiet waters. Rich meadows stretched out on either hand to the verge of a sloping plain that came down from the distant mountains. In strange contrast to the meadows are the plains of blue and lilac-colored, buff and pink, brown and ver-milion rocks, with all these colors clear and bright. A dozen lit-tle streams (dry during the greater part of the year) ran down through the half circle of exposed formations, radiating from the island center to the rim of the basin. Each creek had its sys-tem of side streams, and each side stream its system of laterals, and again these were divided so that this outstretched slope of rock was elaborately embossed. Beds of different colored for-mations ran in parallel bands on either side; the perspective, modified by the undulations, gave the bands a waved appear-ance and the high colors gleamed in the midday sun with the luster of satin. We were tempted to call this "Rainbow Park."

Away beyond these beds were the Uinta and Wasatch Mountains with their pine forests and snow fields, and naked peaks.

Then we turned to the right and looked up Whirlpool Cañon, a deep gorge with a river in the bottom – a gloomy chasm where mad waves roared; but at that distance and altitude the river was but a rippling brook, and the chasm a narrow cleft. The top of the mountain on which we stood was a broad grassy table, and a herd of deer was feeding in the distance. Walking over to the southeast, we looked down into the valley of White River, and beyond that saw the far distant Rocky Mountains in mellow haze, through which came the glint of snow fields.

On the morning of the 25th of June we entered Split Mountain Cañon, and camped that night near the mouth of a cave at the foot of a great rapid. The waves of the rapid dashed in nearly to the farther end of the cave. We could pass along a little shelf at the side until we reached the back part. Swallows had built their nests in the ceiling, and they wheeled in, chattering and scolding at our intrusion, but their clamor was almost drowned by the noise of the waters. Looking out of the cave, we could see far up the river, with a line of crags standing sentinel on either side, and Mt. Hawkins in the distance.

The next day we ran out of Split Mountain Cañon. At the lower end of this gorge the water was very swift, and we ran with great speed wheeling around a rock now and then with a timely stroke or two of the oars. At one point the river turned from left to right in a direction at right angles to the cañon in a long chute and rolled up and struck the right wall where its waters were heaped up in great billows that tumbled back in breakers. We glided into this chute before we could see the danger, and it was too late to stop. Two or three hard strokes were given on the right, and we paused for a moment, expecting to be dashed against the rock; the bow of the boat leaped high on a great wave; the rebounding waters hurled us back, and the peril was past. The next moment the other boats were hurriedly signaled to land on the left. Accomplishing this, the men walked along the shore, holding the boats near the bank and letting them drift around. We started again and the river soon debouched into a beautiful valley. Gliding down its length for ten miles, we camped under a grand old cotton-wood. . . .

Here they rested for awhile at the nearby Uinta Indian Agency. Frank Goodman, who had been on the "No Name" during the wreck upstream, now left the party. The others soon continued downstream through Desolation and Gray Canyons before entering the Canyonlands.

(Canyonlands)

After passing the mouth of the San Rafael, we entered the mouth of another cañon. The walls of this were of orange-colored sandstone, very homogeneous, usually vertical, though not very high at first. Where the river swept around a curve, a vast hollow dome might be seen, with many caves and deep alcoves. The river sweeps in great curves and doubles upon itself many times. Sometimes we went by a great bend for several miles and came back within a stone's throw of points where we had been before. We called this "Labyrinth Cañon."

There was an exquisite charm in our ride down this beautiful gorge; it gradually grew deeper with every mile we traveled; the walls were symmetrically curved, grandly arched, and of a beautiful color. They were reflected in the quiet water in many places so as to almost deceive the eye. We were all in fine spirits, and the badinage of the men was echoed from wall to wall. Now and then a whistle, a shout, or the report of a pistol would reverberate among the cliffs, and the cañon seemed filled with strange weird voices.

Labyrinth Cañon ends abruptly, as did the Cañon of Desolation and Gray Cañon, as the table or great geographical bench through which it is cut terminates on the south in a line of cliffs. . . .

Climb the cliffs at the foot of Labyrinth Cañon and look over the plain below, and you see vast numbers of sharp, angular buttes, and pinnacles, and towers, and standing rocks, scattered about over scores of miles, and every butte, and pinnacle, and tower so regular and beautiful, than you can hardly cast aside the belief that they are works of Titanic art. It seems as if a thousand battles had been fought on the plains below, and on every field the giant heroes had built a monument, compared with which the pillar on Bunker Hill is but a milestone. But no human hand has placed a block in all those wonderful struc-

tures; the rain-drops of unreckoned ages have cut them from the solid rock. . . .

Immediately on leaving Labyrinth Cañon, we entered another with quiet water, so we called it "Still-water Cañon." This cañon is cut through the region of standing rocks which I have before mentioned. The Indians call this "Toom-pin Woo-near Too-weap," the Land of Standing Rocks. It is a weird, grand region. The landscape everywhere away from the river is of rock, a pavement of rock with cliffs of rock, tables of rock, pla-teaus of rock, terraces of rock, crags of rock, buttes of rock, ten thousand strangely carved forms; rocks everywhere, and no vegetation, no soil, no sand. In long gentle curves the river winds about these rocks.

When speaking of them, we must not conceive of piles of bowlders or heaps of fragments, but a whole landscape of naked rock with giant forms carved on it, cathedral-shaped buttes towering hundreds or thousands of feet, cliffs that cannot be scaled, and cañon walls that make the river shrink into insig-nificance, with vast hollow domes and tall pinnacles, and shafts set on the verge overhead, and all the rocks, tinted with buff, gray, red, brown, and chocolate, never lichened, never moss-covered, but bare, and sometimes even polished. Strange, indeed, is "Toom-pin Woo-near Too-weap."

On the 17th of July we reached the junction of the Grand and Green, the head of the Colorado River.

Here we decided to go into camp for several days. The first day was spent in spreading our rations to dry, for we found them badly injured. The flour had been wet many times, and was musty and full of hard lumps; so we made a sieve of mosquito bar and sifted it, losing more than two hundred pounds by the process. Our losses by the wrecking of the "No Name" and by various mishaps, together with the amount now thrown away, left us but little more than two months' supplies, and to make them last this long we must be fortunate enough to lose no more.

On the 19th of July Bradley and I climbed the left wall, below the junction of the streams. The path we selected was up a gulch. After climbing for an hour we found ourselves in a vast

The Gate of Lodore.

*These illustrations by Thomas Moran
appeared in* Scribner's Monthly
for the articles by John Wesley Powell

The Wreck at "Disaster Falls."

The Grand Canyon of the Colorado.

*amphitheater, and our way cut off. We clambered around to the
left for half an hour until we found that we could not go up in
that direction. Then we tried the rocks around to the right, and
discovered a narrow shelf nearly half a mile long. In some
places this was so wide that we passed along with ease; in others it was so narrow and sloping that we were compelled to lie
down and crawl. We could look over the brink of the shelf down
eight hundred feet and see the river rolling and plunging among
the rocks. The edge of the cliff, five hundred feet above, seemed
to blend with the sky. We went on until we came to a point where
the wall was again broken down, and up this we climbed. On
the right there was a narrow mural point of rocks extending
toward the river, two or three hundred feet high, and six or eight
hundred feet long. At last we came back to where this set in, and
found it cut off from the main wall by a great crevice. Into this
we passed, and now a long, narrow rock was between us and
the river. The rock itself was split longitudinally and transversely, and the rains on the surface above had run down
through the crevices and gathered into channels below, and
then run off into the river. The crevices were usually narrow
above, and, by erosion of the streams, wider below, forming a
net-work of caves, but each cave having a narrow, winding sky-
light up through the rocks.*

*We wandered among these corridors for an hour or two, but
found no place where the rocks were broken down so that we
could climb up. At last we determined to attempt a passage by a
crevice, and selected one which we thought wide enough to
admit of the passage of our bodies, and yet narrow enough to
climb out by pressing our hands and feet against the walls; so
we climbed as men would out of a well. Bradley went first; I
handed him the barometer, then climbed over his head, and he
handed the barometer to me; so we passed each other alternately, until we emerged from the fissure on the summit of the
rock .*

*What a world of grandeur was spread before us! Below was the
cañon through which the Colorado runs; we could trace its
course for miles, and at points catch glimpses of the river. From
the north-west came the Green in a narrow, winding gorge.
From the north-east came the Grand through a cañon that
seemed, from where we stood, bottomless. Away to the west
were lines of cliffs and ledges of rock; not such ledges as you*

may see where the quarryman splits his blocks, but ledges from which the gods might quarry mountains; not cliffs where you may see the swallow build its nest, but where the soaring eagle is lost to view before he reaches the summit. Between us and the distant cliffs were the strangely carved and pinnacled rocks of the "Toom-pin Woo-near Too-weap." Away to the east a group of eruptive mountains were seen – the Sierra La Sal. Their slopes were covered with pine, and deep gulches were flanked with great crags, and snow-fields were seen near the summits; so the mountains were in uniform – green, gray, and silver. Wherever we looked there was a wilderness of rocks – deep gorges where the rivers are lost below cliffs, and towers, and pinnacles, and ten thousand strangely carved forms in every direction, and beyond them mountains blending with the clouds.

We started again on the 21st of July, and found the river rough with bad rapids in close succession. In running one of these the "Emma Dean" was swamped, and we were thrown into the river; but we clung to her, and in the first quiet water below she was righted and bailed out; but three of our oars were lost. The larger boats landed above the dangerous place and a portage was made. At night we camped on some rocks on the left bank under a cliff where we could scarcely find room to lie down.

And so much progress was made from day to day with much labor, for we found many rapids and falls more difficult to master than any before. We named this "Cataract Cañon."

Midway down the cañon the more difficult cataracts were passed, the walls were found more regular, and the river, though swift, was rarely beset with rocks. The scenery was grand; there were many side cañons, which we explored from time to time, always finding new wonders. I must describe one of these little excursions. One day Bradley, Captain Powell and myself went up one of the side cañons, entering it through a very narrow passage, having to wade along the course of a little stream until a cascade interrupted our progress. Then we climbed to the right for a hundred feet until we reached a little shelf along which we passed walking with great care, for it was narrow, until we passed around the fall. Here the gorge widened into a spacious sky-roofed chamber. In the farther end was a beautiful grove of cotton-woods, and between us and the cotton-woods the little stream widened out into three clear lakelets with bot-

toms of solid rock. Beyond the cotton-woods the brook tumbled in a series of white, shining cascades, from heights that seemed immeasurable. Turning around, we could look through the cleft by which we came on the river and see towering walls beyond.

Our way the rest of the day was through a gorge, grand beyond description. We seemed to be in the depths of the earth and yet could look down into waters that reflected a bottomless abyss. . . .

After collecting some resin from pine trees on the summit of the cliffs, a terrific storm causes water to stream down the crevices and canyons into the Colorado River.

Near the foot of Cataract Cañon the walls suddenly closed in, so that the gorge was narrower than we had before seen it. The water filled it from wall to wall, giving no landing-place at the foot of the cliffs; the river was very swift, the cañon very tortuous, so that we could see but a few hundred yards ahead. The walls towered overhead, often overhanging so as to almost shut out the light. I stood on deck watching with intense anxiety, lest the way should lead us into danger, but we glided along with no obstruction, no falls, no rapids, and in a mile and a half emerged from the narrow gorge into a more open and broken portion of the cañon. Now that it is past, it seems a very simple thing indeed to run through such a place; but the fear of what might be, made a deep impression upon all of us. Shortly after, we arrived at the foot of Cataract Cañon. Here a long cañon valley comes down from the east, and the river turns sharply to the west in a continuation of the line of the lateral valley. In the bend on the right vast numbers of crags, and pinnacles, and tower-shaped rocks are seen. We called it "Mille Crag Bend."

(Glen Canyon)

On the 29th of July, we entered a cañon with low red walls. A short distance below its head we discovered the ruins of an old building on the left wall. There is a narrow plain between the river and the wall just here, and on the brink of a rock two hundred feet high this old house stood. Its walls were of stone laid in mortar with much regularity. It was probably built three stories high; the lower story was yet almost intact, the second much broken down, and scarcely anything was left of the third.

Great quantities of flint chips were found on the rocks near by, and many arrow-heads, some perfect, others broken, and fragments of pottery were strewn about in great profusion. On the face of the cliff under the building, and along down the river for two or three hundred yards, there were many etchings. Two hours were given to the examination of these interesting ruins, when we ran down fifteen miles further and discovered another group.

The principal building was situated on the summit of the hill. Parts of the walls were standing to the height of eight or ten feet, and the mortar still remained in some places. The house was in the shape of an L, with five rooms on the ground floor; one in the angle and two in each extension. In the space in the angle there was a deep excavation. From what we knew of the people in the province of Tusayan, who are doubtless of the same race as the former inhabitants of these ruins, we concluded that this was a "Kiva" or underground chamber in which their religious ceremonies were performed.

The sandstone through which this cañon is cut is red and homogeneous, being the same as that through which Labyrinth Cañon runs. The smooth naked rock stretches out on either side of the river for many miles, but curiously carved mounds and cones are scattered everywhere, and deep holes are worn out. Many of these pockets were filled with water, and in one of these holes or wells, twenty feet deep, I found a tree growing. The excavation was so narrow I could step from its brink to a limb of the tree, and descend to the bottom of the well down a growing ladder. . . .

Just before sundown I attempted to climb a rounded eminence, from which I hoped to obtain a good outlook over the surrounding country. It was formed of smooth mounds piled one above another, and up these I climbed, winding here and there to find a practicable way, until near the summit, when they became too steep for me to proceed. I searched about for a few minutes for a more easy way; what was my surprise at finding a stairway, evidently cut in the rock by human hands! At one place, where there is a vertical wall ten or twelve feet high, I found an old rickety ladder. It may be that this was a watch-tower of that ancient people whose homes we had found in ruins. On many of the tributaries of the Colorado, I had before examined their deserted dwellings. Those that showed evidences of being built during the latter part of their occupation of the country were usually placed on the most inaccessible cliffs. Sometimes the mouth of caves had been walled across, and there were many other evidences showing their anxiety to secure defensible positions.

Probably the nomadic tribes were sweeping down upon them and they resorted to these cliffs and cañons for safety. It is not unreasonable to suppose that this orange mound was used as a watch-tower.

I stood where a lost people had lived centuries ago, and looked over the same strange country. I gazed off to great mountains in the north-west, slowly covered by the night until they were lost, and then turned toward camp. It was no easy task to find my way down the wall in the darkness, and I clambered about until nearly midnight, before I arrived there.

We made good progress the next day, as the water, though smooth, was swift. Sometimes the cañon walls were vertical to the top, sometimes vertical below with a mound-covered slope above, and in other places the slope with its mounds came down to the water's edge. Farther down we found the orange sandstone cut in two by a group of firm, calcareous strata, the lower bed underlaid by soft gypsiferous shale. Sometimes the upper, homogeneous bed was a smooth vertical wall, but usually it was carried into mounds with gently meandering valley lines. The lower bed, yielding to gravity as the softer shale below worked out into the river, broke into angular surfaces often having a columnar appearance. One could almost imagine that the walls had been carved with the purpose of representing giant architectural forms. In the deep recesses of the walls we found springs with mosses and ferns on the moistened sandstone.

Near our camp, below, there was a low, willow-covered strip of land along the wall on the east, and across this we walked to explore an alcove which was seen from the river. On entering we found a little grove of box-elder and cotton-wood trees, and, turning to the right, found ourselves in a vast chamber, carved out of the rocks. At the upper end there was a clear, deep pool of water bordered with verdure. Standing by the side of this and looking back, we could see the grove at the entrance. The cham-

ber was more than two hundred feet high, five hundred feet long and two hundred feet wide. Through the ceiling and on through the rocks for a thousand feet above there was a narrow winding sky-light, and this was all carved out by a little stream which runs during the few showers that fall now and then in that arid country. The waters, gathering rapidly on the bare rocks back of the cañon into a small channel, have carved a deep side cañon, through which they run until they fall into the farther end of this chamber. The rock at the ceiling is hard, the rock below very soft and friable, and having cut through the upper harder portion down into the lower and softer, these friable sandstones crumble and are washed out by the stream, and thus the chamber has been excavated.

Here we brought our camp, and when "Old Shady" sang us a song at night we were pleased to find this hollow in the rock filled with sweet sounds. It was doubtless made for an Academy of Music by a storm-born architect, so we named it "Music Temple."

Desirous of obtaining a view of the adjacent country, if possible, the men early the next morning rowed me across the river, and I passed along by the foot of the cliff half a mile up stream, and then climbed first up broken ledges, then two or three hundred yards up a smooth, sloping rock, and then passed out on a narrow ridge. Still I found that I had not attained an altitude from which I could overlook the region outside of the cañon; so I descended into a little gulch, and climbed again to a higher ridge all the way along naked sandstone, and at last I reached a point of commanding view, where I could look several miles up the San Juan, and a long distance up the Colorado, and could see, away to the north-west, the Henry Mountains; to the north-east, the Sierra La Sal; to the south-east, unknown mountains, and to the south-west, the meanderings of the cañon. Then I returned to camp.

The features of this cañon are greatly diversified. Vertical walls are usually found to stand above great curves, and the river, sweeping around these bends, has undermined the cliffs in places; sometimes the rocks are overhanging. In other curves curious narrow glens are found. Into these we climbed by a rough stairway, perhaps several hundred feet, to where a spring burst out from under an overhanging cliff, and about the spring cotton-woods and willows stood, while along the curves of the brooklet oaks grew and other rich vegetation was seen, in marked contrast to the general appearance of naked rock. Other wonderful features are the many side cañons or gorges that we passed; sometimes we stopped to explore these for a short distance.

In some places these walls are much nearer each other above than below, so that they looked somewhat like caves or chambers in the rocks. Usually in going up such a gorge we found beautiful vegetation, and our way was often cut off by deep basins or pot holes. On the walls back, and many miles into the country, numbers of monument-shaped buttes were observed, carved walls, royal arches, glens, alcove gulches, mounds, and monuments. From which of these features should we select a name? We finally named this "Glen Cañon."

Past these towering monuments, past these billows of orange sandstone, past these oak-set glens, fern-decked alcoves and mural curves, we glided hour after hour, stopping now and then as our attention was arrested by some new wonder, until we reached a point which is historical. In the year 1776, Father Escalante, a Spanish priest, made an expedition from Santa Fe to the north-west, crossing the Grand and Green, and then passing down the Wasatch Mountains and the southern plateaus, until he reached the Rio Virgin. His intention was to cross to the Mission of Monterey, but from information received from the Indians he decided that the route was impracticable. Not wishing to return to Santa Fe over the circuitous route by which he had just traveled, he attempted to go by one more direct, and which led him across the Colorado at a point known as El Vado de los Padres. From the descriptions which we have read we were enabled to determine the place. A little stream comes down through a very narrow side cañon from the west. It was down this that he came, and our boats were brought up at the point where the ford crosses. A well-beaten Indian trail was seen here still. Between the cliff and the river there is a little meadow. The ashes of many camp fires were seen, and the bones of numbers of cattle were bleaching on the grass. For several years the Navajo Indians have raided on the Mormons who dwell in the valleys to the west, and doubtless cross frequently at this ford with their stolen cattle.

Powell and his men continue to float downstream into another canyon, where he mistakenly labels one of the layers of polished limestone as being marble.

(Grand Canyon)

The limestone of this cañon is often polished, and makes a beautiful marble. Sometimes the rocks are of many colors – white, gray, pink, and purple, with saffron tints. It was with very great labor that we made progress, meeting with many obstructions, running rapids, letting down our boats with lines from rock to rock, and sometimes carrying boats and cargoes around bad places. At one place we camped, after a hard portage, under an overhanging wall, glad to find shelter from the rain, and equally glad to find a few sticks of drift-wood just sufficient to boil a pot of coffee. The water sweeps rapidly in this elbow of river and has cut its way under the rock, excavating a vast half-circular chamber, which, if utilized for a theater, would give sitting for fifty thousand people. Objections might be urged against it from the fact that at high water the floor is covered with a raging flood.

Soon after passing this point the scenery was on a grand scale. The walls of the cañon, twenty-five hundred feet high, were of marble of many beautiful colors, often polished below by the waves, or far up the sides where showers had washed the sands over the cliffs. At one place I had a walk, for more than a mile, on a marble pavement all polished and fretted with strange devices, and embossed in a thousand fantastic patterns. Through a cleft in the wall the sun shone on this pavement, which gleamed in iridescent beauty. Up into this cleft I found my way. It was very narrow, with a succession of pools standing at higher levels as I went back. The water in these pools was clear and cool, coming down from springs. Then I returned to the pavement, which was but a terrace or bench over which the river ran at its flood, but left bare at this time. Along the pavement in many places were basins of clear water, in strange contrast to the red mud of the river. At length I came to the end of this marble terrace, and jumped aboard the boat. Riding down a short distance a beautiful view was presented. The river turned sharply to the east, and seemed enclosed by a wall set with a million brilliant gems. What could it mean! – every one wondered. On coming nearer we found a fountain bursting from the rock high overhead, and the spray in the sunshine formed the gems which bedecked the walls. The rocks below the fountain were covered with mosses and ferns and many beautiful flowering plants. We named it "Vasey's Paradise," in honor of the botanist who traveled with us the previous year.

When it rains in these cañons scarcely do the first drops fall ere little rills are formed and run down the walls; as the storms come on the rills increase in size, until they become streams. Although the walls of this cañon are chiefly limestone, the country adjacent is of red sandstone, and the waters loaded with these sands come in rivers of bright red mud, leaping over the walls in innumerable cascades. It is easy to see why these walls present a polished surface in many places.

We had cut through the sandstones and limestones met in the upper part of this cañon, and through one great bed of marble a thousand feet in thickness. In this, great numbers of caves are hollowed out, and carvings are seen which suggest architectural forms, though on a scale so grand that architectural terms belittle them.

As this great bed forms a distinctive feature of the cañon, we called it Marble Cañon. Along the walls many projections are set out into the river as if they were buttressed for support. The walls themselves are half a mile high, and these buttresses are on a corresponding scale, jutting into the river scores of feet. In the recesses between these projections there are quiet bays of water, except at the foot of a rapid, when they become dancing eddies or whirlpools. Sometimes these alcoves have caves at the back, giving them the appearance of great depth; then other caves were seen above, forming vast dome-shaped chambers; walls and buttresses and chambers are all of marble.

On August 10th, we reached the mouth of the Colorado Chiquito, the foot of Marble Cañon. This stream enters through a cañon on a scale quite as grand as that of the Colorado itself. It is a very small river, and exceedingly muddy and salt. I walked up the stream three or four miles, crossing and recrossing where I could easily wade it; then I climbed several hundred feet at one place and could see up the chasm, through which the river ran for several miles (where Ives had descended in 1858).

I walked down the gorge to the left, at the foot of the cliff climbed to a bench overhead, and discovered a trail deeply worn in the rock; where it crossed the side gulches, in some places steps had been cut. I could see no evidence of its having been traveled for a long time, and it was doubtless a path used by the people who inhabited this region anterior to the present Indian races, – the people who built the communal houses of which mention has been made.

Upon my return to camp the men told me they had discovered ruins and many fragments of pottery, also etchings and hieroglyphics on the rocks. We found, on comparing the readings of the barometers above and below, that the walls were about three thousand feet high – or more than half a mile.

On August 13ᵗʰ we were ready once more to start on our way down the Great Unknown. Our boats, tied to a stake, were chafing each other as they were tossed by the fretful river. They rode high and buoyant, for their loads were lighter than we could desire, indeed we had but a month's rations remaining. The flour had been resifted through the mosquito-net sieve; the spoiled bacon had been dried, and the worst of it boiled; the few pounds of dried apples had been spread in the sun, and had shrunk to their normal bulk; the sugar had all melted and gone on its way down the river, but we had a large sack of coffee.

The lightening of the boats had this advantage, we thought – they would ride the waves better, and we would have but little to carry when we made a portage.

We were three-quarters of a mile down in the depths of the earth, and the great river shrunk into insignificance as it dashed its angry waves against the walls and cliffs that rose to the world above; they were but puny ripples, and we but pygmies running up and down the sands, or lost among the bowlders. We had an unknown distance yet to run, an unknown river yet to explore; what falls there were we knew not, what rocks beset the channel we knew not. The men talked as cheerfully as ever, jests were bandied about freely, but to me the cheer was somber, the jests were ghastly.

With some eagerness and some anxiety, we entered the cañon below and were carried along by swift water, through walls which rose from its very edge. They had the same structure as we noticed the day before, tiers of irregular shelves below, and above these, steep slopes to the foot of marble cliffs.

We ran six miles in little more than half-an-hour, and emerged into a more open portion of the cañon, where high hills and ledges of rock intervened between the river and the distant walls. Just at the head of the open place the river ran across a dike, that is, a fissure in the rocks open to depths below, which has been filled with eruptive matter, which on cooling became harder than the rocks through which the fissure was made.

When these were washed away the harder volcanic matter remained as a wall. The river cuts a gate-way through this, several hundred feet high and as many wide. As it crosses the wall there is a fall below and a bad rapid filled with bowlders of trap, so we were compelled to stop and make a portage.

At daybreak one morning we walked down the bank of the river on a little sandy beach, to take a view of a new feature in the cañon. Heretofore hard rocks had given us a bad river; soft rocks, smooth water. A series of rocks harder than any we experienced now began. The river entered the granite! We could see but a little way into the granite gorge, but it looked threatening. After breakfast we continued our perilous voyage. The cañon was narrower than we had ever before seen it; the water was swift; there were but few broken rocks in the channel, but the walls were set on either side with pinnacles, and crags and sharp angular buttresses, bristling with wind- and wave-polished spires, extended far out into the river. Ledges of rocks jutted into the stream, their tops sometimes just below the surface, sometimes rising few or many feet above, and island ledges, and island pinnacles, and island towers broke the swift course of the stream into chutes, and eddies, and whirlpools. We soon reached a place where a creek came in from the left, and just below the channel was choked with bowlders which had washed down the lateral cañon and formed a dam, over which there was a fall of thirty or forty feet; but on the bowlders we could get foothold, and here we made a portage. Three more such dams were found; over one we made a portage; at the other two we found chutes through which we could run.

About eleven o'clock of the same day we heard a great roar ahead, and approached it very cautiously, the sound growing louder and louder as we ran. As last we found ourselves above a long, broken fall, with ledges and pinnacles of rock obstructing the river. There was a descent of seventy-five or eighty feet, perhaps, in a third of a mile, and the rushing waters were broken into great waves on the rocks, and lashed themselves into foam. We could land just above, but there was no foothold on either side by which a portage could be made. It was nearly a thousand feet to the top of the granite, so it was impossible to carry our boats around, though we could climb to that point ourselves by a side gulch, and passing along a mile or two, could descend to the river. We discovered this on examination, but such a portage would have been impracticable for us, and we were obliged to run the rapid or abandon the river.

We did not hesitate, but stepped into the boats, pushed off, and dashed away, first on smooth but swift water, then striking a glassy wave and riding to its top, down again into the trough, up again on a higher wave, and down and up on the waves, higher and still higher, until we struck one just as it curled back, when a breaker rolled over our little undaunted boat. On we sped, till the boat was caught in a whirlpool and spun around and around. When we managed to pull out again, the other boats had passed us. The open compartment of the "Emma Dean" was filled with water, and every breaker rolled over us. Hurled back from the rock now on this side, now on that, we were carried at last into an eddy, in which we struggled for a few minutes, and then out again, the breakers still rolling over us. Our boat was unmanageable, but she could not sink, and we drifted down another hundred yards through breakers – how, we scarcely knew. We found the other boats had turned into an eddy at the foot of the fall, and were waiting to catch us as we came, for they had seen that our boat was swamped. They pushed out as we came near, and pulled us in against the wall. We bailed out the boat and started on again.

The walls were now more than a mile in height. Stand on the south steps of the Treasury Building in Washington and look down Pennsylvania Avenue to the Capitol Park, measure the distance with your eye, and imagine cliffs extending to that altitude, and you will understand what I mean. Or, stand at Canal Street in New York and look up Broadway to Grace Church, and you have about the distance; stand at Lake Street Bridge in Chicago and look down to the Union Depot, and you have it again.

A thousand feet of this is up through granite crags, then slopes and perpendicular cliffs, rise one above the other to the summit. The gorge is black and narrow below, red and gray and flaring above, and crags and angular projections on walls which, cut in many places by side cañons, seem to be a vast wilderness of rocks. Down through these gloomy depths we glided, always listening; for the mad waters kept up their roar; always watching and peering ahead – for the narrow cañon was winding and the river was closed so that we could see but a few hundred yards, and what might be below we knew not. We strained our ears for warning of the falls and watched for rocks, or stopped now and then in the bay of a recess to admire the gigantic scenery; and ever as we went, there was some new pinnacle or tower, some crag or peak, some distant view of the upper plateau, some deep, narrow side cañon, or some strangely shaped rock. On we went, through this solemn, mysterious way. The river was very deep, the cañon very narrow and still obstructed, so that there was no steady flow of the stream, but the waters wheeled, and rolled, and boiled, and we were scarcely able to determine where we could go with greatest safety. Now the boat was carried to the right, perhaps close to the wall, again she was shot into the stream and dragged over to the other side, where, caught in a whirlpool, she spun about like a chip. We could neither land nor run as we pleased; the boats were entirely unmanageable; now one, now another was ahead, each crew looking after its own safety.

We came to another rapid; two of the boats ran it perforce; one succeeded in landing, but there was no foothold by which to make a portage, and she was pushed out again into the stream; the next minute a great reflex wave filled the open compartment; she was water-logged, and drifted at the mercy of the waters. Breaker after breaker rolled over her, and one tossed her deck downward. The men were thrown out, but they clung to the boat, and she drifted down alongside of us, and we were able to catch her. She was soon bailed out and the men were aboard once more, but the oars were lost; their place being supplied by a pair from the "Emma Dean."

Clouds were playing in the cañon that day. Sometimes they rolled down in great masses, filling the gorge with gloom; sometimes they hung above from wall to wall, covering the cañon with a roof of impending storm, and we could peer long distances up and down this cañon corridor, with its cloud roof overhead, its walls of black granite, and its river bright with the sheen of broken waters. Then a gust of wind would sweep down a side gulch and make a rift in the clouds, revealing the blue heavens, and a stream of sunlight poured in. Again the clouds drifted away into the distance and hung around crags and peaks, and pinnacles, and towers, and walls, covering them with a mantle that lifted from time to time and set them all in sharp relief. Then baby clouds crept out of side cañons, glided around points, and crept back again into more distant gorges. Other clouds stretched in strata across the cañon, with intervening vista views to cliffs and rocks beyond.

Then the rain came down. Little rills were formed rapidly above; these soon grew into brooks, and the brooks into creeks, which tumbled over the walls in innumerable cascades, adding their wild music to the roar of the river. When the rain ceased, the rills, brooks, and creeks ran dry. The waters that fall during the rain on these steep rocks are gathered at once into the river; they could scarcely be poured in more suddenly if some vast spout ran from the clouds to the stream itself. When a storm bursts over the cañon a side gulch is a dangerous place, for a sudden flood may come, and the inpouring water raise the river so as to drown the rocks before your very eyes.

On the 16th of August we were compelled to stop once more and dry our rations and make oars.

The Colorado is never a clear stream, and, owing to the rains which had been falling for three or four days, and the floods which were poured over the walls, bringing down great quantities of mud, it was now exceedingly turbid. A little affluent entered opposite our camp – a clear, beautiful creek, or river, as it would be termed in the Western country, where streams are not so abundant. We had named one stream, above, in honor of the great chief of the bad angels, and as this was a beautiful contrast to that, we concluded to name it "Bright Angel River."

. . . Our rations were rapidly spoiling, the bacon being so badly injured that we were compelled to throw it away, and our saleratus had been lost overboard. We had now plenty of coffee, but only musty flour sufficient for ten days, and a few dried apples. We must make all haste possible. If we met with difficulties as we had done in the cañon above, we should be compelled to give up the expedition and try to reach the Mormon settlements to the north. Our hopes were that the worst places were passed, but our barometers were so badly injured as to be useless, so we had lost our reckoning in altitude, and knew not how much descent the river had yet to make.

It rained from time to time, sometimes all day, and we were thoroughly drenched and chilled, but between showers the sun shone with great power, and the mercury stood at 115°, so that we had rapid changes from great extremes, which were very disagreeable. It was especially cold in the rain at night. The little canvas we had was rotten and useless; the rubber ponchos with which we started from Green River City, were all lost; more than half the party were without hats, and not one of us had an entire suit of clothes, nor had we a blanket apiece. So we gathered drift-wood and built fires, but the rain came down in torrents and extinguished them, and we sat up all night on the rocks shivering. We were, indeed, much more exhausted by the night's discomfort than by the day's toil.

So difficult were the portages on August 18th that we advanced but two miles in this work. I climbed up the granite to its summit and went back over the rust-colored sandstones and greenish-yellow shales to the foot of the marble wall. I climbed so high that the men and boats were lost in the black depths below, and the river was but a rippling brook, and still there was more cañon above than below.

I pushed on to an angle where I hoped to get a view of the country beyond, to see, if possible, what the prospect was of our soon running through this plateau, or, at least, of meeting with some geological change that would let us out of the granite; but, arriving at the point, I could see below only a labyrinth of deep gorges.

After dinner, in running a rapid, the pioneer boat was upset by a wave. We were some distance in advance of the larger boats;

the river was rough and swift and we were unable to land; so we clung to the boat and were carried down stream over another rapid.

The men in the boats above saw our trouble, but were caught in whirlpools, and went spinning about so in the eddies that it seemed a long time before they came to our relief. At last they came. The boat was turned right side up and bailed out, the oars, which, fortunately, had floated along in company with us, were gathered up, and on we went without even landing.

On the 20th, the characteristics of the cañon changed; the river was broader, the walls were sloping, and composed of black slates that stood on edge. These nearly vertical slates are washed out in places; that is, the softer beds are washed out between the harder, which are left standing. In this way curious little alcoves are formed, in which are quiet bays of water, but on a much smaller scale than the great bays and buttresses of Marble Cañon. The river was still rapid, and we stopped to let down with lines several times, but made greater progress, running ten miles.

On a terrace of trap we discovered another group of ruins. Evidently, there was once quite a village here. Again we found mealing-stones and much broken pottery, and upon a little natural shelf in the rock, back of the ruins, we found a globular basket that would hold perhaps a third of a bushel. It was badly broken, and, as I attempted to take it up, it fell to pieces. There were many beautiful flint chips scattered about, as if this had been the home of an old arrow-maker.

The next day, in nearing a curve, we heard a mad roar, and down we were carried with a dizzying velocity to the head of another rapid. On either side, high over our heads, there were overhanging granite walls, and the sharp bends cut off our view. A few moments and we should be carried into unknown waters. Away we went on a long, winding chute. I stood on deck, supporting myself with a strap fastened on either side to the gunwale, and the boat glided rapidly where the water was smooth. Striking a wave, she leaped and bounded like a thing of life, and we had a wild ride for ten miles, which we made in less than one hour. The excitement was so great that we forgot the danger until we heard the roar of a great fall below, when we backed on our oars, and were carried slowly toward its head, and succeeded in landing just above. We found we could make a portage, and at this we were engaged for some hours.

Just here we ran out of the granite. Good cheer returned; we forgot the storms and the gloom, and the cloud-covered cañons, and the raging of the river, and pushed our boats from shore in great glee.

The next day we came to rapids again, over which we were compelled to make a portage. While the men were thus employed I climbed the wall on the north-east to a height of about 2,500 feet, where I could obtain a good view of a long stretch of cañon below. Its course was to the south-west. The walls seemed to rise very abruptly for 2,500 or 3,000 feet, and then there was a gentle sloping terrace on each side for two or three miles, and then cliffs rising from 1,500 to 2,500 feet. From the brink of these the plateau stretches back to the north and south for a long distance. Away down the canon on the right wall I could see a group of mountains, some of which appeared to stand on the brink of the cañon. The effect of the terrace was to give the appearance of a narrow, winding valley with high walls on either side, and a deep, dark, meandering gorge down its middle. It was impossible from this point of view to deter-mine whether there was granite at the bottom or not; but from geological considerations I concluded we should have marble walls below, and this proved to be the case, except that here and there we passed through patches of granite, like hills thrust up into the limestone. At one of these places we made another por-tage, and, taking advantage of this delay, I went up a little stream to the north, wading all the way, sometimes having to plunge in to my neck, and in other places to swim across little basins that had been excavated at the foot of the walls. Along its course were many cascades and springs gushing out from the rocks on either side. Sometimes a cotton-wood tree grew over the water. I came to one beautiful fall of more than a hundred and fifty feet, and climbed around it to the right on broken rocks. As I proceeded the cañon narrowed very much, being but fifteen or twenty feet wide, the walls rising on either side many hundreds of feet – perhaps thousands. In some places the stream had not excavated its channel vertically through the rocks, but had cut obliquely, so that one wall overhung the other. In other places it was cut vertically above and obliquely below, so that it was impossible to see out overhead. But I could go no farther. The time which I estimated it would take to make the portage had now almost expired, so I started back on a round trot, wading in the creek and plunging through basins, and finding the men waiting for me.

Farther on we passed a stream which leaped into the Colorado by a direct fall of more than a hundred feet, forming a beautiful cascade. There was a bed of very hard rock above, thirty or forty feet in thickness, and there were much softer beds below. The harder beds above project many yards beyond the softer, which are washed out, forming a deep cave behind the fall, and the stream poured through a narrow crevice above into a deep pool below. Around on the rocks, in the cave-like chamber, were set beautiful ferns with delicate fronds and enameled stalks; the little frondlets had their points turned down to form spore-cases. It had much the appearance of the maiden-hair fern, but was larger. This delicate foliage covered the rocks all about the fountain and gave the chamber great beauty.

It was curious to see how anxious we were to make up our reckoning every time we stopped, now that our diet was confined to plenty of coffee, a very little spoiled flour, and a very few dried apples. It had come to be a race for dinner. On the 23rd, we ran twenty-two miles, and on the 24th, twenty miles. Such fine progress put all hands in good cheer, but not a moment of daylight was lost, and on the 25th, though we were retarded by a portage, we made thirty-five miles.

During this last day we passed monuments of lava standing in the river, mostly low rocks, but some of them shafts more than a hundred feet high. Three or four miles farther down these increased in number. Great quantities of cooled lava and many cinder-cones were seen on either side, and then we came to an abrupt cataract. Just over the fall on the right wall a cinder-cone, or extinct volcano with a well-defined crater, stands on the very brink of the cañon. From the volcano vast floods of lava have been poured down into the river, and a stream of the molten rock has run up three or four miles, and down we knew not how far. Just where it poured over the cañon wall is the fall. The whole north side as far as we could see was lined with black basalt, and high up on the opposite wall were patches of the same material resting on the benches and filling old alcoves and caves, giving to the wall a spotted appearance. . . .

As we floated along I was able to observe the wonderful phenomena relating to this flood of lava. The cañon was doubtless filled to a height of twelve or fifteen hundred feet, perhaps by more than one flood. This would dam the water back, and in cutting through this great lava-bed a new channel has been formed, sometimes on one side, sometimes on the other. The cooled lava, being of firmer texture than the rocks of which the walls are composed, in some places remains; in others a narrow channel has been cut, leaving a line of basalt on either side. . . .

What a conflict of water and fire there must have been here! Imagine a river of molten rock running down into a river of melted snow!

Up to this time, since leaving the Colorado Chiquito, we had seen no evidence that the Indians inhabiting the plateaus on either side ever approached the river, but one morning we discovered an Indian garden at the foot of the wall on the right, just where a little stream, with a narrow flood-plain, came down through a side cañon. Along the valley the Indians had planted corn, using the water which burst out in springs at the foot of the cliffs for irrigation. The corn was looking quite well, though not sufficiently advanced to give us roasting ears; but there were some nice green squashes. We carried ten or a dozen of these on board our boats, and hurriedly left, not willing to be caught in the robbery. We excused ourselves on the plea of our great want. We ran down a short distance to where we felt certain no Indians could follow, and what a kettle of squash sauce we made! True, we had no salt with which to season it, but it made a fine addition to our unleavened bread and coffee. Never was fruit so sweet to us as those stolen squashes.

At night we found, on making up our reckoning, that we had again run thirty-five miles during the day. What a supper we made – unleavened bread, green squash sauce, and strong coffee! We had been for a day or two on half rations, but now we had no stint of roast squash. A few more days like this and we should be out of prison.

On the 27th the river took a more southerly direction. The dip of the rocks was to the north, and we were rapidly running into the lower formation. Unless our course changed we should very soon run again into the granite – which gave us some anxiety. Now and then the river turned to the west, and gave birth to hopes that were soon destroyed, by another turn to the south. About nine o'clock we came to the dreaded rock. It was with no little misgiving that we saw the river enter those black, hard walls. At the very entrance we were compelled to make a portage, after which we had to let down with lines past some ugly rocks.

At eleven o'clock we came to a place in the river which seemed much worse than any we had met in all its course. A little creek came down from the right, and another, just opposite, from the left. We landed first on the right, and clambered up over the granite pinnacles for a mile or two, but could see no way by which we could let down, and to run it would be sure destruction. Then we crossed to examine it on the left. High above the river we could walk along on the top of the granite, which was broken off at the edge and set with crags and pinnacles, so that it was very difficult to get a view of the river at all. In my eagerness to reach a point where I could see the roaring fall below, I went too far on the wall, and could neither advance nor retreat, and stood with one foot on a little projecting rock and clung, with my hand fixed in a little crevice. Finding I was caught here, suspended four hundred feet above the river, into which I should fall if my footing failed, I called for help. The men came and passed me a line, but I could not let go the rock long enough to take hold of it; then they brought two or three of the longest oars. All this took time, which seemed very precious to me. But at last the blade of one of the oars was pushed into a little crevice in the rock beyond me in such a manner that they could hold me pressed against the wall. Then another was fixed in such a way that I could step on it, and I was rescued.

The whole afternoon was spent in examining the river below by clambering among the crags and pinnacles. We found that the lateral stream had washed bowlders into the river so as to form a dam, over which the river made a broken fall of eighteen or twenty feet; then there was a rapid, beset with rocks for two or three hundred yards, while on the sides points of the wall projected into the river. There was a second fall below, how great we could not tell, and below that a rapid filled with huge rocks for two or three hundred yards. At the bottom of this, from the right wall, a great rock projected half-way across the river. It had a sloping surface extending up stream, and the water, coming down with all the momentum gained in the falls and rapids above, rolled up this inclined plane many feet and tumbled over to the left.

I decided that it would be possible to let down over the first fall, then run near the right cliff to a point just above the second, where we could pull out into a little chute, and, having run over that in safety, to pull with all our power across the stream to avoid the great rock below. On my return to the boats, I announced to the men that we were to run it the next morning.

After supper Captain Howland asked to have a talk with me. We walked up a little creek a short distance, and I soon found that his object was to remonstrate against my determination to proceed; he thought we had better abandon the river here. I learned that his brother, William Dunn and himself had determined to go no farther in the boats. We returned to camp, but nothing was said to the other men.

During the two days previous our course had not been plotted, so I sat down and did this for the purpose of finding where we were by dead reckoning. It was a clear night, and I took out the sextant to make observations for latitude, and found that the astronomic determination agreed very nearly with that of the plot – quite as closely as might be expected from a meridian observation on a planet. I concluded we must be about forty-five miles in a direct line from the mouth of the Rio Virgin. If we could reach that point, we knew there were settlements up that river about twenty miles. This forty-five miles in a direct line would probably be eighty or ninety in the meandering line of the river. But then we knew that there was a comparatively open country for many miles above the mouth of the Virgin, which was our point of destination.

As soon as I determined all this I spread my plot on the sand and awoke Howland, who was sleeping down by the river, and showed him where I supposed we were, and where several Mormon settlements were situated. We had another short talk about the morrow, and he lay down again.

But for me there was no sleep; all night long I paced up and down a little path on a few yards of sand beach along the river. Was it wise to go on? I went to the boats again to look at our rations. I felt satisfied we could get over the danger immediately before us; what there might be below I knew not. From our outlook on the cliffs the cañon seemed to make another great bend to the south, and this, from our previous experience, meant more and higher granite walls. I was not sure we could climb the walls of the cañon here, and I knew enough of the country to be certain, when at the top of the wall, that it was a desert of rocks and sand between this and the nearest Mormon settlement, which on the most direct line must have been seventy-five miles away. True, I believed that the late rains were favorable to us, should we go out; for the probabilities were that we should find water still standing in holes. At one time I almost made up my mind to leave the river. But for years I had been contemplating this trip. To leave the exploration unfinished – to say there was a part of the cañon which we could not explore, having already almost accomplished the undertaking – I could not reconcile myself to this.

Then I awoke my brother and told him of Howland's determination. He, at least, promised to stay with me. Next I called up Hawkins, the cook, and he made a like promise; then Sumner, Bradley, and Hall, and they all agreed to go on.

At last daylight came and we had breakfast, without a word being said about the future. The meal was as solemn as a funeral. After breakfast I asked the three men if they still thought it best to leave us. The elder Howland thought it was, and Dunn agreed with him; the younger Howland tried to persuade them to go on with the party, failing in which, he decided to go with his brother.

Then we crossed the river. The small boat was very much disabled and unseaworthy. With the loss of hands consequent on the departure of the three men we should not be able to run all the boats, so I decided to leave the "Emma Dean." Two rifles and a shot-gun were given to the men who were going out. I asked them to help themselves to the rations and take what they thought to be a fair share. This they refused to do, saying they had no fear but that they could get something to eat; but Billy, the cook, had a pan of biscuits prepared for dinner, and these he left on a rock.

Before starting we took our barometers, fossils, minerals, and some ammunition, and left them on the rocks. We were going over this place as light as possible. The three men helped us lift our boats over a rock twenty-five or thirty feet high, and let them down again over the first falls. Just before leaving I wrote a letter to my wife and gave it to Howland. Sumner gave him his watch, directing that it be sent to his sister, should he not be heard from again.

The records of the expedition had been kept in duplicate, and one set of these was given to Howland; and now we were ready to start. For the last time they entreated us not to go on, and told us that to go on was madness; that we could never get through safely; that the river turned again to the south into the granite, and a few miles of such rapids and falls would exhaust our entire stock of rations, when it would be too late to climb out. It was rather a solemn parting and some tears were shed, for each party thought the other was taking the dangerous course.

My old boat having been deserted, I went on board "The Maid of the Cañon." The three men climbed a crag that overhung the river, to watch us off. The "Maid" pushed out, we glided rapidly along the foot of the wall, just grazing one great rock, pulled out a little into the chute of the second fall, and plunged over it. The open compartment was filled when we struck the first wave below, but we cut through it, and then the men pulled with all their power toward the left wall and swung clear of the dangerous rock below.

We were scarcely a minute in running it, and found that, although it looked bad from above, we had passed many places that were worse. The other boat followed without more difficulty.

We landed at the first practicable point below, fired our guns as a signal to the men above that we had gone over in safety, and remained a couple of hours, hoping they would take the smaller boat and follow us. We were behind a curve in the cañon and could not see up to where we left them. As they did not come we *pushed on again. Until noon we had a succession of rapids and falls, all of which we ran in safety.*

Just after dinner we came to another bad place. A little stream came in from the left, and below there was a fall, and still below another fall. Above, the river tumbled down over and among the rocks in whirlpools and great waves, and the waters were white with foam. We ran along the left, above this, and soon saw that we could not get down on that side, but it seemed possible to let down on the other, so we pulled up stream for two or three hundred yards and crossed. There was a bed of basalt on this northern side of the cañon, with a bold escarpment that seemed to be a hundred feet high. We could climb it and walk along its summit to a point where we were just at the head of the fall. Here the basalt seemed to be broken down again, and I directed the men to take a line to the top of the cliff and let the boats down along the wall. One man remained in the boat to keep her clear of the rocks and prevent her line from being caught on the projecting angles. I climbed the cliff and passed along to a point just over the fall, and descended by broken rocks, and found that the break of the fall was above the break of the wall, so that we could not land, and that still below the river was very bad, and there was no possibility of a portage. Without waiting further to examine and determine what should be done, I hastened back to the top of the cliff to stop the boats from coming down. When I arrived I found the men had let one of them down to the head of the fall; she was in swift water and they were not able to pull her back, nor were they able to go on with the line, as it was not long enough to reach the higher part of the cliff which was just before them; so they took a bight around a crag, and I sent two men back for the other line. The boat was in very swift water, and Bradley was standing in the open compartment holding out his oar to prevent her from striking against the foot of the cliffs. Now she shot out into the stream and up as far as the line would permit, and then wheeling, drove headlong against the rock; then out and back again, now straining on the line, now striking against the cliff. As soon as the second line was brought we passed it down to him, but his attention was all taken up with his own situation, and he did not see what we were doing. I stood on a projecting rock waving my hat to gain his attention, for my voice was drowned by the roaring of the falls, when just at that moment I saw him take his knife from its sheath and step forward to cut the line. He had evidently decided that it was better to go over with his boat as it was, than to wait for her to be broken to pieces. As he leaned over, the boat sheered again into the stream, the stern-post broke away, and she was loose. With perfect composure Bradley seized the great scull oar, placed it in the stern row-lock, and pulled with all his power – and he was a strong fellow – to turn the bow of the boat down stream, for he wished to go bow down rather than to drift broadside on. One, two strokes were made, a third just as she went over, and the boat was fairly turned; she went down almost beyond our sight, though we were more than a hundred feet above the river. Then she came up again on a great wave, and down and up, then around behind some great rocks, and was lost in the tumultuous foam below.

We stood speechless with fear; we saw no boat; Bradley was gone. But now, away below, we saw something coming out of the waves. It was evidently a boat; a moment more and we saw Bradley standing on deck swinging his hat to show that he was all right.

But he was in a whirlpool. The stern-post of his boat remained attached to the line which was in our possession. How badly she was disabled we knew not. I directed Sumner and Powell to run along the cliff and see if they could reach him from below. Rhodes, Hall and myself ran to the other boat, jumped aboard, pushed out, and away we went over the falls. A wave rolled over us and our craft became unmanageable; another great wave struck us, the boat rolled over, and tumbled, and tossed, I know not how. All I know is, that Bradley was soon picking us up. Before long we had all right again, and rowed to the cliff and waited until Sumner and Powell came up. After a difficult climb they reached us, when we ran two or three miles farther, and turned again to the north-west, continuing until night, when we ran out of the granite once more.

At twelve o'clock on August 29th we emerged from the Grand Cañon of the Colorado, and entered a valley from which low mountains were seen coming to the river below. We recognized this as the Grand Wash. . . .

At night we camped on the left bank in a mesquite thicket. The sense of relief from danger and the joy of success were great. When he who has been chained by wounds to a hospital cot until his canvas tent seems like a dungeon, and the groans of those who lie about him are an increasing torture – when such a prisoner at last goes out into the open field, what a world he sees! (John Wesley Powell had been wounded and had lost his arm in the Civil War. This statement likely recalls his personal experience.) *How beautiful the sky, how bright the sunshine, what "floods of delicious music" pour from the throats of the birds, how sweet the fragrance of earth, and tree, and blossom! The first hour of convalescent freedom seems rich recompense for all the pain, the gloom and the terror.*

Something like this was the feeling we experienced that night. Ever before us had been an unknown danger heavier than any immediate peril. Every waking hour passed in the Grand Cañon had been one of toil. We had watched with deep solicitude the steady disappearance of our scant supply of rations, and from time to time when we were hungry had seen the river snatch a portion of the little left. Danger and toil were endured in those gloomy depths where often the clouds hid the sky by day, and but a narrow zone of stars could be seen at night. Only during the few hours of deep sleep consequent on hard labor had the roar of the mad waters been hushed; now the danger was over, the toil had ceased, the gloom had disappeared, and the firmament was bounded only by the wide horizon.

The river rolled by in silent majesty; the quiet of the camp was sweet, our joy was almost ecstasy. We sat till long after midnight talking of the Grand Cañon, of home, and, more than all, of the three men who had left us. Were they wandering in those depths, unable to find a way out? Were they searching over the desert lands above for water? Or were they nearing the settlements with the same feeling of relief that we ourselves experienced?

As they descended the now-quiet river, they saw more Indians, and finally came to the mouth of the Virgin River. There they met three Mormons who led them to the nearest Mormon settlements upstream. Here the party broke up and went their separate ways.

The exploration of the Great Cañon of the Colorado was accomplished.

Chapter VIII

YELLOWSTONE
1870

from "Wonders of the Yellowstone"
in Scribner's Monthly, *May, June, 1871*
by Nathaniel Langford
&
from "Thirty-Seven Days of Peril"
in Scribner's Monthly, *November, 1871*
by Truman Everts

Nathaniel Langford

In the late 1860s, attention was turned to exploring the remaining blank spaces of the American West. One of these regions was the Upper Yellowstone, of which there were many unconfirmed rumors. In fact, many narratives were written down (after Yellowstone was officially discovered) by former trappers, hunters and miners who had visited Yellowstone prior to the Washburn party of 1870. These extended back to the early years of the fur-trapping era in the 1820s and continued up through the 1830s, '40s, '50s and '60s. One can safely say, therefore, that Yellowstone was discovered again and again and again before the johnny-come-latelys of the Washburn expedition. But it was the Langford narrative that made Yellowstone known to the world.

Two expeditions, one in 1869 and another in 1870, followed essentially the same route and discovered the same wonders. The second was Washburn's, following in the footsteps of the first. The first party of Folsom, Cook and Peterson were private citizens of Montana. They returned from Yellowstone somewhat reluctant to relate what they had seen to the local citizens, afraid that they would not be believed. Nevertheless, they tried to have their joint diary published. Yet, magazines were loath to jeopardize their reputations by publishing

Truman Everts

such unreliable material! Poor Folsom, Cook and Peterson. They were true discoverers of Yellowstone and were prepared to share their written account with the public. As it was, they shared their knowledge with the members of the Washburn expedition (and their account finally appeared in one periodical, as we have seen, but attracted little attention). Utilizing that geographical knowledge, they rediscovered many of the same features seen the year before by Folsom, Cook and Peterson. Yet, perhaps the three were not unlucky after all. For, as they themselves noted in their journal, they were privileged to have seen Yellowstone as explorers and not merely as tourists. Langford's narrative of the Washburn expedition gives a complete narrative with references to past explorations of the surrounding region. These past narratives he refers to have been included earlier in the anthology and ties it all together. Evert's narrative is also included, for it is part of the story of this expedition as well.

I had indulged, for several years, a great curiosity to see the wonders of the upper valley of the Yellowstone. The stories told by trappers and mountaineers of the natural phenomena of that region were so strange and marvelous that, as long ago as 1866, I first contemplated the possibility of organizing an expedition for the express purpose of exploring it. During the past year, meeting with several gentlemen who expressed like curiosity, we determined to make the journey in the months of August and September.

The Yellowstone and Columbia, the first flowing into the Missouri and the last into the Pacific, divided from each other by the Rocky Mountains, have their sources within a few miles of each other. Both rise in the mountains which separate Idaho from the new Territory of Wyoming, but the headwaters of the Yellowstone are only accessible from Montana. The mountains surrounding the basin from which they flow are very lofty, covered with pines, and on the southeastern side present to the traveler a precipitous wall of rock, several thousand feet in height. This barrier prevented Captain Reynolds from visiting the headwaters of the Yellowstone while prosecuting an expedition planned by the Government and placed under his command, for the purpose of exploring that river, in 1859.

The source of the Yellowstone is in a magnificent lake, nearly 9,000 feet above the level of the ocean. In its course of 1,300 miles to the Missouri, it falls about 7,200 feet. Its upper waters flow through deep cañons and gorges, and are broken by immense cataracts and fearful rapids, presenting at various points some of the grandest scenery on the continent. This country is entirely volcanic, and abounds in boiling springs, mud volcanoes, huge mountains of sulphur, and geysers more extensive and numerous than those of Iceland.

Old mountaineers and trappers are great romancers. I have met with many, but never one who was not fond of practicing upon the credulity of those who listened to his adventures. Bridger, than whom perhaps no man has experienced more of wild mountain life, has been so much in the habit of embellishing his Indian adventures, that they are received by all who know him with many grains of allowance. This want of faith will account for the skepticism with which the oft-repeated stories of the wonders of the Upper Yellowstone were received by people who had lived within one hundred and twenty miles of them, and who at any time could have established their verity by ten days' travel.

Our company, composed of some of the officials and leading citizens of Montana, felt that if the half was true, they would be amply compensated for all the troubles and hazards of the expedition. It was, nevertheless, a serious undertaking, and as the time drew near for our departure, several who had been foremost to join us, upon the receipt of intelligence that a large party of Indians had come into the Upper Yellowstone valley, found excuse for their withdrawal in various emergent occupations, so that when the day for our departure arrived, our company was reduced in numbers to nine, and consisted of the following-named gentlemen: General H. D. Washburn, who served with distinction during the war of the rebellion, and subsequently represented the Clinton District of Indiana in the Congress of the United States; Samuel T. Hauser, President of the First National Bank of Helena; Cornelius Hedges, a leading member of the bar of Montana; Hon. Truman C. Everts, late United States Assessor for Montana; Walter Trumbull, son of Senator Trumbull; Ben Stickney, Jr.; Warren C. Gillette; Jacob Smith, and the writer.

The preparations were simple. Each man was supplied with a strong horse, well equipped with California saddle, bridle, and cantinas. A needle-gun, a belt filled with cartridges, a pair of revolvers, a hunting-knife, added to the usual costume of the mountains, completed the personal outfit of each member of the expedition. When mounted and ready to start, we resembled more a band of brigands than sober men in search of natural wonders. Our provisions, consisting of bacon, dried fruit, flour, &c., were securely lashed to the backs of twelve broncos, which were placed in charge of a couple of packers. We also employed two colored boys as cooks. . . .

The party rode on to Fort Ellis, where a small military escort under Lieutenant Doane accompanied them into Yellowstone.

Once under way, our little company, now increased to nineteen, presented quite a formidable appearance, as by dint of whip and spur our steeds gaily wheeled across the plain towards the mountains. After a tedious ride of several hours up steep accliv-ities, over rocks, and through dark defiles, we at length passed over the summit of the mountain range, took a last look at the beautiful valley of the Gallatin, and descended into a ravine coursed by the waters of Trail Creek. . . .

The expedition stopped at the ranch of the Boteler brothers, a final outpost of white settlement before entering Yellowstone. They found out that a party of Crows had preceded them a few days earlier on the general path they were to take up the Yellowstone River.

. . . We left Boteler's, plunging at once into the vast unknown which lay before us. Following the slight Indian trail, we trav-eled near the bank of the river, amid the wildest imaginable scenery of river, rock, and mountain. The foot-hills were cov-ered with verdure, which an autumnal sun had sprinkled with maroon-colored tints, very delicate and beautiful. The path was narrow, rocky, and uneven, frequently leading over high hills, in ascent and descent more or less abrupt and difficult. The increasing altitude of the route was more perceptible than any over which we had ever traveled, and the river, whenever visi-ble, was a perfect mountain torrent.

While descending a hill into one of the broad openings of the valley, our attention was suddenly aroused by half a dozen or more mounted Indians, who were riding down the foot-hills on the opposite side of the river. Two of our company who had lin-gered behind, came up with the information that they had seen several more making observations from behind a small butte, from which they fled in great haste on being discovered. They soon rode down on the plateau to a point where their horses were hobbled, and for a long time watched our party as it continued its course of travel up the river. Our camp was guarded that night with more than ordinary vigilance. A hard rainstorm, which set in early in the afternoon and continued through the night, may have saved us from an attack by these prowlers.

When we started the next morning, Gen. Washburn detailed four of our company to guard the pack train, while he, with four others, rode in advance to make the most practicable selection of routes. Six miles above our camp we ascended the spur of a mountain, which came down boldly to the river's edge. From its summit we had a beautiful view of the valley stretched out before us – the river fringed with cottonwood trees – the foothills covered with luxuriant, many-tinted herbage, and over all the snow-crowned summits of the mountains, many miles away, but seemingly rising from the midst of the plateau at our feet. Looking up the river, the valley opened widely, and from the rock on which we stood was visible the train of packhorses, slowly winding their way along the sinuous trail, which followed the inequalities of the mountain-side. The whole formed a scene of great interest. Pursuing our course a few miles farther, we camped just below the lower cañon of the river. Our hunters provided us with a sumptuous meal of antelope, rabbit, duck, grouse and trout.

The night was very cold, the mercury standing at 40° when we broke camp, at eight o'clock the next morning. We remained some time at the lower cañon of the Yellowstone, which, as a single isolated piece of scenery, is very beautiful. It is less than a mile in length, and perhaps does not exceed 1,000 feet in depth. Its walls are vertical, and, seen from the summit of the precipice, the river seems forced through a narrow gorge, and is surging and boiling at a fearful rate – the water breaking into millions of prismatic drops against every projecting rock.

After traveling six miles over the mountains above the cañon, we again descended into a broad and open valley, skirted by a level upland for several miles. . . . We camped at the close of this day's travel near the southwestern corner of Montana, at the mouth of Gardiner's River. (They are now at the border of the park.)

Crossing this stream the next morning, we passed over several rocky ridges into a valley which, for a long distance, was crowded with the spires of protruding rocks, which gave it such a dismal aspect that we named it "The Valley of Desolation." The trail was so rough and mountainous that we were able to travel but six miles before the usual hour for camping. Much of the distance was through fallen timber, almost impassable by the pack train. A mile before camping we discovered on the trail the fresh tracks of unshod ponies, indicating that a party of Indians had recently passed over it. Lieutenant Doane, with one of our company, had left us in the morning, and did not come into camp this evening. One of our horses broke his lariat during the night and galloped through the camp, rousing the sleepers, who grasped their guns, supposing the Indians were really upon them.

We started early the next morning, and soon struck the trail which had been traveled the preceding day by Lieutenant Doane. It led over a more practicable route than the one we left. The marks made in the soil by the travois (lodge-poles) on the side of the trail showed that it had been recently traveled by a number of lodges of Indians – and a little colt, which we overtook soon after making the discovery, convinced us that we were in their immediate vicinity. Our party was separated, and if we had been attacked, our pack-train, horses, and stores would have been an easy conquest. Fortunately we were unmolested, and, when again united, made a fresh resolution to travel as much in company as possible. All precautionary measures, however, unless enforced by the sternest discipline, are soon forgotten – and danger, until actually impending, is seldom borne in mind. A day had scarcely passed when we were as reckless as ever.

From the summit of a commanding range, which separated the waters of Antelope and Tower Creeks, we descended through a picturesque gorge, leading our horses to a small stream flowing into the Yellowstone. Four miles of travel, a great part of it down the precipitous slopes of the mountain, brought us to the banks of Tower Creek, and within the volcanic region, where the wonders were supposed to commence. On the right of the trail our attention was first attracted by a small hot sulphur spring, a little below the boiling point in temperature. Leaving the spring we ascended a high ridge, from which the most noticeable feature, in a landscape of great extent and beauty, was Column Rock, stretching for two miles along the eastern bank of the Yellowstone. At the distance from which we saw it, we could compare it in appearance to nothing but a section of the Giant's Causeway. It was composed of successive pillars of basalt overlying and underlying a thick stratum of cement and gravel resembling pudding-stone. In both rows, the pillars, standing in close proximity, were each about thirty feet high and from three to five feet in diameter. This interesting object, more from the novelty of its formation and its beautiful surroundings of mountain and river scenery than anything grand or impressive in its appearance, excited our attention, until the gathering shades of evening reminded us of the necessity of selecting a suitable camp. We descended the declivity to the banks of Tower Creek, and camped on a rocky terrace one mile distant from, and four hundred feet above the Yellowstone.

Tower Creek is a mountain torrent flowing through a gorge about forty yards wide. Just below our camp it falls perpendicularly over an even ledge 112 feet, forming one of the most beautiful cataracts in the world. For some distance above the fall the stream is broken into a great number of channels, each of which has worked a tortuous course through a compact body of shale to the verge of the precipice, where they re-unite and form the fall. The countless shapes into which the shale has been wrought by the action of the angry waters, add a feature of great interest to the scene. Spires of solid shale, capped with slate, beautifully rounded and polished, faultless in symmetry, raise their tapering forms to the height of from 80 to 150 feet, all over the plateau above the cataract. Some resemble towers, others the spire of churches, and others still shoot up as lithe and slender as the minarets of a mosque. Some of the loftiest of these formations, standing like sentinels upon the very brink of the fall, are accessible to an expert and adventurous climber. The position attained on one of their narrow summits, amid the uproar of waters and at the height of 250 feet above the boiling chasm, as the writer can affirm, requires a steady hand and strong nerves; yet the view which rewards the temerity of the exploit is full of compensations. Below the fall the stream descends in numerous rapids, with frightful velocity, through a gloomy gorge, to its union with the Yellowstone. Its bed is filled with enormous boulders, against which the rushing waters break with great fury. . . .

Early the next morning several of our company left in advance, to explore a passage for our pack-train over the mountains, which were very steep and lofty. We had been following a bend in the river – but as no sign of a change in its course was apparent, our object was, by finding a shorter route across the country, to avoid several days of toilsome travel. The advance party ascended a lofty peak which, in honor of our commander, was called Mount Washburn. From its summit, 400 feet above the line of perpetual snow, we were able to trace the course of the river to its source in Yellowstone Lake. At the point where we crossed the line of vegetation the snow covered the side of the apex of the mountain to the depth of twenty feet, and seemed to be as solid as the rocks upon which it rested. Descending the mountain, we came upon the trail made by the pack-train at its base, which we followed into camp at the head of a small stream flowing into the Yellowstone. . . .

They pass through their first thermal area, Washburn Hot Springs, a place that smelled and looked disagreeable, but was nevertheless fascinating. Soon afterwards they encounter Yellowstone's greatest spectacle.

Our journey the next day still continued through a country until then untraveled. Owing to the high lateral mountain spurs, the numerous ravines, and the interminable patches of fallen timber, we made very slow progress; but when the hour for camping arrived we were greatly surprised to find ourselves descending the mountain along the banks of a beautiful stream in the immediate vicinity of the Great Falls of the Yellowstone. This stream, which we called Cascade Creek, is very rapid. Just before its union with the river it passes through a gloomy gorge, of abrupt descent, which on either side is filled with continuous masses of obsidian that have been worn by the water into many fantastic shapes and cavernous recesses. This we named "The Devil's Den." Near the foot of the gorge the creek breaks from fearful rapids into a cascade of great beauty. The first fall of five feet is immediately succeeded by another of fifteen, into a pool as clear as amber, nestled beneath overarching rocks. Here it lingers as if half reluctant to continue its course, and then gracefully emerges from the grotto, and, veiling the rocks down an abrupt descent of eighty-four feet, passes rapidly on to the Yellowstone. It received the name of "Crystal."

The Great Falls are at the head of one of the most remarkable cañons in the world – a gorge through volcanic rocks fifty miles long, and varying from one thousand to nearly five thousand feet in depth. In its descent through this wonderful chasm the river falls almost three thousand feet. At one point, where the passage has been worn through a mountain range, our hunters assured us it was more than a vertical mile in depth, and the river, broken into rapids and cascades, appeared no wider than a ribbon. The brain reels as we gaze into this profound and solemn solitude. We shrink from the dizzy verge appalled, glad to feel the solid earth under our feet, and venture no more, except with forms extended, and faces barely protruding over the edge of the precipice. The stillness is horrible. Down, down, down, we see the river attenuated to a thread, tossing its miniature waves, and dashing, with puny strength, the massive walls which imprison it. All access to its margin is denied, and the dark gray rocks hold it in dismal shadow. Even the voice of its waters in their convulsive agony cannot be heard. Uncheered by plant or shrub, obstructed with massive boulders and by jutting points, it rushes madly on its solitary course, deeper and deeper into the bowels of the rocky firmament. The solemn grandeur of the scene surpasses description. It must be seen to be felt. The sense of danger with which it impresses you is harrowing in the extreme. You feel the absence of sound, the oppression of absolute silence. If you could only hear that gurgling river, if you could see a living tree in the depth beneath you, if a bird would fly past, if the wind would move any object in the awful chasm, to break for a moment the solemn silence that reigns there, it would relieve that tension of the nerves which the scene has excited, and you would rise from your prostrate condition and thank God that he had permitted you to gaze, unharmed, upon this majestic display of natural architecture. As it is, sympathizing in spirit with the deep gloom of the scene, you crawl from the dreadful verge, scared lest the firm rock give way beneath and precipitate you into the horrid gulf.

We had been told by trappers and mountaineers that there were cataracts in this vicinity a thousand feet high; but, if so, they must be lower down the cañon, in that portion of it which, by *our journey across the bend in the river, we failed to see. We regretted, when too late, that we had not made a fuller exploration – for by no other theory than that there was a stupendous fall below us, or that the river was broken by a continued succession of cascades, could we account for a difference of nearly 3,000 feet in altitude between the head and the mouth of the cañon. In that part of the cañon which we saw, the inclination of the river was marked by frequent falls fifteen and twenty feet in height, sufficient, if continuous through it, to accomplish the entire descent.*

The fearful descent into this terrific cañon was accomplished with great difficulty by Messrs. Hauser and Stickney, at a point about two miles below the falls. By trigonometrical measurement they found the chasm at that point to be 1,190 feet deep.

Their ascent from it was perilous, and it was only by making good use of hands and feet, and keeping the nerves braced to the utmost tension, that they were enabled to clamber up the precipitous rocks to a safe landing-place. The effort was successfully made, but none others of the company were disposed to venture.

From a first view of the cañon we followed the river to the falls. A grander scene than the lower cataract of the Yellowstone was never witnessed by mortal eyes. The volume seemed to be adapted to all the harmonies of the surrounding scenery. Had it been greater or smaller it would have been less impressive. The river, from a width of two hundred feet above the fall, is compressed by converging rocks to one hundred and fifty feet, where it takes the plunge. The shelf over which it falls is as level and even as a work of art. . . . It is a sheer, compact, solid, perpendicular sheet, faultless in all the elements of grandeur and picturesque beauties. The cañon which commences at the upper fall, half a mile above this cataract, is here a thousand feet in depth. Its vertical sides rise gray and dark above the fall to shelving summits, from which one can look down into the boiling, spray-filled chasm, enlivened with rainbows, and glittering like a shower of diamonds. From a shelf protruding over the stream, 500 feet below the top of the cañon, and 180 above the verge of the cataract, a member of our company, lying prone upon the rock, let down a cord with a stone attached into the gulf, and measured its profoundest depths. The life and sound of the cataract, with its sparkling spray and fleecy foam, contrasts strangely with the sombre stillness of the cañon a mile below. There all was darkness, gloom and shadow; here all was vivacity, gaiety, and delight. One was the most unsocial, the other the most social scene in nature. We could talk, and sing, and whoop, waking the echoes with our mirth and laughter in presence of the falls, but we could not thus profane the silence of the cañon. Seen through the cañon below the falls, the river for a mile or more is broken by rapids and cascades of great variety and beauty.

Between the lower and upper falls the cañon is two hundred to nearly four hundred feet deep. The river runs over a level bed of rock, and is undisturbed by rapids until near the verge of the lower fall. The upper fall is entirely unlike the other, but in its peculiar character equally interesting. For some distance above it the river breaks into frightful rapids. The stream is narrowed between the rocks as it approaches the brink, and bounds with impatient struggles for release, leaping through the stony jaws, in a sheet of snow-white foam, over a precipice nearly perpendicular, 115 feet high. Midway in its descent the entire volume of water is carried, by the sloping surface of an intervening ledge, twelve or fifteen feet beyond the vertical base of the precipice, gaining therefrom a novel and interesting feature. The churning of the water upon the rocks reduces it to a mass of foam and spray, through which all the colors of the solar spectrum are reproduced in astonishing profusion. What this cataract lacks in sublimity is more than compensated by picturesqueness. The rocks which overshadow it do not veil it from the open light. It is up amid the pine foliage which crowns the adjacent hills, the grand feature of a landscape unrivaled for beauties of vegetation as well as of rock and glen.

The two confronting rocks, overhanging the verge at the height of a hundred feet or more, could be readily united by a bridge, from which some of the grandest views of natural scenery in the world could be obtained – while just in front of, and within reaching distance of the arrowy water, from a table one-third of the way below the brink of the fall, all its nearest beauties and terrors may be caught at a glance.

We rambled around the falls and cañon two days, and left them with the unpleasant conviction that the greatest wonder of our journey had been seen.

We indulged in a last and lingering glance at the falls on the morning of the first day of autumn. The sun shone brightly, and the laughing waters of the upper fall were filled with the glitter of rainbows and diamonds. Nature, in the excess of her prodigality, had seemingly determined that this last look should be the brightest, for there was everything in the landscape, illuminated by the rising sun, to invite a longer stay. Even the dismal cañon, so dark and gray and still, reflected here and there on its vertical surface patches of sunshine, as much as to say, "See what I can do when I try." Everything had 'put a jocund humor on.' Long vistas of light broke through the pines which crowned the contiguous mountains, and the snow-crowned peaks in the distance glistened like crystal. Catching the spirit of the scene, we laughed and sung, and whooped as we rambled hurriedly from point to point, lingering only when the final moment came to receive the very last impression.

At length we turned our backs upon the scene, and wended our way slowly up the river-bank along a beaten trail. The last vestige of the rapids disappeared at the distance of half a mile above the Upper Fall. The river, expanded to the width of 400 feet, rolled peacefully between low verdant banks. The water for some distance was of that emerald hue which is so distinguishing a feature of Niagara. The bottom was pebbly, and but for the treacherous quicksands and crevices, of which it was full, we could easily have forded the stream at any point between the falls and our camping-place. We crossed a little creek strongly impregnated with alum – and three miles beyond found ourselves in the midst of volcanic wonders of great variety and profusion. The region was filled with boiling springs and craters. Two hills, each 300 feet high, and from a quarter to half a mile across, had been formed wholly of the sinter thrown from adjacent springs – lava, sulphur, and reddish-brown clay. Hot streams of vapor were pouring from crevices scattered over them. Their surfaces answered in hollow intonations to every footstep, and in several places yielded to the weight of our horses. Steaming vapor rushed hissingly from the fractures. . . .

They were now in the vicinity of Mud Volcano, a place with disagreeable odors and hidden dangers.

About a hundred yards distant we discovered a boiling alum spring, surrounded with beautiful crystals. . . . The violent ebullition of the water had undermined the surrounding surface in many places, and for the distance of several feet from the margin had so thoroughly saturated the incrustation with its liquid contents, that it was unsafe to approach the edge. As one of our company was unconcernedly passing near the brink, the incrustation suddenly sloughed off beneath his feet. A shout of alarm from his comrades aroused him to a sense of his peril, and he only avoided being plunged into the boiling mixture by falling suddenly backward at full length upon the firm portion of the crust, and rolling over to a place of safety. His escape from a horrible death was most marvelous, and in another instant he would have been beyond all human aid. . . .

. . . The atmosphere was filled with sulphurous gases, and the river opposite our camp was impregnated with the mineral bases of adjacent springs. The valley through which we had made our day's journey was level and beautiful, spreading away to grassy foothills, which terminated in a horizon of mountains.

We spent the next day in examining the wonders surrounding us. At the base of adjacent foothills we found three springs of boiling mud, the largest of which, forty feet in diameter, encircled by an elevated rim of solid tufa, resembles an immense cauldron. The seething, bubbling contents, covered with steam, are five feet below the rim. The disgusting appearance of this spring is scarcely atoned for by the wonder with which it fills the beholder. . . .

While returning by a new route to our camp, dull, thundering sounds, which General Washburn likened to frequent discharges of a distant mortar, broke upon our ears. We followed their direction, and found them to proceed from a mud volcano, which occupied the slope of a small hill, embowered in a grove of pines. Dense volumes of steam shot into the air with each report, through a crater thirty feet in diameter. The reports, though irregular, occurred as often as every five seconds, and could be distinctly heard half a mile. Each alternate report shook the ground a distance of two hundred yards or more, and the massive jets of vapor which accompanied them burst forth like the smoke of burning gunpowder. It was impossible to stand on the edge of that side of the crater opposite the wind, and one of our party, Mr. Hedges, was rewarded for his temerity in venturing too near the rim, by being thrown by the force of the volume of steam violently down the outer side of the crater. . . .

In contrast, they now passed on to a scene sublime and tranquil.

On our return we followed the trail of the train, fording the river a short distance above the camp. Here we found the first evidence, since leaving Boteler's, that the country had been long ago visited by trappers and hunters. It was a bank of earth two feet high, presenting an angle to the river ingeniously concealed by interwoven willows, thus forming a rifle-pit from which the occupant, without discovery, could bring down geese, ducks, swans, pelicans, and the numerous furred animals with which the river abounds. (Could it be Osborne Russell's campsite?) *Near by we stopped a moment to examine another spring of boiling mud, and then pursued our route over hills covered with artemisia (sage brush), through ravines and small meadows, into a dense forest of pines filled with prostrate trunks which had piled upon each other for years to the height of many feet. Our passage of two miles through this forest to the bank of the lake, unmarked by any trail, was accomplished with great difficulty, but the view which greeted us at its close was amply compensatory. There lay the silvery bosom of the lake, reflecting the beams of the setting sun, and stretching away for miles, until lost in the dark foliage of the interminable wilderness of pines surrounding it. Secluded amid the loftiest peaks of the Rocky Mountains, 8,337 feet above the level of the ocean, possessing strange peculiarities of form and beauty, this watery solitude is one of the most attractive natural objects in the world. Its southern shore, indented with long narrow inlets, not unlike the frequent fiords of Iceland, bears testimony to the awful upheaval and tremendous force of the elements which resulted in its creation. The long pine-crowned promontories, stretching into it from the base of the hills, lend new and charming features to an aquatic scene full of novelty and splendor. Islands of emerald hue dot its surface, and a margin of sparkling sand forms its jeweled setting. The winds, compressed in their passage through the mountain gorges, lash it into a sea as*

*terrible as the fretted ocean, covering it with foam. But now it
lay before us calm and unruffled, save by the gentle wavelets
which broke in murmurs along the shore. Water, one of the
grandest elements of scenery, never seemed so beautiful before.
It formed a fitting climax to all the wonders we had seen, and
we gazed upon it for hours, entranced with its increasing
attractions.*

*This lake is about twenty-five miles long and seventy-five or
eighty in circumference. Doubtless it was once the mighty crater of an immense volcano. It is filled with trout, some of gigantic size and peculiar delicacy. Waterfowl, in great variety, dot in
flocks its mirrored surface. The forests surrounding it are filled
with deer, elk, mountain sheep, and lesser game; and in the
mountain fastnesses the terrible grizzly and formidable amiss
make their lairs.*

*In form, it was by one of our party not inaptly compared to a
"human hand with the fingers extended and spread apart as
much as possible. The main portion of the lake is the northern,
which would represent the palm of the hand. There is a large
southwest bay, nearly cut off, that would represent the thumb,
while there are about the same number of narrow southern
inlets as there are fingers on the hand." Enclosing this watery
palm, is a dense forest of pines, until now untraversed by man.
It was filled with trunks of trees in various stages of decay,
which had been prostrated by the mountain blasts, rendering it
almost impassable; but as the beach of the lake was in many
places impracticable, there was no alternative but to recede
altogether or work our way through it. . . .*

They continued on and made a circuit around the entire southern
end of the lake. The course was difficult and the views were grand.

*Ascending the plateau from the beach, we became at once
involved in all the intricacies of a primeval wilderness of pines.
Difficulties increased with our progress through it, severely trying the amiability of every member of the company. Our packhorses would frequently get wedged between the trees or caught
in the traps of a network of fallen trunks from which labor,
patience, and ingenuity were severely taxed to extricate
them. . . .*

After fifteen miles of unvarying toil we emerged from the forest to the pebbly beach of the lake. . . . The lake was rolling tumultuously, its crested waves rising at least four feet high. The scene was very beautiful and exhilarating.

Our route the next day was divided between the beach of the lake and the forest, and so much impeded by fallen timber that we traveled but ten miles. . . .

Even at this late date, their geography is still confused, mistaking the Absaroka Mountains for the Wind River Mountains in the following passage.

Our course during the two following days was nearly southeast, on a line parallel with the Wind River Mountains – that remarkable range which forms so conspicuous a feature in Mr. Irving's Astoria *and* Bonneville's Adventures. *The faint outline of their distant peaks had been visible on the northeastern horizon for several days. On our right, seventy-five miles distant, were the towering summits of the three Tetons, the great landmarks of the Snake River valley. The close of the day, on Sept. 6th, found us near the southeastern arm of the lake, into which a large river flows* (the Yellowstone). *The ground was low and marshy, and being unable to find a fording-place, we were compelled to make our camp at the base of a range of bluffs half a mile away. During the night we were startled by the shrill and almost human scream of an amiss or mountain lion, which sounded uncomfortably near. This terrible animal is much larger than the panther of the eastern forests, but greatly resembles it in shape, color, and ferocity. It is the terror of mountaineers, and furnishes them with the staple for many tales full of daring exploits.*

Early the next morning our commander and several others left camp in search of a ford, while the writer and Lieutenant Doane started in the direction of a lofty mountain, from the summit of which we expected to obtain a satisfactory observation of the southern shore of the lake. At the expiration of two hours we reached a point in the ascent too precipitous for further equestrian travel. Dismounting, we led our horses for an hour longer up the steep side of the mountain, pausing every few moments to take breath, until we arrived at the line of perpetual snow. Here we unsaddled and hitched our horses, and climbed the apex to its summit, passing over a mass of congealed snow more than thirty feet in thickness. The ascent occupied four hours. We were more than 600 feet above the snow line, and by barometric observation 11,350 feet above the ocean level.

The grandeur and vast extent of the view from this elevation beggar description. The lake and valley surrounding it lay seemingly at our feet within jumping distance. Beyond them we saw with great distinctness the jets of the mud volcano and geyser. But beyond all these, stretching away into a horizon of cloud-defined mountains, was the entire Wind River (Absaroka) range, revealing in the sunlight the dark recesses, gloomy cañons, stupendous precipices, and glancing pinnacles, which everywhere dotted its jagged slopes. Lofty peaks shot up in gigantic spires from the main body of the range, glittering in the sunbeams like solid crystal. The mountain on which we stood was the most westerly peak of a range which, in long-extended volume, swept to the southeastern horizon, exhibiting a continuous elevation more than thirty miles in width; its central line broken into countless points, knobs, glens, and defiles, all on the most colossal scale of grandeur and magnificence. Outside of these, on either border, along the entire range, lofty peaks rose at intervals, seemingly vying with each other in the varied splendors they presented to the beholder. The scene was full of majesty. The valley at the base of this range was dotted with small lakes and cloven centrally by the river, which, in the far distance, we could see emerging from a cañon of immense dimensions, within the shade of which two enormous jets of steam shot to an incredible height into the atmosphere. . . .

From this viewpoint, Langford refers to past western explorers – the expeditions of the Astorians, Captain Bonneville and Captain Reynolds. He quotes from their narratives that were earlier included in this volume, so there is no need to read those passages again. Moving on, they encounter further difficulties, and a misfortune casts a pall over their journey.

We were an hour and a half making the descent of the mountain. At its base we struck the trail of our pack-train, which we followed to a point where the direction it had taken would have been lost, but for the foresight of one of our companions, who had formed a tripod of poles, one of which, longer than the others, pointed to the right.

Obeying this Indian indication, we descended the bank and crossed the bottom to the river, fording which we followed the trail through a beautiful pine forest, free from undergrowth and other obstructions, the distance of a mile. Here night overtook us, and mistaking for the trail a dark serpentine line, we soon found ourselves clambering up the side of a steep mountain. The conviction that we were following a band of Indians, and possibly were near their lodges, suggested no pleasant reflections. Alighting from our horses, we built a fire upon the track, and, carefully examining it, could not find the impression of a single horseshoe. Further investigation revealed the fact that we had been for some time pursuing the path worn by a gang of elk that had crossed the trail of the pack-train since the twilight set in.

A night on the mountain, without supper or blankets, was not to be endured. We retraced our route to the base of the mountain, and struck out boldly in the darkness for the beach of the lake, where we supposed our party had camped. Our ride through fallen timber and morass until we reached the shore was performed more skillfully than if we had seen the obstacles which lay in our path. We reached the lake in safety, and after a ride of two miles on the smooth beach rounded a point from which we saw the welcome watchfire of our company. A loud halloo was responded to by a dozen sympathetic voices, showing that our anxiety had been shared by our companions. Our camp was on the eastern inlet of the south shore of the lake, distant but four miles from the camp of the preceding night.

Thirteen miles of toilsome travel, zigzagged into only seven of progress, found us encamped, at the close of the next day, two miles from the mouth of a small stream flowing into the lake. Our party was separated nearly all day, searching for routes. Two members, after suffering all the early sensations incident to a conviction of being lost in the wilderness, came into camp at a late hour, full of glee at their good fortune. At one of their halts, after they had dismounted to reconnoiter, a huge grizzly jumped at one of them from the bushes, frightening his horse so that he broke his bridle and ran away. They caught him with difficulty. Our commander and Mr. Hauser, in company, while seeking a route for future travel, came suddenly upon a female grizzly and two cubs, about half a mile from camp. On their return, six of the party started in pursuit, but Madame Bruin, meanwhile, had made good her retreat.

Our journey of five miles, the next day, was accomplished with great difficulty and annoyance. Almost the entire distance was through a forest piled full of fallen trunks. Traveling was but another name for scrambling; and as man is at times the least amiable of animals, our tempers frequently displayed alarming activity, not only towards the patient creatures laden with our stores, but towards each other. Once, while involved in the reticulated meshes of a vast net of branches and tree-tops, each man, with varied expletive emphasis, clamorously insisting upon a particular mode of extrication, a member of the party, who was always jolly, restored us to instant good-humor by repeating, in theatrical tone and manner, those beautiful lines from Childe Harold –

> *"There is a pleasure in the pathless woods,*
> *There is a rapture on the lonely shore."*

We were glad, at an early hour in the afternoon, to pitch our tent on one of the small tributaries of Snake River – three miles distant from the lake. In the search made by every member of the party for three routes, our company was unavoidably much scattered

. . . One of our company (the Hon. Truman C. Everts, late U.S. Assessor Montana) had failed to come up with the rest of the company; but as this was a common circumstance, we gave it little heed until the lateness of the hour convinced us he had lost his way. We increased our fire and fired our guns, as signals; but all to no purpose. It had been a sort of tacit agreement among us only the night before, that should any one get parted from the company, he would at once go to the southwest arm of the lake (that being our objective point) and await there the arrival of the train. . . .

Seven miles of struggling took us through the timber to another inlet, five miles farther on our way. No sign of our missing comrade. We built a large fire on a commanding ridge, and ascended a mountain overlooking the north and west shores of the lake, where we kindled another fire, which could be seen at a great distance. Eight hundred feet above Yellowstone Lake,

*nestled in a dark mountain glen, we found two small lakes, com-
pletely environed with frightful masses of basalt and brown
lava, seemingly thrown up and scattered by some terrible convulsion. Two of our company took the backward trail at night,
searching for Mr. Everts; and our anxieties were greatly
increased lest they too should meet with some disaster.*

*We rose early the next morning, after passing a sleepless night.
While at breakfast, our two companions came in. They had followed the beach to a point east of our camp of two days before,
and found no trace of Mr. Everts. More than ever assured that
we should find him at the west arm of the lake, we struck out for
that point – three of our party, Mr. Hauser, Lieut. Doane, and
myself, in advance, to explore a route for the train and make all
possible search by the way. We posted notices on the trees to
indicate the route we had taken, and made caches of provisions
at several points. Late in the afternoon, at the close of a fatiguing day's travel, mostly through forest, we arrived at our objective point, and were greatly distressed to find there no trace of
our lost friend. While gathered around our campfire in the
evening, devising a plan for more systematic search, our ears
were saluted with a screech so terribly human, that, for a
moment supposing it to be our missing comrade, we hallooed in
response, and would have started to his relief but that a mina-
tory growl warned us of the near approach of a mountain lion.*

*Three parties, of two each, struck out the next morning in differ-
ent directions, in pursuit of our companion. One followed the
lake shore; one the back trail through the forest; and the third,
southerly from the lake to a large brown mountain. The party
following the lake shore returned to camp early in the afternoon, with the report that they had seen Indians. The story of
their adventures, written by one of them, runs thus: "He and his
companion having penetrated several miles through the inhospitable wilds of that region, dismounted and unsaddled their
horses. Mr. T. commenced to fish, and prepare them a little dinner, while Mr. S. went ahead with his gun, to continue the
search on foot. The former had just caught four fishes, and kindled a fire, when the latter returned in some haste, but perfectly
cool and self-possessed, and stated that there were six Indians
on a point jutting out into the lake, about a mile distant. They
concluded that neither had a mouth for fish, which they left
sweltering in the noon-day sun, and, saddling their horses, they*

advanced towards the foe. Mr. S. saw them distinctly; but Mr. T. could not, probably because he was somewhat nearsighted. Finally, the former gentleman saw them flitting, phantom-like, among the rocks and trees, at which juncture the party retired to camp in platoons, and in good order, at the rate of a mile in every three minutes." This tribe of Indians, being one of the curiosities of the expedition, and hitherto unknown, was named after the person who discovered it. (It seems likely that they were the Sheepeater Indians, the tribe met by Osborne Russell four decades earlier.)

Both of the other parties returned, after a fruitless search. In their trip to the brown mountain, the two who went south crossed the main range of the Rocky Mountains through a very low pass, which on the western side terminated in a brimstone basin containing forty or fifty sulphur and mud springs, and a large number of craters, from which issued jets of vapor. This slope of the mountain was covered with a hollow incrustation through which the water from the springs, percolating in different channels, had spread out over the little patches of soil with which they came in contact, covering them with bright green verdure. In crossing one of these the horse of one of the party broke through to his haunches, and being extricated, he plunged more deeply into another trap, throwing headlong his rider, whose arm as he fell was thrust violently through the treacherous surface into the scalding morass, from complete submersion in which both man and beast were with great difficulty saved.

At the base of the brown mountain the party saw a lake of considerable size, which they believed to be the headwaters of Snake River – the Lewis fork of the Columbia. They could not approach it nearer than a mile, on account of the treacherous character of the soil. (It seems likely that this is Heart Lake and Geyser Basin, with the brown mountain being Mt. Sheridan.)

The other party were absent two days. They had visited all the camps of the six preceding days, following the trail between them, mostly obliterated by the falling foliage of the pines, with great difficulty, but without discovering the slightest indication that Mr. Everts had come upon it. On full consultation we came to the conclusion that he had either been shot from his horse by an Indian, or had returned down the Yellowstone, or struck out upon some of the headwaters of Snake River, with the intention of following it to the settlements. It was agreed that we should pursue the search three days longer from this point before renewing our journey. Snow began to fall early in the evening. Through the hazy atmosphere we beheld, on the shore of the inlet opposite our camp, the steam ascending in jets from more than fifty craters, giving it much the appearance of a New England factory village.

Snow continued to fall all night and the next day, and we made our camp as comfortable as possible. At night the snow was more than two feet deep. It turned to rain the following morning. Showers, alternated with sunshine through the day, removed the snow rapidly. We were now so completely environed by forest, and so far away from any recognized trail, that all our fear of molestation by Indians, or of danger from any other cause, was thoroughly dissipated. . . .

The five days during which we camped at this locality were occupied by every possible effort to find our missing friend, but the labors of each day only served to increase our fears for his safety. One hope, that of meeting him at Virginia City, was still indulged; but opposed to this were many painful conjectures as to his possible fate – not the least prevalent of which was the one that he might have been shot from an ambush by an Indian arrow. Our provisions were rapidly diminishing, and our longer stay gave promise of unfavorable results. The force of circumstances obliged us to adopt the gloomy alternative of moving forward the next day, leaving one of our own party and two of the calvarymen to prosecute a further search.

The loss of our comrade and friend was to us all a source of much unhappy reflection, and the hope of finding him so entirely absorbed our attention that we had little curiosity to examine, and so escaped very many of the wonders of this region, which we should otherwise have seen. In our constant passing to and fro in different directions through the forest, along the lake, and over the surrounding mountains, we had glances of objects which, had we been free from a heavy charge, it would have been pleasant to visit and describe. These, however, are reserved for future investigation.

The plan of our route led us in a northwesterly direction from the lake towards the headwaters of the Madison. We traveled through a dense pine forest, unmarked by trails and encumbered by fallen timber for most of the distance. The close of the first day's travel found us only twelve miles from the lake, still in the midst of the deep snow, with no place to pitch our tent, and each man seeking, unsuccessfully, a dry spot, whereon to spread his blankets, under the shelter of the trees. The next day we reached the east bank of the Firehole River, the largest tributary of the Madison, down which we traveled, passing several cascades, many craters and boiling springs, to a large basin, two miles above the point of the union of the Firehole and Burnt Hole Rivers.

We bade adieu to Yellowstone Lake, surfeited with the wonders we had seen, and in the belief that the interesting portion of our journey was over. The desire for home had superseded all thought of further exploration. We had seen the greatest wonders on the continent, and were convinced that there was not on the globe another region where, within the same limits, nature had crowded so much of grandeur and majesty, with so much of novelty and wonder. Our only care was to return home as rapidly as possible. Three days of active travel from the headwaters of the Madison, would find us among the settlers in the beautiful lower valley of that picturesque river, and within twelve miles of Virginia City, where we hoped to meet with Mr. Everts, and realize afresh that "all is well that ends well."

Judge, then, what must have been our astonishment, as we entered the basin at mid-afternoon of our second day's travel, to see in the clear sunlight, at no great distance, an immense volume of clear, sparkling water projected into the air to the height of one hundred and twenty-five feet. "Geysers! geysers!" exclaimed one of our company, and, spurring our jaded horses, we soon gathered around this wonderful phenomenon. It was indeed a perfect geyser. . . . It spouted at regular intervals nine times during our stay, the columns of boiling water being thrown from ninety to one hundred and twenty-five feet at each discharge, which lasted from fifteen to twenty minutes. We gave it the name of "Old Faithful." . . .

"The Grotto" was so named from its singular crater of vitrified sinter, full of large, sinuous apertures. Through one of these, on

*our first visit, one of our company crawled to the discharging
orifice; and when, a few hours afterwards, he saw a volume of
boiling water, four feet in diameter, shooting through it to the
height of sixty feet, and a scalding stream of two hundred inches
flowing from the aperture he had entered a short time before, he
concluded he had narrowly escaped being summarily cooked.
The discharge of this geyser continued for nearly half an
hour. . . .*

Langford wrote about several of the geysers seen but one, in particular, made a notable impression on the party.

*Our search for new wonders leading us across the Firehole
River, we ascended a gentle incrusted slope, and came suddenly
upon a large oval aperture with scalloped edges, the diameters
of which were eighteen and twenty-five feet, the sides corrugated and covered with a grayish-white siliceous deposit, which
was distinctly visible at the depth of one hundred feet below the
surface. No water could be discovered, but we could distinctly
hear it gurgling and boiling at a great distance below. Suddenly
it began to rise, boiling and spluttering, and sending out huge
masses of steam, causing a general stampede of our company,
driving us some distance from our point of observation. When
within about forty feet of the surface it became stationary, and
we returned to look down upon it. It was foaming and surging at
a terrible rate, occasionally emitting small jets of hot water
nearly to the mouth of the orifice. All at once it seemed seized
with a fearful spasm, and rose with incredible rapidity, hardly
affording us time to flee to a safe distance, when it burst from
the orifice with terrific momentum, rising in a column the full
size of this immense aperture to the height of sixty feet; and
through and out of the apex of this vast aqueous mass, five or
six lesser jets or round columns of water, varying in size from
six to fifteen inches in diameter, were projected to the marvelous
height of two hundred and fifty feet. . . .*

*This grand eruption continued for twenty minutes, and was the
most magnificent sight we ever witnessed. We were standing on
the side of the geyser nearest the sun, the gleams of which filled
the sparkling column of water and spray with myriads of rainbows, whose arches were constantly changing – dipping and
fluttering hither and thither, and disappearing only to be succeeded by others, again and again, amid the aqueous column,*

while the minute globules into which the spent jets were diffused when falling sparkled like a shower of diamonds, and around every shadow which the denser clouds of vapor, interrupting the sun's rays, cast upon the column, could be seen a luminous circle radiant with all the colors of the prism, and resembling the halo of glory represented in paintings as encircling the head of Divinity. All that we had previously witnessed seemed tame in comparison with the perfect grandeur and beauty of this display. Two of these wonderful eruptions occurred during the twenty-two hours we remained in the valley. This geyser we named "The Giantess.". . .

How many more geysers there are in this locality it would be impossible to conjecture. Our waning stores admonished us of the necessity for a hurried departure, and we reluctantly left this remarkable region less than half explored. . . .

One individual who had entered Yellowstone with the party did not leave with them. His narrative begins here, lost in the wilderness at the southern end of Yellowstone Lake.

Evert's Narrative

On the day that I found myself separated from the company, and for several days previous, our course had been impeded by the dense growth of the pine forest, and occasional large tracts of fallen timber, frequently rendering our progress almost impossible. Whenever we came to one of these immense windfalls, each man engaged in the pursuit of a passage through it, and it was while thus employed, and with the idea that I had found one, that I strayed out of sight and hearing of my comrades. We had a toilsome day. It was quite late in the afternoon. As separations like this had frequently occurred, it gave me no alarm, and I rode on, fully confident of soon rejoining the company, or of finding their camp. I came up with the pack horse, which Mr. Langford afterwards recovered, and tried to drive him along, but failing to do so, and my eyesight being defective, I spurred forward, intending to return with assistance from the party. This incident tended to accelerate my speed. I rode on in the direction which I supposed had been taken, until darkness overtook me in the dense forest. This was disagreeable enough, but caused me no alarm. I had no doubt of being with the party at breakfast the next morning. I selected a spot for comfortable repose, picketed my horse, built a fire, and went to sleep.

The next morning I rose at early dawn, saddled and mounted my horse, and took my course in the supposed direction of the camp. Our ride of the previous day had been up a peninsula jutting into the lake, for the shore of which I started, with the expectation of finding my friends, camped on the beach. The forest was quite dark, and the trees so thick, that it was only by a slow process I could get through them at all. In searching for the trail I became somewhat confused. The falling foliage of the pines had obliterated every trace of travel. I was obliged frequently to dismount, and examine the ground for the faintest indications. Coming to an opening, from which I could see several vistas, I dismounted for the purpose of selecting one leading in the direction I had chosen, and leaving my horse unhitched, as had always been my custom, walked a few rods into the forest. While surveying the ground my horse took fright, and I turned around in time to see him disappearing at full speed among the trees. That was the last I ever saw of him. It was yet quite dark. My blankets, gun, pistols, fishing tackle, matches – everything, except the clothing on my person, a couple of knives, and a small opera-glass were attached to the saddle.

I did not yet realize the possibility of a permanent separation from the company. Instead of following up the pursuit of their camp, I engaged in an effort to recover my horse. Half a day's search convinced me of its impracticability. I wrote and posted in an open space several notices, which, if my friends should chance to see, would inform them of my condition and the route I had taken, and then struck out into the forest in the supposed direction of their camp. As the day wore on without any discovery, alarm took the place of anxiety at the prospect of another night alone in the wilderness, and this time without food or fire. But even this dismal foreboding was cheered by the hope that I should soon rejoin my companions, who would laugh at my adventure, and incorporate it as a thrilling episode into the journal of our trip. The bright side of a misfortune, as I found by experience, even under the worst possible circumstances, always presents some features of encouragement. When I began to realize that my condition was one of actual peril, I banished from my mind all fear of an unfavorable result. Seating myself on a log, I recalled every foot of the way I had traveled since the separation from my friends, and the most probable opinion I could form of their whereabouts was, that they had, by a course but little different from mine, passed by the spot where I had posted the notices, learned of my disaster, and were waiting for me to rejoin them there, or searching for me in that vicinity. A night must be spent amid the prostrate trunks before my return could be accomplished. At no time during my period of exile did I experience so much mental suffering from the cravings of hunger as when, exhausted with this long day of fruitless search, I resigned myself to a couch of pine foliage in the pitchy darkness of a thicket of small trees. Naturally timid in the night, I fully realized the exposure of my condition. I peered upward through the darkness, but all was blackness and gloom. The wind sighed mournfully through the pines. The forest seemed alive with the screeching of night birds, the angry barking of coyotes, and the prolonged, dismal howl of the gray wolf. These sounds, familiar by their constant occurrence throughout the journey, were now full of terror, and drove slumber from my eye-lids. Above all this, however, was the hope that I should be restored to my comrades the next day.

Early the next morning I rose unrefreshed, and pursued my weary way over the prostrate trunks. It was noon when I reached the spot where my notices were posted. No one had been there. My disappointment was almost overwhelming. For the first time, I realized that I was lost. Then came a crushing sense of destitution. No food, no fire; no means to procure either; alone in an unexplored wilderness, one hundred and fifty miles from the nearest human abode, surrounded by wild beasts, and famishing with hunger. It was no time for despondency. A moment afterwards I felt how calamity can elevate the mind, in the formation of the resolution "not to perish in that wilderness."

*The hope of finding the party still controlled my plans. I thought, by traversing the peninsula centrally, I would be enabled to strike the shore of the lake in advance of their camp, and near the point of departure for the Madison. Acting upon this impression, I rose from a sleepless couch, and pursued my way through the timber-entangled forest. A feeling of weakness took the place of hunger. Conscious of the need for food, I felt no cravings. Occasionally, while scrambling over logs and through thickets, a sense of faintness and exhaustion would come over me, but I would suppress it with the audible expression, "This won't do; I **must** find my company." Despondency* *would sometimes strive with resolution for the mastery of my thoughts. I would think of home – of my daughter – and of the possible chance of starvation, or death in some more terrible form; but as often as these gloomy forebodings came, I would strive to banish them with reflections better adapted to my immediate necessities. . . .*

It was mid-day when I emerged from the forest into an open space at the foot of the peninsula. A broad lake of beautiful curvature, with magnificent surroundings, lay before me, glittering in the sunbeams. It was full twelve miles in circumference. A wide belt of sand formed the margin which I was approaching, directly opposite to which, rising seemingly from the very depths of the water, towered the loftiest peak of a range of mountains apparently interminable. The ascending vapor from innumerable hot springs, and the sparkling jet of a single geyser, added the feature of novelty to one of the grandest landscapes I ever beheld. Nor was the life of the scene less noticeable than its other attractions. Large flocks of swans and other water-fowl were sporting on the quiet surface of the lake; otters in great numbers performed the most amusing aquatic evolutions; mink and beaver swam around unscared, in most grotesque confusion. Deer, elk, and mountain sheep stared at me, manifesting more surprise than fear at my presence among them. The adjacent forest was vocal with the song of birds, chief of which were the chattering noises of a species of mockingbird, whose imitative efforts afforded abundant merriment. Seen under favorable circumstances, this assemblage of grandeur, beauty, and novelty would have been transporting; but, jaded with travel, famishing with hunger, and distressed with anxiety, I was in no humor for ecstasy. My tastes were subdued and chastened by the perils, which environed me. I longed for food, friends, and protection. Associated with my thoughts, however, was the wish that some of my friends of peculiar tastes could enjoy this display of secluded magnificence, now, probably, for the first time beheld by mortal eyes.

The lake was at least one thousand feet lower than the highest point of the peninsula, and several hundred feet below the level of Yellowstone Lake. I recognized the mountain which overshadowed it as the landmark which, a few days before, had received from Gen. Washburn the name of Mount Everts; and as it is associated with some of the most agreeable and terrible incidents of my exile, I feel that I have more than a mere discoverer's right to the perpetuity of that christening. The lake is fed by innumerable small streams from the mountains, and the countless hot springs surrounding it. A large river flows from it, through a cañon a thousand feet in height, in a southeasterly direction, to a distant range of mountains, which I conjectured to be Snake River; and with the belief that I had discovered the source of the great southern tributary of the Columbia, I gave it the name of Bessie Lake, after the "Sole daughter of my house and heart."

Apparently, Truman Everts had found his way to Heart Lake, as the search party had earlier. Presumably Mount Everts is now Mount Sheridan.

During the first two days, the fear of meeting with Indians gave me considerable anxiety; but, when conscious of being lost, there was nothing I so much desired as to fall in with a lodge of Bannocks or Crows. Having nothing to tempt their cupidity, they would do me no personal harm, and, with the promise of reward, would probably minister to my wants and aid my deliverance. Imagine my delight, while gazing upon the animated expanse of water, at seeing sail out from a distant point a large canoe containing a single oarsman. It was rapidly approaching the shore where I was seated. With hurried steps I paced the beach to meet it, all my energies stimulated by the assurance it gave of food, safety, and restoration to friends. As I drew near, it turned towards the shore, and oh! bitter disappointment, the object which my eager fancy had transformed into an angel of relief stalked from the water, an enormous pelican, flapped its dragon-wings as if in mockery of my sorrow, and flew to a solitary point farther up the lake. This little incident quite unmanned me. The transition from joy to grief brought with it a terrible consciousness of the horrors of my condition. But night was fast approaching, and darkness would come with it. While looking for a spot where I might repose in safety, my attention was attracted to a small green plant of so lively a hue as to form a striking contrast with the deep pine foliage. For closer examination I pulled it up by the root, which was long and tapering, not unlike a radish. It was a thistle. I tasted it; it was palatable and nutritious. My appetite craved it, and the first meal in four days was made on thistle-roots. Eureka! I had found food. No optical illusion deceived me this time; I could subsist until I rejoined my companions. Glorious counterpoise to the wretchedness of the preceding half-hour!

Overjoyed at this discovery, with hunger allayed, I stretched myself under a tree, upon the foliage which had partially filled a space between contiguous trunks, and fell asleep. How long I slept I know not; but suddenly I was roused by a loud, shrill scream, like that of a human being in distress, poured seemingly, into the very portals of my ear. There was no mistaking that fearful voice. I had been deceived by and answered it a dozen times while threading the forest, with the belief that it was a friendly signal. It was the screech of a mountain lion, so alarmingly near as to cause every nerve to thrill with terror. To yell in return, seize with convulsive grasp the limbs of the friendly tree, and swing myself into it, was the work of a moment. Scrambling hurriedly from limb to limb, I was soon as near the top as safety would permit. The savage beast was snuffling and growling below, apparently on the very spot I had just abandoned. I answered every growl with a responsive scream. Terrified at the delay and pawing of the beast, I increased my voice to its utmost volume, broke branches from the limbs, and, in the impotency of fright, madly hurled them at the spot whence the continued howlings proceeded.

Failing to alarm the animal, which now began to make the circuit of the tree, as if to select a spot for springing into it, I shook, with a strength increased by terror, the slender trunk until every limb rustled with the motion. All in vain. The terrible creature pursued his walk around the tree, lashing the ground with his tail, and prolonging his howlings almost to a roar. It was too dark to see, but the movements of the lion kept me apprised of its position. Whenever I heard it on one side of the tree I speedily changed to the opposite – an exercise which, in my weakened state, I could only have performed under the impulse of terror. I would alternately sweat and thrill with horror at the thought of being torn to pieces and devoured by this formidable monster. All my attempts to frighten it seemed unavailing. Disheartened at its persistency, and expecting every moment it would take the deadly leap, I tried to collect my thoughts, and prepare for the fatal encounter which I knew must result. Just at this moment it occurred to me that I would try silence. Clasping the trunk of the tree with both arms, I sat perfectly still. The lion, at this time ranging round, occasionally snuffing and pausing, and all the while filling the forest with the echo of his howlings, suddenly imitated my example. This silence was more terrible, if possible, than the clatter and crash of his movements through the brushwood, for now I did not know from what direction to expect his attack. Moments passed with me like hours. After a lapse of time which I cannot estimate, the beast gave a spring into the thicket and ran screaming into the forest. My deliverance was effected.

Had strength permitted, I should have retained my perch till daylight, but with the consciousness of escape from the jaws of the ferocious brute came a sense of overpowering weakness which almost palsied me, and made my descent from the tree both difficult and dangerous. Incredible as it may seem, I lay down in my old bed, and was soon lost in a slumber so profound that I did not awake until after daylight. The experience of the night seemed like a terrible dream; but the broken limbs which in the agony of consternation I had thrown from the tree, and the rifts made in the fallen foliage by my visitant in his circumambulations, were too convincing evidences of its reality. I could not dwell upon my exposure and escape without shuddering, and reflecting that probably like perils would often occur under less fortunate circumstances, and with a more fatal issue. I wondered what fate was in reserve for me – whether I would ultimately sink from exhaustion and perish of starvation, or become the prey of some of the ferocious animals that roamed these vast fastnesses. My thoughts then turned to the loved ones at home. They could never know my fate, and would indulge a thousand conjectures concerning it, not the least distressing of which would be that I had been captured by a band of hostile Sioux, and tortured to death at the stake.

I was roused from this train of reflections by a marked change in the atmosphere. One of those dreary storms of mingled snow and rain, common to these high altitudes, set in. My clothing, which had been much torn, exposed my person to its "pitiless peltings." An easterly wind, rising to a gale, admonished me that it would be furious and of long duration. None of the discouragements I had met with dissipated the hope of rejoining my friends; but foreseeing the delay, now unavoidable, I knew that my escape from the wilderness must be accomplished, if at all, by my own unaided exertions. This thought was terribly afflicting, and brought before me, in vivid array, all the dreadful

*realities of my condition. I could see no ray of hope. In this con-
dition of mind I could find no better shelter than the spreading
branches of a spruce tree, under which, covered with earth and
boughs, I lay during the two succeeding days; the storm, meanwhile, raging with unabated violence. While thus exposed, and
suffering from cold and hunger, a little benumbed bird, not
larger than a snow-bird, hopped within my reach. I instantly
seized and killed it, and, plucking its feathers, ate it raw. It was
a delicious meal for a half-starved man.*

*Taking advantage of a lull in the elements, on the morning of
the third day I rose early and started in the direction of a large
group of hot springs which were steaming under the shadow of
Mount Everts. The distance I traveled could not have been less
than ten miles. Long before I reached the wonderful cluster of
natural cauldrons, the storm had recommenced. Chilled
through, with my clothing thoroughly saturated, I lay down
under a tree upon the heated incrustation until completely
warmed. My heels and the sides of my feet were frozen. As soon
as warmth had permeated my system, and I had quieted my
appetite with a few thistle-roots, I took a survey of my surroundings, and selected a spot between two springs sufficiently asun-
der to afford heat at my head and feet. On this spot I built a
bower of pine branches, spread its incrusted surface with fallen
foliage and small boughs, and stowed myself away to await the
close of the storm.*

*Thistles were abundant, and I had fed upon them long enough
to realize that they would, for a while at least, sustain life. In
convenient proximity to my abode was a small, round, boiling
spring, which I called my dinner-pot, and in which, from time to
time, I cooked my roots.*

*This establishment, the best I could improvise with the means at
hand, I occupied seven days – the first three of which were
darkened by one of the most furious storms I ever saw. The
vapor which supplied me with warmth saturated my clothing
with its condensations. I was enveloped in a perpetual steam-
bath. At first this was barely preferable to the storm, but I soon
became accustomed to it, and before I left, though thoroughly
parboiled, actually enjoyed it.*

I had little else to do during my imprisonment but cook, think, and sleep. Of the variety and strangeness of my reflections it is impossible to give the faintest conception. Much of my time was given to devising means for escape. I recollected to have read, at the time of their publication, the narratives of Lieutenant Strain and Doctor Kane, and derived courage and hope from the reflection that they struggled with and survived perils not unlike those which environed me. The chilling thought would then occur, that they were not alone. They had companions in suffering and sympathy. Each could bear his share of the burden of misery which it fell to my lot to bear alone, and make it lighter from the encouragement of mutual counsel and aid in a cause of common suffering. Selfish as the thought may seem, there was nothing I so much desired as a companion in misfortune. How greatly it would alleviate my distress! What a relief it would be to compare my wretchedness with that of a brother sufferer, and with him devise expedients for every exigency as it occurred! I confess to the weakness, if it be one, of having squandered much pity upon myself during the time I had little else to do.

Nothing gave me more concern than the want of fire. I recalled everything I had ever read or heard of the means by which fire could be produced; but none of them were within my reach. An escape without it was simply impossible. It was indispensable as a protection against night attacks from wild beasts. Exposure to another storm like the one just over would destroy my life, as this one would have done, but for the warmth derived from the springs. As I lay in my bower anxiously awaiting the disappearance of the snow, which had fallen to the depth of a foot or more, and impressed with the belief that for want of fire I should be obliged to remain among the springs, it occurred to me that I would erect some sort of monument, which might, at some future day, inform a casual visitor of the circumstances under which I had perished. A gleam of sunshine lit up the bosom of the lake, and with it the thought flashed upon my mind that I could, with a lens from my opera-glasses, get fire from Heaven. Oh, happy, life-renewing thought! Instantly subjecting it to the test of experiment, when I saw the smoke curl from the bit of dry wood in my fingers, I felt, if the whole world were offered me for it, I would cast it all aside before parting with that little spark. I was now the happy possessor of food and fire. These would carry me through. All thoughts of failure were instantly aban-

doned. *Though the food was barely adequate to my necessities – a fact too painfully attested by my attenuated body – I had forgotten the cravings of hunger, and had the means of producing fire. I said to myself, "I will not despair."*

My stay at the springs was prolonged several days by an accident that befell me on the third night after my arrival there. An unlucky movement while asleep broke the crust on which I reposed, and the hot steam, pouring upon my hip, scalded it severely before I could escape. This new affliction, added to my frost-bitten feet, already festering, was the cause of frequent delay and unceasing pain through all my wanderings. After obtaining fire, I set to work making preparations for as early departure as my condition would permit. I had lost both knives since parting from the company, but I now made a convenient substitute by sharpening the tongue of a buckle which I cut from my vest. With this I cut the legs and counters from my boots, making of them a passable pair of slippers, which I fastened to my feet as firmly as I could with strips of bark. With the ravelings of a linen handkerchief, aided by the magic buckle-tongue, I mended my clothing. Of the same material I made a fish-line, which, on finding a piece of red tape in one of my pockets better suited to the purpose, I abandoned as a "bad job." I made of a pin that I found in my coat a fish-hook, and, by sewing up the bottoms of my boot-legs, constructed a very good pair of pouches to carry my food in, fastening them to my belt by the straps.

Thus accoutered, on the morning of the eighth day after my arrival at the springs I bade them a final farewell, and started on my course directly across that portion of the neck of the peninsula between me and the southeast arm of Yellowstone Lake. It was a beautiful morning. The sun shone bright and warm, and there was a freshness in the atmosphere truly exhilarating. As I wandered musingly along, the consciousness of being alone, and of having surrendered all hope of finding my friends, returned upon me with crushing power. I felt, too, that those friends, by the necessities of their condition, had been compelled to abandon all efforts for my recovery. The thought was full of bitterness and sorrow. I tried to realize what their conjectures were concerning my disappearance; but could derive no consolation from the long and dismal train of circumstances they suggested. . . .

A change in the wind and an overcast sky, accompanied by cold, brought with them a need of warmth. I drew out my lens and touchwood, but alas! there was no sun. I sat down on a log to await his friendly appearance. Hours passed; he did not come. Night, cold, freezing night, set in, and found me exposed to all its terrors. A bleak hillside sparsely covered with pines afforded poor accommodations for a half-clad, famishing man. I could only keep from freezing by the most active exertion in walking, rubbing, and striking my benumbed feet and hands against the logs. It seemed the longest, most terrible night of my life, and glad was I when the approaching dawn enabled me to commence retracing my steps to Bessie Lake (Heart Lake). *I arrived there at noon, built my first fire on the beach, and remained by it, recuperating, for the succeeding two days.*

The faint hope that my friends might be delayed by their search for me until I could rejoin them now forsook me altogether. I made my arrangements independent of it. Either of three directions I might take would effect my escape, if life and strength held out. I drew upon the sand of the beach a map of these several courses with reference to my starting-point from the lake, and considered well the difficulties each would present. All were sufficiently defined to avoid mistake. One was to follow Snake River a distance of one hundred miles or more to Eagle Rock bridge; another, to cross the country between the southern shore of Yellowstone Lake and the Madison Mountains (Red Mountains), *by scaling which I could easily reach the settlements in the Madison Valley; and the other, to retrace my journey over the long and discouraging route by which I had entered the country. Of these routes the last-mentioned seemed the least inviting, probably because I had so recently traversed it, and was familiar with its difficulties. I had heard and read so much concerning the desolation and elemental upheavals and violent waters of the upper valley of the Snake, that I dared not attempt to return in that direction. The route by the Madison Range, encumbered by the single obstruction of the mountain barrier, was much the shortest, and so, most unwisely as will hereafter appear, I adopted it.*

Filling my pouches with thistle-roots, I took a parting survey of the little solitude that had afforded me food and fire the preceding ten days, and with something of that melancholy feeling experienced by one who leaves his home to grapple with untried adventures, started for the nearest point on Yellowstone Lake. All that day I traveled over timber-heaps, amid tree-tops, and through thickets. At noon I took the precaution to obtain fire. With a brand which I kept alive by frequent blowing, and constant waving to and fro, at a late hour in the afternoon, faint and exhausted, I kindled a fire for the night on the only vacant spot I could find amid a dense wilderness of pines. The deep gloom of the forest, in the spectral light which revealed on all sides of me a compact and unending growth of trunks, and an impervious canopy of somber foliage; the shrieking of night-birds; the supernaturally human scream of the mountain lion; the prolonged howl of the wolf, made me insensible to all other forms of suffering.

The burn on my hip was so inflamed that I could only sleep in a sitting posture. Seated with my back against a tree, the smoke from the fire almost enveloping me in its suffocating folds, I vainly tried, amid the din and uproar of this horrible serenade, to woo the drowsy god. My imagination was instinct with terror. At one moment it seemed as if, in the density of a thicket, I could see the blazing eyes of a formidable forest monster fixed upon me, preparatory to a deadly leap; at another I fancied that I heard the swift approach of a pack of yelping wolves through the distant brushwood, which in a few moments would tear me from limb to limb. Whenever, by fatigue and weakness, my terrors yielded to drowsiness, the least noise roused me to a sense of the hideousness of my condition. Once, in a fitful slumber, I fell forward into the fire, and inflicted a wretched burn on my hand. Oh! with what agony I longed for day!

A bright and glorious morning succeeded the dismal night, and brought with it the conviction that I had been the victim of uncontrollable nervous excitement. I resolved henceforth to banish it altogether; and, in much better spirits than I anticipated, resumed my journey towards the lake. Another day of unceasing toil among the treetops and thickets overtook me, near sunset, standing upon a lofty headland jutting into the lake, and commanding a magnificent prospect of the mountains and valley over an immense area. In front of me, at a distance of fifty miles away, in the clear blue of the horizon, rose the arrowy peaks of the three Tetons. On the right, and apparently in close proximity to the eminence I occupied, rolled the picturesque range of the Madison, scarred with clefts, ravines, *gorges, and cañons, each of which glittered in the sunlight or deepened in shadow as the fitful rays of the descending luminary glanced along their varied rocky irregularities. Above where I stood were the lofty domes of Mounts Langford and Doane, marking the limits of that wonderful barrier which had so long defied human power in its efforts to subdue it. Rising seemingly from the promontory which favored my vision was the familiar summit of Mount Everts, at the base of which I had dwelt so long, and which still seemed to hold me within its friendly shadow. All the vast country within this grand enclosure of mountains and lake, scarred and seamed with the grotesque ridges, rocky escarpments, undulating hillocks, and miniature lakes, and steaming with hot springs, produced by the volcanic forces of a former era, lay spread out before me like a vast panorama.*

I doubt if distress and suffering can ever entirely obliterate all sense of natural grandeur and magnificence. Lost in the wonder and admiration inspired by this vast world of beauties, I nearly forgot to improve the few moments of remaining sunshine to obtain fire. With a lighted brand in my hand, I effected a most difficult and arduous descent of the abrupt and stony headland to the beach of the lake. The sand was soft and yielding. I kindled a fire, and removing the stiffened slippers from my feet, attached them to my belt, and wandered barefoot along the sandy shore to gather wood for the night. The dry, warm sand was most grateful to my lacerated and festering feet, and for a long time after my wood-pile was supplied, I sat with them uncovered. At length, conscious of the need of every possible protection from the freezing night atmosphere, I sought my belt for the slippers, and one was missing. In gathering the wood it had become detached, and was lost. Darkness was closing over the landscape, when, sorely disheartened with the thought of passing the night with one foot exposed to a freezing temperature, I commenced a search for the missing slipper. I knew I could not travel a day without it. Fearful that it had dropped into the lake, and been carried by some recurrent wave beyond recovery, my search for an hour among fallen trees and bushes, up the hill-side and along the beach, in darkness and with flaming brands, at one moment crawling on hands and feet into a brush heap, another peering among logs and bushes and stones, was filled with anxiety and dismay. Success at length rewarded my perseverance, and no language can describe the joy with which I drew the cause of so much distress from beneath the limb that, as I passed, had torn it from my belt. With a feeling of great relief, I now sat down in the sand, my back to a log, and listened to the dash and roar of the waves. It was a wild lullaby, but had not terrors for a worn-out man. I never passed a night of more refreshing sleep.

When I awoke my fire was extinguished save a few embers, which I soon fanned into a cheerful flame. I ate breakfast with some relish, and started along the beach in pursuit of a camp, believing that if successful I should find directions what to do, and food to sustain me. The search which I was making lay in the direction of my pre-arranged route to the Madison Mountains, which I intended to approach at their lowest point of altitude.

Buoyed by the hope of finding food and counsel, and another night of undisturbed repose in the sand, I resumed my journey along the shore, and at noon found the camp last occupied by my friends on the lake. I struck their trail in the sand some time before I came to it. A thorough search for food in the ground and trees revealed nothing, and no notice to apprise me of their movements could be seen. A dinner-fork, which afterwards proved to be of infinite service in digging roots, and a yeast-powder can, which would hold half a pint, and which I converted into a drinking-cup and dinner-pot, were the only evidences that the spot had ever been visited by civilized man. "Oh!" thought I, "why did they forget to leave me food!" It never occurring to me that they might have cached it, as I have since learned they did, in several spots nearer the place of my separation from them. I left the camp in deep dejection, with the purpose of following the trail of the party to the Madison. Carefully inspecting the faint traces left of their course of travel, I became satisfied that from some cause they had made a retrograde movement from this camp, and departed from the lake at a point farther down stream. Taking this as an indication that there were obstructions above, I commenced retracing my steps along the beach. An hour of sunshine in the afternoon enabled me to procure fire, which, in the usual manner, I carried to my camping-place. There I built a fire, and to protect myself from the wind, which was blowing violently, lashing the lake into foam, I made a bower of pine boughs, crept under it, and very soon fell asleep. How long I slept I know not, but I was aroused by the snapping and cracking of the burning foliage, to find my shelter and the adjacent forest in a broad sheet of flame. My left hand was badly burned, and my hair singed closer than a barber would have trimmed it, while making my escape from the semicircle of burning trees. Among the disasters of the fire, there was none I felt more seriously than the loss of my buckle-tongue knife, my pin fish-hook, and tape fish-line.

The grandeur of the burning forest surpasses description. An immense sheet of flame, following to their tops the lofty trees of an almost impenetrable pine forest, leaping madly from top to top, and sending thousands of forked tongues a hundred feet or more athwart the midnight darkness, lighting up with lurid gloom and glare the surrounding scenery of lake and mountains, fills the beholder with mingled feelings of awe and astonishment. I never before saw anything so terribly beautiful. It was marvelous to witness the flash-like rapidity with which the flames would mount the loftiest trees. The roaring, cracking, crashing, and snapping of falling limbs and burning foliage was deafening. On, on, on traveled the destructive element, until it seemed as if the whole forest was enveloped in flame. Afar up the wood-crowned hill, the overtopping trees shot forth pinnacles and walls and streamers of arrowy fire. The entire hill-side was an ocean of glowing and surging fiery billows. Favored by the gale, the conflagration spread with lightning swiftness over an illimitable extent of country, filling the atmosphere with driving clouds of suffocating fume, and leaving a broad and blackened trail of spectral trunks shorn of limbs and foliage, smoking and burning, to mark the immense sweep of its devastation.

Resolved to search for a trail no longer, when daylight came I selected for a landmark the lowest notch in the Madison Range. Carefully surveying the jagged and broken surface over which I must travel to reach it, I left the lake and pushed into the midst of its intricacies. All the day, until nearly sunset, I struggled over rugged hills, through windfalls, thickets, and matted forests, with the rock-ribbed beacon constantly in view. As I advanced it receded, as if in mockery of my toil. Night overtook me with my journey half accomplished. The precaution of obtaining fire gave me warmth and sleep, and long before daylight I was on my way. The hope of finding an easy pass into the valley of the Madison inspired me with fresh courage and deter-

mination; but long before I arrived at the base of the range, I scanned hopelessly its insurmountable difficulties. It presented to my eager vision an endless succession of inaccessible peaks and precipices, rising thousands of feet sheer and bare above the plain. No friendly gorge or gully or cañon invited such an effort as I could make to scale this rocky barrier. Oh for the faith that could remove mountains! How soon should this colossal fabric open at my approach! What a feeling of hopeless despair came over me with the conviction that the journey of the last two days had been in vain! I seated myself on a rock, upon the summit of a commanding hill, and cast my eyes along the only route which now seemed tenable – down the Yellowstone. How many dreary miles of forest and mountain filled the terrible panorama!. . .

In his fevered state, Truman Everts says that a friendly apparition appears and urges him to turn back. He resolves to return by the same long path he and the other party have come thus far – around the eastern side of Yellowstone Lake and down the Yellowstone River. He barely mentions the many days of traveling until reaching the Grand Canyon of the Yellowstone.

I lost all sense of time. Days and nights came and went, and were numbered only by the growing consciousness that I was gradually starving. I felt no hunger, did not eat to appease appetite, but to renew strength. I experienced but little pain. The gaping sores on my feet, the severe burn on my hip, the festering crevices at the joints of my fingers, all terrible in appearance, had ceased to give me the least concern. The roots which supplied my food had suspended the digestive power of the stomach, and their fibres were packed in it in a matted, compact mass. . . .

It was a cold, gloomy day when I arrived in the vicinity of the falls. The sky was overcast and the snow-capped peaks rose chilly and bleak through the biting atmosphere. The moaning of the wind through the pines, mingling with the sullen roar of the falls, was strangely in unison with my own saddened feelings. I had no heart to gaze upon a scene which a few weeks before had inspired me with rapture and awe. One moment of sunshine was of more value to me than all the marvels amid which I was famishing. But the sun had hid his face and denied me all hope of obtaining fire. The only alternative was to seek shelter in a thicket. I penetrated the forest a long distance before finding one that suited me. Breaking and crowding my way into its very midst, I cleared a spot large enough to recline upon, interlaced the surrounding brushwood, gathered the fallen foliage into a bed, and lay down with a prayer for sleep and forgetfulness. Alas! neither came. The coldness increased through the night. Constant friction with my hands and unceasing beating with my legs and feet saved me from freezing. It was the most terrible night of my journey, and when, with the early dawn, I pulled myself into a standing posture, it was to realize that my right arm was partially paralyzed, and my limbs so stiffened with cold as to be almost immovable. Fearing lest paralysis should suddenly seize upon the entire system, I literally dragged myself through the forest to the river. Seated near the verge of the great cañon below the falls, I anxiously awaited the appearance of the sun. That great luminary never looked so beautiful as when, a few moments afterwards, he emerged from the clouds and exposed his glowing beams to the concentrated powers of my lens. I kindled a mighty flame, fed it with every dry stick and broken tree-top I could find, and without motion, and almost without sense, remained beside it several hours. The great falls of the Yellowstone were roaring within three hundred yards, and the awful cañon yawned almost at my feet; but they had lost all charm for me. In fact, I regarded them as enemies which had lured me to destruction, and felt a sullen satisfaction in morbid indifference.

. . . At many of the streams on my route I spent hours in endeavoring to catch trout, with a hook fashioned from the rim of my broken spectacles, but in no instance with success. The tackle was defective. The country was full of game in great variety. I saw large herds of deer, elk, antelope, occasionally a bear, and many smaller animals. Numerous flocks of ducks, geese, swans, and pelicans inhabited the lakes and rivers. But with no means of killing them, their presence was a perpetual aggravation. At all the camps of our company I stopped and recalled many pleasant incidents associated with them.

One afternoon, when approaching "Tower Falls," I came upon a large hollow tree, which, from the numerous tracks surrounding it, and the matted foliage in the cavity, I recognized as the den of a bear. It was a most inviting couch. Gathering a needful supply of wood and bough, I lighted a circle of piles around the tree, crawled into the nest, and passed a night of unbroken slumber. I rose the next morning to find that during the night the fires had communicated with the adjacent forest, and burned a large space in all directions, doubtless intimidating the rightful proprietor of the nest, and saving me from another midnight adventure.

At "Tower Falls" I spent the first half of a day in capturing a grasshopper, and the remainder in a fruitless effort to catch a mess of trout. . . .

Soon after leaving "Tower Falls," I entered the open country. Pine forests and windfalls were changed for sage brush and desolation, with occasional tracts of stinted verdure, barren hillsides, exhibiting here and there an isolated clump of dwarf trees, and ravines filled with the rocky debris of adjacent mountains. My first camp on this part of the route, for the convenience of getting wood, was made near the summit of a range of towering foothills. Towards morning a storm of wind and snow nearly extinguished my fire. I became very cold; the storm was still raging when I arose, and the ground white with snow. I was perfectly bewildered, and had lost my course of travel. No visible object, seen through the almost blinding storm, reassured me, and there was no alternative but to find the river and take my direction from its current. Fortunately, after a few hours of stumbling and scrambling among rocks and over crests, I came to the precipitous side of the cañon through which it ran, and with much labor, both of hands and feet, descended it to the margin. I drank copiously of its pure waters, and sat beside it for a long time, waiting for the storm to abate, so that I could procure fire. The day wore on, without any prospect of a termination to the storm. Chilled through, my tattered clothing saturated, I saw before me a night of horrors unless I returned to my fire. The scramble up the side of the rocky cañon, in many places nearly perpendicular, was the hardest work of my journey. Often while clinging to the jutting rocks with hands and feet, to reach a shelving projection, my grasp would unclose and I would slide many feet down the sharp declivity. It was night when, sore from the bruises I had received, I reached my fire; the storm, still raging, had nearly extinguished it. I found a few embers in the ashes, and with much difficulty kindled a flame. Here, on this bleak mountain side, as well as I now remember, I must have passed two nights beside the fire, in the storm. Many times during each night I crawled to the little clump of trees to gather wood, and brush, and the broken limbs of fallen tree-tops. All the sleep I obtained was snatched from the intervals which divided these labors. It was so harassed with frightful dreams as to afford little rest. I remember, before I left this camp, stripping up my sleeves to look at my shrunken arms. Flesh and blood had apparently left them. The skin clung to the bones like wet parchment. A child's hand could have clasped them from wrist to shoulder. "Yet," thought I, "it is death to remain; I cannot perish in this wilderness."

Taking counsel of this early formed resolution, I hobbled on my course through the snow, which was rapidly disappearing before the rays of the warm sun. Well knowing that I should find no thistles in the open country, I had filled my pouches with them before leaving the forest. My supply was running low, and there were yet several days of heavy mountain travel between me and Boteler's ranch. With the most careful economy, it could last but two or three days longer...

Two or three days before I was found, while ascending a steep hill, I fell from exhaustion into the sage brush, without the power to rise. Unbuckling my belt, as was my custom, I soon fell asleep. I have no idea of the time I slept, but upon awaking I fastened my belt, scrambled to my feet, and pursued my journey. As night drew on I selected a camping-place, gathered wood into a heap, and felt for my lens to procure fire. It was gone. If the earth had yawned to swallow me I would not have been more terrified. The only chance for life was lost. The last hope had fled. I seemed to feel the grim messenger who had been so long pursuing me knocking at the portals of my heart as I lay down by the side of the wood-pile, and covered myself with limbs and sage brush, with the dreadful conviction that my struggle for life was over, and that I should rise no more. The floodgates of misery seemed now to be opened, and it rushed in living tide upon my soul. With the rapidity of lightning, I ran over every event of my life. Thoughts doubled and trebled upon me, until I saw, as if in vision, the entire past of my existence. It was all before me, as if painted with a sunbeam, and all seemingly faded like the phantoms of a vivid dream.

As calmness returned, reason resumed her empire. Fortunately, the weather was comfortable. I summoned all the powers of my

*memory, thought over every foot of the day's travel, and con-
cluded that the glass must have become detached from my belt
while sleeping. Five long miles over the hills must be retraced
to regain it. There was no alternative, and before daylight I had
staggered over half the distance. I found the lens on the spot
where I had slept. No incident of my journey brought with it
more of joy and relief.*

*Returning to the camp of the previous night, I lighted the pile I
had prepared, and lay down for a night of rest. It was very cold,
and towards morning commenced snowing. With difficulty I
kept the fire alive. Sleep was impossible. When daylight came, I
was impressed with the idea that I must go on despite the storm.
A flash – momentary but vivid – came over me, that I should be
saved. Snatching a lighted brand, I started through the storm.
In the afternoon the storm abated and the sun shone at intervals. Coming to a small clump of trees, I set to work to prepare
a camp. I laid the brand down which I had preserved with so
much care, to pick up a few dry sticks with which to feed it, until
I could collect wood for a camp-fire, and in the few minutes
thus employed it expired. I sought to revive it, but every spark
was gone. Clouds obscured the sun, now near the horizon, and
the prospect of another night of exposure without fire became
fearfully imminent. I sat down with my lens and the last remaining piece of touchwood I possessed to catch a gleam of sunshine, feeling that my life depended on it. In a few moments the
cloud passed, and with trembling hands I presented the little
disk to the face of the glowing luminary. Quivering with excitement lest a sudden cloud should interpose, a moment passed
before I could hold the lens steadily enough to concentrate a
burning focus. At length it came. The little thread of smoke
curled gracefully upwards from the Heaven-lighted spark,
which, a few moments afterwards, diffused with warmth and
comfort my desolate lodgings.*

*I resumed my journey the next morning, with the belief that I
should make no more fires with my lens. I must save a brand, or
perish. The day was raw and gusty; an east wind, charged with
storm, penetrated my nerves with irritating keenness. After
walking a few miles the storm came on, and a coldness unlike
any other I had ever felt seized me. It entered all my bones. I
attempted to build a fire, but could not make it burn. Seizing a
brand, I stumbled blindly on, stopping within the shadow of*

every rock and clump to renew energy for a final conflict for life. A solemn conviction that death was near, that at each pause I made my limbs would refuse further service, and that I should sink helpless and dying in my path, overwhelmed me with terror. Amid all this tumult of the mind, I felt that I had done all that man could do. I knew that in two or three days more I could effect my deliverance, and I derived no little satisfaction from the thought that, as I was now on the broad trail, my remains would be found, and my friends relieved of doubt as to my fate. Once only the thought flashed across my mind that I should be saved, and I seemed to hear a whispered command to "struggle on." Groping along the side of a hill, I became suddenly sensible of a sharp reflection, as of burnished steel. Looking up, through half-closed eyes, two rough but kindly faces met my gaze.

"Are you Mr. Everts?"

"Yes. All that is left of him."

"We have come for you."

"Who sent you?"

"Judge Lawrence and other friends."

"God bless him, and them, and you! I am saved!" and with these words, powerless of further effort, I fell forward into the arms of my preservers, in a state of unconsciousness. I was saved. On the very brink of the river which divides the known from the unknown, strong arms snatched me from the final plunge, and kind ministrations wooed me back to life. . . .

My narrative is finished. In the course of events the time is not far distant when the wonders of the Yellowstone will be made accessible to all lovers of sublimity, grandeur, and novelty in natural scenery, and its majestic waters become the abode of civilization and refinement; and when that arrives, I hope, in happier mood and under more auspicious circumstances, to revisit scenes fraught for me with such thrilling interest; to ramble along the glowing beach of Bessie Lake; to sit down amid the hot springs under the shadow of Mount Everts; to thread unscared the forest maze, retrace the dreary journey to the

Madison Range, and with enraptured fancy gaze upon the mingled glories and terrors of the great falls and marvelous cañon, and to enjoy, in happy contrast with the trials they recall, their power to delight, elevate, and overwhelm the mind with wondrous and majestic beauty.

Chapter IX

BRYCE – ZION – GRAND CANYON
1870

from "An Overland Trip to the Grand Cañon"
in Scribner's Monthly, *Oct. 1875*
by John Wesley Powell

Following his first descent of the Colorado River, John Wesley Powell continued his exploration of the Colorado Plateau, a region little known at that time. Jacob Hamblin had made a number of excursions throughout the region, but this information was limited to the Mormon community. During this excursion, Powell finds out the fate of the three men who abandoned the first expedition by climbing out of the Grand Canyon. Herein, Powell first describes the pink cliffs of Bryce and his passage through two narrow river canyons of Zion, the Parunuweap and Mukoontuweap (Virgin River Narrows).

The explorations of the cañons of the Colorado gave birth to a desire to see more of that wonderful country, and in the summer of 1870 I organized a party at Salt Lake City for another trip by land through that difficult region. We had in fact determined to make a more thorough exploration of the entire Valley of the Colorado, and for this purpose decided to descend the river once more in boats, and use the stream as a base line, from which excursions should be made into the country on either side. We expected to devote several years to this work, but the summer and fall of 1870 were to be given to the exploration of roads from the settlements in Utah to the Colorado River, by which rations might be taken to suitable points along that stream, so that in the final trip down the river we might have depots of supplies at different points. (The second descent of the Colorado would be in 1871.)

I wish now to give a narrative of these preliminary explorations.

Between Gunnison's Crossing and the foot of the Grand Cañon we knew of only two points where the river could be reached by land; one at the Crossing of the Fathers, thirty or forty miles north of the Arizona line, and another a few miles below at the mouth of the Paria, on a route which had been explored by Jacob Hamblin, a Mormon missionary. These two points are so near each other that only one of them could be selected for the purpose above mentioned; and we wished to go down to the mouth of the Paria and determine with certainty the practicability of that route. We had been unable up to this time to obtain from either Indians or white men any information which would give us a clue to any other trail down to the river.

Having organized at Salt Lake City, we made our way southward to the valley of the Sevier River, and then up to the headwaters of that stream. There we were at the summit of a great watershed. The Sevier itself flows north, and then westward into the lake of the same name. The Rio Virgen, rising near by, flows to the southwest, and enters the Colorado sixty or seventy miles below the Grand Cañon. The Kanab, also rising near by, runs south into the heart of the Grand Cañon. The Paria, which has its source in the same vicinity, runs a little south of east, and enters the river at the head of Marble Cañon. To the northwest of this point other streams, which run into the Colorado, have their sources. Forty or fifty miles away we reach the southern branches of the Dirty Devil River, the mouth of which stream is but a short distance below the junction of the Grand and the Green.

The Pauns-a-gunt Plateau terminates in a point which is well marked by a line of beautiful pink cliffs. At the foot of this plateau on the west, the minute upper branches of the Rio Virgen and Sevier Rivers are dovetailed together; the upper surface of the plateau inclines to the northwest, so that its waters roll off into the Sevier; but from the foot of the cliffs, quite around this sharp angle of this plateau for a dozen miles, we find numerous springs, whose waters unite to form the Kanab; and a little farther to the northwest the springs gather into streams that feed the Paria.

Here, by the springs of the Kanab, we established a rendezvous camp, and from this point we were to radiate in a series of trips southward and eastward to the Colorado.

Hamblin, the Mormon missionary, who had been among the Indians for more than twenty years, had collected a number of Kaibabbits, with Chu-ar-ru-um-peak their chief, and they were camped with us. They were certain that we could not make our way to the river, but promised to show us the spring and water-pockets, which are very scarce in that region, and to give us all the information in their power, so that we might examine the country for ourselves.

Here we fitted up a pack-train for the transportation of our supplies, bedding, and instruments, and for a day or two we were engaged in preparation for a difficult trip.

Powell and two companions depart from the rest of the party for awhile and head up into the higher region of Bryce.

One day, while this general work of preparation was going on in camp, I took with me a white man and an Indian, and started on a climb to the summit of the Pauns-a-gunt Plateau. Our way for a mile or more was over a great peat-bog that trembled under our feet; now and then a mule sank through the broken turf, and we were compelled to pull him out with ropes. Passing the bog, our way was up a gulch at the foot of the Pink Cliffs, which form the escarpment or wall of the great plateau. We soon left the gulch, and climbed a long ridge which winds around the right toward the summit of the great table.

Two hours riding, climbing, and clambering brought us near the top. We looked below and saw clouds drifting up from the south, rolling tumultuously toward the foot of the cliffs beneath us. Soon all the country below was covered with a sea of vapor – a billowy, raging, noiseless sea; and as the vapory flood still rolled up from the south, great waves dashed against the foot of the cliffs, and rolled back toward the south, and another tide came in and was hurled back, and another and another, lashing the cliffs until the fog rose to the summit and covered us all.

There is a heavy pine and fir forest above, beset with dead and fallen timber, and we made our way through the undergrowth to the east.

And then it rained! The clouds discharged their moisture in torrents, and we made for ourselves shelters of boughs, which were soon abandoned, and we stood shivering by a great fire of pine logs and boughs, which we kindled, but which the pelting storm half extinguished. One, two, three, four hours of the storm, and at last it partially abated.

During this time our animals, which we had turned loose, sought shelter for themselves under the trees, and two of them wandered away beyond our sight. I went out to follow their tracks, and came near the brink of a ledge of rocks, which, in the fog and mist, I supposed to be a little ridge. Here I looked for a way by which to go down. While I stood there, a rift was made in the fog below, by some current or blast of wind, and an almost bottomless abyss was revealed. I looked from the brink of a great precipice, more than two thousand feet high; the forms below were half obscured by the mist, and all reckoning of distance was lost; it seemed ten thousand feet, ten miles, any distance the imagination might make it.

Catching our animals, we returned to camp, and found that the little streams which came down from the plateau were greatly swollen. At camp, however, they had had no rain. The clouds which drifted up from the south, striking against the plateau, were lifted up into colder regions, and discharged their moisture on the summit and against the sides of the plateau, but there was no rain in the valley below.

"Valley of Babbling Waters, Southern Utah"
by Thomas Moran.

They have now left Bryce and are heading on into the canyons of Zion.

On the ninth of September we made a fair start from the beautiful meadow at the head of the Kanab, and crossed the line of little hills at the head of the Rio Virgen, and at ten o'clock came to the brink of a great geographic bench – a line of cliffs. Behind us were cool springs, green meadows, and forest-clad slopes; below us, stretching to the south until the world was lost in blue haze, was a painted desert – not a desert plain, but a desert of rocks cut by deep gorges and relieved by towering cliffs and pinnacled rocks, naked rocks brilliant in the sunlight.

By a difficult trail, we made our way down the basaltic ledge, through which innumerable streams here gather into a little river running in a deep cañon. The river was close to the foot of the cliffs on the left-hand side, and the trail passes along to the right. At noon we rested, and our animals grazed on the luxuriant grass.

After slow progress along a stony way, we camped at night under an overarching cliff, on the side of a beautiful glen or park, which is enclosed with high rocks on all sides except up and down the river. Here the river turns to the west, and our way properly was to the south, but we wished to explore the cañon that was below us. The Indians told us that the cañon narrowed gradually a short distance below, and that it would be impossible to take our animals much farther down the river. Early in the morning I went down to examine the head of this narrow part. After breakfast, having concluded to explore the cañon for a few miles on foot, we arranged that the main party should climb the cliff, and go around to a point eighteen or twenty miles below, at the foot of the cañon; three of us started on the exploration of the gorge called by the Indians Pa-ru-nu-weap or Roaring-Water Cañon. Between the little river and the foot of the walls was found a dense growth of willows, vines, and wild-rose bushes, and with great difficulty we made our way through this tangled mass. It is not a wide stream – only twenty or thirty feet across, in most places – shallow, but very swift. After spending some hours in breaking our way through the mass of vegetation, and climbing rocks here and there, it was determined to wade along the stream. In some places this was an easy task, but here and there we came to deep holes where we had to wade to our arm-pits. We soon reached places so narrow that the river filled the entire channel and compelled us to wade. In many places the bottom was a quicksand, into which we sank, and it was with great difficulty that we made progress. In some places the holes were so deep that we had to swim, and our little bundles of blankets and rations were fixed to a raft made of drift-wood and pushed before us. Now and then there was a little flood-plain, on which we could walk, and we crossed and re-crossed the stream and waded along the channel, where the water was so swift as almost to carry us from our feet; we were in danger every moment of being swept down, until night came on. We estimated we had traveled eight miles that day. We found a little patch of flood-plain on which there was a huge pile of drift-wood and a clump of box-elders, and near by a great stream bursting from the rocks.

Here we soon had a huge fire; our clothes were spread to dry; we made a cup of coffee, took out our bread and cheese and dried beef, and enjoyed a hearty supper.

The next morning we were wading again, sinking in the quicksands, swimming the deep waters, and making slow and painful progress, the waters still being swift and the bed of the stream rocky.

The day before, the cañon was 1,200 feet deep, but we found it steadily increasing in depth, and in many places exceedingly narrow – only twenty or thirty feet wide below, and in some places even narrower – for hundreds of feet overhead. There are places where the river, in sweeping past curves, has cut far under the rocks, but still preserves its narrow channel, so that there is an overhanging wall on one side, and an inclined wall on the other. In places a few hundred feet above, it becomes vertical again, and thus the view to the sky above is entirely closed. Everywhere this deep passage is dark and gloomy, and resounds with the noise of rapid waters. At noon we were in a cañon sixteen hundred feet deep, and we came to a fall where the walls were broken down, and the channel was beset by huge rocks, on which we obtained a foothold to reach a level two hundred below. Here the cañon was again wider, and we found a floodplain along which we could walk, now on this and now on that side of the stream. Gradually the cañon widened; steep rapids, cascades, and cataracts were found along the river. We waded only when it was necessary to cross. We made progress with very great labor, having to climb over many piles of broken rocks.

Late in the afternoon we came to a little clearing in the valley where we saw signs of civilization, and by sundown arrived at the Mormon town of Schunesburg, where we met the train, and feasted on melons and grapes.

Our course for two days had been directly west through Pa-ru-nu-weap Cañon. Another stream comes down from the north and unites near Schunesburg with the main branch of the Rio Virgen. We determined to spend a day in the exploration of this stream. The Indians call the cañon through which it runs Mu-koon-tu-weap, or Straight Cañon (Zion Canyon and Narrows). *Entering this, we were compelled to wade upstream; often the water filled the entire channel, and although we traveled many miles, we found no flood-plain, talus, or broken pile of rocks at the foot of the cliff. The walls have smooth, plain faces, and are everywhere very regular and vertical for a thousand feet or more, and then they seem to break back in shelving slopes to higher altitudes. Everywhere as we went along we found springs bursting out at the foot of the walls, and, passing these, the river above becoming steadily smaller, the great body of water which runs below bursts out from beneath this great bed of red sandstone; as we went up the cañon it came to be but a creek, and then a brook. On the western wall of the cañon stand some buttes and towers, and high, pinnacled rocks. Going up the cañon we gained glimpses of them here and there. After our trip through the cañons of the Colorado the year before, on our way from the mouth of the Virgen to Salt Lake City, we could see these buttes as conspicuous landmarks from a distance of sixty or seventy miles, away to the southwest. These tower-rocks are known as the Temples of the Virgen.*

Having explored this cañon to its head, we returned to Schunesburg, arriving quite late at night.

Sitting in camp that evening, Chu-ar, the chief of the Kaibab-bits, told us one of the traditions of the tribes. Many years ago, he said, a great light was seen somewhere in this region by the Pa-ru-sha-pats, who lived to the southwest. They supposed it to be a signal kindled to warn them of the approach of the Nava-

jos, who lived to the east beyond the Colorado River. Then other signal fires were kindled on the Pine Valley Mountains, Santa Clara Mountains, and U-in-ka-ret Mountains, so that all the tribes of northern Arizona, southern Utah, southern Nevada, and southern California, were warned of the approaching danger; but when the Pa-ru-sha-pats came near they discovered that it was a fire on one of the Great Temples, and then they knew that the fire was not kindled by men, for no human being had scaled the rocks. The Tu-mu-ur-ru-gwait-si-gaip, or Rock Rovers, had kindled a fire to deceive the people, and so this is called in the Indian language Rock Rovers' Land.

The party now proceeds to survey the region north of the Grand Canyon and south of Bryce/Zion, today known as the Arizona strip. Here Powell would meet up with the Indian tribe responsible for the deaths of his three men during the first descent of the Colorado River.

The next day, September 13th, we started very early, for we had a long day's travel before us. Our way was across the Rio Virgen to the south. Coming to the bank of the stream, we found a strange metamorphosis; the streams, as we had seen them above, ran in narrow channels, leaping and plunging over the rocks, raging and roaring in their course; but here they united, and spread in a thin sheet several hundred yards wide, and only a few inches deep; they were running over a bed of quicksand. Crossing the stream, our trail led up a narrow cañon, not very deep, and then among the hills of golden, red and purple shales and marls – a region of bad lands. Climbing out of the valley of the Rio Virgen, we passed through a forest of dwarf cedars, and came out at the foot of the Vermilion Cliffs. We followed this Indian trail toward the east all day, and at night camped at a great spring, known to the Indians as "Yellow Rock Water," but to the Mormons as Pipe Spring. Nearby there was a cabin in which some Mormon herders found shelter.

Pipe Spring is a point in Arizona just across the Utah line, and we supposed it to be about sixty miles from the river. Here we found that the Mormons designed building a fort another year as an outpost for protection against the Indians. From this point we sent a part of our Indians to the rendezvous camp, keeping two with us, Chu-ar and Shuts, for the purpose of showing us the trails and springs; the latter are very scarce, very small, and not easily found. Not more than half a dozen are known in a dis-

trict of country large enough to make as many good-sized counties in Illinois. There are no running streams, and these springs and water-pockets – that is, holes in the rocks that hold water from shower to shower – were our only dependence.

As we started on, we left behind a long line of cliffs, many hundred feet high, composed of orange and vermilion sandstones. I have named them "Vermilion Cliffs." When we were out a few miles I looked back and saw the morning sun shining in splendor on their painted faces, and the retreating angles were buried in shade. I gazed and gazed until my vision dreamed, and the cliffs appeared a long bank of purple clouds piled from the horizon high into the heavens. At noon we passed along a ledge of chocolate cliffs, and, taking out our sandwiches, we made dinner as we rode along.

The day before, our Indians had discussed for hours the route which we should take. There was one way that was farther by ten or twelve miles, with sure water; another, the shorter, where water was found sometimes; their conclusion was that water would be found there, and that was the way we went. All day long we were anxious about it. To be out two days with only the water that could be carried in two small kegs was to have our animals suffer greatly. At five o'clock we came to the spot, and to our great relief found a huge water-pocket containing several barrels. Here we camped for the night.

We were up at daybreak the next morning, for it was a long day's march to the next water, so the Indians said. Our course was southward. From Pipe Spring we could see a mountain, and I recognized it as one I had seen the previous summer from a cliff overlooking the Grand Cañon. It was just behind this mountain that I wished to strike the river. There were Indians living in the group of which it is the highest, whom I wished to visit on the way. These mountains are of volcanic origin, and we soon came to ground that was covered with fragments of lava. The way became very difficult; we had to cross deep ravines, the heads of cañons that run into the Grand Cañon. It was curious now to observe the knowledge of our Indians; there was not a trail they did not know; every gulch and every rock seemed familiar. I have prided myself on being able to grasp and retain in my mind the topography of a country, but these Indians put me to shame. My knowledge is only general, embracing the

*most important features of a region which remains as a map
engraved on my mind; theirs is specific; they know every rock
and ledge, every gulch and cañon – just where to wind among
these to find a pass, and their knowledge is unerring; they cannot describe a country to you, but they can tell you all the
details of a route.*

*The two had been furnished with but one pony, which they were
to ride "turn about," but Chu-ar managed to keep the horse to
himself. Shuts, the one-eyed, bare-legged, merry-faced pigmy,
walked, and pointed the way with a slender cane, and would
leap and bound by the shortest way, and sit down on a rock and
wait demurely until we came, always meeting us with a jest, his
face a rich mine of humor.*

*At dusk we reached the water-pocket. It was found in a deep
gorge on the flank of this great mountain. During the rainy season the water rolls down the mountainsides, plunging over
precipices, and excavating a deep basin in the solid rock below.
This basin, hid from the sun, holds water the year round. High
rocks of black basalt stand about it, and above are overhanging
cedars. The Indians call it U-nu-pin Pi-ka-vu, that is, Elfin
Water-Pocket.*

*The next morning, while the men were packing the animals, I
climbed a little mountain near camp to obtain a view of the
country. It was a huge pile of volcanic scoria, loose and light as
cinders from a forge, which gave way under my feet as I
climbed with great labor. Reaching the summit, and looking to
the southeast, I could see once more the labyrinth of deep
gorges that flank the Grand Cañon; in the multitude I could not
determine whether the latter was in view or not. The memories
of grand and awful months spent in their deep gloomy solitudes
came up, and I lived that life over again for a time. I supposed
before starting that I could get a good view of the great mountain from this point, but it was like climbing a chair to look at a
castle. I wished to discover some way by which it could be
ascended, as it was my intention to go to the summit before I
returned to the settlements. I saw a steep and apparently
impassable cliff stretching across the face of the mountain, and
my problem was still unsolved. I hurried down again, sliding on
the cinders, and making them rattle and clang.*

The Indians told us that we were to have a short ride that day, and that we would reach an Indian village by way of a good spring. Our way was across spurs that put out from the great mountain as we passed it to the left. Up and down we went across deep ravines, the fragments of lava clanking under our horses' feet; now among cedars, now among pines, and now across mountain-side glades. At one o'clock we descended into a lovely valley with a carpet of grass. We were told by Chu-ar that at some seasons of the year water runs through this valley from a spring above, but that he supposed it would be dry at this time; yet he was not sure, and thought it possible that some of the Indians whom we were seeking might be found near the spring. So he rode on to find them, and to say that we were friends, for should we come without notice, they would run away, or propose to fight. Soon we saw Chu-ar riding at full speed, and heard him shouting at the top of his voice, and away in the distance were two Indians scampering up the mountain-side. One stopped, the other still ran on, and was soon lost to view. We rode up and found Chu-ar talking with the one who had stopped. It was one of the ladies resident in those mountain glades, whom we called Godiva. She told us that her people were at the large spring, that it was only two hours' ride, and that her own good master, whom we had seen running so lustily, had gone on to tell them we were coming. We sat down and ate our luncheon, and shared our biscuit with the lady of the mountain, who had been gathering seeds. Then we sent Chu-ar on to the village to apprise them of our coming, and to allay any fears they might have, keeping with us Shuts and Godiva. We rode along the trail another half-hour until we came to a pass between two high cinder-cones, of which I concluded to climb the one to the left. So, leaving the train to pursue its way, I rode my horse as far as possible, and then tugged up afoot to the summit, from which I could see the Grand Cañon. I now knew where I was. I recognized some landmarks on its brink which I had observed the year before. Below me to the northwest the Indian village was plainly seen. They had a lovely little park for their home – a meadow in front, and a grove of tall pines behind. I could see the smoke curling up from their fires, and with my glass could watch the approach of the little train, and see the people coming out to meet it. The men unsaddled their horses, and an Indian boy took them out to graze. I descended the mountain, and reached camp at sunset.

After supper, we put some cedar boughs on the fire; the dusky villagers sat around, and we had a smoke and a talk. I explained the object of my visit, and assured them of my friendly intentions. Then I asked them about a way down into the cañon. They told me that, years ago, a way was discovered by which parties could go down, but that no one had attempted it for a long time; that it was a very difficult and dangerous undertaking to reach the "Big Water." Then I inquired about the Shuwits, the tribe that lives about the springs on the mountain-sides and cañon cliffs to the southwest. They said that their village was about thirty miles away, and promised to send a messenger for them the next morning. . . .

Around the camp-fire, the Indians related a long story from their repertoire of legends and myths. The next day, they would begin their descent into the Grand Canyon by way of the Kanab.

The story finished, I took Chu-ar aside for a talk. The three men who left us in the cañon the year before found their way up the lateral gorge, by which they went on the Shi-wits Plateau, lying to the west of this, where they met with the Indians, and camped with them one or two nights, and were finally killed. I was anxious to learn the circumstances, and as the people of the tribe who committed the deed live but a little way from these people, and are intimate with them, I asked Chu-ar to make inquiry for me. Then we went to bed.

Early the next morning the Indians came up to our camp. They had concluded to send out a young man after the Shi-wits. The runner fixed his moccasins, put some food in a sack, and some water in a little wicker-work jug lined with pitch, strapped them on his back, and started off at a good round pace.

We concluded to go down the cañon, hoping to meet the Shi-wits on our return. Soon we were ready to start, leaving the camp and pack animals in charge of the two Indians who came with us. As we moved out, our new guide came up – a blear-eyed, wizen-faced, quiet old man, with his bow and arrows in one hand, and a small cane in the other. These Indians all carry canes with a crooked handle, they say to kill rattlesnakes, and to pull rabbits from their holes. The valley is high up in the mountain, and we descended from it by a rocky, precipitous, trail down, down, down, for two long weary hours, leading our ponies, and stumbling over the rocks.

At last we were at the foot of the mountain, standing on a little knoll, from which we could look into a cañon below. Into this we descended, and then we followed it for miles, clambering down, and still down. Often we crossed beds of lava that had been poured into the cañon by lateral channels, and these angular fragments of basalt made the way very rough for the animals. About two o'clock the guide halted us with his wand, and, springing over the rocks, was soon lost in a gulch. In a few minutes he returned and told us there was a little water below in a pocket. But it was vile and nauseating, and our ponies refused to drink it. We passed on, still ever descending. A mile or two from the water-basin we came to a precipice more than a thousand feet to the bottom. There was a cañon running at a greater depth, and at right angles to this, and into which this entered by the precipice, and this second cañon was a lateral one to the greater one, in the bottom of which we were to find the river. Searching about, we found a way by which we could descend to the left along the shelves and steps and piles of broken rocks.

We started, leading our ponies, a wall upon our left, unknown depths on our right. At places our way was along shelves so narrow or so sloping that I ached with fear lest a pony should make a misstep and knock a man over the cliff with him. Now and then we started the loose rocks under our feet, and over the cliff they went thundering down, and the echoes rolled through distant cañons. At last we passed along a level shelf for some distance, then we turned to the right, and zigzagged down a steep slope to the bottom. Now we passed along this lower cañon for two or three miles to where it terminates in the Grand Cañon; as the other ended in this, the river was only eighteen hundred feet below us, and it seemed at this distance to be but a creek. Our withered guide, the human pickle, seated himself on a rock, and seemed wonderfully amused at our discomfiture, for we could see no way by which to descend to the river. After some minutes he quietly rose, and, beckoning us to follow, he pointed out a narrow sloping shelf on the right, which was to be our way. It led along the cliff for half a mile to a wider bench beyond, which, he said, was broken down on the other side in a great slide, and there we could get to the river. So we started out on the shelf; it was so steep we could hardly stand on it, and to

"Temples and Towers of the Virgen"
by William Henry Holmes

"Panorama from Point Sublime" by William Henry Holmes

Continuation of "Panorama from Point Sublime" by William Henry Holmes

fall would be to go – we dared not look to see where. It was soon manifest that we could not get the ponies along the ledge. The storms had washed it down since our guide was here last, years ago. One of the ponies had gone so far that we could not turn him back until we had found a wider place, but at last we got him off. With part of the men, I took the horses back where there were a few bushes growing, and turned them loose. In the meantime the other men were looking for some way by which we could get down to the river. When I returned, one, Captain Bishop, had found a way, and gone down. We packed bread, coffee, sugar, and two or three blankets among us, and set out. It was then nearly dark, and we could not find the way by which the Captain went, and an hour was spent in fruitless search. Two of the men went around an amphitheater more than a fourth of a mile, and started down a broken chasm that faced us who were behind. These walls that are often vertical, or nearly so, are often cut by chasms where the showers run down, and the tops of these chasms will be back a distance from the face of a wall, and the bed of the chasm will slope down with here and there a fall, and at some places be choked with huge rocks which have fallen from the cliff. Down such a one the two men started. We worked our way for a time, until we came to the "jumping-off place," where we could throw a stone and hear it faintly strike away below. We feared that we should have to stay there clinging to the rocks until daylight.

There is a curious plant growing out from the crevices of the rocks in this region: a dozen stems will start from one root and grow to the length of eight or ten feet and not throw out a single branch or twig. At this crisis our little Indian, who seemed fully to comprehend the circumstances, gathered a number of these dry stems and tied them together in a bundle, forming a fascine. Then he lighted one end, and held it up. With this we could see a way out of our trouble; and helping one another, and clinging to one another's hands, we worked our way still farther into the depths of the cañon. While we were doing this, we noticed that the party coming down the gulch on the opposite side of the amphitheater would occasionally kindle a fire in a bunch of dried stems; and while these fires served them to find a way down difficult points, it marked to us their progress down the gulch. Then Captain Bishop kindled a huge fire in the driftwood on the bank of the river. Soon every man of our party had a torch of his own, and the light by the river, and the lights in the opposite gulch, and our own torches, made more manifest the awful darkness which filled the stupendous gorge. Still on we went, for an hour or two, and at last we saw Captain Bishop coming up the gulch, with a huge torchlight on his shoulders. He looked like a fiend waving brands and lighting the flames of hell, and the men in the opposite gulch were imps lighting delusive fires in inaccessible crevices over yawning chasms; while our little Indian was surely the king of wizards. So I thought, as I stopped to rest for a moment on a rock. At last we met Captain Bishop, with his flaming torch, and as he had learned the way, he soon piloted us to the side of the great Colorado. We were hungry and athirst and almost starved, and we lay down on the rocks to drink. Then we made a cup of coffee, and, spreading our blankets on a sand beach, were lulled to sleep by the roaring Colorado.

The next morning we looked about us to see if there were no better way by which we could bring rations down to the river, and finally concluded that we could make that point a depot of supplies, should it be necessary; that we could pack rations to the point where we left our animals the night before, and employ Indians to carry them down to the water's edge. (Powell would use this as a place to cache supplies for his second descent of the Colorado in 1871.) *While looking about we discovered, on a broad shelf, the ruins of an old house, the walls of which were broken down, and could see where the ancient people who lived here had made a garden, and used a great spring that comes out of the rocks for irrigation. On some rocks near by we discovered some curious etchings. Still searching about we found an obscure trail up the cañon wall, marked here and there by steps which had been built in the loose rock. Elsewhere there were hewn stairways, and we found a much easier way to go up than that by which we came down in the darkness the night before.*

We were in the Grand Cañon, by the side of the roaring Colorado, more than six thousand feet below our camp on the mountain-side, eighteen miles away; but the miles of horizontal distance represented but a small part of the day's labor before us. It was the mile and a quarter of altitude to be compassed that made it a Herculean task.

We started early, and soon reached the place where we had left our horses, and found them mad with thirst. It was with difficulty that we were able to catch them, though they were hobbled; but at last they were all secured, and we started up the cañon with our jaded ponies until we reached the second cliff. Up this we climbed by easy steps, leading our animals. Then we reached the vile water-pocket found the day before. Our ponies had had no water for thirty hours, and were eager even for this foul fluid. We carefully strained a kettleful for ourselves, then divided what was left between them, two or three gallons for each; but this did not satisfy them, and they raged around, refusing to eat the scanty grass. We boiled our kettle of water and skimmed it; straining, boiling, and skimming made it a little better, and plenty of coffee took away the bad odor, and so modified the taste that most of us could drink it. Our little Indian, however, seemed to prefer the original mixture. We reached camp about sunset, and were glad to rest. . . .

Back on the plateau north of the Grand Canyon, Powell finally manages to meet up with the Shi-wits, the Indians responsible for killing the three men who had left the Colorado River expedition by climbing out of the Grand Canyon.

That evening, the Shi-wits, for whom we had sent, came in, and after supper we held a long council: a blazing fire was built, and around this we sat: the Indians living here, the Shi-wits, Jacob Hamblin, and myself. This man Hamblin speaks their language well, and has a great influence over all the Indians in the region round about. He is a silent, reserved man, and when he speaks, it is in a slow, quiet way that inspires great awe. His talk was so low that they had to listen attentively to hear, and they sat around him in death-like silence. When he finished a measured sentence, the chief repeated it and they all gave a solemn grunt. But first, I filled my pipe, lit it, and took a few whiffs, then passed it to Hamblin; he smoked and gave it to the man next, and so it went around. When it had passed the chief, he took out his own pipe, filled, and lit it, and passed it around after mine. I could smoke my own pipe in turn, but when the Indian pipe came round I was nonplussed. It had a large stem, which, at some time, had been broken, and now there was a buckskin rag wound around it and tied with sinew, so that the end of the stem was a huge mouthful. To gain time I refilled it, then engaged in very earnest conversation, and all unawares I passed it to my neighbor unlighted.

I told the Indians that I wished to spend some months in their country during the coming year, and that I should like them to treat me as a friend. I did not wish to trade, did not want their lands. Heretofore I had found it very difficult to make the natives understand my object, but the gravity of the Mormon missionary helped me much. I told them that all the great and good white men are anxious to know very many things, that they spend much time in learning, and that the greatest man is he who knows the most; that they want to know all about the mountains, and the valleys, the rivers, and the cañons, the beasts, and birds, and snakes. Then I told them of many Indian tribes, and where they live; of the European nations, of the Chinese, and Africans, and all the strange things about them that came to my mind. I told them of the ocean, of great rivers and high mountains, of strange beasts and birds. At last I told them I wished to learn about their cañons and mountains, and about themselves, to tell other men at home, and that I wanted to take pictures of everything, and show them to my friends. I told them that I could stay with them but a short time then, but that I should be back again and stay with them many months. All this occupied much time, and the matter and manner made a deep impression.

Then their chief replied, "Your talk is good, and we believe what you say. Your heart is good. We believe in Jacob, and look upon you as a father. When you are hungry you may have our game. You may gather our sweet fruits. We will give you food when you come to our land. We will show you the springs and you may drink; the water is good. We shall be friends, and, when you come, we shall be glad. We shall tell the Indians who live on the other side of the great river that we have seen Kah-pu-rats, and he is the Indian's friend. We shall tell them he is Jacob's friend. We are very poor. Look at our women and children; they are naked. We have no horses; we climb the rocks, and our feet are sore. We live among rocks, and they yield little food and many thorns. When the cold moons come, our children are hungry. We have not much to give; you must not think us mean. You are wise; we have heard you tell strange things. We are ignorant. Last year we killed three white men. Bad men said they were our enemies. They told great lies. We thought them true. *We were mad; it made us big fools. We are very sorry. Do not think of them; it is done; let us be friends. We are ignorant, like little children in understanding compared with you. When we do wrong, do not get mad, and be like children too.*

"When white men kill our people, we kill them. Then they kill more of us. It is not good. We hear that the white men are a great number. When they stop killing us, there will be no Indian left to bury the dead. We love our country; we know not other lands. We hear that other lands are better; we do not know. The pines sing, and we are glad. Our children play in the warm sand; we hear them sing, and we are glad. The seeds ripen, and we have to eat, and we are glad. We do not want their good lands; we want our rocks and the great mountains where our fathers lived. We are very poor; we are very ignorant; but we are very honest. You have horses and many things. You are very wise; you have a good heart. We will be friends. Nothing more have I to say."

Kah-pu-rats is the name by which I am known by the Utes and Shoshones, meaning "no right arm." There was much more repetition than I have given, and much more emphasis. After this a few presents were given, we shook hands, and the council broke up.

Mr. Hamblin then fell into conversation with one of the men, and held him until the others had left, and learned more of the particulars of the death of the three men. It seems that they came upon the Indian village almost starved and exhausted with fatigue. They were supplied with food, and put on their way to the settlements. Shortly after they had left, an Indian from the east side of the Colorado arrived at their village and told them about a number of miners having killed a squaw in a drunken brawl, and no doubt these were the men. No person had ever come down the cañon; that was impossible; they were trying to hide their guilt. In this way he worked them into a great rage; they followed, surrounded the men in ambush, and filled them full of arrows.

That night I slept in peace, although these murderers of my men, and their friends, the U-in-ka-rets, were sleeping not five hundred yards away. While we were gone to the cañon, the pack train, and supplies enough to make an Indian rich beyond his wildest dreams, were all left in their charge, and all was safe; not even a lump of sugar was pilfered by the children. . . .

The next day the train started back to the Elfin Water-Pocket, while Captain Bishop and I climbed Mt. Trumbull. The U-in-ka-ret Mountains are volcanic – great irregular masses of lava, and many cones, one hundred and eighteen in number. . . . Then we rode through a cedar forest up a long ascent until we came to cliffs of columnar basalt. Here we tied our horses, and prepared for a climb among the columns. Through crevices we worked, still toiling up, till at last we were on the mountain; a thousand acres of pine-lands spread out before us, gently rising to the other edge. There are two peaks on the mountain. We walked two miles to the foot of the one that seemed the highest, then made a long hard climb to its summit. And there, oh! what a view was before us. A vision of glory! Peaks of lava all around below us; the vermilion cliffs to the north, with their splendor of colors; the Pine Valley Mountains to the northwest, clothed in mellow perspective haze; unnamed mountains to the southwest towering over cañons bottomless to my peering gaze; and away beyond, the San Francisco Mountains lifting their black heads into the heavens. We found our way down the mountain, reaching the trail made by the pack train just at dusk, and following it through the dark until we descried the campfire – a welcome sight.

Two days more, and we were at Pipe Spring, and another, at the bank of the Kanab.

Chapter X

MT. RAINIER
1870

from "The Ascent of Takhoma"
in The Atlantic Monthly, Nov. 1876
by Hazard Stevens

Takhoma is the Yakima word meaning 'the mountain.' Kautz had nearly made it to the top of the mountain in 1857, Stevens and Van Trump did in 1870. This is not an anthology that is concerned so much with the first ascents of prominent peaks, but some are included as they are early narratives of exploration in the western parklands. Stevens and Van Trump took a different route up Rainier than Kautz, and thereby provide a different perspective. They were guided to the upper slopes of Rainier by Sluiskin, a local Yakima Indian.

. . . After a few more hours of this climbing, we stood upon the summit of the last mountain-ridge that separated us from Takhoma. We were in a saddle of the ridge; a lofty peak rose on either side. Below us extended a long, steep hollow or gulch filled with snow, the farther extremity of which seemed to drop off perpendicularly into a deep valley or basin. Across this valley, directly in front, filling up the whole horizon and view with an indescribable aspect of magnitude and grandeur, stood the old leviathan of mountains. The broad, snowy dome rose far among and above the clouds. The sides fell off in vertical steeps and fearful black walls of rock for a third of its altitude; lower down, vast, broad, gently sloping snow-fields surrounded the mountain, and were broken here and there by ledges or masses of the dark basaltic rock protruding above them. Long, green ridges projected from this snow-belt at intervals, radiating from the mountain and extending many miles until lost in the distant forests. Deep valleys lay between these ridges. Each at its upper end formed the bed of a glacier, which closed and filled it up with solid ice. Below the snow-line bright green grass with countless flowers, whose vivid scarlet, blue, and purple formed bodies of color in the distance, clothed the whole region of ridges and valleys, for a breadth of five miles. The beautiful

balsam firs, about thirty feet in height, and of a purple, dark-green color, stood scattered over the landscape, now singly, now in groves, and now in long lines, as though planted in some well-kept park. Farther down an unbroken fir forest surrounded the mountain and clad the lower portions of the ridges and valleys. In every sheltered depression or hollow lay beds of snow with tiny brooks and rivulets flowing from them. The glaciers terminated not gradually, but abruptly, with a wall of ice from one to five hundred feet high, from beneath which yeasty torrents burst forth and rushed roaring and tumbling down the valleys. The principal of these, far away on our left front, could be seen plunging over two considerable falls, half hidden in the forest, while the roar of waters was distinctly audible.

At length we cautiously descended the snow-bed, and, climbing at least fifteen hundred feet down a steep but ancient landslide by means of the bushes growing among the loose rocks, reached the valley, and encountered a beautiful, peaceful, limpid creek. Van Trump could not resist the temptation of unpacking his bundle, selecting one of his carefully preserved flies, and trying the stream for trout, but without a single rise. After an hour's rest and a hearty repast we resumed our packs, despite Sluiskin's protests, who seemed tired out with his arduous day's toil and pleaded hard against traveling farther. Crossing the stream, we walked through several grassy glades, or meadows, alternating with open woods. We soon came to the foot of one of the long ridges already described, and ascending it followed it for several miles through open woods, until we emerged upon the enchanting emerald and flowery meads which clothe these upper regions. Halting upon a rising eminence in our course, and looking back, we beheld the ridge of mountains we had just descended stretching from east to west in a steep, rocky wall; a little to the left, a beautiful lake, evidently the source of the stream just crossed, which we called Clear Creek, and glimpses of which could be seen among the trees as it flowed away to the right, down a rapidly descending valley along the foot of the lofty mountain wall. Beyond the lake again, still farther to the left, the land also subsided quickly. It was at once evident that the lake was upon a summit, or divide, between the waters of the Nisqually and Cowlitz rivers. The ridge which we were ascending lay north and south, and led directly up to the mountain.

We camped, as the twilight fell upon us, in an aromatic grove of balsam firs. A grouse, the fruit of Sluiskin's rifle, broiled before the fire and impartially divided, gave a relish to the dry bread and coffee. After supper we reclined upon our blankets in front of the bright, blazing fire, well satisfied. The Indian, when starting from Bear Prairie, had evidently deemed our intention of ascending Takhoma too absurd to deserve notice. . . . But his views had undergone a change with the day's march. The affair began to look serious to him, and now in Chinook, interspersed with a few words of broken English and many signs and gesticulations, he began a solemn exhortation and warning against our rash project.

Takhoma, he said, was an enchanted mountain, inhabited by an evil spirit, who dwelt in a fiery lake on its summit. No human being could ascend it or even attempt its ascent, and survive. At first, indeed, the way was easy. The broad snowfields, over which he had so often hunted the mountain goat, interposed no obstacle, but above them the rash adventurer would be compelled to climb up steeps of loose, rolling rocks, which would turn beneath his feet and cast him headlong into the deep abyss below. The upper snow slopes, too, were so steep that not even a goat, far less a man, could get over them. And he would have to pass below lofty walls and precipices whence avalanches of snow and vast masses of rock were continually falling; and these would inevitably bury the intruder beneath their ruins. Moreover, a furious tempest continually swept the crown of the mountain, and the luckless adventurer, even if he wonderfully escaped the perils below, would be torn from the mountain and whirled through the air by this fearful blast. And the awful being upon the summit, who would surely punish the sacrilegious attempt to invade his sanctuary – who would hope to escape his vengeance? Many years ago, he continued, his grandfather, a great chief and warrior, and a mighty hunter, had ascended part way up the mountain, and had encountered some of these dangers, but he fortunately turned back in time to escape destruction; and no other Indian had ever gone so far.

Finding that his words did not produce the desired effect, he assured us that, if we persisted in attempting the ascent, he would wait three days for our return, and would then proceed to Olympia and inform our friends of our death; and he begged us to give him a paper (a written note) to take to them, so that they

*might believe his story. Sluiskin's manner during this harangue
was earnest in the extreme, and he was undoubtedly sincere in
his forebodings. After we had retired to rest, he kept up a most
dismal chant, or dirge, until late in the night. The dim, white,
spectral mass towering so near, the roar of the torrents below
us, and the occasional thunder of avalanches, several of which
fell during the night, added to the weird effect of Sluiskin's song.*

*The next morning we moved two miles farther up the ridge and
made camp in the last clump of trees, quite within the limit of
perpetual snow. Thence, with snow-spikes upon our feet and
Alpine staff in hand, we went up the snowfields to reconnoitre
the best line of ascent. We spent four hours, walking fast, in
reaching the foot of the steep, abrupt part of the mountain. After
carefully scanning the southern approaches, we decided to
ascend on the morrow by a steep, rocky ridge that seemed to
lead up to the snowy crown.*

*Our camp was pitched on a high knoll crowned by a grove of
balsam firs, near a turbulent glacial torrent. About nine
o'clock, after we had lain down for the night, the firs round our
camp took fire and suddenly burst out in a vivid conflagration.
The night was dark and windy, and the scene – the vast, dim
outlines of Takhoma, the white snowfields, the roaring torrent,
the crackling blaze of the burning trees – was strikingly wild
and picturesque.*

*In honor of our guide we named the cascade at our feet Slu-
iskin's Falls; the stream we named Glacier Creek, and the mass
of ice whence it derives its sources we styled the Little Nisqually
Glacier.*

*Before daylight the next morning, Wednesday, August 17, 1870,
we were up and had breakfasted, and at six o'clock we started
to ascend Takhoma. Besides our alpine staffs and creepers, we
carried a long rope, an ice axe, a brass plate inscribed with our
names, our flags, a large canteen, and some luncheon. We were
also provided with gloves, and green goggles for snow blind-
ness, but found no occasion to use the latter. Having suffered
much from the heat of the sun since leaving Bear Prairie, and
being satisfied from our late reconnaissance that we could
reach the summit and return on the same day, we left behind our
coats and blankets. In three hours of fast walking we reached*

the highest point of the preceding day's trip, and commenced the ascent by the steep, rocky ridge already described as reaching up to the snowy dome. We found it to be a very narrow, steep, irregular backbone, composed of a crumbling basaltic conglomerate, the top only, or backbone, being solid rock, while the sides were composed of loose broken rocks and débris. Up this ridge, keeping upon the spine when possible, and sometimes forced to pick our way over the loose and broken rocks at the sides, around columnar masses which we could not directly climb over, we toiled for five hundred yards, ascending at an angle of nearly forty-five degrees. Here the ridge connected, by a narrow neck or saddle, with a vast square rock, whose huge and distinct outline can be clearly perceived from a distance of twenty-five miles. . . . Crossing by the saddle from the ridge, despite a strong wind which swept across it, we gained a narrow ledge formed by a stratum more solid than its fellows, and creeping along it, hugging close to the main rock on our right, laboriously and cautiously continued the ascent. The wind was blowing violently. We were now crawling along the face of the precipice almost in mid-air. On the right the rock towered far above us perpendicularly. On the left it fell sheer off, two thousand feet, into a vast abyss. A great glacier filled its bed and stretched away for several miles, all seamed or wrinkled across with countless crevasses. We crept up and along a ledge, not of solid, sure rock, but one obstructed with the loose stones and débris which were continually falling from above, and we trod on the upper edge of a steep slope of this rubbish, sending the stones at every step rolling and bounding into the depths below. Several times during our progress showers of rocks fell from the precipices above across our path, and rolled into the abyss, but fortunately none struck us.

Four hundred yards of this progress brought us to where the rock joined the overhanging edge of the vast névé or snowfield that descended from the dome of the mountain and was from time to time, as pressed forward and downward, breaking off in immense masses, which fell with a noise as of thunder into the great canyon on our left. The junction of rock and ice afforded our only line of ascent. It was an almost perpendicular gutter, but here our ice axe came into play, and by cutting steps in the ice and availing ourselves of every crevice or projecting point of the rock, we slowly worked out way up two hundred yards higher. Falling stones were continually coming down, both from

*the rock on our right and from the ice in front, as it melted and
relaxed its hold upon them. Mr. Van Trump was hit by a small
one, and another struck his staff from his hands. Abandoning
the rock, then, at the earliest practicable point, we ascended
directly up the ice, cutting steps for a short distance, until we
reached ice so corrugated, or drawn up in sharp pinnacles, as
to afford a foothold. These folds or pinnacles were about two or
three feet high, and half as thick, and stood close together. It
was like a very violent chop sea, only the waves were sharper.
Up this safe footing we climbed rapidly, the side of the mountain becoming less and less steep, and the ice waves smaller
and more regular, and, after ascending about three hundred
yards, stood fairly upon the broad dome of mighty Takhoma. It
rose before us like a broad, gently swelling headland of dazzling white, topped with black, where the rocky summit projected above the névé. Ascending diagonally towards the left,
we continued our course. The snow was hard and firm under
foot, crisp and light for an inch or two, but solidified into ice a
foot or less beneath the surface. The whole field was covered
with the ice-waves already described, and intersected by a number of crevasses which we crossed at narrow places without difficulty. About half-way up the slope, we encountered one from
eight to twenty feet wide and of profound depth. The most beautiful vivid emerald-green color seemed to fill the abyss, the
reflection of the bright sunlight from side to side of its pure ice
walls. The upper side or wall of the crevasses was some twelve
feet above the lower, and in places overhung it, as though the
snowfield on the lower side had bodily settled down a dozen
feet. Throwing a bight of the rope around a projecting pinnacle
on the upper side, we climbed up, hand over hand, and thus
effected a crossing. We were now obliged to travel slowly, with
frequent rests. In that rare atmosphere, after taking seventy or
eighty steps, our breath would be gone, our muscles grew tired
and strained, and we experienced all the sensations of extreme
fatigue. An instant's pause, however, was sufficient to recover
strength and breath, and we would start again. The wind, which
we had not felt while climbing the steepest part of the mountain,
now again blew furiously, and we began to suffer from the cold.
Our course — brought us first to the southwest peak. This is a
long, exceedingly sharp, narrow ridge, springing out from the
main dome for a mile into mid-air. The ridge affords not over
ten or twelve feet of foothold on top, and the sides descend
almost vertically. On the right side the snow lay firm and*

smooth for a few feet on top, and then descended in a steep, unbroken sheet, like an immense, flowing curtain, into the tremendous basin which lies on the west side of the mountain between the southern and northern peaks, and which is inclosed by them as by two mighty arms. The snow on the top and left crest of the ridge was broken into high, sharp pinnacles, with cracks and fissures extending to the rocks a few feet below. The left side, too steep for the snow to lie on, was vertical, bare rock. The wind blew so violently that we were obliged to brace ourselves with our Alpine staffs and use great caution to guard against being swept off the ridge. We threw ourselves behind the pinnacles or into the cracks every seventy steps, for rest and shelter against the bitter, piercing wind. Hastening forward in this way along the dizzy, narrow, and precarious ridge, we reached at length the highest point. Sheltered behind a pinnacle of ice we rested a moment, took out our flags and fastened them upon the Alpine staffs, and then, standing erect in the furious blast, waved them in triumph with three cheers. We stood a moment upon that narrow summit, bracing ourselves against the tempest to view the prospect. The whole country was shrouded in a dense sea of smoke, above which the mountain towered two thousand feet in the clear, cloudless ether. A solitary peak far to the southeast, doubtless Mount Adams, and one or two others in the extreme northern horizon, alone protruded above the pall. On every side of the mountain were deep gorges falling off precipitously thousands of feet, and from these the thunderous sound of avalanches would rise occasionally. Far below were the wide-extended glaciers already described. The wind was now a perfect tempest, and bitterly cold; smoke and mist were flying about the base of the mountain, half hiding, half revealing its gigantic outlines; and the whole scene was sublimely awful.

It was now five p.m. We had spent eleven hours of unremitted toil in making the ascent, and, thoroughly fatigued, and chilled by the cold, bitter gale, we saw ourselves obliged to pass the night on the summit without shelter or food, except our meagre lunch. It would have been impossible to descend the mountain before nightfall, and sure destruction to attempt it in darkness. We concluded to return to a mass of rocks not far below, and there pass the night as best we could, burrowing in the loose débris.

The middle peak of the mountain, however, was evidently the highest, and we determined to first visit it. Retracing our steps along the narrow crest of Peak Success, as we named the scene of our triumph, we crossed an intervening depression in the dome, and ascended the middle peak, about a mile distant and two hundred feet higher than Peak Success. Climbing over a rocky ridge which crowns the summit, we found ourselves within a circular crater two hundred yards in diameter, filled with a solid bed of snow, and inclosed with a rim of rocks protruding above the snow all around. As we were crossing the crater on the snow, Van Trump detected the odor of sulphur, and the next instant numerous jets of steam and smoke were observed issuing from the crevices of the rocks which formed the rim on the northern side. Never was a discovery more welcome! Hastening forward, we both exclaimed, as we warmed our chilled and benumbed extremities over one of Pluto's fires, that here we would pass the night, secure against freezing to death, at least. . . .

A deep cavern, extending into and under the ice, and formed by the action of heat, was found. Its roof was a dome of brilliant green ice with long icicles pendent from it, while its floor, composed of the rocks and débris which formed the side of the crater, descended at an angle of thirty degrees. Forty feet within its mouth we built a wall of stones, inclosing a space five by six feet around a strong jet of steam and heat. Unlike the angular, broken rocks met with elsewhere, within the crater we found well-rounded bowlders and stones of all sizes worn as smooth by the trituration of the crater as by the action of water. Nowhere, however, did we observe any new lava or other evidences of recent volcanic action excepting these issues of steam and smoke. Inclosed within the rude shelter thus hastily constructed, we discussed our future prospects while we ate our lunch and warmed ourselves at our natural register. The heat at the orifice was too great to bear for more than an instant; but the steam wet us, the smell of sulphur was nauseating, and the cold was so severe that our clothes, saturated with the steam, froze stiff when turned away from the heated jet. The wind outside roared and whistled, but it did not much affect us, secure within our cavern, except when an occasional gust came down perpendicularly. However, we passed a most miserable night, freezing on one side, and in a hot steam sulphur bath on the other.

The dawn at last slowly broke, cold and gray. The tempest howled still wilder. As it grew light, dense masses of driven mist went sweeping by overhead and completely hid the sun, and enveloped the mountain so as to conceal objects scarce a hundred feet distant. We watched and waited with great anxiety, fearing a storm which might detain us there for days without food or shelter, or, worse yet, snow, which would render the descent more perilous, or most likely impossible. And when, at nine a.m., an occasional rift in the driving mist gave a glimpse of blue sky, we made haste to descend. First, however, I deposited the brass plate inscribed with our names in a cleft in a large bowlder on the highest summit – a huge mound of rocks on the east side of our crater of refuge, which we named Crater Peak – placed the canteen alongside, and covered it with a large stone. I was then literally freezing in the cold, piercing blast, and was glad to hurry back to the crater, breathless and benumbed.

We left our den of refuge at length, after exercising violently to start the blood through our limbs and, in attempting to pass around the rocky summit, discovered a second crater, larger than the first. . . . The rim of the second crater is higher, or the snow field inside lower, than that of the first. . . . From the summit we obtained a view of the northern peak, still partially enveloped in the driving mist. It appeared about a mile distant, several hundred feet lower than the centre peak, and separated from it by a deeper, more abrupt depression or gap than that separating Crater and Success peaks. . . . The weather was still too threatening, the glimpses of the sun and sky through the thick, flying scud, were too few and fugitive, to warrant us in visiting this peak, which we named Peak Takhoma, to perpetuate the Indian name of the mountain.

Our route back was the same as on the ascent. At the steepest and most perilous point in descending the steep gutter where we had been forced to cut steps in the ice, we fastened one end of the rope as securely as possible to a projecting rock, and lowered ourselves down by it as far as it reached, thereby passing the place with comparative safety. We were forced to abandon the rope here, having no means of unfastening it from the rock above. We reached the foot of the rocky ledge or ridge, where the real difficulties and dangers of the ascent commenced, at 1:30 p.m., four and a half hours after leaving the crater. We had been seven and a half hours in ascending from this point to the summit of Peak Success, and in both cases we toiled hard and lost no time.

We now struck out rapidly and joyfully for camp. When nearly there Van Trump, in attempting to descend a snow bank without his creepers, which he had taken off for greater ease in walking, fell, shot like lightning forty feet down the steep incline, and struck among some loose rocks at its foot with such force as to rebound several feet into the air; his face and hands were badly skinned, and he received some severe bruises and a deep, wide gash upon his thigh. Fortunately the camp was not far distant, and thither with great pain and very slowly he managed to hobble. Once there I soon started a blazing fire, made coffee, and roasted choice morsels of a marmot, Sluiskin having killed and dressed four of these animals during our absence. Their flesh, like the badger's, is extremely muscular and tough, and has a strong, disagreeable, doggy odor.

Towards the close of our repast, we observed the Indian approaching with his head down, and walking slowly and wearily as though tired by a long tramp. He raised his head as he came nearer, and, seeing us for the first time, stopped short, gazed long and fixedly, and then slowly drew near, eyeing us closely the while, as if to see whether we were real flesh and blood or disembodied ghosts fresh from the evil demon of Takhoma. He seemed both astonished and delighted to find us safe back, and kept repeating that we were strong men and had brave hearts: "Skookum tilicum, skookum tumtum." He expected never to see us again, he said, and had resolved to start the next morning for Olympia to report our destruction. . . .

Chapter XI

GRAND STAIRCASE-ESCALANTE –
CAPITOL REEF
1872

from A Canyon Voyage
by Frederick S. Dellenbaugh

This book concerns Powell's second descent of the Colorado River, written by a young member of the expedition who continued to have an interest in exploration throughout his life. Along with this personal narrative, he would later write a history of the exploration of the Colorado River from earliest times up to his own exploration with John Wesley Powell. On this second expedition, side excursions were made from the river throughout southern Utah. These expeditions finished Powell's work to learn the topography of this last major blank space on the map of the American West. After the descent of the Colorado was finished, other expeditions were sent out by land. This land expedition, which Dellenbaugh accompanied and wrote about, was led by Almon Harris Thompson. They left from the Mormon town of Kanab heading in a northeast direction, skirted the present border of Grand Staircase-Escalante, ascended the high plateau east of Capitol Reef, and then crossed the middle portion of Capitol Reef itself along Pleasant Creek. On the way, they discovered an unknown river, which they named the Escalante. From the Aquarius Plateau, they had impressive views over the desert country of Capitol Reef. Not included is the crossing of the Henry Mtns. back to the Colorado River. By discovering an unknown river and mountain range, they filled in the last major geographical mystery of the West.

. . . All the next morning, June 1ˢᵗ, our way led over rolling meadows covered with fine grass, but about noon this ended and we entered the broken country of the upper Paria, with gullies and gulches barren and dry the rest of the day, except two, in which we crossed small branches of the Paria. In one of the dry gulches we passed a grave, marked by a sandstone slab with E. A. cut on it, which the wolves had dug out, leaving the human bones scattered all around. We could not stop to re-inter them. They were the remains of Elijah Averett, a young Mor-

mon, who was killed while pursuing Pai Utes in 1866. Just before sunset we arrived at the banks of the Paria, where we made camp, with plenty of wood, water, and grass. Captain Dodds during the afternoon recognized a place he had been in when hunting a way the autumn before, and we followed his old trail for a time. Leaving the Paria the following day where it branches, we followed the east fork to its head, twelve miles, climbing rapidly through a narrow valley. We could plainly see on the left a high, flat, cliff-bounded summit, which was called Table Mountain, and early in the afternoon we reached a series of "hog-backs," up one of which the old Indian trail we were now following took its precarious way. The hog-backs were narrow ridges of half-disintegrated clay-shale, with sides like the roof of a house, the trail following the sharp summit-line. Before we had fairly begun this very steep, slippery, and narrow climb, the thunder boomed and the heavens threw down upon us fierce torrents of rain, soaking everything and chilling us through and through, while making the trail like wet soap. Part way up, at one of the worst places, a pack came loose, and, slipping back, hung on the rump of the horse. There was no room for bucking it off, and there was no trouble so far as the beast of burden was concerned, for he realized fully his own danger. Two of us managed to climb along past the other animals to where he meekly stood waiting on the narrow ridge, with a descent on each side of eight hundred or nine hundred feet, and set things in order once more, when the cavalcade continued the ascent, the total amount of which was some twelve hundred feet.

Arriving at the top we found ourselves almost immediately on the edge of a delightful little valley, mossy and green with a fresh June dress, down which we proceeded two or three miles to a spring where Dodds and Jacob had made a cache of some flour the year before. The flour had disappeared. We made a camp and dried out our clothes, blankets, etc., by means of large fires. Though it was summer the air was decidedly chilly, for we were at an altitude of nearly 6,000 feet. . . . There was a pretty creek in this valley flowing eastward, which Dodds said was the head of the Dirty Devil, the same stream he had followed down the year before in the attempt to find a way to bring us rations. The weather was very bad but we kept on down Potato Valley as it had been named, crossing three or four swift tributaries. About four o'clock we stopped beside a raging torrent and went into camp to reconnoitre. There were signs of *some one having been here about a month before, and as the animals were shod we judged it was some prospector. . . . Prof. and Dodds rode away to the south on a dim trail to find out what move to make; how far we might be able to go down the Dirty Devil the next day. When they got back they reported finding a canyon twelve miles farther on, with many water-pockets, and concluded to go there.*

We arrived about noon Thursday, June 6th, making camp. Prof. and Dodds then climbed to where they could get a wide view, and Dodds pointed out the locality he had before reached when he thought himself so near the mouth of the Dirty Devil. No sooner had he done so than Prof. perceived at once that we were not on the river we thought we were on, for by this explanation he saw that the stream we were trying to descend flowed into the Colorado far to the southwest of the Unknown Mountains, whereas he knew positively that the Dirty Devil came in on the northeast. Then the question was, "What river is this?" for we had not noted a tributary of any size between the Dirty Devil and the San Juan. It was a new river whose identity had not been fathomed (the Escalante). *This discovery put a different complexion on everything. The problem was more complicated than Dodds had imagined when he was trying to reach the mouth the year before.*

Prof. declared it was impossible to proceed farther in this direction towards our goal. The canyon of the river was narrow, and with the stream swimming high it was out of the question as a path for us now, and even had we been able to go down far enough to get out on the other side, the region intervening between it and the distant mountains was a heterogeneous conglomeration of unknown mesas and canyons that appeared impassable. He concluded the only thing to do was to go north to the summit of the Wasatch cliffs and keep along the high land northeast to an angle where these slopes vanished to the north. From that point we might be able to cross to the Dirty Devil or Unknown Mountains. Once at these mountains we felt certain of finding a way to our former campground at the mouth of the Dirty Devil River. . . . (Here the two parties separated, one going back to Kanab. Dellenbaugh continues with the other party high above 10,000 feet onto the Aquarius Plateau.) *A prettier mountain region than this could not be imagined, while the magnificent outlook to the south and east across the broken*

*country was a bewildering sight, especially as the night envel-
oped it, deepening the mystery of its entangled gorges and cliffs*
(Capitol Reef). *From every point we could see the Navajo
Mountain and at least we knew what there was at the foot of its
majestic northern slope. I climbed far above camp and crossing
over a promontory looked down upon the nebulous region to the
eastward that we were to fathom, and it seemed to me one of the
most interesting sights I had ever beheld. The night was so cold
that ice formed in our kettles, for our altitude in feet above sea
was in the ten thousand still.*

*. . . All day we traveled over a rancher's paradise, meeting no
Indians and seeing no recent signs of any except in some filmy
smoke mounting mysteriously from canyons in the tangled sandstone labyrinth below. Who were they, how many, and what
might be their temper? were questions that came to us as we
reflected on the presence there of unknown human beings, and
furthermore would we meet them, and if so when? As on the
preceding day we crossed many fine brooks which in the dry
season probably would not make so vigorous a showing. Late in
the afternoon, having traveled fifteen miles, we reached the
point where the end of the . . . Aquarius Plateau, the high slope
of which we were using as a bridge from Potato Valley to the
Unknown Mountains, broke back to the north, cutting us off
once more from our objective, for a wide stretch, twenty-five
miles in an airline, of ragged desert apparently impassable still
intervened. We camped there at a convenient little spring. In the
morning I was sent with Johnson . . . in one direction down the
mountain to look for some old trail, while Prof. with Dodds
went in another. Scarcely had I gone half a mile when I found
tolerably fresh Indian sign, and a mile or two farther on we
struck a recently traveled trail. The horses that had gone over it
were unshod and there were moccasin tracks indicating Indians
without a doubt, but what kind of course the track did not
reveal. The trail led towards the Dirty Devil Mountains, and we
followed it three or four miles to ascertain with certainty its
general course. There was a possibility of our stumbling upon
the Indians in camp at some bend, and as this was not desirable
for only two of us we turned back as soon as we felt sure of the
direction. Prof. had seen no trail at all, and he said he would
take the one I had found and follow it. That night was disagreeable and rainy with numberless mosquitoes, but worst of all one
of our new men always snored till the ground shook, and owing*

to the rain we could not get away from him, for we had to remain in the improvised tent to keep dry.

The morning light never was more welcome and we were all up early. The day was fair. We were soon off and made our way down from the grassy heights to the trail, tracing its wearisome twists and turns, sometimes thinking it was not going our way at all when the next turn would be exactly right. In general its course was about east. The land was desolate and dry, and exactly as the region appeared from above, a complete labyrinth of variously colored cliffs and canyons. Besides being very crooked on account of the nature of the topography, the trail at times was indistinct because of the barren rocks, smooth as a floor, with nothing to take an imprint. In these places we were obliged to make the best guess we could. We came to a place where a valley lay about 1,800 feet below us, with the descent to it over bare, smooth, white sandstone almost as steep as a horse could stand on. We traveled a mile and a half over this and then found ourselves in a better looking region where, after a few miles, we discovered a beautiful creek flowing rapidly. There was plenty of good grass and we made our camp beneath some cottonwood trees, having accomplished twenty miles the way we came. Smoke of an Indian fire was rolling up about three miles below us, but we paid little attention to it. Every man delayed putting down his blankets till the champion snorer had selected the site of his bed, and then we all got as far away as the locality would permit. Having slept little the night before, we hardly stirred till morning, and in gratitude we called the stream Pleasant Creek without an attempt at originality. . . .

Chapter XII

GRAND TETON
1872

*from "The Ascent of Mount Hayden"
in* Scribner's Monthly, *June 1873,
by Nathaniel Langford*

Following the official discovery of Yellowstone by the Washburn party in 1870, Ferdinand Hayden led an even larger party into the Yellowstone in 1871. From the Hayden survey came the paintings of Thomas Moran and the photographs of William Henry Jackson that so impressed the public and convinced Congress to set aside Yellowstone as the first national park. Nathaniel Langford accompanied another Hayden survey into Yellowstone during 1872, who had earlier joined the initial Washburn expedition and written the article for Scribner's Monthly. This time, the Hayden survey is broken up into several groups approaching Yellowstone from more than one direction. Langford accompanied the group approaching Yellowstone from the south past the Tetons. An important goal was to ascend Grand Teton, which Langford dubbed Mount Hayden – a name that did not stick. Although, there is some controversy for various reasons over whether Langford and Stevenson did actually reach the top of the peak, it seems obvious that they, at least, came very close to the summit of the Grand Teton (or of a neighboring peak). In any case, previous explorers had been to the Tetons and crossed over its passes, but this is the first account of explorers ascending into the high alpine region of the mountain chain.

> . . . *As we looked before us and beheld, rising through the morning vapors, the glinting sides and summits of the Tetons, we felt that even this country, desolate and virgin as it was, had a thrilling history. Those grand old mountains covered with eternal snow had, by their very isolation, pointed the way to the Pacific to all the early explorers, from the days of Lewis and Clarke, through the mountain passes and river mazes of this the most intricate part of the continent. Guided by them, Hunt in 1811 led his little half-starved band out of the almost inextricable wilderness of the Bighorn Mountains, and pursued his long*

and tortuous journey to the Columbia. Often did they serve during his years of wandering to guide Bonneville to the friendly wigwams of the Bannacks or Shoshones. . . . Rough, jagged and pointed, they stood out before us nearer than I had ever before seen them, shining like gigantic crystals in the morning sunbeams. . . . Beaver Dick told us, that though many times attempted, the ascent of the great Teton had never been accomplished. And this was the opinion of the Indians. Indeed, as late as the visit of Captain Reynolds to this region in 1860, the opinion was prevalent that the Tetons were surrounded by a tract of country so full of rocks and wild streams and perpetual snows as to be entirely inaccessible. . . .

The great theme of talk about our campfire was the proposed ascent of the Tetons. Beaver Dick said our design was not new. The ascent had been often tried, and always without success. An old trapper by the name of Michaud, as long ago as 1843, provided himself with ropes, rope-ladders, and other aids, and spent days in the effort, but met with so many obstructions he finally gave it up in despair. "You can try," said Dick, significantly; "but you'll wind up in the same way."

After a ride of ten miles, we arrived at mid-day at the Middle Fork of the Snake, or the Mad river of Mr. Hunt. It is not as large as the North Fork, but much more rapid. All day the Tetons reared their heads in full view. From the summit, midway to the base, they seemed to be covered with perpetual snow. In the buttressed sides, as the eye scanned them critically, many places were seen where the rocks were nearly vertical, and which it would be impossible to scale. They were apparently entrenched in a wilderness of rocks, as inaccessible as their summits.

Our camp, the next day, was thirteen miles nearer the Tetons, which assumed a loftier appearance and seemed more distant than ever. . . .

Eight miles of difficult travel took us fairly into the Teton basin. This basin, hid away among the mountains, is like an oasis in the desert. It embraces an area of about eight hundred square miles, and is carpeted with the heaviest and largest bunch-grass I have ever seen. It is bounded on three sides by a range of snow-capped mountains, and forms a complete cul-de-sac. . . .

"Gate of Lodore" by John K. Hillers

*Photos taken during Powell's second descent of
the Colorado River in 1872.*

"The Heart of Lodore" by John K. Hillers

"Echo Rock" by John K. Hillers

*Photo of Powell's armchair boat in the Grand Canyon
by John K. Hillers.*

"Mist in Kanab Canyon" by Thomas Moran.

*Photo shows Jackson and companion developing
photos high in the Grand Tetons
during the 1872 survey.*

*All the resources of our camp were now put in requisition to
favor the ascent of the Great Teton. Mr. Adams, who had
returned to Fort Hall from North Fork, was daily expected. He
was to bring with him barometric instruments necessary to
determine the altitude of the lofty peaks. Mr. Stevenson and the
writer concluded to occupy the time until he should arrive in a
preliminary reconnaissance of the mountains. Accordingly, on
the morning of the 24th of July, after an early breakfast, we
mounted our horses and proceeded up the cañon above our
camp. Following the main stream, we passed in the distance of
three miles thirty or forty beautiful cascades. For that entire
distance the walls of the cañon seemed full of their reverbera-
tions. Many of them were fashioned by the descent of lateral
streams into the main Teton, and followed each other in almost
continuous succession down the rocks. Their noisy laughter (we*

could not call it roar) was the only sound that broke the silence of the chasm through which we were passing.

On every hand we saw them through the pines, at a height of thousands of feet, veiling the rocks and leaping into pools of foamy whiteness.

There was no trail up the cañon, and we were obliged, as best we might, to pick our way over fallen trunks, through narrow ravines, and amid innumerable rocks. On our right the massive walls of fossiliferous limestone, nearly vertical, towered three thousand feet above us. Looking up, we could see, at that amazing height, huge projections of shelving rock just over our heads, and lofty towers rising above them into the clear blue atmosphere. A feeling of dread, lest some of these mighty masses should be loosed and hurled upon us, was mingled with those sublimer emotions which this spectacle evoked. . . .

In traveling the distance of ten miles from our camp, we had accomplished an ascent of two thousand feet, when we struck the line of snow. Our horses were tired out, and the ravine up which we had advanced was now so full of rocks and bowlders as to render further progress on horseback impossible.

We lariated our horses, and proceeded to clamber over the immense granite bowlders that jutted from the side of the chasm. . . .

Following in the direction of the Tetons, which were hidden by intercepting rocks, after three hours' scrambling over yawning precipices, immense bowlders and vast snow-fields, we stood upon the summit of the ridge, at an elevation of 10,500 feet above ocean level. Expecting here to find ourselves upon a plateau which stretched to the base of the mountains, what was our disappointment at beholding, between us and it, an immense gorge with perpendicular sides, two thousand feet deep, and more than three thousand feet in width. A field of snow of measureless depth concealed the bottom of the chasm, and the hollow murmur of a creek which struck our ears seemed to come from the center of the earth. It must have been at least twelve hundred feet beneath the surface of the snow. On the right, in the midst of the snow-field, was a large lake of marvelous beauty. Upon its dark blue bosom swans and other aquatic fowl

*were sporting. . . . It is located in that portion of the Teton range
known among the early trappers as Jackson's Hole.*

*From our point of observation we discovered a smaller lake,
lying at the base of the Tetons, the surface of which was covered
with ice and snow. The perspiration occasioned by the severe
exercise we had taken soon disappeared before the chill blasts
from the mountains, and we found it necessary to shelter ourselves beneath some friendly rocks, whence we made a critical
examination of the Grand Teton, and the slopes ascending to
the ridge or plateau which isolates those three peaks from all
surrounding mountains. This immense bench, though not
divided by erosions, seems at some former time to have been the
base of one enormous mountain, the summit of which, by time
and the elements, has been divided into the three Teton peaks.
The view from where I stood was unlike any other I had ever
beheld: in all the elements of savage grandeur, I doubt if it
could be surpassed. Rocks and snow, with a few patches of
trees, composed the entire scenery; but these were arranged in
such fantastic forms and on so unlimited a scale as to defy all
effort at description. It was bewildering – overpowering – but
needed something beautiful, something upon which the eye
could rest pleasurably, to relieve the stern lineaments everywhere revealed.*

*The ascent of the Grand Teton, to look at the lofty peak of rug-
ged granite, seemed impossible. On either side, the angle at
which it rose was apparently a continuous precipice from top to
bottom. Even to clamber up the plateau to its base was a labor
full of difficulty. After crossing the glacier in the chasm beneath
us, we would have to select a pathway up the plateau between
the confronting ridges which everywhere swelled from its irregular sides, and crept in tortuous protuberances to its very summit. A mistake in the selection would be fatal to success, and we
would be compelled to return and commence anew, for we
could not cross laterally from one to another of these walled
ravines. Two hours of observation, if they failed to exalt, did not
dampen our courage, and we returned to our horses more
determined than ever that the enterprise should not fail for want
of effort. We selected a spot for a temporary camp, at the first
grass we met with while descending the cañon, intending from
that point to accomplish the ascent and return in a single day.*

Night was now approaching, and we hastened towards the camp. . . .

Langford mentions the photographer, William Henry Jackson, who is with the party, taking a number of pictures in the scenic vicinity of their camp.

Our ascending party, fourteen in number, being fully organized, we left camp at 10 o'clock, on the morning of the 28th July, and followed up the cañon nine miles, to the spot chosen for our temporary camp. Here we rested, and dined; after which Messrs. Adams and Taggart ascended a mountain on the left of the camp to a plateau 3,000 feet above it, from which they were able to determine the general features of the route to the base of the Great Teton. That peak rose majestically in the distance above a hundred smaller peaks, its sharp sides flecked with snow, and its bold gray summit half buried in fleecy clouds. It was indeed the lord of the empyrean. Pressing on toward it, they ascended a point of the plateau separated by an intervening chasm of nearly a thousand feet in depth from the elevation over which their pathway lay. The setting sun admonished them that they had barely time to return to camp before dark. They reached there in time to join the boys in a game of snow-balling, a singular amusement for the last days of July.

At half past four the next morning, the thermometer being 11° above zero, the party was aroused, and after partaking of a hearty breakfast, each man provided with an alpine staff, and a bacon sandwich for mid-day lunch, departed from camp, intent upon reaching the topmost summit of the loftiest Teton. The first two miles of the journey lay directly up the cañon, and over countless heaps of fallen trees. This tedious course of travel only terminated to give place to another, still more wearisome, through a ravine, and up a steep acclivity which we were enabled only to ascend by clinging to the points and angles of projecting rocks. Pausing at the summit to take breath, we saw lying between us and the first icy ridge a vast field of snow. Our aneroid showed that we were 9,000 feet above the ocean level – a height which entirely overlooked the walls of the cañon we had ascended, and took in an immense view of the surrounding country. Far as the eye could reach, looking northward, peak rose above peak, and range stretched beyond range, all glistening in the sunbeams like solid crystal. In the immediate vicinity of our position, the eye roamed over vast snow-fields, rocky chasms, straggling pine forests, and countless cascades.

The snow-field over which we next traveled, instead of the smoothness of a freshly covered plain, was as irregular, as full of hummocks and billows as the rocks beneath it and the storms which for years had swept over could possibly make it. It presented the appearance of an ocean frozen when the storm was at its height. Clambering over the first ridge, we traveled on in the direction of the second, which obstructed our view of the Tetons. Our route was over huge bowlders alternated with snow, and at this hour of the morning, before the sun had visited it, no traveling could be more unpleasant. We found our alpenstocks of infinite service, and we may thank them for the many falls we escaped upon the slippery surface, as well as for the comparative safety of many we made. Two miles of this kind of exercise brought us to the second ridge, which was composed of crumbling rock, and at least six hundred feet above the level of the field we had passed over. The view from this point was magnificent, but almost disheartening, from the increasing obstruction it presented to our progress. Another stretch of snow, rising to a sharp ridge, lay in front of us, at least five miles in length, across which, in our line of travel, was another upheaval of crumbling rock. On our right, a thousand feet below, was the open, blue Lake Cowan.

Resuming labor, some of our party crawled around the side of the gorge, preferring rather to cross over the snowy ridge on our left, than to descend the slippery side of the elevation upon which we stood. Several projecting ledges of crumbling rock lay between them and the snow, from which, as they passed over them, detached masses rolled down the bank endangering the lives of all below. Mr. Beckler, by a sudden jump, barely escaped being crushed by a large rock, which whistled by him like an avalanche. As he jumped he fell, and rolled down upon an out-cropping bowlder, receiving an injury which disabled him. Others of the party slid down the ridge unharmed, and encountered fewer difficulties in their journey along its base than its sides. The snow in the long ridge was at least two hundred and fifty feet in depth, and apparently as solid as the granite it covered. After a walk of more than a mile upon its glassy surface, we made a long descent to the right, and passed over a lake about 600 yards long by 200 wide, covered with ice from twelve to fifteen feet thick. There was nothing about this frozen water to indicate that it had ever been open. The ice which bound it, as well as the snow surrounding, seemed eternal. So pure and clear was this frozen surface, that one could see, even at its greatest thickness, the water gurgling beneath. At the distance from which we first saw it, we supposed this lake lay at the very base of the Tetons, but after we passed over it, there still stretched between us and that point two miles of corrugated snow. Still receding and receding, those lofty peaks seemed to move before us like the Israelites' pillar of cloud, and had we not seen this last snow-field actually creeping up to the top, and into the recesses of that lofty crest, from which the peaks shoot upward to the heavens, we should most willingly have turned our face campward from the present point of vision, and written over the whole expedition, "Impossible."

There is no greater wonder in mountain scenery on this continent, than the tendency it has to shorten distance to the eye and lengthen it to the feet. A range of mountains apparently ten miles distant may be fifty miles away. A plain, to all appearances as smooth as a floor, is often broken into deep ravines, yawning chasms, and formidable foot-hills. Everything in distance and surface is deceptive.

Beyond the lake we ascended the last rocky ridge, more precipitous than the others, to take a last look at the dreary landscape.

We seemed to be in the midst of an arctic region. All around was snow and rock and ice. Forward or backward everything was alike, bleak, barren and inhospitable; but our great labor was still unperformed. Encouraged by the certainty that we were upon the last of those great snow environments which lay at the feet of the mountains, we pushed onward to the base of the immense saddle between them. At this point several of the party, worn out with the day's exertions, and despairing of reaching the lofty summit which still towered five thousand feet in mockery above them, abandoned all further effort. Our kind surgeon, Dr. Reagles, had considerately accompanied us to the base of the ridge, provided with instruments and bandages in case of accident.

We lost no time in selecting from the numerous ravines that were made by the erosion of the friable rock from between the ascending granite ledges, such a one as we believed might be traversed to the top of the ridge without meeting lateral obstructions. Some of our party, mistaken in this, encountered when midway up the side a precipitous wall of granite, which made their return imperative. Five only of the company, after clambering over a snow-slide a thousand feet or more in width, reached the depression upon the right of the Grand Teton which we called "The Saddle." The ascent thus far had tested the endurance of all who made it. It was only difficult or dangerous to those who had selected the wrong passage through the ledges. We ate part of our luncheon while upon "The Saddle," which we reached about noon, and rested there a quarter of an hour beneath the shadow of the Great Teton. It seemed, as we looked up its erect sides, to challenge us to attempt its ascent. As we gazed upon the glaciers, the concavities, the precipices which now in more formidable aspect than ever presented themselves to us, we were almost ready to admit that the task we had undertaken was impossible to perform.

The mountain side, from the Saddle to the summit of the Grand Teton, arose at an angle of sixty degrees; broken by innumerable cavities and precipices.

Our leader, Captain Stevenson, had pushed on ahead, and when Messrs. Hamp, Spencer and the writer had reached "The Saddle," he was far up the mountain, lost to view in its intricacies. Our fears concerning him were allayed by occasionally seeing his footprints in the debris. Very soon after we commenced the ascent, we found ourselves clambering around projecting ledges of perpendicular rocks, inserting our fingers into crevices so far beyond us that we reached them with difficulty, and poising our weight upon shelves not exceeding two inches in width, jutting from the precipitous walls of gorges fifty to three hundred feet in depth. This toilsome process, which severely tested our nerves, was occasionally interrupted by large banks of snow, which had lodged upon some of the projections or in the concavities of the mountain side – in passing over the yielding surface of which we obtained tolerable foothold, unless, as was often the case, there was a groundwork of ice beneath. When this occurred, we found the climbing difficult and hazardous. In many places, the water from the melting snow had trickled through it, and congealed the lower surface. This, melting in turn, had worn long openings between the ice and the mountain side, from two to four feet in width, down which we could look two hundred feet or more. Great care was necessary to avoid slipping into these crevices. An occasional spur of rock or ice, connecting the ice-wall with the mountain, was all that held these patches of snow in their places. In Europe they would have been called glaciers. Distrustful as we all were of their permanency, we were taught, before our toil was ended, to wish there had been more of them. As a general thing, they were more easily surmounted than the bare rock precipices, though on one occasion they came near proving fatal to one of our party.

Mr. Hamp, fresh from his home in England, knew little of the properties of snow and ice, and at one of the critical points in our ascent, trusting too much to their support, slipped and fell. For a moment his destruction seemed inevitable, but with admirable dexterity he threw himself astride the icy ridge projecting from the mountain. Impelled by this movement, with one leg dangling in the crevice next the mountain side, and the other sweeping the snow outside the glacier, he slid with fearful rapidity, at an angle of forty-five degrees, for the distance of fifty feet, falling headlong into a huge pile of soft snow, which prevented his descent of a thousand feet or more down the precipitous side of the mountain. I saw him fall, and supposed he would be dashed to pieces. A moment afterwards he crawled from the friendly snow-heap and rejoined us unharmed, and we all united in a round of laughter, as thankful as it was hearty. This did not quiet that tremulousness of the nerves, of which extreme and sudden danger is so frequent a cause, and underlying our joy there was still a feeling of terror which we could not shake off. Pressing carefully forward, we attained a recess in the rocks, six hundred feet below the summit, where we halted.

While resting here, far above us, we heard the loud shouts of Captain Stevenson, which we answered. Soon he joined us, with the information that he had been arrested in his ascent, at a point two hundred feet above us, by an intervening rock, just too high for him to scale. It was perpendicular, and surmounted by a wide sheet of ice stretching upward towards the summit, and covered with snow. He had made several ineffectual efforts to reach the overhanging edge of the rock, and at one time lost his foothold, his entire weight coming upon his hands while he hung with his face to the wall. It was impossible without a leap to reach a standing place, and by loosening his hold without one he would drop several hundred feet down the mountain. Fortunately, there was a coating of ice and snow, which reached midway from his feet to his arms, and into this, by repeated kicks with the toe of his boot, he worked an indentation that afforded a poise for one foot. This enabled him to spring on one side to a narrow bench of rock, where he was safe.

We had periled life and limb to little purpose, if the small matter of five hundred feet was to prevent the accomplishment of our task. We determined, therefore, to ascend with Captain Stevenson, and make another effort to scale the rock. When I saw the perilous position from which he had escaped, I could not but regard his preservation as almost miraculous. In spite of nervous exhaustion, Mr. Hamp had persevered in the attempt to climb the mountain, but as all upward progress from this point was extremely hazardous, he and Mr. Spencer were persuaded to avail themselves of a foot-hold in the rocks, while Captain Stevenson and I made a last essay to reach the pinnacle.

A rope which I had brought with me, cast over a slight projection above our heads, enabled me to draw myself up so as to fix my hands in a crevice of the rock, and then, with my feet resting on the shoulders of Captain Stevenson, I easily clambered to the top. Letting the rope down to Captain Stevenson, he grasped it firmly, and by the aid of his staff soon worked his way to my side. The shelving expanse of ice, overlying the rocky surface at an angle of 70°, and fastened to it by slight arms of the same brittle material, now presented an obstacle apparently insurmountable. Beside the danger of incurring a slide which would insure a rapid descent to the base of the mountain, there was the other risk, that the frail fastenings which held the ice-sheet to the rocks might give way while we were crawling over it, and the whole field be carried with us down the terrible precipice. But the top was just before us, not three hundred feet away, and we preferred the risk to an abandonment of the task. Laying hold of the rocky points at the side of the ice-sheet, we broke with our feet in its surface a series of steps, up which we ascended, at an angle deflecting not more than twenty degrees from a vertical line, one hundred and seventy-five feet, to its topmost junction with the rock.

The peril to which this performance exposed us was now fully revealed, and had we seen it at the foot of the ice-sheet, the whole world would not have tempted us to the effort we had made. Why the entire mass of ice, yielding to our exertions, was not detached from its slender fastenings and hurled down the mountain is a mystery. On looking down through the space which separated it from the rock, I could see half a dozen icy tentacles, all of small size, reaching from wall to wall. Seemingly the weight of a bird would have loosened the entire field. We felt, as we planted our feet on the solid mountain, that we had escaped a great peril – and quenching our thirst from one of the numerous little rivulets which trickled down the rock, set resolutely at work to clamber over the fragments and piles of granite which lay between us and the summit. This was more tedious than difficult, but we were amply rewarded when, at three p.m., after ten hours of the severest labor of my life, we stepped upon the highest point of the Grand Teton. . . .

The several pinnacles of the Grand Teton seen from the valley seem of equal height, but the inequality in this respect was very apparent at the top. The main summit, separated by erosions from the surrounding knobs, embraced an irregular area of thirty by forty feet. Exposure to the winds kept it free from snow and ice, and its bald, denuded head was worn smooth by the elemental warfare waged around it. With the unshorn beams of a summer sun shining full upon us, we were obliged to don our overcoats for protection against the cold mountain breeze. Indeed, so light was the atmosphere that our respiration from its frequency became almost burdensome, and we experienced, in no slight degree, how at such an elevation one could at a single exposure suffer the opposite intensities of heat and cold. Above the ice-belt, over which we had made such a perilous ascent, we saw in the debris the fresh track of that American Ibex, the mountain sheep – the only animal known to clamber up the sides of our loftiest peaks. Flowers also, of beauteous hue, and delicate fragrance, peeped through the snow, wherever a rocky jut had penetrated the icy surface.

On the top of an adjacent pinnacle, but little lower than the one we occupied, we found a circular enclosure, six feet in diameter, composed of granite slabs, set up endwise, about five feet in height. It was evidently intended, by whomsoever built, as a protection against the wind, and we were only too glad to avail ourselves of it while we finished our luncheon. On entering it we found ourselves a foot deep in the detritus, which had been worn by the canker of time from the surrounding walls. . . .

Far away on the northern horizon, scarcely distinguishable from the clouds with which they are intermingled, we saw the Belt, Madison and Main Rocky ranges, from which long, lateral spurs stretch down on either side, and close up the immense amphitheater by uniting with the Malade Range on the south. Within this vast enclosure, and more immediately beneath us, we overlooked the valley of the Snake, the emerald surface of Pierre's Hole with its mountain surroundings, the dark defile leading into Jackson's Hole, and Jackson and DeLacy lakes, Madison Lake, the source of the Snake River – Henry's Lake, the source of the North Fork, and afar off, beyond these, the cloud defined peaks of the Wind River mountains, and the peaks surrounding the great lake of the Yellowstone. Our elevation was so great that the valley beneath us, filled as it was with knobs and cañons and foot-hills, had the appearance of a vast and level plain, stretching away to, and imperceptibly blending with the distant mountains.

We gazed upon the varied beauties of this wondrous panorama until reminded by the position of the sun that we had scarcely time to effect our descent, and return to camp before dark. Great caution was necessary while passing down the ice belt lest it should become detached, but it was our only passage-way to the bottom, and we were greatly relieved when we reached in safety the cranny occupied by Hamp and Spencer. At this point Captain Stevenson separated from us, and was the first to reach the base of the mountain. We clambered over the rocks and precipices with all possible expedition, and stood in safety upon the saddle, just as the sun was setting.

The interval between sunset and evening in these high altitudes is very brief, and we had yet to descend the ridge. In our haste to accomplish this, we selected a pathway between ledges too abrupt to scale, which led directly to a precipice, thirty-five feet in height, at the base of which was a mass of granite fragments and debris from three to four feet deep. We were now in a dilemma. Either we must pass the declivity or re-ascend the steep mountain side, five hundred feet or more, and select another passage. Crawling to the edge, I saw at a distance of twenty-five feet a jutting point, which would afford standing room for a single person, and about eight feet below it, a smaller projection, too sharp on the face for a safe foothold. Passing the rope alternately around the bodies of my comrades, I let them down the perpendicular wall to the base, then throwing the middle of the rope over a projecting crag, and seizing the two ends, I lowered myself to the narrow shelf first described, whence a well-directed leap enabled me to poise myself on the smaller projection below, and gather for a final jump into the pile of debris, where my comrades stood. Our safe descent being thus accomplished, we had yet the snowfields, ridges and gorges to traverse, before we arrived in camp. Fatigued with the exercise of ascending and descending the Teton, the passage of these ridges was the most exhaustive effort of our lives. It was after nine o'clock, and very dark, when we first caught sight of our campfire, afar down the chasm. After a rough walk over prostrate trunks, through deep depressions, amid pine thickets, climbing bowlders, penetrating chaparral, wading streams – at just thirty minutes past ten, when all our comrades had thought some serious and perhaps fatal accident had befallen us, we entered camp amid cordial greetings and shouts of delight. The joy of reunion, after even so brief a separation, was as earnest and sincere as if we had been parted a year.

Chapter XIII

LAVA BEDS
1873

from the correspondence of Robert Bogart,
reporter for the San Francisco Chronicle,
March 2, 1873

In late 1872, war broke out between settlers and the Modoc Indians of northern California. During the conflict, Captain Jack and his Modoc followers retreated from their Lost River homeland across Tule Lake into the Lava Beds. As is clear from the following narrative, this was an excellent defensive stronghold to hold off attacks. For in January, 1873, the Modoc warriors were able to inflict heavy losses upon an invading American Army at the Stronghold Battle. There was an attempt later among representatives on both sides to negotiate a peaceful settlement. To this end, it was agreed that a Peace Commission would be allowed to enter the Modoc stronghold. The newspaper correspondent, Robert Bogart, accompanies the group and reports upon the proceedings. He writes a vivid description of the region as they are led into the Lava Beds. Although, other whites had entered the area, such as the many soldiers who perished in the Stronghold Battle, it is one of the earliest descriptions of the Lava Beds. In the report, whenever Robert Bogart refers to the Chronicle correspondent, he is referring to himself.

. . . Mr. Steele made preparations to start on the journey the next morning. He selected to accompany him Bogus Charley, the Indian who came out the other day; John A. Fairchild, Frank G. Riddle, and the Modoc squaw with whom the latter lives – these two to act as interpreters; the Chronicle War Correspondent and the Secretary of the Peace Commission. The night before the party packed their traps for the trip. As they would have to spend a night in the lava bed, they took their blankets, plenty of warm clothing, a good stock of provisions and provender for their horses. These were packed on a horse, the region where Jack has his lair being utterly inaccessible to anything on wheels. When the morning broke, a fierce snowstorm was raging, and the wind blew out from the north in furi-

ous blasts. Time was precious, though, and Mr. Steele would not defer the trip, so about 9 o'clock the whole party set out. The distance from Fairchild's to Jack's rocky camp is twenty-five miles over the roughest road, or rather trail, that I ever saw or dreamed of. The first ten miles is traveled by the regular Lost River wagon road, which is pretty fair, but after that the trail is taken, and then comes the hard part of the journey: over bluffs whose steepness makes it a miracle that anything animate can ever descend them; through rocky gorges, that to look at one thinks it impossible for even a mountain sheep to find a foothold; through sagebrush and across lava rock plains, and into narrow ravines and caverns, the narrow path leads and winds and turns till one is lost in the rugged labyrinth. Almost every hour we were obliged to dismount and lead the horses through some yawning rocky chasm, or down a steep declivity that no mounted man could descend. The horses, though, were sure-footed and got through such places safely, though very slowly. Twelve miles of such perilous travel brought us to the summit of the last bluff before descending to the edge of the great bed of scoria. . . . We reached this point at 4 o'clock. The snowstorm had broken away, and the setting sun, directly behind us, shed a brilliant glare over the rocky valley below. The scene was one of the grandest I ever saw. The point where we stood on the bluff was directly at the southwestern corner of Tule Lake. From our position the lake was immediately to the left, its waters washing the base of the hill beneath us. Beyond, slightly to the left and across the glassy sheet of water, rose a range of high mountains, imbedded in a fleecy snow covering, and reflecting back the golden sunlight into the mirror-like surface at their foot. Immediately in front and due east was the famed lava bed, of which so much has been said and written. As far as the eye could reach in one direction, and back to the rugged volcanic hills to the southward, this remarkable formation extended from our position at least one thousand feet above it. It had merely the appearance of a sagebrush plain as level as a marble floor. Not a single unevenness could be detected, except away off miles away on the lake shore the faintest suspicion of a ridge showed itself, but it was so slight that at first glance it failed to catch the eye. Fairchild pointed out this little break in the almost painful regularity of the surface, and said that this was the scene of Jack's triumph. This is the place in which he defied the power of all the troops on the Pacific Coast. The party stood looking at the wonderful scene for fifteen minutes, and then, again dismounting, prepared to descend the steep slope. A narrow trail led down in a zigzag direction, and over this the horses had to be led slowly, step by step. Down, down we went, groping cautiously, expecting almost every instant that an unlucky slip or a careless step would send some horse and leader whirling down the sharp incline. Fifteen minutes of this perilous work, in which no one dared scarcely cast his eyes off his own or his horse's feet, and we were at the edge of the lava.

But what a change! What from the summit seemed a level plain was now transformed to ridges, mounds and piles of hard, jagged, flinty rocks, reaching as far as the eye could see. To pass over them seemed impossible. To go through and around them appeared like a task that a man would hardly undertake, to say nothing of a horse; but a little trail led off for a hundred yards or so and then was lost behind a ridge of rocks, and into this the Indian, Bogus Charley, boldly led the way. . . . The trail was narrow, crooked, and so filled with lava rocks that the horses had difficulty in finding places to put their feet; hence the progress was slow and tedious. Once in a while a clear place was found on the edge of the lake, but only for a few yards, and then the path led off again into the hard, jagged scoria, and through the thick, tangled sagebrush. Whenever a rise in the surface was reached we could see the ridge where Jack's camp lay, rising higher and higher, and something of its terrible grandeur became apparent. We had gone a mile or more through this bed, when suddenly coming where the narrow trail turned around a ledge, we came full upon an Indian, Captain Jack's outpost sentinel. The Indian had seen us from behind a rock long before we had seen him, but discovering Charley at the head of the file of horsemen, he had made no sign until we were well up. Then he came out into the trail and advanced to meet us. When Charley rode up he spoke a few words and sent him across the rocks by a cut-off, to apprise Jack who it was; for, of course, every Indian in the camp had seen the party before they began to descend the bluff. The Indian bounded off like a deer when he learned that it was Squire Steele, and long before we reached the camp every Indian there knew that we were friends, so nothing further was seen of sentinels or lookouts, though I have no doubt we passed several.

As we passed along, Fairchild called our attention to many points of interest; the place where he and Dorris held their first

*interview with Jack in December last – the one attended with so
much peril; also where the troops were formed for the last fight,
and the positions occupied by the several companies; the bluffs
they carried and those they didn't carry; where he and his men
passed around the edge of the lake and formed their junction
with Bernard, and many other things calculated to give one a
complete understanding of that lamentable failure to drive Jack
from his stronghold. Finally the big ledge was reached; and
turning up from the lake into a steep rocky ravine, where the
trail was so narrow that our stirrups scraped the flinty bowlders
and the horses were obliged to creep along, Charley announced
that we were within 300 yards of the Indian stronghold. Riding
along slowly and with almost bated breath – for the party now
began to realize their position – some of the horses gave a
snort, and pricking up their ears stopped. The Chronicle correspondent's horse, which was immediately behind Charley's
pony, seemed particularly averse to going ahead; and as his
rider could see nothing to frighten him, he said, "Charley,
what's the matter? What does this horse see?" "Oh! nothing. I
guess he smell dead soldier there in rocks. We pile up rocks
there over two or three, and that what scare him. Come along."
After another hundred yards were passed, the trail widened a
little, and we began to see signs of the proximity of Jack's camp.
Rounding a turn in the ravine we saw on a high ledge ahead the
Indian battle-flag pole planted. The flag that floated from it was
the tail of a wolf, and as it dangled back and forth in the wind it
seemed the most significant war banner I had ever seen. A few
minutes more and the party made a sharp turn in the rocks,
which brought them suddenly on the Indian camp.*

*The whole force was out waiting for us in front of their little
houses, which were huddled together like bee hives. For the
next five minutes the scene was lively. Men, women and naked
children came running up to see us dismount, and then began
such a hand-shaking as is only seen at a Presidential levee. The
warriors were all there: Scar-faced Charley, Shack Nasty Jim,
Hocker Jim, the Doctor, old Schonchin, Black Jim, Long Jim,
and dozens of others more or less noted. Captain Jack was ill in
his cave and could not come, but he had sent word to the "Bos-
ton men" that he wanted to see them as soon as they had had
their supper, and his message was delivered by Scar-Face. As
soon as Steele dismounted, all the Indians were delighted to see
him, and huddled around him like children. They were all*

armed with revolvers, but their guns had been put away, Bogus Charley having sent them word by the scout that the whites were unarmed. They were probably too proud to make a display of their strength, when they knew we trusted them completely. After much hand-shaking and a great display of curiosity on all sides, the Indians gave way and some of them showed us where to put the horses for the night. Hocker Jim led the pack-horse and the rest followed. The place selected was a little further up the ravine, where a smooth, level place was found, and here they were fed and tethered for the night. . . . While Mrs. Riddle was fixing the supper the Chronicle man went outside the tent, ostensibly to look after his horse, but really to get a look at the Indian stronghold before night set in. To the unmilitary eye of the correspondent the place seemed absolutely impregnable. The principal portion of the camp is situated in a huge opening or widening of the ravine, of perhaps an acre in area. On all sides of this opening, which seems more like a huge washbowl than anything else, the natural wall rises a hundred feet or more; but it is easily scaled, for the inner side is inclined and the rocks are sharp and jut out all over it. Once in this basin there is but one open way out, and that is by the trail we entered. There are other ways out, but they are by tunnels leading to the many caves or sink-holes in another part of the lava bed, and which will be more fully described further. On the outside of this basin there is a succession of ridges as high as that which encloses it, but these do not extend all the way around. To the west of the basin is a flat, table-like surface of lava, extending from the very summit of the rim clear back for more than a mile. In this level place are the sink-holes or caves formed thousands of years ago, perhaps in the cooling of this immense body of molten earth. The openings of the holes are very small; indeed, one does not see them until he has almost fallen in. But they widen as they go down, and their sides being sloping, one can pick his way to the bottom without difficulty. Most of these caves are connected with each other and with the large basin by subterranean passages, so that one can go for half a mile in the bed without coming to the surface at all. This is of incalculable benefit in defending the stronghold, for one man can keep a hundred at bay almost anywhere in it without fear of being smoked out or having his retreat cut off.

After supper, which, by the way, was shared with a keen relish by about a dozen naked Indian babies, Bogus Charley came and said he would conduct us to Captain Jack. So the whole party gathered up their blankets and followed. Charley led the way up one side of the basin, through a little trail, not easy of ascent by unpracticed feet, and across the level place about fifty yards, when we came suddenly to the mouth of a pit-hole at least forty feet deep. The hole inclined as it led downward, and at the bottom widened and formed a perfect cave, extending under the rock at least fifty feet. At the mouth of the cave proper, but yet thirty or forty feet below the surface, a piece of canvas was stretched. This was Captain Jack's front door, and the cave behind it was his abiding place – the palace of the Modoc King. Behind the canvas we could see a bright fire burning and nearly the whole tribe encircled around it ready for the talk, which they knew was to come. The descent into the cave was somewhat perilous, but by a vigorous clinging to the rocks and careful stepping we managed to reach the canvas. Then, throwing that back, we stood in the presence of Captain Jack. . . .

These peace efforts ultimately failed when the Modocs murdered a future party of peace commissioners in April. In a second attack on the Stronghold, the Modocs retreated from the area when their supply of water was cut off. Finally, the Modocs surrendered in June of 1873 and were transplanted to a reservation in Oklahoma. Captain Jack and some other leaders were hanged.

Chapter XIV

BLACK HILLS
1874

from Report of a Reconnaissance
of the Black Hills of Dakota
by Bvt. Lieut. Colonel William Ludlow

The Black Hills had been recognized by treaty as a homeland for the Sioux. The discovery of gold there, however, confirmed by the following expedition led by General Custer, brought an end to this state of affairs. The military reconnaissance started from Ft. Lincoln, near present-day Bismarck, North Dakota, and headed southwestward, skirting past the Little Missouri Badlands and just missing Devils Tower. The selection begins with the expedition entering the heart of the Black Hills from the west side.

Photos taken during Custer's 1874 Black Hills
Expedition

July 25 – The course ascended the valley to the southeast; the hills were limestone covered with pine. . . . The valley . . . filled with the greatest profusion of wildflowers, in almost incredible numbers and variety, General Custer named Floral Valley. As we ascended through these beds of color, the hills became lower, and tamarack and spruce appeared on the slopes. . . . An old and deeply cut lodge-trail ran up the valley, and, halting the command, the valleys leading out of Floral Valley were explored. . . . Near the highest point many old camps and abandoned lodge-poles were seen. Pursuing the lodge-trail a spring was reached, the waters of which flowed north and east. The fog, which had been sweeping up from the eastward, became very dense. The flowers were if anything more abundant than in the morning, the hills . . . covered with pine and aspen, tamarack and spruce. The wood and open seemed to share the country about equally. All vegetation was luxuriant and fresh, and we had no doubt that a portion, at least, of the park country we were in search of had been reached. The valleys radiated in all directions, connecting with each other, and a more beautiful wild country could not be imagined. Signs of bear and deer were abundant, and the woods frequently resounded with the clangorous cry of the crane. July 26 – Still ascending Floral Valley, the divide was reached, and we almost insensibly passed into the valley of another stream, falling rapidly to the southeast. The hills became gradually higher and the valley wider. . . . From a high hill near camp, the first well-defined view was gained of Harney's Peak, twenty miles to the southeast. The position of this peak, on the southeast slope of the hills, was known from Warren's map. We were nearly in the heart of the unexplored portion of the hills. . . . The high limestone ridges surrounding the camp had weathered into castellated forms of considerable grandeur and beauty, and suggested the name of Castle Valley. The valley itself was luxuriantly rich and grassy, a fine stream meandering through it. . . . July 27 – The command remained in camp, to give time to examine the neighboring country, and the gold-hunters were very busy all day with shovel and pan exploring the streams. Several surveying parties were sent out in various directions. Each tributary valley had its springs and little streams; was heavily grassed and often filled with flowers. The grass in places was as high as a horse's shoulder. . . . July 28 – After dinner made a reconnaissance with General Custer up the creek below camp. A good road was found up the valley, which is heavily grassed and flowered for two and one-half miles. Then ascended a hill on the left and reached, through some timber, the open prairie I was on in the afternoon. Harney's Peak was visible from the top of a high, bare hill, and the sun having just set, we were in a few minutes well rewarded for the ride of five miles. The moon was rising just over the southern shoulder of Harney, and masked by heavy clouds. A patch of bright blood-red flame was first seen, looking like a brilliant fire, and soon after another, so far from the first that it was difficult to connect the two. A portion of the moon's disk became presently visible, and the origin of the flame was apparent. While it lasted the sight was superb. The moon's mass looked enormous and blood-red, with only portions of its surface visible, while the clouds just above and to the left, colored by the flame, resembled smoke drifting from an immense conflagration. The moon soon buried herself completely in the clouds, and under a rapidly darkening sky we returned to camp. . . . July 30 – We traveled all day through a beautiful pastoral country, half wood, half glade, full of deer and abundantly grassed. Harney's Peak was passed eight or nine miles on the left. A few high hills were scattered about. Granite appeared for the first time, and the range of which Harney is the chief, appeared granitic and very rugged. . . .

July 31 – The command remained in camp, while surveying parties were sent out, and the gold hunters redoubled their efforts. General Custer and myself, with Professors Winchell and Donaldson and Mr. Wood, escorted by a company of cavalry, set out to ascend Harney. A rough ride of eight or nine miles over high hills and heavily-timbered ravines, in some of which birch was seen for the first time, brought us to the foot of a granite elevation with a creek flowing eastward. . . . Leaving the horses at the foot of the clear granite, the ascent was made on foot. Halting to rest and lunch, another summit, two or three miles west, was seen, rising higher than the one we were on. Reaching the summit of this, still another, several hundred feet higher, and a mile more west, showed that we had more work to do. A stiff climb brought us to the top, whence nothing more lofty could be seen, and we stood on the most elevated portion of the hills some 9,700 feet above the sea, except that alongside us rose a mass of granite 40 feet in height, with perpendicular sides that forbade an attempt to scale them without the aid of ropes and ladders. A stunted spruce was growing under its pro-

tection, and a few ferns and harebells obtained sustenance near by. The view was superb, extending over the intervening peaks and hills to a broad expanse of prairie and hills from north by east round to southwest. The course of the Forks of the Cheyenne could be distinctly traced, and a dim line visible to the southeast was even thought to be the hills of White River, fifty or sixty miles distant. Bear Butte, forty-odd miles to the north, was again seen over the wooded ranges; and all but Inyan Kara of the principal peaks were in view. Two of the prominent ones I have named for General Terry and General Custer. The return to camp was a struggle against almost every possible obstacle – rocks, creeks, marshes, willow and aspen thickets, pine timber, dead and fallen trees, steep hillsides and precipitous ravines. Every difficulty multiplied by the darkness, and with only the stars for a guide, camp was finally reached at 1:30 in the morning.

Chapter XV

OLYMPIC
1885

from "O'Neil's Exploration"
in Seattle Press, *July 16, 1890*

In 1890, the year of the census that marked the official closing of the frontier, Seattle newspapers were reporting a number of explorations in the Olympic Mountains. Most were taking place in the years 1889 and 1890. One, however, occurred in 1885, and stands as the first written account of an expedition into the Olympic interior. For a long time, shipmen had spotted the mountains of Olympus from the sea and strait that surround it. Settlement had come to the nearby ports, but the topography of the Olympics was still a mystery. The O'Neil expedition of 1885 cut a path from Port Angeles into the northeastern portion of the present park. He apparently ascended into the northern reaches of Hurricane Ridge, and more or less followed the alpine country to Obstruction Point and well beyond. Occasional forays were made into the adjoining river and stream valleys before Lieutenant O'Neil was ordered to return to post.

While stationed at Fort Townsend in 1884 and 1885 I was attracted by the grand noble front of the Jupiter hills, rising with their boldness and abruptness, presenting a seemingly impenetrable barrier to the farther advance of man and civilization.

Inquiries about them elicited very little reliable information, and it seemed to me that Jupiter hills and the Olympic mountains were almost as unknown to us as the wilds of Alaska.

A few bold, adventurous spirits, for the sake of a shot at game, or lured on by the thought of mineral wealth, had made some endeavors to penetrate the outer barrier of forest and under brush, and the steep ridges and passes of the interior, but their efforts seemed crowned with so little success that their undertakings were either given up or the results so barren that the termination of their adventures are unknown to us.

Photos taken W. H. Illingworth

After spending a good deal of time and work clearing a path through the tangled underbrush, the group breaks through into the high country.

Mr. Smith and myself followed an elk trail for about six miles and came into a most beautiful valley, surrounded by lofty peaks, completely enclosed by the mountains, and forming one of the finest grazing grounds I have ever seen. These mountains seem to be a distinct range. . . .

Passing through this valley and climbing a steep ascent on the south, after a toilsome march we reached the summit of Victor pass, and here the scene changes. Looking east, west and south mountains, free from timber, some covered with snow, rise in wild, broken confusion. The grandest sight is of a cluster of mountains about thirty miles or so due south of Freshwater Bay. This cluster I set down as Mount Olympus. For this mountain, famous as it is, seems to be a source of mystery as to where it really is located; sailing around on the ocean a mountain, or rather cluster of peaks, is seen, and very probably some mariner gave that name to these. I have never found or heard of any one who had, up to this time, been on or near it. This cluster is snow covered, and seems to be the center of a mountain range, the formation of which much resembles a coil. It has no pronounced direction, but seems to circle on itself, and guard, as the walls of a citadel, the great gem, the pride of the particular territory, its central peaks. . . . There seems to be a river running by the outer circle, whose canyon is lost to sight in the center of the mountains. This river I pronounced to be the Elwha. . . .

While in the mountains and valleys, the group hunts elk and bear. At night, they often hear the panther's cry. The steep topography creates dangers and mishaps.

Late in the afternoon, while trying to get from a mountain to the valley below and following the bed of a dry creek, whose banks were covered with brushes, which overhanging, concealed the pathway to a great extent, I lost my footing and fell. The incline was so great that my fall started the loose dirt, and after sliding with it some distance my pack caught between two rocks and stopped my headway for the moment. This gave me time to recover myself, and with the assistance of the shrubbery on the bank I pulled myself out. Glancing around, I discovered that just below me, and not ten feet away, was a fall where, in the spring, I suppose, the water made a magnificent jump. The fall was at least 50 feet deep, and the huge, ungainly boulders at its base did not look inviting. With great difficulty I got below the falls, and made the creek again.

The scenery in these mountains is grand – waterfalls and canyons, valleys, and snow-covered mountains. One fall attracted my special attention. It was of a stream about 10 feet wide, with a descent of about 150 feet, then seething and foaming for a short distance, made another leap nearly as large as the first. Large fields of ice and snow were often passed, and trees dotting a landscape of green in the valleys.

During the several days we traveled on this trip we passed numerous bands of elk and small game in great plenty. They were all so tame and almost confiding that it was like going into a herd of domestic cattle, selecting your beast and killing him. . . .

While traveling in the valley you come every now and then to what I called an elk yard, the winter home of the elk. These yards are sometimes hundreds of acres in extent. The trees are denuded of their bark, the bushes cut down and the ground as trampled as the picket ground of a cavalry troop. They seem to be always found on the southern slope of a ridge or mountain, and so hemmed in that they are, to a great extent, protected on all sides. Elk are generally found in the valleys in the morning and evening. During the heat of the day they climb a mountainside and rest in a cool snowfield. . . .

Passing this we continued on our way towards a peak from which I wished to take observations. This we gained about noon time, and ascended with some difficulty. From here I could see Mounts Baker and Rainier rising in their massive grandeur. Mounts Constance, Adams and St. Helens were distinctly visible, as was also the Sister Peaks of the Sherman Miles range . . . Johnson and myself in making our way back came to the snow field, in which rises the east fork of the Elwha.

Here I had an irresistible urge to cross and not follow the trail around the ridge, which was much longer; so leaving Johnson with instructions to watch me for a signal to come if it was thought best, or to go around by trail if not, I started. The snow was hard packed and in many places pure ice, very slippery about half way down, and the incline was rather steep. Here a crevasse about 10 feet wide yawned before me. It was impossible even to estimate its depth; to return, was on account of the steepness of the grade, the smoothness of the ice and lack of spikes in our shoes, impossible. So taking the only alternative I leapt it. In alighting, I lost my balance and fell. Sliding down, I reached the bottom much quicker and more bruised than I had anticipated. But on recovering, I immediately signaled to Johnson to go back by trail.

He was much excited by my mishap, and in trying to come to me as quickly as possible attempted a short cut, but got bewildered among the many ravines and wandered away, lost. After waiting a sufficient time for him to come up, I slowly made my way to camp, thinking to find him there; but when I found the camp deserted, my anxiety was aroused. Lighting huge fires on all the points around, I sought by this means to show him to camp. The night slowly passed but no Johnson came. After wandering around firing off my gun and doing all things else that could possibly attract attention, I started for the pack train camp with the hope of finding him there, but I was disappointed. Everyone was sent out to look for the missing man, thinking that he might have fallen and injured himself, but on searching every part of the trail over which we had passed, we felt that he was lost and his only chance of safety lay in his own judgment. . . . After several days of fruitless search no signs of Johnson were found.

When I arrived at camp I found a courier with an order directing me to proceed to Fort Leavenworth for duty. I delayed as long as I possibly could looking for our lost man. Leaving the party in charge of Sergeant Weagraff to continue the search, I left for Port Angeles and on the 26th of August took the boat to return.

Johnson followed down the Elwha River and managed to find his way back to the settlements. O'Neil would return to the Olympics in 1890 to explore further.

Chapter XVI

BIG BEND
1899

from "Running the Cañons of the Rio Grande"
in Century Magazine, *Jan. 1901*
by Robert T. Hill, U.S.G.S.

Since the boundary survey of 1852, the Big Bend region was not completely unexplored. In 1859-60, an experiment was made using camels to carry supplies through the deserts of America. One of these camel expeditions passed through Dog Canyon into Big Bend. Camels proved to be more durable pack animals through desert terrain than the more popular mules and horses. However, the railroads were soon built and there was no follow-up on the experiment. In 1881, Captain Nevill led another surveying trip through some of the river canyons of the Big Bend region. Not until 1899 (as told in the following article) were all the canyons of the Big Bend successfully navigated. These include the canyons of the present-day Big Bend Ranch State Park (Murderers Canyon and Black Rock Canyon in the report), Big Bend National Park and the Lower Canyons beyond (still one of the most remote regions in the lower 48.

The author and leader of the expedition discusses how the canyons of the Big Bend had not yet been fully explored and described. He presents an overall picture of the hard and strange landscape of the Big Bend region, and the expected dangers of the planned expedition. Boats, supplies and crew had to be transported by rail and wagon to the border town of Presidio, where the river trip would begin.

At noon, October 5, 1899, we pushed out into the river at Presidio, and started on our long journey into the unknown. I do not claim to be the only man who has traveled the tortuous and dangerous channel of the frontier stream; for one man, and one only, James MacMahon, has made at least three trips down the river. Mine, however, was the first exploring expedition to pass the entire length of the cañons, and, with the exception of MacMahon's, was the only attempt that succeeded. Others, like Gano and Neville, have passed the fearful twelve miles of the Grand Cañon de Santa Helena. The only government expedi-

tion, the International Boundary Survey, pronounced the cañons impassable, and gave up the attempt to survey them, except the lower hundred miles of the course, which Lieutenant Micheler passed through.

MacMahon was interested neither in science, exploration, nor travel. He ventured the stream without knowledge of its dangers, and merely because, as a lifelong hunter and trapper, he knew that the beaver probably lived along its unmolested banks. These animals alone interested him, and a map made by him, if he could make such a thing, would note only beaver banks and danger spots, for these were all that he saw. Unguided and alone, he loaded his boats with traps, placed it in the stream, and slowly drifted down to Del Rio, braving a thousand dangers and making the first successful passage. This man, whose name has perhaps never before appeared in print, had spent his long life in such exploits, and is one of the few old-time trappers still to be found in the West.

The finding of MacMahon was the first of the dozen fortuitous circumstances, which made my trip possible, and there was not a day that his knowledge of the dangers of the stream did not save us from loss and destruction. Always kind and unobtrusive, he was as cautious as a cat, being at times apparently over-careful. He was ever on the lookout for a safe channel in the treacherous current, beaver slides on the banks, and border Mexicans in the bushes.

Hardly had we begun to enjoy the pleasant sensation of drifting down the stream when a roaring noise was heard ahead. This came from seething and dangerous torrents of water foaming over huge rounded boulders of volcanic rock which everywhere form the bottom of the river. Reaching these rapids, we had to get out of the boats and wade beside them, pushing them off or over the stones, or holding them back by the stern-lines. This process had to be repeated many times a day for the entire distance, and, as a consequence, all hands were constantly wet. The swift current and uncertain footing of the hidden rocks make these rapids very dangerous. A loss of balance or a fall meant almost certain death. It was our very good fortune not to upset a boat or lose a man. Ware was especially cautious at such places, for only a year before, while upon a hunting and *fishing expedition of the Lower Rio Grande, his companion had been drowned in a place of this character.*

The first twenty miles lay through a low, broken desert country. The river banks were of muddy silt, with here and there a lone cottonwood or willow. Ahead of us loomed the Bofecillos Mountains of Texas and the San Carlos Sierra of Mexico, closing in upon the river.

This region is infested by thieves and murderers, and MacMahon was watchful. Our loaded rifles lay beside our oars, and every bush and stone was closely scanned for men in ambush. The special objects of terror were a famous Mexican, Alvarado, and his associates. Alvarado possessed a mustache one side of which was white and the other black. From this he was called "Old White Lip." To his hand had been charged the murder of several men who had attempted the river route, and it was he who, MacMahon avowed, the year before had riddled his sleeping camp with rifle balls. At night we secreted our camps in thickets of carrizo, a kind of cane which grew on the low sand banks, and each man slept with a loaded Winchester beneath his pillow.

The second morning we reached the appropriately named village of Polvo ("dust"), the last settlement for one hundred and fifty miles. It consists of half a dozen dreary adobe houses on a mud bank, the remains of the old United States military post of Fort Leaton. Here the hospitable storekeeper, an agreeable white man who for some unknown reason had chosen this dreary place of exile, entertained us by showing us the splotches of blood upon the floor and wall behind his counter, where his predecessor had been robbed and murdered the year before, supposedly by Alvarado and his friends. Before I saw this gruesome sight I had not entertained sufficient respect for MacMahon's precautions. Thereafter I was more careful to keep my firearms handy. While at this store, remarks were made by some of my men which led me to suspect that they were secretly planning to retaliate upon Alvarado. Here was a possible motive for undertaking a journey the dangers of which they depicted in vigorous terms. In vain I protested that this expedition was for scientific purposes, and not for vengeance. They only replied that they would shoot Alvarado on sight, "like any other varmint."

A few miles below Polvo the huge chocolate-colored cliffs and domes of the Bofecillos Mountains began to overhang the river, and before night we entered the first of the series of cañons of the Rio Grande, in which we were to be entombed for the succeeding weeks. This bears the cheerful name of Murderer's Cañon, for here, a year or two before, the body of a supposed victim of Alvarado was found lodged on a sandbar. . . .

Toward sunset I scaled a break in the cañon to reach the upland and obtain a lookout. Above the narrow alluvial bench forming the green ribbon of river verdure I suddenly came upon the stony, soil-less hills forming the matrix out of which the valley is cut, glaring in the brilliant sunshine and covered with the mocking desert flora. The sight of this aridity almost within reach of the torrent of life-giving waters below, the blessing of which it was never to receive, was shocking and repulsive. It also recalled a danger which ever after haunted us. Should we lose our boats and escape the cañons, what chance for life should we have in crossing these merciless, waterless wastes of thorn for a hundred miles or more to food and succor?

Below the mouth of Murderer's Cañon the rapids were unusually bad and dangerous, and it required all hands but one, who stood guard with cocked rifle, to wade beside the boats and preserve them from destruction. As the cañon suddenly ends, its vertical walls continue north and south, as the front of the mountain which it has crossed. We then entered a valley which presents a beautiful panorama of desert form and color. The hills are of all sizes and shapes. Those on the outer border are dazzlingly white, chalky rocks, surmounted here and there by black caps of volcanic rock. The slopes are vermilion foothills of red clay. Still lower are the river terraces of the desert yellow clay and gravel, the whole threaded by the narrow fringe of fresh green along the river.

In this wild country lived the notorious Alvarado. Only a most fortunate mistake prevented my men from carrying out their threat to exterminate this bandit. Alvarado had a surname as well as a Christian name, and when they were told that the next ranch down the river was Ordonez's, they did not understand that this was another name for Alvarado until after we had passed him with an infant in his arms, serenely watching us float down the stream. I breathed easier on finding this out, but the men swore audibly and long at their misfortune in not recognizing the supposed monster.

Still lower down the river this region becomes more weird. Immediately adjacent to the stream there are great bluffs of a dirty yellow volcanic tuff, which weather into many fantastic, curvilinear forms. One of these, two hundred feet high, stands out conspicuously from its surroundings, an almost perfect reproduction of the Egyptian Sphinx. This, with the sterility of the surroundings and the dirty mud colors, constantly recalled the character of the Nile.

We were relieved to see before us the entrance of another vertical "shut-out," or cañon, into which we passed at about four o'clock in the afternoon, and found a suitable camping ground, hemmed in on each side by vertical walls and out of rifle range from above. This cañon was only a mile or two long, and was very similar to Murderer's Cañon in its scenic and geologic features.

The next day the river followed a sinuous course through a most picturesque district which we named the Black Rock Cañon. . . .

Toward evening a graceful sweep of the river brought us into a more open basin opposite the mouth of the San Carlos Creek. This stream, which can barely be said to flow, comes in from the Mexican side, and is the only flowing tributary of the Rio Grande that we passed between the Conchos and the Pecos. Near its headwaters in the wild and rugged San Carlos Mountains is a little settlement of Indians, the remnant of a once famous desperate tribe from which the creek and the mountains take their names.

Opposite is a wide, sloping plain of limestone, from the center of which rises a wonderful symmetrical butte a thousand feet high, the summit of which is a head presenting the profile of an old man, which we named the Sentinel, from the watch which it kept over the entrance of the Grand Cañon.

We traveled fully one hundred miles to this point by river, but as the crow flies it is only about fifty miles below Presidio. We camped upon the Texas side, beneath a limestone bluff. A mile below us down the river was a vast mountain wall, the vertical escarpment of which ran directly north and south across the path of the river, and through which the latter cuts its way. The river disappears in a narrow vertical slit in the face of the escarpment. This mountain is the Sierra Santa Helena, and the rift in its face is the entrance to the so-called Grand Cañon of the Rio Grande. . . .

The next morning, after the customary involuntary wetting at the rapids by which we made our nightly camps, we rowed straight for the narrow slit in the mountain. The river makes a sudden bend as it enters the cañon, and almost in the twinkling of an eye we passed out of the desert glare into the dark and silent depths of its gigantic walls, which rise vertically from the water's edge to a narrow ribbon of sky above. Confined in a narrow channel less than twenty-five feet wide, without bench or bank upon which to land, our boats glided along without need of oars, as we sat in admiration of the superb precipices which hemmed us in on each side. The solemnity of the scene was increased by the deathlike stillness which prevailed and by the thought of those who had tried the journey and either lost their lives or narrowly escaped destruction. The walls rose straight toward the sky, unbroken by bench or terrace, and marked only by an occasional line of stratification in the cream-colored marbles and limestone which composed them. The waters flowed noiselessly and swiftly through this cañon, with hardly a ripple or gurgle except at one place. Their flow is so silent as to be appalling. With the ends of our oars we could almost touch either wall. The solemnity and beauty of the spectacle were overwhelming.

We had gone only a few miles when a halt was suddenly forced upon us. Directly ahead was a place where one side of the great cliffs had caved away, and the debris spread across the narrow passage of the river. This obstacle was composed of great blocks of stone and talus rising two hundred feet high, which, while obstructing the channel, did not dam the waters, but gave them way through the interstices of the rocks. The boulders were mostly quadrangular masses of limestone fifty feet or more in height, dumped in a heterogeneous pile, like a load of bricks from a tip-cart, directly across the stream. At this place, which we appropriately named "Camp Misery," trouble began. Although the obstruction was hardly a quarter of a mile in length, it took us three days to get our boats across it.

He discusses the many difficulties of portaging the boats and supplies over the rocky obstruction. After the exhausting labor of the day, the nights were passed in discomfort trying to find places to sleep upon narrow ledges. Nevertheless, his aesthetic senses were not dulled by the experience.

During our three days' stay at Camp Misery we had abundant opportunity to observe the majestic features of the great gorge in which we were entombed. The scene within this cañon is of unusual beauty. The austerity of the cliffs is softened by colors which camera or pen cannot reproduce. These rich tints are like the yellow marbles of Portugal and Algiers, warmed by reddening tones which become golden in the sunlight. The cliffs are often rigid and geometrically vertical, but usually the severity is modulated by gently swelling curves which develop at the edges of the horizontal strata or vertical joint-seams. In many instances the profiles are overhanging or toppling. This was forcibly illustrated on one occasion, when, having selected a spot upon which to make my bed, my attention was directed by the men to an immense boulder so delicately poised upon the very edge of the cliff immediately above me that the vibration of a rifle-shot would apparently have dislocated it and sent it thundering down. . . .

From above the sky-line was of never ceasing interest, whether bathed in sunshine while shadows filled the vast crevices below, or flooded with the glorious moonlight which is one of the characteristics of the desert. Frequently there were vast caverns a hundred feet or more below the crest-line, into which we could look from below and see their other ends opening out upon the plain above. Castellated and turreted forms in natural mimicry of the feudal structures of the Rhine were frequent. One of these, opposite our camp, was so natural that, upon awakening one moonlit night and seeing it above me, it took several moments for me to dispel the idea that it was a genuine castle, with towers, bastions, portcullis, and port-holes. . . .

While buried in this cañon at Camp Misery we were constantly impressed by the impossibility of escaping from it in case we should lose our boats or be overwhelmed by sudden floods. Leisure moments were devoted to looking for some possible manner by which the vertical walls could be scaled. For its entire length there is no place where this cliff can be climbed by man. . . .

Having finally succeeded in crossing the obstruction early one morning, we transported our baggage to the boats, preparatory to leaving. Before the boats were loaded a tremendous roaring sound like distant thunder was heard up the cañon, and we saw that what we most dreaded was happening – the river was rising. A big flood of the ordinary kind would have veneered the dangerous rocks with water, and our prospects for escape would have been small. We hastily piled our baggage into the boats and sprang aboard. It was either stay and starve or go and chance it. Fortunately, this particular rise proved to be a small one, just sufficient to give the desired impetus to our craft, and our course through the cañon was rapid. The walls increased in altitude as we descended the stream, and just as they reached their greatest height, some seventeen hundred and fifty feet, our boats suddenly emerged into the sunlit desert.

Floating downstream, Hill looks back and admires the huge escarpment from which the Santa Helena Canyon emerges, still visible to the group up to a week later further downstream. He also observes the bizarre features of the Terlingo Desert spreading out before them, particular the mountain cluster dominating the horizon – impressing him as it had the other survey party fifty years earlier.

The crowning feature of this desert is the lofty and peculiar group of peaks known as Los Chisos ("the ghosts"). These weird forms are appropriately named —. Wherever one climbs out of the low stream groove these peaks stare him in the face like a group of white-clad spirits rising from a base of misty gray shadow and vegetation. Many are the weird forms and outlines which the peaks assume. Two specially conspicuous rocks are known as "Mule Ears," and, seen from a distance of twenty miles or more, are remarkably suggestive of the objects for which they are named. They are separated from the main summits by a valley which, from its inaccessibility, the cowboys have named "Cow Heaven." Surrounding these peaks on all sides is an area of lower hills and old terraces covered with desert gravel and vegetation, some of which are black-capped volcanic hills, others are of dazzling yellow sandstone; still others show stripes of stratified vermilion and chocolate colors.

Day after day we drifted through this weird desert, hemmed in by low bluffs of dirty yellow soil, and seeing few signs of human habitation. One day we ran across three or four Mexicans leisurely driving a herd of stolen cattle across the river into Mexico. This is the chief occupation of the few people who choose this wild region for a habitation. A little later we were greeted at our camp on the Mexican side by a white man accompanied by seven or eight Mexicans, all fully armed. Ware recognized him as a notorious ex-convict known in Texas as "Greasy Bill." Later, upon my return to Marathon, I learned from the rangers that he was the outlaw most wanted in Texas, and that only the year before he had murdered an old man named Reed, who kept a store on the Texas side.

After following the meandering of the river, they finally rounded the bend and changed their direction from a southeast to a northeast direction, entering another canyon.

Just after making the turn we entered the first of the two cañons known as the Little and the Big San Vincente cañons respectively. These cut through a long, low sierra within the general area of the Terlingo valley. Directly through and across the front of the sierra a vertical black line could be seen marking the vast chasm through which the stream makes its way. As we neared the entrance, the river presented the appearance of apparently plunging into a seething hole without visible outlet. . . .

The passage of the San Vincente cañons took only a few hours, and at noon we found ourselves in the eastern or Tornillo extension of the Terlingo Desert, near the ruins of the old Mexican Presidio de San Vincente. These ruins were seen in 1852 by the Mexican Boundary Survey, and were apparently as ancient and deserted then as today. They consist of extensive roofless walls of old adobe buildings standing in an uninhabited region, upon a low mesa a mile or two from the river. The people of the Big Bend region have a tradition that in the days of the Spanish régime they were the site of a prison where convicts were kept and worked in certain mythical mines in the Chisos Mountains. They are the ruins of an old Spanish frontier military post.

They passed through an area of hot springs and came to the Mexican village of Boquillas. At that time, there were about two thousand

Mexicans and some American inhabitants in the settlement extracting
silver from a nearby mine. This was a temporary anomaly that Hill
correctly predicted would soon end.

*East of the Boquillas group of settlements the wonderful west-
ern escarpment of the Sierra del Carmen rises straight above
our path. Although the crest, which makes a gentle arch, is less
regular than that of the opposing escarpment of the plateau of
Santa Helena, it is higher and of grander relief. Surmounting
the center of the arch of the plateau is a single steeple-like peak,
which may be termed the Boquillas Finger. This landmark, like
the Chisos summits, was often in sight from points one hundred
miles away.*

*Across the center of the Sierra del Carmen, which rises seventy-
five hundred feet above the sea, the river cut another vertical
chasm, which is even more worthy of the name of the Grand
Cañon than that of the Sierra de Santa Helena. The Mexican
Boundary Surveyors, upon encountering it, were obliged to
make a detour of fifty miles around the mountain to approach
the river again, where they finally gave up the attempt of further
exploration, and reached the lower Texas country by a long
journey through Mexico. The cañon profile presents a summit
nearly five thousand feet above the river. The river itself, in
approaching this mountain, first turns from side to side in short
stretches, as if trying to avoid the mighty barrier above it, and
then, as if realizing that it is constantly becoming involved in
the maze of foothills, suddenly starts across the sierra.*

*In crossing this mountain the river pursues a tortuous course
made of many small rectangular bends, around each of which a
new and more surprising panorama is presented. The walls of
the cañon are of the same rich cream-colored limestone rocks
as those which make the cañons of Santa Helena and San Vincente. Owing to the dislocation of the strata, the rocks are more
varied in form, and are broken into beautiful pointed salients
and vertical columns. Wonderful indeed are the remarkable
forms of rock sculpture. Among these was a vast cylindrical
tower like the imaginary pictures of Babel, standing outward of
the cliff-line and rising, through perspective, far above. Upon
the opposite side was another great Rhine castle. Frequently
lonely columns of rock five hundred feet or more in height stood
out from the front of the cliff in an apparent state of unstable*

equilibrium. Caverns of gigantic proportions also indented the cliff at many places. Again, the great yellow walls were cut from base to summit by wonderful fissures filled with white calcite or vermilion-colored iron ore. Huge piles of talus here and there encumbered the bases of the cliffs.

The moon was full while we were in this cañon, and the effects of its illuminations were indescribably beautiful. Long before its face could be seen, its light would tip the pinnacles and upper strata of the cliffs, still further gilding the natural yellows of the rocks. Slowly this brilliant light sank into the magma of darkness which filled the cañon, gently setting from stratum to stratum as the black shadows fled before it, until finally it reached the silent but rapid waters of the river, which became a belt of silver. Language cannot describe the beauty of such nights, and I could never sleep until the glorious light had ferreted out the shadows from every crevice and driven darkness from the cañon.

After several days our boats suddenly drifted out of the shades and beauties of the Carmen Cañon and emerged into the last of the open desert basins. . . .

Beyond the little Stillwell Desert we entered Temple Cañon. The severity of its walls was frequently broken by ravines, so that at nearly every bend there stood before one a beautifully sculptured mountain, golden in the sunlight, with pinnacled summits, and cliffs carved into exquisite panels and grottoes. . . .

Beyond Temple Cañon the cliffs recede, leaving a valley from one to five miles in width between the distant walls. Through a huge gap in these the mouth of Maravillas Creek has been cut. This is a horrible desert arroyo, leading northward for one hundred miles or more to Marathon. It has a channel sufficient for the Hudson, but is utterly void of water. Now and then, in the intervals of years, great floods pour down its stony bottom, giving the boulders and other desert debris a further push toward the Rio Grande and the sea. Such floods, however, are so unusual and sporadic that I have never found a man who knew this stream to run from source to mouth. No profounder testimonial to the slowness of nature's great geological processes can be found than these vast waterless waterways. . . .

Below the mouth of the Maravillas the river continues in a narrow valley between the now more widely separated cliffs of the cañon, which are great buttes and mesas, the dissected fringe of a high limestone plateau above us. These cliffs are cut into many lobes and buttes. Occasionally one of these stands out and apart from the main cliff-line in lonely grandeur. Of this nature is Castle Butte, a notable landmark. This rises fully fifteen hundred feet above the river. Its circular, flat top, the square-cut escarpment cornice, and the gracefully sloping pediment are beautiful illustrations of the wonderful symmetrical sculpture seen along the river. These wider vistas are only of brief duration. Soon the rocky walls again approach each other, and the stream resumes its crowded channel between vertical walls, presenting only at rare intervals a place where one can land and find a small spot to camp.

We had now been nearly a month on the river, and the necessities of the occasion forced us to push on as fast as possible. In the steep cañons there had always been a tense feeling of anxiety, accompanied by a longing to escape their dangers as soon as possible. This feeling, as well as our limited commissary, ever drove us onward.

A welcome stop at a large pool formed by a hot spring was a delightful respite. The men were able to take a long hot bath before continuing downstream.

In the eastern course of the river the rock forms and sculpture become more varied, and one is constantly surprised by new types of architecture and scenery. For miles we passed through a perpendicular cañon the cliffs of which were serrated by rough and cavernous indentations and great vertical seams, between which the ledges were molded into ragged forms like the Badlands of Dakota. Below this, in another cañon, the sculpture is marked by queer, eccentric pinnacles projecting above the ragged skyline – spires, fingers, needles, natural bridges, and every conceivable form of peaked and curved rocks.

About the center of the eastern stretch of the river the altitudes of the cañon walls decrease slowly and almost imperceptibly until the river completely surmounts the great limestone formation which has been the chief matrix of its prison walls. These walls, to their termination, lock in the river securely from approach. In this eastern stretch the immediate gorge of the river is generally a cañon within a cañon. Within a double cañon of this type MacMahon had once been caught by a flood. He endeavored to escape to the uplands, in order to make his way to the railway. After three days of attempt he finally reached the summit of the immediate cañon, only to find another wall, invisible from the river, which it was utterly impossible to surmount. Fortunately, the river had meanwhile subsided, and he escaped by resuming his boats.

There is a break in the continuity of the cañon near where the river crosses the 102nd meridian. This interruption is only a short one, for the stream soon begins to descend again into a rock-bound trough. In this portion, and as far east as the mouth of Devil's River, some of the most beautiful and picturesque effects are found. The walls are no longer of orange color, but are of chalky limestone of purest white, which weathers into great curves rather than vertical ledges. In one cañon, for instance, the walls are carved into the most remarkable perpendicular pillars, resembling columns of the Egyptian type, each of which is over one hundred feet in height. . . .

Beautiful as were these cañons, and prolific as they were in game and in caves of wild honey, the hardships we had endured were telling upon the temper of the party, and we no longer appreciated the noble surroundings. We longed only to escape from the walls, upon which we now began to look as a prison. Ten hours of hard rowing each day, every one of which was burdened with the additional labor of dragging the boats over dangerous rapids, constant wetting by wading and ducking, the baking due to a merciless sunshine, the restricted diet, made no better by Serafino's ignorance of hygienic cooking and Shorty's constant additions of bacon grease to every article, together with the ever-present apprehension of danger, had put us all in a condition of quarrelsome, nervous tension, which is a dangerous state in camp, no matter how friendly all may be, and it was with pleasure that we finally sighted a longed-for landmark indicating a point where we could abandon the river.

Opposite the village of Langtry, near the top of a vertical cliff some three hundred feet high, is a small bluff cavern. Poised on the edge of this inaccessible cavern is a huge pile of sticks skill-

fully entwined into what is perhaps the largest birds' nest in America. . . .

We landed the contents of our boat upon a little beach opposite this nest. A messenger proceeded a mile and a half to the village of Langtry and secured a packhorse, which conveyed our belongings to the railway station. It was gratifying to see once more even the crudest habitation of man. We were received by a famous old frontiersman, whose hospitable house is decorated with a peculiar sign reading:

*Law West of the Pecos.
Roy Bean,
Justice of the Peace
and Notary Public.
San Antonio Lager Beer.*

We had successfully navigated and mapped three hundred and fifty miles of a portion of one of America's greatest rivers which hitherto had been considered impassable; we had made a geologic section directly across the eastern sierra of the great American Cordilleras from the interior deserts to the coastal plain, procuring light upon some of our least-known country; we had escaped dangers which had overwhelmed those who had attempted the cañons before; and our little party dispersed contented with its success.

Chapter XVII

BLACK CANYON OF THE GUNNISON
1901

from "Exploration of the Cañon"
by Abraham Lincoln Fellows
in History of Agriculture in Colorado
by Alvin Steinel

In 1853, the Gunnison expedition passed by some of the deep chasms in the vicinity but not the Black Canyon itself. The Hayden survey saw it in 1873 and a party did descend into a part of the Black Canyon in 1887. Not until 1901 were the canyon depths explored from end to end. The practical purpose of the journey was to find a suitable place for a tunnel to be built toward the end of diverting waters for irrigation in the region.

It was my good fortune to have charge of the government hydrographic work in the state of Colorado at that time and the general direction of the survey, which was made in the summer of 1901, was turned over to me. From the very commencement of the survey I felt that it would be necessary, before its conclusion, to make an exploration in detail of the Grand Cañon of the Gunnison, which was generally supposed to be impassable. Other parties had tried in vain to explore the gloomy recesses of the cañon. Efforts had been made in the winter time to pass through on the ice, but had failed on account of the existence of falls and rapids where no ice could form and these expeditions had been given up. Surveying parties had attempted to go through it with complete outfits but had failed and had given up the efforts after losing their equipment and had painfully worked their way out over the rim of the cañon before the most inaccessible points had been reached. In the year 1900, a party of five residents of the Uncompaghre Valley, under the leadership of John E. Pelton of Montrose, had made the best planned and boldest attempt yet undertaken to force their way through the gloomy passages, but after traversing about half the distance, that is to say about twenty miles out of a total of about forty, and after losing one boat and a large part of their sup-

plies, they were forced to abandon their remaining boat and return to their homes by a most toilsome and perilous detour of more than a hundred miles. The veteran old trapper and hunter of that region, Moccasin Bill, offered the encouraging ultimatum that it was impossible for mortal man to go through the cañon and live, that he himself had been about half way through and he knew no man could go farther.

Fellows decided that swimming the Gunnison would be the best way to go, using rubber rafts to carry their instruments and supplies by day, and to sleep on at night. He took William W. Torrence as his one companion, who had been with the Pelton party the previous summer in their unsuccessful attempt to pass through the entire canyon. He selected a friend, A. W. Dillon, to carry food down to the bottom of the canyon, at three strategic points along the canyon.

Exploration was actually commenced August 12, 1901. At the head of the Grand Cañon of the Gunnison is the mouth of the Cimarron River. The Denver and Rio Grande Railroad comes out of the Black Cañon of the Gunnison to this point, then climbing out of the cañon by way of the Cimarron and one of its tributaries. It was at this point that our toilsome journey was commenced. The conductor kindly stopped the train upon the exact spot where I told him we wished to get off. Turning immediately down the cañon, we started upon our perilous journey. The packs on our shoulders were not light, although we had limited their size as much as we could. It was frequently necessary to wade through deep water, even when we were obliged to swim, and all walking was along boulders which formed the talus of the cañon walls. Easy walking was never to be found unless it was a very few feet upon some gravel bar. We would proceed along one side of the river until we came to a point where it was absolutely necessary either to cross, or to swim for some distance out into the stream, making as rapid progress as we could.

Our surroundings were of the wildest possible description. The roar of the waterfalls was constantly in our ears and the walls of the cañon towering half a mile in height above us, were seemingly vertical. Occasionally a rock would fall from one side or the other, with a roar and crash, exploding like a ton of dynamite when it struck bottom, making us think our last day had come. At times the cañon would become so narrow that it would almost, but never quite, be possible to step across the river. At times, great gorges of rock that had fallen in from the sides would hem in the water to such an extent that it would be nearly concealed. On the second day of our trip, we were so unfortunate as to get into a veritable cul-de-sac, from which it took us the entire afternoon to extricate ourselves, camping that night just across the river from where we had eaten our lunch at noon. Our most dangerous work, possibly, was that of clambering along the sides of precipices, traversing old mountain sheep trails, at points where it was impracticable to swim without too great danger to life and limb.

Upon one of these occasions I was so unlucky as to fall about 20 feet, but so fortunate, if it might be so called, as to land in a bed of wild gooseberry bushes, which kept me from breaking any bones, but had other unpleasant features. Naturally, one gets tired after springing like a mountain goat from one rock to another and swimming whirlpools and rapids, and when the rocks are sharp, as they usually are, they are hard upon shoes. On the third day, when we arrived along toward evening at the mouth of Trail Gulch, where Dillon was first to meet us, we were more than glad at a chance to rest and to send to Montrose for new shoes and fresh supplies. We remained at this point two nights and one whole day, sleeping nearly all of the time.

. . . At times we would traverse along reaches looking like mill ponds with the sky and cañon walls reflected in the depth of the blue water, but again we would come to rapids and waterfalls as turbulent as the waters of Lodore. The cañon walls appeared more and more to be hemming us in from the outer world. One remarkable point which we passed on the 16th, I called the Giant Stairway. The walls looked almost as if cut into enormous steps by some Titan of old, while statues, turrets and pinnacles adorned the rugged precipices on either side. Leaning out a little from one of the Giant steps was a long, thin rock, like a needle, apparently not more than two or three feet in thickness and apparently over 150 feet in height, entirely detached from the cliff, except at its base. It seemed extraordinary that it could so hold its position for centuries, as it had apparently done. That evening we reached a point which we named Beaver Camp, from the fact that a colony of beaver had lived there at no distant date and had cut down some of the great trees growing in

the little flat, which formed a delightful camping ground where we stopped for the night.

On the morning of the 17th, we again started out upon what we expected would be the most perilous portion of our journey. Others had been as far as this point and escaped with their lives, but no one had ever gone far beyond. We had made good time the preceding day and were farther along than I had expected, so I thought it best to make great bonfires of the huge piles of driftwood which lined the stream, to indicate to Dillon above that we had passed this point. We made an early start, for we expected the day would be a hard one, and about 11 o'clock that morning we reached what had hitherto been the Ultima Thule of other explorers. Legends existed of a party which many years before had attempted to pass through the jaws of the cañon which now appeared to be closing in upon us. The legend runs that they lost their entire effort, with one of their party, and being unable to retrace their steps, had, with the utmost difficulty, scaled the sides of the cañon. Pelton's party, too, had reached this point with their second boat and we found a piece of the rope still fastened to the rocks and some of the provisions and supplies left by them. They, too, had abandoned everything and climbed out of the cañon, glad to escape with their lives. Their leader had told me that it was impossible for a man to pass through the gorge and live.

When about noon, we reached the lowest point attained by earlier explorers and saw before us the mighty jaws, past which there was to be no escape, I believe I might be pardoned for the feeling of nervousness and dread which came over me for the first time. It was not so much for myself that I feared, but because I was leading another man into a place from which there might be no escape. Right then I made the only discouraging speech that was made during the entire trip. I said to Torrence:

"Will, your last chance to go out is to the right. You can make it there if you wish, but if we cross the river at this point there can be no return, we must go on. I do not ask you to go, but leave the decision entirely to yourself. As for me, I am going through."

Torrence said: "Here goes nothing!" And he commenced to pull off his coat.

Nothing further was said. We swam the river, reaching a similar point of rocks on the other side, but still above the gorge. And, lo, we beheld as a beacon of hope through the narrow opening, where the water was of unknown depth and velocity, and below which it was believed there were high falls, a bonfire kindled by Dillon on a huge rock below the jaws of the cañon. He had come down by a most precipitous path, risking life and limb for our encouragement. The very sight of this man in the jaws of the gorge was a wonderful inspiration. Again we plunged into the foaming water and in a few minutes we had passed through the jaws of the gorge and were safe among the enormous boulders below.

Here we lunched heartily upon provisions brought by Dillon and then we were once more on our way. Another gorge was below, apparently more dangerous than the preceding one, with a longer and, worse still, for the most part invisible distance to traverse by swimming. This, too, was safely passed at last and we resumed our tiresome journey along the cañon side.

We were soon obliged to cross the river again, where we clambered along gigantic boulders, often as large as a good sized house, the peculiar characteristic of which was that the nearer the water the larger and more impassable the boulders seemed to be. In consequence, we kept ascending the side of the talus until, when darkness fell, we were a long way above the water, and we made camp under a huge shelving rock against which the roaring of the river reverberated and echoed like demons howling over their prey. We were so far above the water that it took an hour to make a trip down for a coffee pot full, the distance being augmented by the difficulties in climbing.

On the morning of the 18th, we hoped that our greatest difficulties were passed, but we were doomed to disappointment, for on that day we encountered some of the most trying experiences of the trip. At the very start we came to a gorge where gigantic boulders had fallen in from the cliffs, the water flowing 100 feet or more beneath these boulders. They were packed closely enough, however, so that they formed a dam in high water. The boulders were smooth and polished to such an extent that it was only with the greatest difficulty they could be surmounted. It took us six hours to traverse less than a quarter of a mile. At times it would be necessary for one of us to climb upon the shoulders of the other, clamber to the top of some huge rock and draw our supplies and the other man up by means of the rope which we carried with us. Again on the other side there might be a deep pool where we were obliged to swim, into which the water boiled from the caves above and was sucked out again through the crevices between the boulders below. In one of these pools I was drawn completely under water in an eddy. I fully expected to be drawn down into the crevices of the rocks below, but by dint of the hardest kind of swimming, succeeded in getting into still water. At this time, Torrence felt that he would never see me again.

All things have an end, however, and about 1 or 2 o'clock we passed this gorge and emerged to where the cañon opened out to a slight degree. Here we met an experience most unusual to hunters or explorers. To appreciate the situation the reader must understand that we were now out of provisions, have lost or spoiled those with which we had been supplied. We were hungry, sick and exhausted and were losing flesh, as we had through the entire trip, at the rate of about two pounds a day. At this critical stage, while climbing along the side of the cañon thirty or forty feet above the stream, I stepped out from behind a large rock to a spot where there were some small bushes. As I forced my way through these bushes, up sprang two mountain sheep which apparently had been lying asleep and which I had come within three feet of stepping upon. One of them was so dazed that it sprang over the cliff and broke its shoulders upon the rocks below. It was hard upon the poor sheep, but I could easily understand why it had been so frightened, when I saw the reflection of myself in a mirror after we had once more reached civilization. Although hard on the sheep, it was our salvation. Though the game laws of Colorado forbade one having any portion of a mountain sheep in possession, a hind quarter was immediately added to our supply and a goodly portion cooked and eaten.

Soon after this we came to what, in my opinion, is the most beautiful part of the entire cañon. The river pitches down over a succession of falls which I named in honor of my companion, Torrence Falls. At the foot of this cataract is a beautiful little grove of cottonwood trees and there we found shelter from the rain that was falling, building a fire and making ourselves as comfortable as possible. We were compelled to move on soon and so until dark trudged along through the rain, crossing the river a number of times in the hope that we might be able to reach the mouth of Red Rock Cañon, where we expected Dillon to meet us again. In this, however, we were disappointed and darkness came upon us when we were still a mile above the longed-for spot. We camped for the night under the sheltering cliffs, putting up our rubber sacks to keep off the rain, and making an enormous fire out of driftwood.

On the morning of the 19th it was still raining and the first thing we had to do was to swim the river. We found it bad enough to swim the ice cold water when the sun was shining, but when rain was falling and everything gloomy, it was far more disagreeable and trying. At about 10 o'clock, without having encountered any very serious difficulties, we came to where Dillon was waiting for us. He had come up the river about three quarters of a mile and met us and I was glad, indeed, to turn my pack over to him for a time. By noon we were at the camp which he had made at the mouth of Red Rock Cañon and he was soon busily engaged in cooking us a good dinner. It rained all that afternoon and was still cloudy the next morning. We were seriously tempted to leave the cañon, for we had passed through all the most important part of it and I hardly expected to be able to obtain any information of value below. But the fever was upon us and we thought it would be a great pity when we were so fully equipped not to go entirely through the cañon, and moreover there were still some doubtful points that needed to be cleared up.

Accordingly, on the following morning, we started out once more, this time without our packs, except a luncheon, as I intended to go downstream rapidly as possible, hoping to be able to reach a ranch house which I thought was some eight miles below. In this we were disappointed as the distance proved to be considerably greater. We traversed 8 or 10 miles and it was the hardest day's trip that we had as yet endured. At night we camped without bedding and without food or water upon a bleak hillside. Having passed through all of the cañon that was of any interest to us and having reached a horse trail, we decided we had gone far enough and directed our course toward Delta. We arrived there in time to take the train to Montrose, reaching there at 12:45 p.m.

We were strange looking objects. Our clothing and shoes were ragged and worn and, with a luxuriant growth of beard and a covering of dirt acquired in the last few miles of our trip, we would hardly have been candidates for positions in polite society.

We had been obliged to swim the river, the water of which was as cold as ice, 76 times. The swimming was naturally fraught with great danger, it being necessary for us often to land on sharp points of rock where the water was flowing swiftly. We were bruised from head to foot. Each had lost at least fifteen pounds in the ten days' trip. So ended this portion of the exploration and survey.

EPILOGUE

The first national parks were set aside in the American West. Later ones were created back east. Later still, large wilderness parks were set aside in Alaska. In time, they spread to other nations around the world. Yet, it was the encounter with the exotic features and titanic formations of the American West that engendered its beginnings. This was a circumstance that resulted from a concatenation of historical forces. One of these was the closing of the frontier.

As an historical process, the American frontier was an ongoing movement of settlement and utilization. Its logical end was to ever push back the boundaries of the frontier until it would disappear, which it eventually did. The consequent creation of parklands after the closing of the frontier was an attempt to stop and even reverse the historical process so that the frontier might never disappear.

The first parkland set aside was Yosemite as a state park in 1864. Some years later it was placed in the national park system. The first official national park was Yellowstone in 1872. When Langford wrote about their discovery of Yellowstone, he envisioned villas dotting the shores of Yellowstone Lake and a bridge spanning the Yellowstone canyon. Yet, as it turned out, he was one of the individuals who championed the creation of a national park to spare its natural settings from the intrusions of present-day structures. In this way, the illusion of wilderness was maintained.

The national park movement received great impetus under the presidency of Theodore Roosevelt. Here at the dawn of the twentieth century, while Roosevelt was having the Panama Canal dug and a modern naval fleet constructed, America was flexing its economic, technological and military muscle. Henry Ford was mass-producing automobiles for public use. The Wright brothers had a successful airplane flight at Kitty Hawk. The vast distances crossed laboriously by Lewis and Clark a century before were shrinking rapidly. America's vast forests were being cut

Theodore Roosevelt and John Muir at Yosemite in 1906.

down. By presidential fiat, Theodore Roosevelt set aside many forest preserves and national monuments, such as Olympic, Devils Tower and Grand Canyon. The forest service and the first wildlife refuges were created.

Roosevelt's own personal experiences had prepared him for taking these critical steps. In 1884, after personal tragedy in his life, he had headed west to be a rancher in the North Dakota Badlands. In three years, a harsh winter killed off most of his herd and he lost a considerable sum of his fortune. However, he wrote lyrical works on his experience, the landscape, the flora and fauna. As an avid hunter, he became aware of the decimation of the vast buffalo herds in the Great Plains. He saw the need to preserve the animals and habitats of natural America. He was well-acquainted with George Bird Grinnell, who had traveled and hunted extensively in the Glacier region and had championed the cause of setting it aside as a national park. Both were members of the conservationist Boone and Crockett Club. Roosevelt was also acquainted with John Muir and went on camping trips with him to Yosemite and Yellowstone. As president, he was in a position to realize many of their dreams. Fittingly, the North Dakota Badlands, where Roosevelt had ranched, were later set aside as Theodore Roosevelt National Park after his death. And so it continued.

Narratives of western discovery had been exciting the imagination of readers for many years prior to the establishment of parklands. Thomas Jefferson eagerly anticipated Lewis' report of the geography, flora, fauna, fossils, native tribes, etc. What was out there? He was curious to know it all. Then, Washington Irving turned his literary talents to tell the tales of early westering expeditions. John Charles Fremont inspired a mass exodus of overlanders. Curiosity to fill in the gaps of western geography continued to spur expeditions, reaching a crescendo with the popular reports, sketchings, paintings and photos of the great surveys. Articles about our western wonderlands appeared in popular magazines and were read avidly in the late 19th century. Awareness of the wonders of the west intensified, paving the way for the creation of parklands. This anthology comprised many of their narratives from America's multi-generational odyssey, recording the thrill of discovery and revealing the mysteries of the West step by step.

FURTHER READING

For a secondary history of western exploration in the 19th century, I would recommend *Exploration and Empire: The Explorer and the Scientist in the Winning of the American West* by William Goetzmann.

A number of the excerpts included in this anthology can be read in their entirety. Some are available through Narrative Press. These include *The Adventures of Captain Bonneville* by Washington Irving, *The Adventures of Zenas Leonard* written by himself, *Journal of a Trapper* by Osborne Russell, and *Death Valley in '49* by William Lewis Manley. Other recommended titles available elsewhere are the *Journals of Lewis and Clark* of which there are many editions, *Astoria* by Washington Irving, and *A Canyon Voyage* by Frederick Dellenbaugh.

Deciding which first-hand accounts to exclude from this anthology was problematic. The intent was to bring together the exploration narratives of the western parklands. There is not a clear dividing line where and when exploration ends and tourism begins. Many well-known narratives of early naturalists have been excluded that followed close behind the exploration narratives chosen for this book. Clarence King's *Mountaineering in the Sierra Nevada* includes his account of the ascent and descent of Mt. Tyndall, which occurred during the California Geological Survey and immediately after Brewer's ascent of another peak in Kings Canyon (part of this anthology). Clarence Dutton's *Tertiary History of the Grand Canon District* and *Report on the Geology of the High Plateaus of Utah* are the works of one who was part of the Powell survey of the Colorado Plateau. John Muir wrote a number of works about the parklands of the Sierra Nevada and elsewhere in the latter third of the 19th century. Theodore Roosevelt wrote of his experiences as a rancher in the Little Missouri Badlands during the mid-1880s in *Hunting Trips of a Ranchman* and *The Wilderness Hunter*. These excluded works are literary classics and can be found in anthologies of nature writings or in their entirety. Other excluded works are more obscure and difficult to find, that also followed close behind the exploration narratives herein. These include *Travels in the Interior of North America* by Prince Maximilian of Wied, where Karl Bodmer's illustrations first appeared, detailing an ascent by boat to the Upper Missouri in the 1830s. Other excluded works include Thaddeus Culbertson's geological and fossil-finding journey sponsored by the Smithsonian in *Journal of an Expedition to the Mauvaises Terres and the Upper Missouri in 1850*. There were plenty of discoveries of Yellowstone before Ferdinand Hayden's official survey in 1871, so it was excluded as well; along with George Bird Grinnell's articles in *Forest & Stream* about his hunting expeditions in Glacier during the late 1880s; and the further exploration of Olympic by Wickersham and Christie in 1889-90, whose accounts appeared in *The Seattle Press* on July 16, 1890. Some early exploration narratives were excluded because of their extreme brevity; such as Harrison Roger's journal of Jedediah Smith's travels that included passage through the Redwoods in 1828, Philip St. George Cooke's *Journal of the March of the Mormon Battalion* past Saguaro at the opening of the Mexican War in 1846, and John Hillman's article in the *Portland Oregonian* on June 7, 1903 about his discovery of Crater Lake in 1853. Major archeological discoveries were also excluded; for example, Lieutenant James Simpson's discovery of the Chaco Canyon ruins, Canyon de Chelly, and Inscription Rock in his drab and detailed *Journal of a Military Reconnaissance from Santa Fe, New Mexico to the Navaho County, made in 1849*.

Journals included in this anthology, not cited in the table of contents, can be found in the following sources: Journal of William Ashley in *Ashley-Smith Explorations and the Discovery of a Central Route to the Pacific, 1822-1829*, edited by Harrison Clifford Dale; Journal of William Brewer in *Up and Down in California in 1860-1864*, edited by Francis Farquhar; Journal of Cook and Folsom in *Valley of the Upper Yellowstone*, edited by Aubrey Haines; Journal of Captain R. B. Marcy in *Marcy and the Gold Seekers*, edited by Grant Foreman; a portion of the Journal of Henry Custer in "First Crossing of the Picket Range, 1859" in *Northwest Discovery*, May 1984, edited by Harry Majors; and Journal of James Clyman in *James Clyman, American Frontiersman, 1792-1881*, edited by Charles Camp.

THE NARRATIVE PRESS
HISTORICAL ADVENTURE & EXPLORATION

The Narrative Press publishes only true, first-person accounts of historical adventure and exploration. These books are first-hand journals, diaries, and memoirs, written by the explorers, mountain men, prospectors, scientists, spies, pioneers, lawmen, and fortune hunters themselves.

Most of these adventures are classics, about people and places now long gone. They take place all over the world – in Africa, South America, the Arctic and Antarctic, in America (in the Old West and before), on islands everywhere, and on the open seas.

Some of our authors are famous – Ernest Shackleton, Kit Carson, Henry Stanley, David Livingston, William Bligh, John Muir, Richard Burton, Elizabeth Custer, Teddy Roosevelt, Charles Darwin, Osborne Russell, John Fremont, Joshua Slocum, William Manley, Tom Horn, Philip St. George Cooke, Apsley Cherry-Garrard, Richard Henry Dana, Jack London, and Buffalo Bill, to name a few.

One thread binds all of our books: every one is historically important, and every one of them is fascinating.

Visit our website today. You can also call or write to us for a free copy of our printed catalogue.

THE NARRATIVE PRESS
P.O. BOX 2487
SANTA BARBARA, CALIFORNIA 93120 U.S.A.
(800) 315-9005
www.narrativepress.com